ECONOMIC INTERDEPENDENCE
IN SOUTHEAST ASIA

PROCEEDINGS OF A CONFERENCE

HELD AT BANGKOK, 1967

SPONSORED BY THE

UNIVERSITY OF WISCONSIN RESEARCH PROJECT

ON ECONOMIC INTERDEPENDENCE IN SOUTHEAST ASIA

WITH FINANCIAL SUPPORT FROM THE

UNITED STATES AGENCY FOR INTERNATIONAL DEVELOPMENT

ECONOMIC INTERDEPENDENCE IN SOUTHEAST ASIA

EDITED BY

THEODORE MORGAN

AND

NYLE SPOELSTRA

PUBLISHED FOR THE

CENTER FOR INTERNATIONAL ECONOMICS

AND ECONOMIC DEVELOPMENT

BY THE

UNIVERSITY OF WISCONSIN PRESS

MADISON, MILWAUKEE, AND LONDON: 1969

Published for
the Center for International Economics and Economic Development
by the University of Wisconsin Press
Box 1379, Madison, Wisconsin 53701
The University of Wisconsin Press, Ltd.
27–29 Whitfield Street, London W.1
Copyright © 1969 by the Regents of the University of Wisconsin
All rights reserved
Printed in the United States of America by
Kingsport Press, Inc., Kingsport, Tennessee
Standard Book Number 299–05150–1
Library of Congress Catalog Number 68–9021

Contributors

A. N. Bhagat
Research and Planning
Economic Commission for Asia and
  the Far East
Bangkok

Amado A. Castro
Dean, School of Economics
University of the Philippines
Manila

K. R. Chou
Head, Department of Economics
Nanyang University
Singapore

Everett D. Hawkins
Department of Economics
University of Wisconsin
Madison

Nurul Islam
Director, Pakistan Institute of Devel-
  opment Economics
Karachi

H. N. S. Karunatilake
Research Department
Central Bank of Ceylon
Colombo

Hiroshi Kitamura
Director, Research and Planning
Economic Commission for Asia and
  the Far East
Bangkok

D. T. Lakdawala
Member, Fifth Finance Commission,
Government of India, New Delhi, and
Director, Department of Economics
University of Bombay
Bombay

Robert J. Lampman
Department of Economics
University of Wisconsin
Madison

Lim Chong Yah
Reader in Economics
University of Singapore
Singapore

Theodore Morgan
Director, Research Program on Eco-
  nomic Interdependence in Southeast
  Asia
University of Wisconsin
Madison

Ken'ichi Odawara
Faculty of Economics, Sophia Uni-
  versity
Tokyo

Douglas S. Paauw
Director, Center for Development
  Planning
National Planning Association
Washington, D.C.

J. Panglaykim
Senior Research Fellow
The Australian National University
Canberra

R. H. Patil
Research Officer, Economics Department
Reserve Bank of India
Bombay

John H. Power
School of Economics
University of the Philippines
Manila

D. V. Ramana
Development Economist
Asian Institute for Economic Development and Planning
Bangkok

Gerardo P. Sicat
School of Economics
University of the Philippines
Manila

Nyle Spoelstra
Adviser, National Institute of Development Administration
Bangkok

I-Shuan Sun
Deputy Governor
Central Bank of China
Taipei

Suparb Yossundara
Director, Research Department
Assistant to the Governor
Bank of Thailand
Bangkok

Anthony Tang
Department of Economics
Vanderbilt University
Nashville

Kenneth D. Thomas
Lecturer in Economics
La Trobe University
Melbourne

Wu Ta-Yeh
Adviser, Economic Development Board
Singapore

Yune Huntrakoon
Research Department
Bank of Thailand
Bangkok

Preface

Among recent proposals for accelerating the rate of economic growth among less-developed countries, few have excited more interest among professional economists, government policy makers, and the general public than regional economic cooperation and integration. Proposals for, and agreements on, joint investment ventures, multinational river development, free-trade areas, customs unions, economic unions, and other varieties of economic cooperation among nations have become routine news.

The extent and nature of economic interdependence in Southeast Asia, and the possibilities for increasing the region's interdependence, has been the subject of a three-year research program conducted in the Department of Economics at the University of Wisconsin.

The contributors of the central papers in this book are economists in university and government work in and near various countries of South, Southeast, and East Asia. They were invited to examine trends and prospects in national economic growth and trade relationships, and the implications of these relationships for economic interdependence in Southeast Asia. These papers, and comments on them, were presented at a conference in Bangkok in January, 1967, held under the auspices of the University of Wisconsin with support from the United States Agency for International Development.

This volume contains shortened and revised versions of the conference papers along with selected proceedings of the conference. Prefatory and supplementary material has been drawn from some of the studies made by the research group working at the University of Wisconsin.

Our debts are many. We are grateful to the Agency for International Development for financial support and critical encouragement, during the whole of the three-year research program. We appreciate, also, financial aid from the Research Committee of the Graduate School of the University of Wisconsin.

For the conference itself, we should like to thank General Netr, Secretary-General of the National Research Council, who, representing the Government of Thailand, arranged for our use of Sala Santitham for the conference sessions. Dr. Hiroshi Kitamura, Director of Research and Planning at ECAFE, smoothed our path in many ways. Dr. Fred R. von der Mehden, in Thailand on leave from the University of Wisconsin at the time, now at Rice University, Houston, assisted us in several ways in the months preceding the conference.

The Economic Research Centre, University of Singapore, and the Center for Development at the University of Wisconsin—both supported with grants from the Ford Foundation—generously made facilities available to the editors during the final preparation of this book. Everett D. Hawkins, Seiji Naya, and George W. Betz provided helpful comments at various points in assembling the book. Finally, we should like to thank Marjorie Hill and Mary Louise Munts for careful and perceptive editorial assistance in preparing the manuscript.

The views presented here are, of course, personal ones and do not necessarily reflect those of the United States Agency for International Development, the University of Wisconsin, or the organizations with which various contributors are or have been associated.

Theodore Morgan
Nyle Spoelstra

April, 1969

Contents

Tables

Figures

ECONOMIC INTERDEPENDENCE
IN SOUTHEAST ASIA

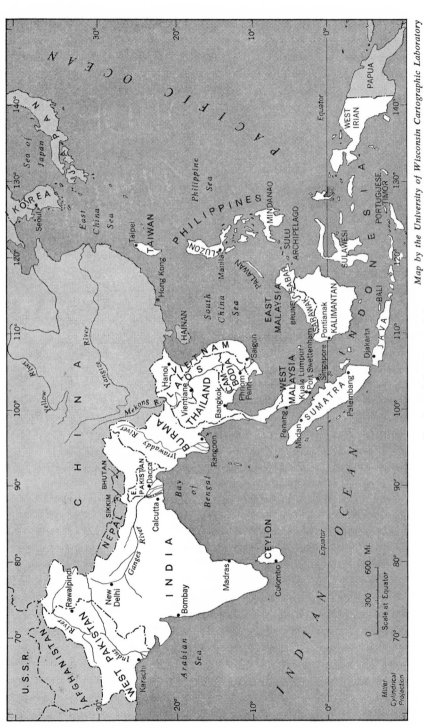

South and Southeast Asia

Map by the University of Wisconsin Cartographic Laboratory

Introduction

I

Since the end of World War II, many proposals have emerged for some sort of economic cooperation or integration among less-developed countries.[1] Most of these plans exist only on paper; of those that have come into existence, most have had a checkered history; a few have become useful servants of economic growth. The African and Middle Eastern countries have spawned a bewildering number of supranational organizations, most of which so far have had only minor economic substance. The two major trading blocs that have emerged in Latin America appear to be stable and productive. Southeast Asian experience falls somewhere between, both in the number of regional arrangements that have been formed or suggested and in the variety of forms these arrangements have taken.

Our working definition of Southeast Asia, for the purpose of tracing economic interdependence, is deliberately generous: the countries of Southeast, South and East Asia that stretch from Pakistan to Taiwan (see Map). In addition to the nine countries of Southeast Asia proper (Burma, Thailand, South Vietnam, Laos, Cambodia, Malaysia, Singapore, Indonesia, and the Philippines), our definition includes the South Asian countries of Ceylon, India, and Pakistan, and Hong Kong and Taiwan in East Asia. Although we draw on their experiences for comparative purposes, we do not include in this volume papers for Burma, Cambodia, Laos, Singapore, or South Vietnam. The omissions result more from our inability to obtain representatives from those countries, plus our feeling that each is in a special or temporary situation, or is economically small, than from any judgment about the composition of the region.

Even the most casual examination of ventures in regional cooperation in Southeast Asia and elsewhere suggests that the causes for varying degrees of success and failure lie in the potential participants' assessment of the relative economic, political, and social costs and benefits of regionalism. This book is concerned primarily with the economics of regional interdependence, although important interrelations between economic, political, and historical factors are apparent at several points. In general, we have not been concerned with questions of regional political alliances or security arrangements.

In Southeast Asia, as elsewhere, the possibilities for greater regional interdependence are in large measure dependent on national sentiments and policies. Most of the papers in this book are concerned with the economic growth and trading experiences of individual countries and the implications of these experiences for regional economic cooperation and integration. A nation's recent economic history, or at least its perception of it, conditions strongly that nation's willingness to participate in cooperative ventures. Nations that find their performance acceptable may resist changing policies that have had the great merit of tolerable success. Nations that are dissatisfied, or that anticipate problems in the future, may within certain limits search for new policies, including regional cooperation, in order to try to improve their growth performance. But countries with relatively poor performance may resist cooperative measures for fear that they will be left farther behind than ever.

Differences in economic policy among nations are important for explaining variations in growth performance, and they also affect the chances for regional cooperation. We asked contributors to attempt to relate observed patterns of trade and growth to national economic policy, not only because of the intrinsic interest of the relationship, but also because the type of economic policy followed plainly limits the range of feasible economic cooperation. Two decades of relatively independent policymaking have led not only to diversity among nations, but also to certain rigidities in approach that must be taken into account in any proposal for regional cooperation. Experience and analysis indicate that steps toward cooperation are technically more difficult—even among strongly motivated participants—if there are substantial disparities either in the types of trade policies followed (e.g., tariffs versus quotas or payments restrictions) or in the levels at which a particular policy is employed (e.g., high tariff countries versus low tariff countries).

The two papers in Part I take a general view of the region and explore in some detail the context for economic interdependence in Southeast

Asia. Mr. Wu provides an introduction to the nature and extent of economic interdependence in Southeast Asia and surveys the various cooperative and integrative measures that have been or might be taken in the region. Dr. Kitamura and Dr. Bhagat explore what to them appears to be the most promising approach to increased interdependence in Southeast Asia—the harmonization of national development plans, with provisions for agreed specialization and trade among the participating countries.

The papers on individual countries in Parts II, III, and IV reflect fully the variety of ways in which national economic problems may impinge on regional economic interdependence. Part II opens with a highly original analysis of tariff protection in Pakistan, with implications for future patterns of comparative advantage, and of exports and imports. Pakistan is in some ways a country that has yet to fulfill its early promise; the second country discussed, Taiwan, is a major success story. Dr. Sun describes the events and policies that account for Taiwan's performance and looks at the implications of its trade and tariff structure for the growth process. Thailand's success story is of a different type, in which exporting new types of primary products mainly to Asian markets has been a successful means of growth.

The papers of Part III give concrete expression to the diversity of Asia. In terms of structure, background, policy, and performance, it is hard to imagine greater contrasts than those between Hong Kong and India. Hong Kong is unique: because of special circumstances, it has an admirable record as an exporter and is endowed with remarkable capital and human resources. India is also unique: it has the largest potential market and the largest industrial and agricultural capabilities in the region. Between these extremes come accounts of two countries that seem to approximate most closely the "typical" Asian country. The Philippines and Malaysia are both medium-sized countries which is recent years have relied on their traditional primary product exports. But their past economic performance and policies and their prospects for the future are quite different.

Part IV explores some of the problem areas of Asian economic development and trade. Mr. Karunatilake describes the effects of and responses to foreign exchange problems in Ceylon. Dr. Ramana and Dr. Odawara trace statistically the impact of deficit financing and inflation on the Indian economy. Part IV concludes with an examination of recent trends in Indonesia's major export industries and of future prospects.

Part V presents first some selected summary statements by the conference participants on the broader implications of the country studies for regional cooperation and integration in Southeast Asia. The final chapter considers some of the major issues raised by the contributors in the light of research done at the University of Wisconsin.

II

The papers and discussions that follow will refer to various kinds of regional cooperation and integration, and from different points of view. It is useful to preface them with a bit of taxonomy, setting out logically the wide range of regional measures that are possible, and illustrating them with some Asian examples.

Cooperative activity can go on under either private or government auspices, and measures for regional cooperation can be classified by degree of formality and government commitment. The most informal are occasional meetings of private societies in various countries, and exchanges of information, advice, and published documents. Examples are meetings of and exchanges between technical and professional societies, literary groups, cooperatives, and political groups.

Occasional ad hoc meetings of government officials and groups to deal with special problems as they arise are a little more formal. There may be understandings or agreements to consult, or to hold regular meetings on matters of joint interest. The Association of Southeast Asia (ASA) has held ad hoc consultations and maintained continuing joint committees and working parties during its active periods from 1961 to 1963 and after 1965. Many activities of the United Nations Economic Commission for Asia and the Far East (ECAFE) involve this type of cooperation.

There may be commitments to take cooperative action on matters of a public service type, where provision by one state of a service useful also to others causes no decreased supply of the service domestically. Among these are research activities, technical education, radio and television programs, films, exchanges of artists and art exhibits, exchange visits of specialists and of groups. ASA carried on such exchanges.

Similar services may be provided through international or regional organizations. ECAFE carries on research in regional economic problems. The Southeast Asia Treaty Organization (SEATO) has conducted research in tropical medicine; ASA also initiated some studies of the possibilities of such research. Technical advice has been supplied and programs of technical education have been undertaken by ECAFE, SEATO, and also by the Colombo Plan and the Asian Productivity Organization (APO). ASA, again, has done some planning in the area.

There may be significant commitment of resources in the joint interest of contiguous countries in individual fields, like road or river valley development. The Committee for Coordination of Investigations of the Lower Mekong Basin, on which four bordering states are represented, Thailand, Laos, Cambodia, and South Vietnam, envisages this kind of joint commitment. Resources may be contributed for regional purposes. Cooperative deep-sea fishing and fish canning, and the setting up of regional air and shipping lines have been discussed by several organizations including ASA and ECAFE. A cooperative regional development bank, like the Asian Development Bank (ADB) at Manila, can be established. There can be joint efforts to expand exports of products like tea, and to conduct research in and explore markets for products like rubber and fiber, and to increase tourism. ASA carried on some investigations in this area.

In the meetings at New Delhi in February, 1968, of the United Nations Conference on Trade and Development (UNCTAD), a joint position was established by the trade union of countries from the different underdeveloped regions on certain trade and commodity marketing policies. With such agreement they judged they could face the high income countries in a better bargaining position.

The forms of cooperation listed above require little or no abrogation of sovereignty through commitments to change domestic government policies. But regional cooperation may require changes in domestic policies. These changes can have varying degrees of political significance. Promotion of traditional exports may require agreement to enforce standard sanitary regulations within individual countries, and to set up a standard grading system for ensuring the quality of regional products. Promotion of tourism may persuade nations to simplify or ease health and immigration regulations.

Large benefits from regional cooperation are often expected to come from increased intraregional trade. Trade may be encouraged between two or more countries of the region by joint simplifying and standardizing of customs regulations. ECAFE has recommended such measures, and ASA to some extent undertook to unify national customs codes.

There may be agreement for a regional payments union, to cut the need for restrictions on intraregional trade by deficit countries. Possibilities for an Asian payments union were discussed as long ago as 1955 at the Simla Conference. ECAFE sponsored a meeting in July of 1967 on this question. The Regional Cooperation for Development (RCD) composed of two ECAFE members, Pakistan and Iran, and a non-ECAFE member, Turkey, reached an agreement in June 1967 to establish a clearinghouse for regional payments.

Trade may be encouraged within the region by lowering or eliminating tariffs and other trade barriers. In 1963 ASA urged study of the possibility of setting up a regional free-trade area. There have been suggestions that the Association of Southeast Asian Nations (ASEAN) which includes Singapore and Indonesia along with the ASA countries, may evolve into a free-trade area or customs union.

Most writers distinguish between regional cooperation of the types described above, and regional integration in the form of a free-trade area, a customs union, a common market, or economic and political union. Regional integration requires a substantial commitment from governments to remove economic barriers and other forms of discrimination among themselves. Countries that form a free-trade area must reduce or eliminate tariff barriers against each other. A customs union requires that participating countries also adopt a common external tariff against non-member countries. A common market provides additionally for free movements of the factors of production.

The desire for stable trade and payments relationships and factor movements exerts pressure toward coordinating monetary and tax policies so that prices will be stable or change at similar rates. Coordination of these and other economic policies and regulations are the features of an economic union. Efficient functioning of an economic union requires a high degree of political coordination which may lead eventually to a political union.

Finally, there may be more or less complete political union, as exemplified in one form by the assimilation of West Irian (West New Guinea) into Indonesia and by India's absorption of Goa, and in another by the checkered history of Malaysia.

Would establishing a free-trade area in part or all of the region imply prior or concomitant agreement on the location of given industries? The argument for such a policy is that duplicating investment should be avoided, in order to avoid the resulting excess capacity and high average costs due to small-scale production. Agreed-upon specialization would be expected to insure that new investment and economic activity do not concentrate in the more economically-advanced countries of the region. This line of reasoning, in turn, implies that major investments would have to be decided upon, within each country, in the main by government policy; that private decisions and competitive pressures would not or could not be allowed to be effective in determining an acceptable pattern for location, growth of industry, and contraction of production.

ECAFE has been in the forefront in urging this kind of policy (see Chapter 2). A 1963 ministerial meeting of ECAFE member nations responded to an earlier economists' report by accepting as an aim of policy the establishment of a customs union or free-trade area within the region, and agreed that national development plans should be harmonized in order to achieve rational location and size of new industries. The RCD shows elements of an agreed specialization approach to regional cooperation. In the summer of 1967 ECAFE sponsored working parties of experts who explored possibilities for agreed specialization in the iron and steel, aluminum, and petrochemical industries among the ASEAN nations.

The range of regional cooperation and integration measures, listed above according to their formality and the degree of commitment of resources, is only one possible pattern of classification of experience and alternatives. The cases mentioned may also be arranged according to comprehensiveness of geographical and economic coverage. Some regional projects require the agreement of two or more countries of the region, while other regionally useful enterprises can be set up by one government, perhaps with support from the United Nations or other international organizations, the United States or other governments, or private foundations.

Cooperation can exist *within* the region: ASA has fitted this category as does ASEAN; and so did Maphilindo (Malaya, the Philippines, Indonesia). Or cooperation can exist among one or more countries of the region and countries outside. The Asian Development Bank, set up in 1966 in Manila, fits this category. The Lower Mekong Committee is composed of four regional countries but draws extensive technical and financial assistance from outside the region. The Asian Productivity Organization has its nine members in Asia, from Pakistan to Japan. ECAFE has twenty-three Asian members, in Southeast Asia and beyond. SEATO has Thailand, the Philippines, and Pakistan and some non-Asian members. The Colombo Plan has fifteen Asian members, from Afghanistan to South Korea, plus countries outside. The Asian and Pacific Council (ASPAC), founded in 1966 at meetings in South Korea, is also a mixed grouping.

Regional projects may involve major physical investment (the Asian Highway, the Mekong River project), or mainly educational and technical outlays (the International Rice Research Institute at Los Baños, the Philippines, the Institute for Economic Development and Planning at Bangkok, APO, the United Nations technician-exchange agreements, any well-thought-of education or research program that attracts students from other countries of the region).

Intergovernmental agreements may be mainly economic (trade and payments treaties) or may have only small or indirect economic significance as in political, cultural, education, and research pacts.

Regional arrangements may or may not have invidious economic and/or military implications: SEATO, or trade and investment agreements prescribing the national location of strategic industry, *versus* educational and research projects with entry open to students from other countries, and research findings freely available.

Finally, there are organizations that have functioned (ECAFE, SEATO, ASA except from 1963 to 1965 when Malaysia and the Philippines broke diplomatic relations, the Colombo Plan, APO). In contrast there are proposals advanced for domestic or foreign political effect that have not functioned (Maphilindo was hardly more than a slogan and sentiment; Sukarno's NEFO, Newly Emerging Forces, is another example).

The bars to mutually useful regional cooperation in Southeast Asia have normally been, as elsewhere in the world, political. And in major part the causes of such cooperation as has gone on have also been political.

Maphilindo, a purely political vehicle, died getting born. ASA's imaginative efforts were halted mainly due to the political falling-out between Malaysia and the Philippines. SEATO survives mainly because of its political-military implications. Other organizations (ECAFE, APO, the Colombo Plan) survive and are effective in large part because of continuing outside support—which is also partly political-economic in motivation, and only partly disinterested.

Both old and new antagonisms divide the countries of the region, causing acute sensitivity to the political and military implications of regional measures. *Confrontasi* between Indonesia and Malaysia had deeper roots than Sukarno's fancy. The roots are still there even though Confrontation is over. There is long-standing antagonism between Cambodia on the one hand, and Vietnam and Thailand on the other. Malaysia and the Philippines have quarreled over North Borneo.

Southeast Asia is a major cold war arena. Indonesia, Laos, Cambodia, and Burma have been mainly neutral between East and West, though the West has often thought they leaned toward Peking or Moscow. Now Indonesia again leans West. Malaysia, Singapore, Thailand, the Philippines, and Taiwan have been sympathetic toward the West.

And basic economic policies differ. Burma, Indonesia, and India have been "inward looking," relying on direct controls and controlling trade. Malaysia, Thailand, the Philippines, and Taiwan have been "outward looking," choosing to rely more on private enterprise and relatively free trade. These differences in patterns of economic decision-making are usually highly charged with domestic and international political significance.

The political and economic differences and sensitivities point a moral. Regional cooperation measures have the best chance of success when they achieve a net maximum of two goals: the maximum contribution for the obvious economic and other advantages of the region, and a maximum of intraregional political neutrality and colorlessness. The avoidance of political suspicions and antagonisms is an absolute requisite.

NOTE

1. In this book the terms "less developed," "developing," and "under-developed" are synonymous; "more developed" and "developed" are also synonymous. In the editors' opinion, the most accurate terms are "less developed" and "more developed." From the perspective of a century or so of successful economic growth ahead, all countries today will be less developed. Among today's lower income countries, a few are regressing economically, not going forward. All higher income countries are increasing their average incomes. The editors have not attempted to enforce conformity in the use of these terms, however, especially since the terms "developed" and "developing" are used in United Nations documents. frequently cited in these chapters.

I

The Context of
Economic Cooperation

Chapter 1

PROBLEMS AND PROSPECTS OF ECONOMIC COOPERATION IN SOUTHEAST ASIA

WU TA-YEH

THE SOUTHEAST ASIA REGION AND ITS ECONOMIC BACKGROUND

Southeast Asia—defined for the purposes of this paper as the area extending from Burma to Hong Kong and Taiwan—includes Cambodia, Laos, Malaysia, Singapore, Thailand, and Vietnam, Brunei, Indonesia, and the Philippines. Geographical closeness, comparable climate, and limited domestic markets cause similar problems which justify closer cooperation among some or all of the countries of the region. This region has a total area of 4,000,000 square kilometers and a total population of 270,000,000 in twelve politically separate territories. About 40 percent of the area and population belongs to Indonesia. The eleven other political units possess a total area of 2,600,000 square kilometers and a total population of 165,000,000. Most of these territories are too small in natural resources and population to be economically independent, and this problem is intensified by their low levels of income, technical training, and purchasing power.

All of these countries except Thailand were colonies of the metropolitan countries, and, of these colonies, all except Brunei and Hong Kong became independent only after World War II. With the exception of Hong Kong and Singapore, which handled a large volume of entrepôt trade before the war, all were countries producing agricultural products and minerals, with very little manufacturing. After the war, prices of the primary products fluctuated greatly, often with falling trends due, in part, to substitution of synthetic for natural products. Industrialization and diversification are therefore generally considered necessary and urgent.

These countries also identify economic independence with political independence and, whenever possible, aim at self-sufficiency, with strong reliance on government efforts. Although their economic development cannot be patterned closely on that of the centrally planned economies because of basic differences in political and economic systems, these countries are inclined to follow lines of development somewhat similar to those in the centrally planned economies and to accord special priority to manufacturing. Capital goods and capital-intensive industries are judged to play the most dynamic role in economic development.

The indiscriminate development of industries in countries without sufficient domestic markets and efficient management often requires government subsidies or high protection. When the market does not permit the efficient operation of more than one production unit, partial monopoly leads to inefficiency and high cost or low quality. Limited size of market may prevent the industry from being operated at optimum capacity. If a second unit should be established, the scale of production will be even smaller.

Sometimes consumers pay unreasonably high prices for the protected products because of lack of experience or inefficiency on the part of management and labor. Capacity may be underutilized because of irregular flow of raw material and spare parts caused by inefficient exchange and trade controls, difficulties in transportation and marketing, and problems of obtaining working capital. It is not uncommon for some of the protected industries to have a negative value added (that is, world-market price of the product is less than the delivered price of imported raw materials and the depreciation on imported equipment), although these industries may still increase employment.

A common phenomenon in most developing countries is that the inefficient agricultural sector does not receive sufficient attention despite its potential for increased employment and for a greater return from a given amount of capital. The experience of Taiwan indicates the potential scope of agricultural diversification and of rapid increase of per-hectare yield. Although agricultural development is always included in development plans, sometimes with fairly sizeable budgetary provisions, the intention is usually not fully implemented.

Insufficient attention is given to agriculture because of the comparative ease with which industries can be established with imported equipment and the application of techniques developed in the West, in comparison with the formidable task of organizing and training the millions of individual farmers scattered widely throughout the country. Emphasis on the sector in which the countries have the least experience, and neglect of the sector that might provide quicker employment and income at the present stage of development, have generally resulted in a very slow rate of overall growth save where foreign aid or foreign expenditure in the country is large,[1] and where, as in Hong Kong, cheap, skilled labor and relatively experienced entrepreneurs are available. Taiwan is an exception: agricultural development has been given considerable emphasis, and the high rate of overall growth was made possible only because of the success in agriculture.

The slow rate of increase of national income and export earnings, the rapid rate of population growth, and the emphasis on industrial development bring about a continuously increasing need of foreign exchange for the import of capital goods, of intermediate goods, and sometimes also of consumption goods. It is not possible to produce many of these capital goods in the small Southeast Asian countries, however, because of inadequate demand and of the limited availability of capital and technical ability. The same applies to many consumer goods such as paper, and to intermediate goods such as basic chemicals. The serious limitations of individual countries lead to one of the strongest arguments for regional cooperation.

THE NATURE OF INTRAREGIONAL TRADE

In 1962, intraregional exports of the twelve Southeast Asian countries amounted to US$1,583 million and intraregional imports to US$1,641 million (see Table 1.1). Intraregional exports equalled 31 percent of total exports and intraregional imports equalled 26 percent of total imports. These percentages are higher than the intraregional trade of all developing ECAFE countries partly because of the entrepôt trade. Intraregional trade consisted mainly of food and live animals, crude materials, and mineral fuels (Standard International Trade Classification [SITC] groups 0, 2, and 3). These commodities constituted 66 percent of total intraregional exports and 77 percent of total intraregional imports. Of the region's exports of food, crude materials, and mineral fuels—which amounted to US$3,618

TABLE 1.1—Intraregional trade of Southeast Asia,[a] 1962
(Million US$)

SITC Section	Exports[b]			Imports		
	Total	Intraregional exports	% of intra-regional exports in total exports	Total	Intraregional imports	% of intra-regional imports in total imports
0 Food and live animals	1,034	389	38	1,052	414	39
1 Beverages and tobacco	73	39	53	116	21	18
2 Crude material excluding fuels	2,060	348	17	767	509	66
3 Mineral fuels, etc.	524	302	58	585	338	58
4 Animal and vegetable oils and fats	95	18	19	50	17	34
5 Chemicals	70	50	72	522	42	8
6 Basic manufactures	587	204	35	1,505	157	10
7 Machinery and transport equipment	158	130	82	1,197	53	4
8 Miscellaneous manufactured goods	417	76	18	326	64	20
9 Goods not classified	50	27	55	79	26	32
Total	5,068	1,583	31	6,199	1,641	26

[a] Trade statistics for Southeast Asia cover Brunei, Burma, Cambodia, Taiwan, Hong Kong, Indonesia, Laos, Malaysia, Singapore, the Philippines, Thailand, and South Vietnam.

[b] For Hong Kong, only domestic exports are included.

Source: Basic statistics were taken from United Nations, *Foreign Trade Statistics of Asia and the Far East, 1962*, 1, no. 1 (1965).

million—only 29 percent went to the region. On the other hand, 52 percent of the import requirements for these commodities (US$2,404 million) were imported from countries within the region. A large part of the intraregional trade is transit trade, as well as reexports after some simple processing or grading. Producing countries are now increasing their efforts to export these products directly to the developed countries.

Similar climates result in the production of similar agricultural products such as rice, rubber, timber, hides and skins, coconuts, other oil seeds, and hard fibers. The region also produces certain minerals such as tin, iron ore, petroleum, and some other products, but most of the products are exported to the developed countries. Rice is the major commodity traded mainly within the region, but most of the rice-deficit countries, such as Indonesia, Malaysia, and the Philippines, are attempting to achieve self-sufficiency. The final result will probably be a reduction or a slowing down in the rate of increase of rice trade. The prospect for expanding intraregional trade in other primary products is also limited.

The prospects for intraregional trade in manufactured articles are brighter. Table 1.1 shows that 72 percent of the region's chemical exports and 82 percent of the region's exports of machinery and transport equipment were within the region. This trade, however, constituted only a very small fraction of total import requirements of these commodities: 8 percent of the US$522 million imports of chemicals and 4 percent of the US$1,197 million imports of machinery and transport equipment. The region also depends heavily on the countries outside the region for its trade in other manufactures (SITC 6 and 8). Of the US$1,004 million of such exports, only 28 percent went to the region. On the other hand, only 12 percent of the US$1,831 million imports of these articles came from the region. Since economic development and increase in per-capita income will further increase the demand for manufactured goods, there is a large potential market to be captured by the developing countries.[2]

At present, countries which developed their industries a few years ahead of the others are exporting manufactured products to neighboring countries. Instead of developing different types of industries, however, the lagging countries tend to develop industries similar to those of their exporting neighbors, at least partially offsetting any complementarities. This is easily understandable. Many of these industries, such as textiles, sugar, plastic wares, monosodium glutamate, and cement, cater to domestic consumption needs; produce things relatively easy to manufacture; and do not require substantial capital investment. Other industries, once they have shown themselves to be successful in the neighboring countries, are chosen for development with the belief or the hope that they will be similarly successful. These include textile fabrics, garments, plywood, and electrical appliances—industries in which the developing countries compete among themselves in the world market.

During the colonial period, the metropolitan countries controlled their colonies economically as well as politically, and there was a wide discrepancy between the income level and the economic power of the controlling and the controlled people. As a result, the developing countries (most of which attained independence only after the Second World War) often identify economic independence with political independence and have adopted various policies to avoid foreign economic domination. In some cases, they have nationalized industry and commerce. They have reserved for nationals the right to own and operate certain industries, commerce, and services and have limited direct foreign-capital participation in business to no more than 49 percent of total capital. They have restricted the employment of foreign personnel and the immigration of both unskilled and skilled workers. Diversification and self-sufficiency policies often cause the development of industries the optimum size of which far exceeds domestic demand and in which engineering and administrative requirements are beyond the local competence. Some countries even desire to have the highest possible domestic content in products despite much higher cost and lower quality. These policies constitute formidable obstacles to international and regional economic cooperation.

BILATERAL ECONOMIC COOPERATION

Despite the obstacles, there is a certain amount of economic cooperation among the Southeast Asian developing countries. Countries tend to formulate industrial and export-promotion policies like those of their neighbors. There is intraregional transfer of capital for direct investment, although the amount is not large. Intraregional capital flow is sometimes stimulated by quota restrictions in industrial countries on imports. Some countries recruit technical personnel or skilled workers from neighboring countries whose industrial development is a few years ahead of their own. Technical and skilled personnel recruited from certain developing countries in Southeast Asia have the reputation of being hard working and responsible, and the cost of this kind of cooperation is extremely low in comparison with the cost of technical personnel from the highly developed countries. There are also successful cases in Southeast Asia in which one developing country has supplied another with complete plant equipment, together with all technical personnel and most of the skilled workers.

Relaxation of immigration restrictions can easily expand the intraregional flow of labor, but limitations are obvious. Industrial experience in developing countries is extremely limited; the industries that can successfully compete in the world market in cost and quality are few in number. Most of the needed assistance has to be sought from the highly developed countries. Regional cooperation must, therefore, be supported by international cooperation.

COMMON MARKET

The widest scope for economic cooperation among Southeast Asian countries lies in promoting the common welfare by concerted action of several, if not all, countries. This may be done at different levels, according to the degree of cooperation required. At one extreme is complete economic integration in the form of economic union; at the other is closer contacts among countries for an exchange of views, including the various meetings sponsored or convened by international organizations. The more extensive the cooperation, the greater will be the difficulties encountered.

The success of the European Economic Community has influenced an increasing number of people to think about creating a similar common market among Asian countries. The advantages of such a plan are most obvious. It would pool capital and trained personnel—both of which are scarce in the region—for better use. In comparison with several small factories, one in each country, one or two large factories for the region would economize on the use of these scarce resources for many industries. With a larger market, optimum scale can be achieved. Even if the combined market is still not large enough, the possibility for export to countries outside the region is brighter, because a larger, protected market can absorb the fixed cost of production so that the price of exports may be based on variable cost alone. This practice is already followed in many industrial countries for numerous commodities. With a wider market assured it is also easier to attract foreign capital and to receive cooperation from the developed countries. Foreign firms in developed countries, accustomed to large-scale operation, do not find it attractive to establish several independent factories in different countries, each with a small domestic market. The increased possibility of specialization according to factor endowment also increases overall productivity, promotes growth, and realizes external economies by establishing a cluster of related industries. With an expanded market for each country's product and increased imports from the member countries, more foreign exchange resources can be made available for purchase, from the developed countries, of capital equipment or other essentials not produced within the common-market countries.

A common market in Asia has special problems, however. During the colonial period, most countries had closer economic ties and personal contacts with their metropolitan countries than with their neighboring countries. The contacts among Asian countries after the war, although increasing, are still not frequent enough to create the mutual understanding and cooperation needed to implement a common-market scheme. Nor is there a common language as in Latin America (although the increasing popularity of English is a great help). The basic hindrance, however, is the desire for economic independence fomented by strong nationalist sentiments.

In addition, different countries vary in the degree to which they are attractive for industrial development. The location of industry depends not only on supply of raw materials, the availability of skilled and unskilled labor, marketing and transport facilities, and other economic and social infrastructure, but also on political and social stability, and the economic policies and administrative efficiency of the government. A simple and unconditional common market in Southeast Asia will not benefit all countries equally, because of the unequal economic, social, and political assets of the various countries. Countries that have low-cost, skilled, and disciplined labor; enterprising entrepreneurs; good infrastructure; and adequate transport facilities—e.g., Hong Kong—will benefit most. Other countries where these factors are lacking—e.g., Laos—might not be able to have any modern industry at all. Although Hong Kong and Laos are extreme cases, they illustrate the range in investment potential of the various countries. Even among countries with similar backgrounds, there is usually a fear of opening the country's domestic market freely to the competition of other members, because most industries are at an infant stage of development.

A common market, as such, may not be enough to promote development. Without supplementary measures, the rate of development in some countries would accelerate at the cost of retardation in others. Negotiations on a commodity-by-commodity basis appear necessary. Trade liberalization among the participating countries can be accomplished more easily if the negotiations involve only a few commodities at first. The number can then be increased gradually. For this purpose, it is easier to group a smaller number of countries with similar conditions. In the long run, all countries will benefit, especially if there is free movement of the factors of production. Countries will also be stimulated by the examples set by their partners who have been successful in improving their own investment environment.

Economic independence for a small territory with a small population and limited purchasing power does not maximize income. Countries must realize that economic cooperation, or even integration, is not necessarily in conflict with nationalism and that economic integration of the smaller countries, even if it is not immediately practicable, will be the only ultimate solution. If countries take these considerations into account before industrialization has proceeded too far, they will greatly reduce or eliminate the waste of later readjustment. The choice of industries should be based on the long-term comparative advantages of different industries in different countries of the region. Such a choice should not be based on their present relative positions, but should allow for expected changes after a period of initial development.

There are, of course, difficulties in putting this principle into practice. In theory, the principle is most readily applicable to government industries and to industries established with government initiative or assistance. The majority of such industries, however, are chosen by the governments because they are felt to have security or prestige value or to have chain effects that will help in training workers or that will lead to the establishment of allied industries. If self-sufficiency and prestige value are the main purposes, the choice may not take sufficient account of long-term objectives. Similarly, private industries aiming at immediate profits will not be influenced by long-range considerations unless government plays a role through tariffs, quotas, or export subsidies. Where there is a wide choice of industries to be sponsored or encouraged by the government, consideration at an early stage of long-term regional goals would facilitate future economic cooperation or integration, would reduce readjustments, and would leave such forward-planning countries one step ahead of the others.

PLAN HARMONIZATION AND SPECIALIZATION

One method suggested for incorporating long-term economic considerations at an early stage is the coordination and harmonization of development plans. Although this idea was proposed several years ago, nothing concrete has emerged. The major difficulty is that draft development plans are always considered confidential—not even available for open discussion within the respective countries. Plans in the draft stage sometimes represent only tentative thinking, and so publicity is shunned. If the public in individual countries do not have a chance to comment on the draft plans, it is not likely that governments can be expected to consult each other before the plans are adopted. Unlike the Common Market countries of Europe, these countries have no common incentive like the Marshall Plan to encourage coordination. Many countries are more interested in trade with developed countries than with neighboring countries. There is more complementarity between the developing and the developed countries, and exports to the developed countries usually claim a higher priority because the foreign exchange earned may be used to import scarce capital goods and technical knowledge.

National development plans vary in the amount of detail: some include production targets for individual industries or commodities, while others merely outline the general direction of development, leaving the details to be spelled out in the implementation stage, or to the choice of private investors. It is doubtful whether harmonization of plans at this general level is useful. Few countries implement their plans exactly as they are published. Changes evolve from the uncertain response of the private sector and from the uncertain flow of foreign capital. At the project level, to the extent that foreign-capital participation is involved, secrecy during the negotiation stage is preferred for many industries, because of the fear of losing the project to other countries.

Although strict coordination of development plans is difficult, it

338.9159 Ec74e
c. 1

should at least be possible to agree on general lines of initial specialization. The goal of many countries is to become as economically
diversified as possible, in order to avoid the difficulties of overspecialization experienced by countries dependent on a few primary products.
Any rigid restriction on industrial specialization is not likely to be
welcome. Countries feel they should be free to develop any industry,
especially if the cost of production is not very far above the world
price.

But it is not possible for the smaller countries to establish a wide
variety of industries, especially industries subject to economies of
scale and requiring substantial capital and a high level of technique. It
is, therefore, to the joint interest of these countries to agree on some
initial division of labor. Industrial efficiency not only requires large
enough markets for a single plant, but also depends on the proper
functioning of a whole complex of related industries. Instead of select-
ing a number of industries at random for development, it is more
advantageous to develop a cluster of related industries. For example,
one country might develop its industries centering around machinery
manufacturing, another around chemicals, another around electrical
equipment, and another around precision instruments. Within each
field, there would be, ultimately, a large enough variety of commodities for diversification, including the products and by-products of
allied industries. Yet there would still be a high degree of specialization and important external economies, thus encouraging the development of greater skills and improvements in design and technology.

Alternatively, each country could specialize in different types of
engineering products, chemicals, or pharmaceutical goods in order to
attain diversification among various industrial groups. For the highly
complex industries such as automobiles, each country might also
specialize in the manufacturing of certain groups of spare parts. Any
agreed specialization will, of course, require adjustment in the overall
economic-development plans, including planning in the trade sector.

Demand for the products of industries such as fertilizer and paper
may be quite low at first but can be expected to expand greatly over
time. In such cases, it would be more economical, initially, to have
one or two countries in the region set up plants of optimum size and
supply their neighboring countries in exchange for other products for
which the optimum scale of production is also large. It would be
unreasonable, however, permanently to prohibit other countries from
establishing their own plants.

If successful, initial specialization may, of course, make it difficult for other countries to compete at a later date. Specialization may continue, with a second or third factory established in the same country. Such multiplication of units can successively increase external economies. If, however, the country assigned a given industry fails to develop it as expected, the free entry of other countries, after the lapse of a specified period of time, will undercut the high-cost country. In the long run, free competition within a common market is still the best way to achieve high quality and low cost. Allocation of industries for initial specialization should be made among countries only after sufficient consideration has been given to long-term economic feasibility.

Problems will arise concerning how to ensure the initial market for these products, particularly since the new industry may have high costs in its early stages. The most common measure is to lower, or to remove completely, intraregional import tariffs on the agreed products, so that the regional products can outcompete those from outside the region. However, most of these products, whether capital equipment or basic materials, are free from import duties, and levying them would increase the production cost of the industries utilizing the products. Nevertheless, the result should not be worse than that of producing these articles in each country. If each of the participating countries in such a cooperative scheme expands the market for its own products, there are mutual benefits.

When deciding upon the fields of specialization, there should also be decisions on quality standards and on the price differentials which would be permissible in comparison with the world price. In consumer goods such as paper, developing countries may agree to accept lower quality products at lower cost to suit their standard of living. Capital goods, however, affect the productivity of equipment for many years to come, and so the quality standard should always be sufficiently high. High standards should be applied to medicines also, since they affect the health of the population.

If accompanied by reduced tariffs among the participating countries on the agreed products or by a common external tariff on the agreed products and free trade among the participating countries, agreed specialization encourages a common market. A common external tariff may have to be applied, not only to the direct products based on specialization, if these products are intermediate goods, but possibly extended to the final products produced with these intermediate goods.

For example, if a given article, X, is produced with capital equipment from Country A, and materials from countries B and C, all under the specialization scheme, the production cost of X may be too high as compared with the import price from outside the region. Under such circumstances, a common external tariff on X may also have to be introduced, together with free trade or reduced tariffs among the participating countries. This situation could gradually force the inclusion of an increasing number of commodities in a common market.

One of the major problems in developing countries is how to import capital equipment and intermediate goods without the means to pay for them. The payments problem will be eased if each participating country produces some of these items to exchange with other participating countries. Countries producing final consumption goods with regionally produced equipment and materials may also ease their payments problem if these products share the privilege of a common external tariff on the one hand and free trade or reduced tariffs among the participating countries on the other.

Organization of agreed specialization may take various forms and should be flexible. If a group of countries agrees on fields of special emphasis for initial specialization, the agreement may also specify that other developing countries making use of these intermediate goods will also enjoy the privilege of a reduced tariff, or tariff exemption, when manufactured goods using the intermediate goods are imported into the participating countries. Arrangements such as these may expand the market of the specialized products beyond the participating countries. With specialization and an expanding market, the new industries should have a better chance to raise quality and to lower costs, and even to compete in the world market.

JOINT VENTURES

Even if there are no agreed fields of specialization, large-scale industries may be developed through joint ventures. This form of cooperation was proposed at the Manila Ministerial Conference on Asian Economic Cooperation, and a number of projects have been suggested to the Asian Industrial Development Council. Flexibility of participation is greater on a project basis. Different countries may participate in various joint projects, and fields of specialization need not be pre-agreed among countries. The forms of participation may range from contributing capital, management, technical knowledge, and technical personnel, to sharing in the market for the products. In addition to the benefits of pooled resources, joint ventures also may attract more external assistance.

Marketing problems will be minimized if the industry is well selected from the point of view of availability of high-quality raw materials, central location, and availability of skilled labor at a reasonable cost, and if economies of scale are realized. If the cost is still not competitive, special marketing arrangements will be necessary. There will be no problem if the products are used by the governments of the participating countries. Nor will problems arise if the investors in the joint ventures are private firms which will make use of the products. For example, the plywood manufacturers in Malaysia, the Philippines, and Singapore may invest jointly in the production of methanol from Brunei natural gas and may share in the market for the products. Without some linkage of this kind, any industry with a cost higher than the world price, but requiring an export market, will not be attractive for joint capital participation unless the purpose is to maintain a sure and steady flow of imports, or unless the arrangement is to supply a given quantity of the product per year in payment for the interest and amortization on the loan capital. Competitive cost is therefore most important.

The largest joint venture in Asia is the Asian Development Bank (ADB). The authorized capital of $1,100 million is small—only slightly more than one dollar per capita—compared with the needs of the developing Asian countries. But the provision that the Bank will give special regard to the needs of the smaller and less-developed countries in financing multinational projects[3] may enable it to play an important role in developing Southeast Asia, especially with respect to the joint projects.

The Asian Conference on Industrialization was held in Manila in 1965 under the sponsorship of ECAFE. It recommended the establishment of an Asian Industrial Council as a permanent organ to promote the progressive harmonization of industrial development plans, to identify joint industrial projects, and to provide assistance in the preparation of industrial feasibility studies and in other aspects of industrial development. The council is also expected to assist the ADB in the various studies and surveys necessary for the negotiation of loans and, together with the ADB, to play an important role in the industrialization of Asian countries.[4]

In Southeast Asia, the largest joint project at present is the development of the Lower Mekong basin, involving four countries: Cambodia, Laos, Thailand, and South Vietnam. The project is made possible by the efforts of ECAFE and by substantial external assistance. But joint efforts of the riparian countries thus far have been confined to investigation and planning. Separate dams are being constructed on the tributary rivers in individual countries, although it is expected that closer cooperation will follow in various areas such as electricity supply, navigation, industry, agriculture, and fisheries. Dams on main streams at the common border of two countries will also be constructed at a later time.

An important experiment in regional cooperation, still in an early stage, is the Association of Southeast Asia (ASA), composed of Malaysia, the Philippines, and Thailand. The success or failure of the ASA may affect future cooperation among other countries. While the ASA may, in the long run, intend to form a common market, the three countries are approaching this possibility cautiously, beginning their cooperation on a project basis. Three groups of projects were approved at the third meeting of the foreign ministers of the three countries in August, 1966: joint projects for external financial aid, projects for economic cooperation, and projects for technical cooperation. Joint projects for external financial assistance include telecommunications projects linking ASA countries, expansion and improvement of port and airport facilities, and a marine fisheries training and development center. Projects for economic cooperation include an ASA fund, trade liberalization, commerce and navigation agreements, a products display center, a customs-study tour, promotion of tourism, and an ASA shipping line. Projects for technical cooperation include research on coconuts, rice, rubber, palm oil, sugar technology, pulp and paper technology, and cholera and other diseases.

Other programs agreed upon include studies of preferential tariff treatment, of cargo movements, and of primary commodities; and consultation and sharing of experience on the problem of human resources development. These projects certainly mean closer economic cooperation and may finally lead to a common market. The combined markets and resources of the three countries are, however, meager for many purposes. An expansion of the Association, or an extension of some of the joint ventures to include other Southeast Asian countries, may provide additional benefits.

For example, the ASA shipping line is a good proposal. The practice of discriminatory ocean-freight rates against Asian developing countries has been discussed repeatedly at ECAFE meetings, but nothing useful has yet been achieved. Since there is resistance on the part of the existing steamship lines to altering their practice, an effective strategy would be to establish a large shipping company with the participation of the interested Southeast Asian countries. It could handle the freight between Asian ports and also between the ports of Asian countries and the rest of the world. The competition would help to lower the other shipping lines' rates for Asian products. An expansion of the proposed ASA shipping line to include a larger number of countries would make it more effective.

If a multinational shipping company is not feasible, cooperation among existing national lines of several Southeast Asian countries (such as synchronized schedules at Asian ports, agreed routes to non-Asian countries, and mutual reduction of freight rates) would also bring about fuller utilization of the present shipping facilities and lower costs. Through cooperation, member countries could be assured of a certain freight volume, making it possible to expand present facilities.

One of the joint ventures already proposed, but temporarily dropped, is the formation of a joint ASA airline, patterned on the Scandinavian Airlines System. Although this proposal has been temporarily shelved because of the advent of supersonic jets that may make present purchase of new aircraft unprofitable, the consolidation of separate national airlines for international flights should prove to be a sound project; if not, small Asian airlines have no hope of competing with the big Western airlines. The expansion of the original proposal to include other Southeast Asian countries may make the airline even more profitable, because it would increase passengers and freight from Asian countries and would provide access to additional amounts of capital.

OTHER POSSIBLE TYPES OF COOPERATION

It is not the intention of this paper to compile a list of possible measures for regional economic cooperation, but rather to outline some of the problems involved in a few of the more commonly discussed measures. There is no doubt that closer economic cooperation is necessary and that ultimately there will be a common market at least among the smaller countries. But, since more extensive cooperation always encounters greater difficulties, it is often easier to start from partial cooperation on a project basis or from cooperation among a smaller number of countries. The lead taken by ASA is a good sign, although progress is still slow. A cooperative arrangement among the three ASA countries may be easier to achieve than one among more countries or among countries with less similar economies. But, since the combined ASA market is small at present, the expansion of the Association to include other Southeast Asian countries may be necessary for many types of projects.

Similarly, although the subject of this paper is the economic cooperation of Southeast Asia, extension of cooperation to other small developing countries like Ceylon and Korea can expand the market and increase the resources available. For example, if Ceylon has or develops a comparative advantage in certain products which can be exchanged for rice under trade agreements or other arrangements, both Ceylon and the rice-producing countries may benefit. At present, the cost of producing rice in the rice-exporting countries is considerably lower than it is in Ceylon, and the subsidy to rice producers in Ceylon therefore appears to discourage the best utilization of its human, land, and financial resources. If Ceylon's special products are not required directly by the rice-producing countries, tripartite or quadripartite trading arrangements might be concluded.

Cooperation in certain areas might also be expanded to include the larger developing countries such as India and Pakistan. Some of their present mineral and agricultural products are not produced in Southeast Asia. Their large population can not only provide a market for goods produced in Southeast Asia but may also support certain large-scale industries that might not be profitably established in the smaller countries. Cooperation with the developed countries, whether in Asia or in other continents, is especially needed to secure technical personnel, patent rights, equipment, financial resources, and marketing arrangements for primary and manufactured goods.

Most of the more comprehensive forms of cooperation require joint sacrifice in order to gain the benefits derived from them. Naturally, countries will weigh expected benefits against sacrifices. Sacrifice may be immediate, while benefits are long term.

There are types of regional cooperation that do not require much, if any, national sacrifice and that yield more immediate benefits, at least to some of the participating countries. For example, there is usually no objection to cooperation in the field of research and training, particularly if it is supported by external resources. The United Nations Asian Institute for Economic Development and Planning, which trains economic planners and policymakers, is an outstanding example. There are other fields of research and planning that are also beyond the individual capacity of small countries but that could be gone into effectively if collective action is taken.

The arts of public administration and of industrial management, for example, are unfamiliar to the newly independent developing countries. Western experts in Asian countries have reported that the lower efficiency prevalent in industry is generally the fault, not of workers, but of management. Often, efficiency has dropped immediately after Western management experts left the country. While college graduates of Western countries receive in-service training before they take more responsible jobs, graduates in the developing countries have to learn by trial and error—sometimes in advanced or senior administrative posts.

Because of the differences in social background and the inertia of centuries-old traditions, Western administrative techniques may not always be as directly applicable as science and technology. Regional institutes could help identify and study the special problems of Asia and could devise methods for improving administrative and productive efficiency, since very few of the smaller developing countries can afford to establish national institutions to provide high-quality training. Such institutes should not duplicate the regular courses of national universities but should aim instead at the training of policymaking executives. The help of experienced personnel from developing countries would be needed in studying administrative problems and in developing new approaches. As experience accumulates, the research and training staff of regional institutions could also serve as administrative or management consultants to different countries.

Regional cooperation in science and technology is another area in which there are immediate benefits. Most industrial techniques and processes developed in the West can be directly applied, but it is also possible to lower costs by substituting cheap labor for expensive machinery. Labor substitution is only applicable to a limited number of processes in manufacturing as developed in the West, but new processes may be devised. There is also greater scope for such substitution in material handling if labor is well organized. Joint efforts can be made to develop cheaper production processes and to find ways to utilize raw material, by-products, and wastes that are abundant in the region. The costs of services of the foreign experts required will often be too high for any small country to bear alone. The Asian Council for Industrial Research and Technology, the Engineering Panel, and the Prototype Production and Training Centers proposed for the Asian Industrial Development Council should meet some of these needs. Although the initial costs are high, income can also be derived from the services rendered.

Cooperation on standards and promotion of Southeast Asian exports is another promising area for regional cooperation. Most countries still do not have a good system of export quality control. Even in countries that have such a system, the standards and the examination procedures are not always satisfactory and may not command the confidence of foreign importers and consumers. Certification by a regional bureau—in which Western experts are in key positions and help prescribe standards for selected articles, examine sample products, and certify the quality—would command much higher respect than that obtained by national bureaus. Adherence to prescribed standards must be the responsibility of the national bureaus, although the regional bureau may provide technical assistance to the national bureaus. Charges for such assistance might partly or largely cover the cost of such a regional bureau. A regional standards committee is now being proposed for the Asian Industrial Development Council. The objective of the committee appears to be confined to the prescription of standards only, but perhaps this function may be expanded to cover wider regulatory activities.

Joint efforts in export promotion also would be more economical and effective than individual efforts by small countries. The first Asian trade fair was organized in 1966 with considerable success, and product display centers have been proposed by ASA. Other promotional measures might also be considered. A regional export-promotion board, with offices in the main importing countries, could do promotion work at a smaller cost to each of the member countries.

Some Asian manufactured products are unquestionably inferior in quality. But many products of the developing countries are not generally recognized or accepted even though they are comparable in quality with those of the industrially developed countries. This is partly because of traditional prejudice and partly because small-scale production cannot afford the high costs of international, or even domestic, advertising. Many consumers are brand conscious or prestige conscious and prefer to buy the high-cost goods produced in Western countries even if they are of the same quality as Asian products. Experience in the Republic of Korea demonstrates that appeals to patriotism can be used to get people to use local products. Joint efforts at promotion, together with the certification by a regional bureau of standards, might make a considerable contribution toward acceptance of Southeast Asian products.

The developing countries are also handicapped by their inability to grant credit to importers, thus placing their exports in a less favorable position than the exports of developed countries, which are backed by large financial resources for export credit. The export of manufactured goods is particularly handicapped; it would be useful to assign a part of the resources of the ADB to finance the export of manufactured goods. The half of the capital of the Bank to be paid in national currencies of member countries could be very useful toward financing intraregional trade among the participating countries.

At present, Southeast Asia depends heavily on the export of primary and manufactured products to the developed countries and on the import of capital equipment and industrial supplies from them. Until the developing countries can produce these items, or unless the currencies of the developing countries become fully convertible, exporting to developed countries will continue to claim higher priority. Organized efforts might persuade the developed countries to buy more by giving the developing countries larger import quotas or preferential duties and by corresponding changes in the production patterns of the developed countries.

Tourist trade is one source of foreign-exchange earnings that has increased rapidly in recent years. The number of tourists visiting Thailand, for example, increased twenty-five times in the ten years from 1955 to 1965, and those visiting Hong Kong and Taiwan increased eight times. Regional cooperation may promote tourism both for business and for pleasure. The cost to Europeans or Americans of visiting a few additional countries in Southeast Asia is very small. A regional tourist-promotion center advertising various tourist attractions and trade opportunities in the region could induce more tourists to visit the region and to visit more countries. Each country would have to improve its hotel, travel, recreation, shopping, and related facilities, as well as its hygienic conditions. Visa and customs formalities should also be simplified. Promotion of tourism has been considered one of the joint projects of ASA, but ASA countries may benefit even more if such activities can be carried out in cooperation with other Southeast Asian countries.

Recent discussions on regional cooperation have concentrated on industry and trade. Regional cooperation in agriculture has not received sufficient attention.

In most countries, agriculture still provides the most employment and generates the most income, but the slow rate of growth of the agricultural sector has pulled down the rate of general economic growth. Regional cooperation in agriculture probably requires less assistance from the developed countries, because of regional similarities of climate, agricultural technique, and social institutions. The International Rice Research Institute in the Philippines, for example, has found several species of rice that will considerably raise yields all over Southeast Asia. The experience in Malaysia of planting a new variety of rubber tree that raised the yield from three to five times has influenced other rubber-producing countries. Many agricultural improvements may be observed in Taiwan: a method for successful land reform; the organization of farmers to operate various activities such as food processing, marketing, distribution of farm inputs, distribution of irrigation water, and agricultural credit; ways to convey the results of agricultural research and experiments to the farmers for practical use; various price and other incentives given to the farmers; the selection of crops and seeds and methods of planting to allow for multiple cropping; farming practices that have raised the per-hectare output per annum to a level among the highest in the world;[5] and the close linkage of industries with agriculture. Farming demonstration teams have been sent from Taiwan to distant lands in the Middle East, Africa, and Latin America to demonstrate the cultivation of rice and other crops and to help promote farmers' organizations and better farm management. This kind of cooperation could justifiably be considerably expanded in Southeast Asia. Because Taiwan's social background is more similar to that of the other Southeast Asian countries than to that of the more remote countries, even larger benefits might possibly be derived from such cooperation within the region. If other Southeast Asian countries could raise their per-hectare yield per annum to the level reached in Taiwan, food and agricultural problems could be solved in spite of the present population growth rate, and substantial savings in the agricultural sector could be channelled to finance industrial development.[6]

The recent Tokyo conference on agricultural development in Southeast Asia recommended the establishment of a special fund in the ADB to finance agricultural development, particularly in Southeast Asia. It is hoped that this will be a starting point for larger-scale regional cooperation in agriculture. The conference also recommended cooperation in fishery research and development to increase food supplies and to improve nutritional standards.

It is not possible or necessary to exhaust the list of the types of economic cooperation. The immediate difficulties in undertaking more comprehensive types of economic cooperation should not deter countries from starting to cooperate on a project basis. Such project cooperation may improve mutual understanding, may cultivate a cooperative spirit, and may possibly lead to more comprehensive cooperation in the future.[7]

NOTES

1. For a comparison of rates of growth, see United Nations, *Economic Survey of Asia and the Far East, 1965* (1966), p. 157.
2. See Table 1.1. Although only domestic exports from Hong Kong are included in the statistics, total imports of Hong Kong and total imports and exports of Singapore are used in the table because of the lack of alternative statistics. There are therefore distortions in the real trade relations. But the relative positions of the intraregional trade in primary and manufactured products as stated in the text should not be seriously affected. The 1962 statistics were chosen because that was the year immediately before Confrontation.
3. United Nations Conference of the Plenipotentiaries on the Asian Development Bank (Manila, 1965), *Agreement Establishing the Asian Development Bank* (1966).
4. ECAFE, "Operational Procedures and Arrangements for Implementation of the Resolution on Asian Industrialization," mimeographed (E/CN.11/L.156), March 4, 1966.
5. See Food and Agricultural Organization, *The State of Food and Agriculture, 1963* (Rome, 1963), p. 110.
6. For statistics showing the increasing role of the agricultural sector in financing nonagricultural development in Japan and Taiwan, see United Nations, *Economic Survey of Asia and the Far East, 1964* (1965), pp. 55–63.
7. This paper expresses the personal views of the author and does not necessarily reflect those of the United Nations or of the Government of Singapore.

COMMENT ON CHAPTER 1

LIM CHONG YAH

Several general features characterize the economies of Southeast Asia. Excluding, as does Mr. Wu, India and Pakistan from the definition of the region, we find that all the Southeast Asian countries are primary producers, except for Singapore and Hong Kong. Except for Thailand, all were colonies, and all achieved their independence only after the Second World War. The countries all share the same anxiety to industrialize as quickly as possible, often at the expense of agricultural development, and, except for Indonesia, all are small in economic size and have limited markets, so that the case for regional and international cooperation appears to be strong.

Intraregional trade in the region is small, however, because the economies are not complementary, and much of the trade that does take place is entrepôt in nature. Other difficulties limiting the possibilities for a regional common market are traditional ties with the former metropolitan powers, language barriers, difficulties of fixing acceptable criteria for the location of industry, and the popular prevailing concept of economic independence. Some degree of harmonization of development plans and agreement on fields of specialization seems to be called for, although, as Mr. Wu notes, there are problems associated with this strategy.

Mr. Wu does not seem to give the price system much place as a guide to the countries in the region for producing goods in which they might have a comparative advantage. Mr. Wu also seems disturbed by the fact that many Southeast Asian countries are competing to produce the same types of manufactured goods. Such competition will not necessarily be unhealthy, however, and may, indeed, be required for efficiency. The expertise gained in the production of various goods may well be a prelude to later cooperation.

The author rightly points out that intraregional trade in Southeast Asia consists largely of entrepôt trade, but, to my knowledge, no estimate of the size of this trade exists—either for major exports and imports for individual countries or for the region as a whole. I think that it would be much more useful if the discussion of economic cooperation could be carried on against a background of statistical tables on the exact nature of intraregional and interregional trade.

One wonders whether agreed specialization and the requirements of equity might require some countries with an actual or potential comparative advantage in a commodity not to produce it or to stop producing it. If the commodity were a primary product, however, there would be nothing to stop countries outside the region from joining in the competitive race to produce it.

More generally, it would be undesirable to overemphasize the importance of regional cooperation and to underemphasize cooperation with countries outside the region. There is normally no reason why a country must attain self-sufficiency in a number of economic fields; neither is there any unchallengeable reason why a region must try to attain a greater degree of economic independence. Countries may well find that, given the political and economic conditions of the times, it is more to their advantage to trade and cooperate, not only with neighboring countries, but with the entire world. As a general rule, the countries in Southeast Asia are following this pattern.

Finally, Southeast Asia is one of the most politically unstable regions in the world. To this fact, I think, Mr. Wu has not given enough emphasis in terms of the actual impediments to more and closer economic cooperation in the region. Countries can cooperate better if they are politically stable and if there is better political understanding among the nations of the region.

CHAPTER 2

ASPECTS OF REGIONAL HARMONIZATION OF NATIONAL DEVELOPMENT PLANS

HIROSHI KITAMURA AND A. N. BHAGAT

INTRODUCTION

The main objectives of this paper are to suggest an operational approach to economic integration among the developing countries in the ECAFE region,[1] and to spell out the salient features of the experiences so far accumulated in the region. Both harmonization of national development plans and trade liberalization are proposed as important elements in the strategy of economic integration in the region, while the strategy of economic integration itself is viewed as a way of overcoming some of the obstacles encountered by the developing countries in the region in accelerating their economic growth.

The paper does not go into the details of the theoretical merits of economic integration, nor does it examine at length various obstacles experienced by the developing countries in the path of rapid economic development. The available literature in both these areas is already profuse and of high quality. Instead, the paper concentrates on some practical problems and feasible patterns of economic integration in the specific context of the prevailing conditions in the developing ECAFE region. As the implementation of any comprehensive integration scheme in this region belongs to the future, much of the discussion in the following pages must inevitably be based on the acceptance of certain hypotheses that have been only partially tested on empirical grounds.

The following section deals with the rationale of harmonization of national development plans in the ECAFE region. The second section suggests feasible patterns of plan harmonization, and the third section touches upon possible patterns of trade liberalization in the context of plan harmonization. The final section attempts to describe the salient features of schemes of subregional integration observed in the ECAFE region.

THE RATIONALE OF REGIONAL
PLAN HARMONIZATION

Defining the term "economic integration" in a clear-cut manner is not easy. Economic integration may be either a process or a state of affairs.[2] In the former sense, economic integration is simply a process of bringing together certain autonomous national economies by, in Tinbergen's words, "removing artificial hindrances to the optimal operation and introducing deliberately all desirable elements of co-ordination and unification."[3] In the latter sense, it is a state of affairs in which the autonomous national economies have already been brought together with such optimizing effects. Such a definition is not precise, but it can be taken as a useful starting point for discussion. The term definitely suggests that economic integration includes any preconceived and deliberate attempts to intensify economic relations between two or more national economies.

In both its static and its dynamic versions, the theory of economic integration deals with the benefits to be derived from integration for the participating countries' economies and with the possible effects on the rest of the world. The static version[4] of integration concentrates mainly on the beneficial effects of reallocating given resources through free commodity movements and possibly through factor movements as well. The dynamic version deals with the interrelationship between market size and economic growth via various internal and external economies, as well as other dynamic considerations relating to technological change and competition in a larger integrated market.[5] For the purpose of this paper, both the statics and the dynamics of economic integration will be discussed in relation to the problems facing the developing countries. In particular, the dynamic theory of economic integration implies that the larger the size of the market, the better are the chances of economic growth, other things being equal.[6]

The growth problems of the small countries have been extensively discussed in the context of the changed environment of international economic relations in general and of foreign trade in particular.[7] The small nations are generally handicapped in their economic growth by the limited size of their domestic markets, but the changes in the structure of the twentieth-century world economy have made export markets a poor alternative basis for growth. It is thus argued that the small developing countries can hope to overcome obstacles to accelerated economic growth only by merging their domestic markets and reaping the static and dynamic gains of economic integration. In this connection, it can be shown that both balanced growth strategy (as propounded mainly by Rosenstein-Rodan, Nurkse, and Lewis[8]) and unbalanced growth strategy (as advocated mainly by Hirschman[9]) are subject to some serious limitations within national bounds. Balanced growth strategy—based on the simultaneous development of mutually supporting industries that would create markets for each other's products—is hamstrung mainly by deficiencies in resource supply. Unbalanced growth strategy—aimed at concentrated development of a few industries having strong backward and forward linkage effects and based on the creation of pressures, tensions, and incentives and challenges—is faced with the problem of narrow domestic markets and lack of adequate export outlets. The argument is therefore put forward that integration, by widening the market and by releasing opportunities for specialization, can be an important means of accelerating economic growth, regardless of what growth strategy is adopted.[10]

The importance of economic integration in accelerating the economic growth of developing Asian countries (many of which are small) is not in dispute here. But the means or methods of attaining the goals of integration deserve serious consideration. Through widening of the markets and greater division of labor and specialization, integration—either global, regional, or subregional (even between two countries)—will lead to greater efficiency in the use of resources and to exploitation of various internal and external economies. The fact that integration is prevented by restrictions on commodity and factor movements and by other protectionist policies adopted by the countries concerned leads a liberal-minded classical economist to the free-trade argument. The acceptance of the spirit of free trade and currency convertibility was evident in the working of the trade liberalization that took place within the framework of the Organization for European Economic Cooperation (OEEC), and is evident in the functioning of the European Common Market (EEC). But even in the context of economically developed regions, although free trade may lead to higher real income or a faster rate of growth, it may not lead to other goals of integration, such as greater equality of opportunity or greater equality of incomes among the participating countries. This is more likely to occur if free trade is applied within a group of countries at different levels of development.

Paul Streeten indicates that, where free trade results in a less equal distribution of benefits and in narrower opportunities, "integration requires either opposing or supplementing the market forces." As he has forcefully put it: "It is, therefore, possible to share the ultimate beliefs of the classics without sharing their faith in the methods."[11] The goals of integration can be attained, at least in principle, by the alternative means of "agreed specialization" through intergovernmental negotiations without subjecting the participating countries to brutal and blind market forces and to the disruptive side effects[12] of free trade.[13]

The above observations seem to be particularly applicable to the developing ECAFE region. The introduction of a free-trade regime of the European Common Market type in the ECAFE region is fraught with difficulties and dangers. First, planning is recognized in almost all countries as the main instrument of development policy. Where national development plans are not geared deliberately to the requirements of the new situation, the introduction of free trade as such is bound to give rise to certain disturbances and disruptions in the production and consumption programs of the countries concerned. Mere free-trade arrangements, if not supported by some degree of plan harmonization, would hardly be acceptable to many countries in the region. Second, the market mechanism under a free-trade regime tends to favor investment in countries where the initial conditions are favorable and the profit prospects are bright. A free-trade regime may lead to concentration of investment in some countries that have the initial advantages of a certain industrial infrastructure and a larger market and may prejudice the chance of growth in other, less fortunate countries. Thus, there is a danger that free trade may lead to an inequitable distribution of benefits from integration.[14]

Given the current conditions in the ECAFE region, there are several reasons why the case for optimum reallocation of resources through the market mechanism of free trade would not appear to be very strong. First, the existing pattern of production and trade in the region is not such that the mere lifting of trade barriers among the countries in the region would considerably increase the intraregional flow. The economic structures of most countries in the region lack complementarity to such an extent that there is not much prospect for expanding the commodity flow through measures of trade liberalization.

Second, even assuming that mutual trade liberalization can expand the volume of intraregional trade to some extent, it is doubtful whether this approach to freer trade would have the impact on the economic growth of the developing ECAFE countries postulated in the free-trade doctrine. In theory, the case for free trade as a means of economic growth is based on the assumption of elastic supply and perfect mobility of internal resources. Removal of trade barriers, it is argued, will enable the countries concerned to specialize on those lines of production in which they have a comparative advantage, and such specialization will lead to more efficient use of the region's resources. This argument may well apply to Western Europe, where the reallocational effects of trade liberalization can be assumed to be important. In a developing region, however, the price mechanism cannot be expected to work efficiently enough to bring about a more rational allocation of resources: market criteria will be far from satisfactory guides in reallocating resources. Demand may have been an important limiting factor to growth in Western Europe, and hence a widening of the market itself may contribute to economic growth considerably. In most developing countries in the ECAFE region, however, growth has been inhibited mainly by the factors on the supply side. Free trade would hardly solve the problems of supply deficiency and internal immobility with which many developing countries are faced.

The experience of the Latin American Free Trade Association is relevant for deciding upon the course of action best suited to the goals of integration in a developing region. The method chosen was to establish a free-trade area through gradual liberalization of traditional exports and imports on the basis of selective negotiations. Although this approach did not ensure a speedy realization of the far-reaching targets of integration, no other method would have been acceptable to developing countries that inevitably encounter great difficulties in abandoning restrictive trade practices. This procedure involved the risk that each country would agree to free only those items in the production of which it had no interest. As a paper by the secretariat of the Economic Commission for Latin America (ECLA) puts it, "It should be recognized that under the present system the vast majority of the tariff items in which really active trade is to be expected . . . are being excluded from the negotiations."[15] The sober spirit in which the Latin American countries embarked upon their economic integration in 1960 found its expression in the realistic undertaking of selective negotiations. Despite the initial progress that was made in the reduction of intraregional trade barriers, it is now clear that this free-trade approach to integration is reaching its limits. The experience in Latin America has shown that "the aims of economic integration cannot be achieved through the mere liberalization of trade, which must be accompanied by other agreements that constitute a real program for the achievement of a series of major common objectives,"[16]—that is, by a regional investment policy.

Regional investment planning can be conceived of as a necessary complement to the regional scheme of trade liberalization. Since the free-trade approach is subject to narrow limits in the typical circumstances of developing regions, a better course of action may be to start with regional coordination or harmonization of investment and production programs. The plan-harmonization approach to integration would appear to be an alternative to the classical prescription of free trade.

The plan-harmonization approach seems to hold special appeal for the developing ECAFE countries, since most of them have adopted national planning as an important instrument of development policy. As a concept, the harmonization of national development plans may be defined as partial or comprehensive extension of national economic planning to a regional or subregional plan for the allocation of productive resources. It will lead sooner or later to the formulation of investment and production policies which would take into account the entire region. In the absence of a supranational authority, however, regional investment planning will aim at a conscious and deliberate harmonization of national production efforts and investment policies. Intergovernmental agreements on specialization will be required after an exchange of information, consultations, and negotiations. Such agreements will also include trade in those products directly and indirectly affected by the agreements. Trade liberalization thus will act as a permissive circumstance of plan harmonization. Freedom of commodity movements will be a dictated rather than a dictating circumstance in the plan-harmonization strategy. This is one important reason why the plan-harmonization approach to integration is likely to be more acceptable to Asian countries than the free-trade approach.

The operational approach to plan harmonization suggested here will (a) enable the participating countries to exploit internal and external economies and to reap other gains of integration; (b) help overcome resource supply deficiencies by avoiding the wasteful proliferation of competitive production and investment efforts; (c) widen the area of useful exchange of goods and services and render new patterns of trade more certain;[17] and (d) remove the possibilities of serious distortions in the distribution of the gains from integration.

The plan-harmonization approach to integration applies the strategy of import substitution to the regional market. Although one possible basis for economic growth could conceivably be exports of primary products and manufactures, the export prospects of the developing ECAFE countries have not proved, and are not likely to prove, very encouraging.[18] But the strategy of using import substitution to accelerate economic growth has encountered the limitations of resource-supply deficiencies and narrow domestic markets, except for some agricultural products and simple and light manufactures. For intermediate products and capital goods, plan harmonization would replace national import-substitution policies with regional or subregional import-substitution policies that would include a good deal of specialization and would have greater chances of success. By pooling their markets and resources, the countries in the ECAFE region would be able to achieve a higher level of efficiency and an accelerated rate of growth.

PATTERNS OF PLAN HARMONIZATION

Serious thought needs to be given to the country and commodity coverage of plan harmonization and to some of the implications of suggested patterns of plan harmonization in the ECAFE region.

A) The developing ECAFE region is one of vast geographical expanse, sociocultural diversity, and political and economic complexity. The evolution of a common political outlook in the ECAFE region has proved to be slow and halting due mainly to certain localized political conflicts centering around specific groups of countries and often involving territorial disputes. The groups of countries which have much in common in terms of history and culture are infested with territorial conflicts, while those countries without political tensions are geographically far apart and dissimilar in their sociocultural heritages.[19] The problem of regional cooperation and economic integration has to be viewed in this perspective. Economic cooperation itself could be a cohesive factor in welding various nation-states into a region, but economic cooperation certainly presupposes a minimum degree of political understanding and a preparedness to discuss matters of common interest.

Localized political conflicts within the ECAFE region and the lack of social and cultural cohesion on a wider regional plane may hamstring the task of regional plan harmonization. These considerations, along with the practical and administrative difficulties of dealing with the entire region, suggest plan harmonization on a subregional level.[20] The importance of subregional groupings is already recognized both within the ECAFE region and elsewhere in the world. Examples within the ECAFE region are the Regional Cooperation for Development (the RCD, comprising Pakistan, Iran, and Turkey[21]) and the Association of Southeast Asia (the ASA, comprising Malaysia, the Philippines, and Thailand). Outside the ECAFE region, the formation of the EEC in Western Europe; the establishment of the Regime for Central American Integration Industries within Latin America; and the functioning of the subregional meetings on economic cooperation in East Africa, in North Africa, and in Central Africa are all attempts to arrive at feasible patterns of subregional groupings within a given region.

The above discussion suggests that the integrating elements in the formation of subregional groupings in the ECAFE region can be geographical contiguity, a certain degree of sociocultural cohesion, absence of political tensions, and a potential for economic complementarity and cooperation. Subregional integration should not lead away from the ideal of wider regional integration, however, and efforts should be made to seek cooperation and coordination among various subregional groupings.[22]

B) Consideration must be given to the scope of development activities to be harmonized and coordinated even at the subregional level. Ideally, harmonization strategy should be comprehensive, because economic activities are interdependent. Some practical and administrative difficulties can be expected, however, if comprehensive plan harmonization is attempted at one stroke.[23] Harmonization and coordination in specific sectors or relating to specific commodities may be the most feasible method of plan harmonization.[24] Balassa raises some theoretical objections to sector-by-sector integration through a free-trade mechanism but admits that integration in one sector will be beneficial if "political obstacles hinder integration in all areas."[25] Some of these theoretical objections can be removed through intergovernmental negotiations and agreements on plan harmonization.[26] And, as the ECAFE secretariat puts it, "with the experience and habits of mutual cooperation implanted in the process of negotiations the commodity or sectoral coordination at sub-regional levels may lead to recognition of the need for overall plan harmonization and thus may pave the way for coordination of development plans of the sub-region as a whole."[27]

Selective plan harmonization can be fruitfully adopted first for developing intermediate- and capital-goods industries. These industries offer scope for various internal and external economies, and their development is crucial in accelerating economic growth. Furthermore, it is in the development of these industries that purely national efforts have been limited by narrow domestic markets and by supply deficiencies.

C) Selective subregional plan harmonization will require careful preparation and study and may entail certain changes in, and coordination of, the participating countries' domestic economic policies.

The necessary steps to arrive at appropriate locational decisions include careful assessment of the subregion's market potential for specific products and country-by-country studies of cost structure, economic potential, and profitability of industries or activities for which plan harmonization is contemplated. Decisions on product specialization will have to be translated into concrete agreements by industrial treaties between the producer countries and the user countries. Agreements or "trade treaties" will have to be reached also regarding trade liberalization for products directly and indirectly involved in agreed areas of specialization. Such products will need some protection against third-country competition, and this protection will entail short-run costs to realize the long-term gains of integration. Prices of the products for which production specialization and trade liberalization are agreed upon will have to bear a certain relation to world prices, however, in order to ensure some protection for the consumer.[28]

Plan-harmonization strategy based on intergovernmental agreements on specialization faces one danger that may prevent the realization of some of the gains of integration. The danger is that the market forces of competition may not operate. Possible abuses can be prevented, however, by devising suitable criteria for accounting and pricing procedures, incentives to improve production techniques, and other safeguards.

SCOPE FOR TRADE LIBERALIZATION

In our discussion so far, it has been argued that, in the context of the developing ECAFE region, the market mechanism of free trade cannot be relied upon as the principal method of regional integration, dictating new spectrums of production patterns. Trade liberalization has a role to play in the developing ECAFE region, however. Not only is trade liberalization a necessary concomitant to agreed areas of specialization, but there is also scope for trade expansion without going to the extreme of blind worship of free trade. What is needed is a pragmatic look at the problems facing the developing ECAFE region.

While neither the item-by-item negotiations used in the Latin American approach to integration nor the Western European scheme of automatic trade liberalization is suitable at present for the ECAFE region,[29] there is scope for an approach to "freer" trade in the region. Less far-reaching measures of trade liberalization are not only practicable but would also greatly benefit the participating countries by increasing the intraregional trade flow to some extent. Some degree of preference for imports from the region may be established by means of regional quotas for selected commodities. Or, preferential tariff rates may be established by annual reductions, on an agreed basis, of the duties applicable to imports from the region, while the tariffs applicable to imports from outside the region remain constant. If the intraregional trade flow increases through such agreements, producers and governments may become keenly aware of the possible advantages of specialization and joint investment policies. The scope for regional plan harmonization will thus be considerably broadened.

The advantage of trade liberalization on a limited scale is that some regional outlook and discipline is imposed on national economic decisions. Otherwise, continued neglect of regional possibilities by economic decisionmakers tends to create vested interests which may hamper progress towards an integrated market at some decisive later stage.

The risk of vested interests may even arise in a developing region in which the formation of subregional groupings is promoted as a step towards wider regional integration. In order to reduce the risk that the initial grouping might harden into an exclusive inward-looking bloc, the United Nations Conference on Trade and Development (UNC-TAD) secretariat suggests that "it is possible to envisage a combination of commitments both in the regional and in the sub-regional framework."[30] If, at the same time that subregional economic cooperation is expanded, the constituent countries agree with other subregions or with individual countries to establish a minimum degree of preference for imports from each other, or an upper limit to protective measures toward each other, then the subregional markets would be embedded in a regional framework providing for a preference and a reasonable degree of protection at the regional level. The trade commitments at the regional level, though less far-reaching, would effectively support the plan harmonization commitments at the subregional level and would underscore the determination of the subregional groups not to forget the advantages of trade liberalization in the geographically wider framework.

Trade liberalization with regard to the products directly involved in sectoral plan harmonization will be conditional upon coordination of investment programs. Because this approach runs the risk of introducing distortions between industrial sectors covered by the harmonization scheme and those not covered, a limited program of trade liberalization can encourage progress towards an integrated market. The UNCTAD secretariat suggests that "the sectoral agreements might be accompanied by less far-reaching trade liberalization measures regarding the products not covered by them; if the sectoral agreements were embedded in a framework of commitments covering also the producers outside the sectors concerned, the risks of distortions would be reduced and the consequences of the widening of the market more widely spread."[31]

Intraregional trade expansion will have to proceed on the selective basis of intergovernmental trade negotiations and agreements. These agreements can be either bilateral or multilateral. Agreements can also be negotiated between various subregional groupings which might have individually adopted a plan-harmonization strategy.

The extent to which bilateral and multilateral trade agreements contribute to trade expansion will depend upon the ability and willingness of countries to exchange mutually useful goods and commodities. Trade will expand if the region can move in the direction of producing intermediate and capital goods and can emerge with complementary production patterns. Subregional plan-harmonization strategy has been suggested as the way to make the region capable of producing greatly needed intermediate and capital goods.

In the meantime, possibilities for bilateral and multilateral trade agreements, preferably long-term, should be explored for primary products such as rice, rubber, jute, tin and minerals, and manufactures such as cotton and jute textiles, electric goods, and other consumer durables.

Institutional machinery is needed to facilitate intergovernmental negotiations and agreements. Within the ECAFE framework, such machinery already exists in the form of the Intra-Regional Trade Promotion Talks that are held at frequent intervals. As a result of these talks, several bilateral agreements leading to increased trade and improved commercial relations within the region have been concluded. It has been maintained, however, that the effectiveness of these agreements from the point of view of long-term trade expansion has been restricted because of inadequate review of targets and of the actual working of the agreements. It was therefore recommended that the trade delegations of member countries of ECAFE should systematically review at the Intra-Regional Trade Promotion Talks these bilateral agreements in the light of new developments that might have taken place since their conclusion.[32] The talks can provide an appropriate forum also for multinational trade agreements.

A selective approach to trade liberalization will lead to production harmonization among participating countries and will thus eliminate the mutually harmful proliferation of production activities. This type of trade liberalization will widen national markets and will lead to greater efficiency in resource use, while minimizing the operation of ruthless competitive forces. The types of products included in trade agreements will ultimately be governed by the countries' relative resource endowments and by dynamic comparative cost considerations. Thus, either trade liberalization followed by production coordination, or plan harmonization followed by trade liberalization constitute important elements in economic integration.

EXPERIENCE IN SUBREGIONAL
INTEGRATION IN THE ECAFE REGION

The ECAFE region has carried out a few experiments in economic cooperation and integration over the last few years. The process of economic integration has not proceeded very far, but the results achieved so far are encouraging, and the current burst of activity seems to bode well for the future. The regional organizational machinery to carry out effectively the programs of integration or plan harmonization has yet to emerge except, in some cases, at the subregional level. The day when such organizational machinery will be established under the aegis of ECAFE may not be very far distant, however.[33] Some of the experiments in economic cooperation and integration are undertaken solely on the initiative of the countries concerned, while others are inspired, initiated, and encouraged by ECAFE. The purpose here is not to review all such experiments[34] but to focus attention on salient features of some subregional schemes which have potentially great implications for the future.

THE REGIONAL COOPERATION FOR DEVELOPMENT. The RCD is a subregional grouping of Iran, Pakistan, and Turkey. These countries share feelings of amity, and aim at closer economic and cultural cooperation. The historical links binding these countries go back more than a thousand years. Their peoples share a common faith and a common cultural heritage. Geographical contiguity and absence of political conflicts have proved to be positive factors in the formation of this subregional grouping.

The RCD came into being in July, 1964, following the summit conference attended by the heads of state of the three countries. The conference reached an agreement on a number of objectives: (*a*) harmonization and coordination of the countries' development plans for selected industries and implementation of joint-purpose projects; (*b*) trade liberalization through trade agreements within the subregion; and (*c*) improvement of transport and communication links between the countries. The conference also led to the establishment of organizational machinery to implement the programs. The RCD has already created: (*a*) a Ministerial Council, composed of the three foreign ministers, to direct the program of integration and cooperation; (*b*) a Regional Planning Council, composed of the heads of the planning agencies of the three countries, to make recommendations to the Ministerial Council about coordination of national development plans and joint-purpose ventures; and (*c*) various sectoral committees to examine the scope for harmonization in specific fields such as shipping, air transport, communications, trade, tourism, banking, petroleum, and technical assistance, thereby assisting the Regional Planning Council.

The results and the experience achieved so far with subregional and sectoral plan-harmonization strategy are significant. Agreements on selective plan harmonization relate to three industrial projects: aluminum, banknote paper, and carbon black.

Under the joint scheme proposed for aluminum, Iran would establish (using imported alumina) a plant with a minimum capacity of 20,000 metric tons per annum of aluminum ingots. Under a proposed long-term agreement, Pakistan would buy about 10,000 metric tons per annum of aluminum ingots from Iran at world-market prices. Pakistan is expected to take up 10 percent of the equity capital of the project. Similarly, Iran is expected to set up a carbon-black plant, part of the production of which will be sold to Pakistan. Pakistan is expected to have up to 25 percent of equity participation in this project. Conversely, Pakistan proposes to undertake a banknote-paper project that would supply banknote-paper requirements of both Iran and Turkey at competitive world prices. Iran would contribute 10 to 15 percent of the equity capital of the project, and Turkey is also expected to take up part of the equity capital.[35]

Locomotives and pulp and paper have also been identified as suitable projects for development on a joint basis, and studies of these industries are underway by the RCD expert groups with a view to formulating harmonization proposals. Detailed studies are also nearing completion relating to other industries such as diesel engines; textile machinery; plant and equipment for chemical, sugar, and cement factories; electric goods; and shipbuilding.[36] The RCD experiments appear to indicate that plan-harmonization strategy can be implemented fruitfully among a limited number of countries on the basis of agreements on selected industrial ventures.

ASSOCIATION OF SOUTHEAST ASIA. The ASA, composed of Malaysia, the Philippines, and Thailand, was launched in 1961 to promote economic and cultural cooperation among the three countries. Areas of cooperation include trade liberalization; joint action to develop industries and to establish shipping lines and airlines; joint efforts to stabilize primary-commodity markets; technical training and research; and promotion of educational development and of cultural ties among the countries.

ASA has had a short and checkered life, with little progress toward these goals. It received a setback at an early stage of its existence from the diplomatic break in 1962 between the Philippines and Malaysia over the Sabah issue. It was revived in 1964 with the reestablishment of consular relations between the two countries and was revitalized in June, 1966, with the complete normalization of the relations between the two. Since then, ASA's activities have gathered momentum, and the association can be expected to begin to move in the direction of limited coordination of industrial development plans.

ASA has demonstrated that it is not inward-looking in nature by its declared willingness to include other Asian countries such as Singapore, Indonesia, Laos, Burma, South Vietnam, and Cambodia, as well as India, Ceylon, and Pakistan.[37]

THE MEKONG RIVER PROJECT. Preliminary studies for a comprehensive development project of the Lower Mekong basin, one of the earliest experiments in economic cooperation in Asia, started in the late 1950's. The project seeks to harness the water and energy potential of the Mekong River for the mutual benefit of 55 million people living in the four participating riparian countries: Cambodia, Laos, Thailand, and South Vietnam. The Committee for Coordination of Investigations of the Lower Mekong Basin is expected to develop into a committee for the comprehensive development of the Lower Mekong basin. The committee's present work, directed toward systematic development of the basin's water resources through irrigation, electric-power generation, and navigation improvement, is divided into four categories: "(a) pre-investment planning (including basic data collection, overall basin planning, planning individual mainstream and tributary projects, planning navigation improvements and ancillary projects); (b) construction; (c) finance; and (d) management."[38]

Cooperative projects involving exchanges of electric power are already being undertaken between Laos and Thailand. Mining and mineral-processing industries are likely to be established on the basis of mineral surveys of northeast Thailand and Laos. Electric power from the committee's hydroelectric projects will find its markets in these industries. Experimental and demonstration farms for irrigated agriculture have been established in all four countries.

Up to now, the Mekong project has been a scheme of sectoral development of water and energy resources. The development of one particular sector has to be carried out within the proper framework of overall economic development, however. Given more favorable political conditions, the Mekong area may witness evolution towards an integrated subregional market through joint investment policy and through limited trade liberalization.

Apart from these three subregional groupings—the RCD, the ASA, and the Mekong project—other measures have played a significant role in creating a climate of cooperation in the region and in fostering the spirit and habits of mutual help.[39] Thus, the region is beginning to acquire the infrastructure and experience that can pave the way for other far-reaching measures of regional and subregional economic integration.[40]

NOTES

1. The developing ECAFE countries are Afghanistan, Burma, Cambodia, Ceylon, Hong Kong, Indonesia, Iran, Laos, Malaysia, North Borneo (Sabah), Pakistan, the Philippines, Sarawak, Singapore, South Korea, South Vietnam, Taiwan, and Thailand.
2. Bela Balassa, *The Theory of Economic Integration* (Homewood, Ill.: Richard D. Irwin, 1961), p. 1.
3. J. Tinbergen, *International Economic Integration* (Amsterdam: Elsevier, 1954), p. 95.
4. See the significant contributions of Jacob Viner, *The Customs Union Issue* (New York: Carnegie Endowment for International Peace, 1950); and J. E. Meade, *The Theory of Customs Union* (Amsterdam: North Holland Publishing Co., 1955).
5. See particularly Balassa, *Theory of Economic Integration,* and T. Scitovsky, *Economic Theory and Western European Integration* (London: Allen and Unwin, 1958).
6. Balassa, *Theory of Economic Integration,* part 2.
7. See particularly the papers contributed by R. Triffin, "The Size of the Nation and its Vulnerability to Economic Nationalism"; G. Marcy, "How Far Can Foreign Trade and Customs Agreements Confer Upon Small Nations the Advantages of Large Nations?"; T. Scitovsky, "International Trade and Economic Integration as a Means of Overcoming the Disadvantages of a Small Nation"; I. L. Tarshis, "The Size of the Economy and its Relation to Stability and Steady Progress"; C. N. Vakil and P. R. Brahmananda, "The Problems of Developing Countries"; and S. Kuznets, "Economic Growth of Small Nations"; in *The Economic Consequences of the Size of Nations: Proceedings of a Conference held by the International Economic Association,* ed. E. A. G. Robinson (London: Macmillan and Co., 1960).
8. P. N. Rosenstein-Rodan, "Problems of Industrialization of Eastern and Southeast Europe," *Economic Journal,* 53, no. 2 (1943): 202–11; R. Nurske, *Problems of Capital Formation in Under-developed Countries* (Oxford: Oxford University Press, 1953); and W. A. Lewis, *The Theory of Economic Growth* (London: Allen and Unwin, 1955).

9. Albert O. Hirschman, *The Strategy of Economic Development* (New Haven: Yale University Press, 1958).

10. Balassa, *Theory of Economic Integration,* pp. 154–55.

11. Paul Streeten, *Economic Integration* (Leyden: A. W. Sythoff, 1961), p. 16. On the same page, while explaining the confusion between ends and means of integration, Streeten argues that, "Since it would be wrong to prejudge the issue, integration should not be defined in terms of the means (free trade, unified market, convertibility, liberalization, etc.) but in terms of the ends: equality, liberty, prosperity. Otherwise, we exercise a fraud on those who share the ideals, by substituting possibly ineffective means for these ends."

12. These side effects will be markedly unequal distribution of industries, unemployment, bankruptcies, and severe balance of payments difficulties.

13. For example, see Hiroshi Kitamura, "Economic Theory and Regional Economic Integration of Asia," *Pakistan Development Review,* 2, no. 2 (1962): 485–504; Streeten, *Economic Integration,* p. 16; J. Tinbergen, *Shaping the World Economy* (New York: The Twentieth Century Fund, 1962), chaps. 6 and 7; Michael Kaser, *COMECON—Integration Problems of the Planned Economies* (Oxford: Oxford University Press, 1962), chap. 3; and ECAFE, "Approaches to Regional Harmonization of National Development Plans in Asia and the Far East," *Economic Bulletin for Asia and the Far East,* 15, no. 3 (1964): 33–81.

14. See ECAFE, "The Rationale of Plan Harmonization and Economic Cooperation in the Ecafe Region," mimeographed (RP/WPH.1/A.3), November 7, 1966.

15. United Nations, Economic Commission for Latin America, "A Contribution to Economic Integration Policy in Latin America," mimeographed (E/CN.12/728), April 20, 1965, p. 51.

16. *Ibid.,* p. 52.

17. It may be noted that, in the absence of deliberate efforts to create a complementary production structure and pattern, intraregional trade in the developing ECAFE region declined over the past few years. For a detailed analysis see ECAFE, "Approaches to Regional Harmonization."

18. For details, see United Nations, *Economic Survey of Asia and the Far East, 1962* (1963), part 1.

19. This, at best, is a broad generalization, and exceptions can be cited. Sometimes, geographical proximity itself is a factor in political conflicts.

20. Such a suggestion is made in ECAFE, "Rationale of Plan Harmonization."

21. A country outside the ECAFE region.

22. See ECAFE, "Report of the First Working Group of Planning Experts on Regional Harmonization of Development Plans," *Economic Bulletin for Asia and the Far East,* 18, no. 1 (1967): 1–11.

23. Similar difficulties are present in the free-trade type of integration, as provisions for escape clauses and exceptional circumstances indicate.

24. See ECAFE, "Rationale of Plan Harmonization." In Western Europe, the sectoral approach of the European Coal and Steel Community preceded the present attempts at economic integration in the EEC.

25. These objections are related to lack of compensating changes; to disturbances of new and temporary equilibria of prices, costs, and resource allocation resulting from isolated steps to integration; and to possible burdens on external payments and lack of coordination in monetary, fiscal, and other policies. See Balassa, *Theory of Economic Integration,* pp. 15–17.

26. Scitovsky, while discussing the European Coal and Steel Community, draws attention to the possibility of attaining integration in sectors other than coal and steel in such a way that compensation can be provided to countries losing in coal and/or steel production, and equity can be maintained. From this, he argues for extension of "integration by sectors" and for "co-ordinated planning of investment on an all-European scale." See Scitovsky, *Economic Theory,* p. 149.

27. ECAFE, "Rationale of Plan Harmonization," p. 12.

28. Ideas contained in this paragraph are taken from ECAFE, "Approaches to Regional Harmonization."

29. For a similar conclusion, see ECAFE, "Report of the Working Group of Experts on Trade Liberalization," in *Regional Economic Co-operation in Asia and the Far East: The Asian Development Bank and Trade Liberalization,* United Nations, Regional Economic Co-operation Series, no. 2, part II (1965), p. 85.

30. United Nations Conference on Trade and Development, *Trade Expansion and Economic Integration among Developing Countries* (1966), p. 129.

31. *Ibid.,* p. 107.

32. ECAFE, "Report of the Working Group of Experts on Trade Liberalization," pp. 86–87.

33. See the recommendations in ECAFE, "Report of the First Working Group of Planning Experts on Regional Harmonization."

34. For a comprehensive review: ECAFE, "Review of Past Progress in Regional Cooperation and Plan Harmonization," mimeographed (RP/WPH.1/B.2), November 10, 1966.

35. See ECAFE, "Sub-regional Plan Harmonization: A Case Study of the Regional Co-operation for Development (RCD) (Turkey, Pakistan, and Iran)," mimeographed (RP/WPH.1/B.3), November 11, 1966.

36. *Ibid.*

37. "ASA, A Southeast Asian Landmark," in "Malaysia Supplement," *The Bangkok Post,* August 31, 1966, pp. 16–17.

38. ECAFE, Committee for the Co-ordination of Investigation of the Lower Mekong Basin, *Annual Report, 1965* (E/CN.11/WRD/MKG/L.159), p. 3.

39. See ECAFE, "Report of the First Working Group of Experts on Regional Harmonization."

40. The authors are members of the Secretariat of ECAFE. The views expressed in this paper are their personal views and do not necessarily reflect those of ECAFE.

COMMENT ON CHAPTER 2

ANTHONY TANG

Drs. Kitamura and Bhagat take the position that harmonization of national development plans and trade liberalization will both be important elements in any strategy of economic integration in the region. Subsequent amendment makes it clear that plan harmonization is to be the means to integration, while trade liberalization merely assists in the process. Stated differently, division of economic activities and investment decisions is to be made on a regional basis through negotiation among national planners which will take into consideration regional efficiency and other goals such as equity. Trade liberalization plays a passive role, serving to insure a fuller realization of the fruits of regional planning. To allow market forces to influence allocation is, to the authors, "going to the extreme of blind worship of free trade."

When pitted against an idealized model in which reasoned and reasonable planners would sit together and devise a regionally "efficient" plan, the free-trade position is, of course, untenable. The argument is merely an extension to a regional grouping of the well-known case for national planning. That the planning problems would be greatly magnified on a supranational basis needs no elaboration. Even on a national basis, the distortions resulting from planning as commonly practiced in the developing nations are so staggering that pragmatism and realism increasingly require economists and planners to rely less on controls and more on market signals as the second-best solution. It is surprising, therefore, that Kitamura and Bhagat should argue their case for regional plan harmonization on grounds of pragmatism and realism. A realistic look, it is tempting to suggest, is likely to point to trade liberalization of the common-market type as a more promising approach than grandiose supranational planning.

The fundamental problems of the developing countries can be traced in large measure to the "lock-in" effect of a basically inward-looking trade and development policy. Once an outward-looking stance is adopted, one of the crucial *raisons d'être* for regional plan harmonization, the limited size of national markets, loses much of its substance. And one must question further the limiting of the outward horizon by regionalism. Why not consider as an alternative a supraregional, two-way grouping of nations into the developed and the developing? This alternative taxonomy is implicit in the United Nations Conference on Trade and Development (UNCTAD) trade-preference scheme. If properly envisioned, the scheme may serve as a vehicle for transferring resources to the developing countries and for inducing outward-looking industrialization in these countries.

The Kitamura-Bhagat chapter, as well as the one by Mr. Wu, points out the similarity of economic background among most Southeast Asian countries, but there is little indication how such similarities would influence the ease with which various types of regional cooperation may be achieved. Homogeneity is helpful for certain forms of cooperation—for example, in organizing a united front in the region's economic "confrontation" with the outside world. But homogeneity also implies competitiveness rather than complementarity among the constituent nations and is apt to be a hindrance in such matters as intraregional decisionmaking regarding location and specialization. Even this twofold distinction suggests that we need to attempt to delineate useful areas for regional cooperation after first sorting out the conceptual and analytical problems of what constitutes a meaningful region for the purposes at hand.

COMMENT ON PART I

NURUL ISLAM

Both Drs. Kitamura and Bhagat and Mr. Wu have argued that meaningful regional economic integration has to take the form of harmonization, or at least of a partial integration and coordination of sectoral programs and plans and that trade liberalization relating to existing exports and imports is not going to achieve much expansion of trade. The basic problems in any scheme for harmonization or sectoral integration are how to distribute the gains among the participating countries and how to compensate for any losses. Is it necessary that the participating countries gain equally, or should the aim be rather that each partner country achieve some increase in welfare or real income, but not necessarily an equal increase? In any event, it is necessary to ensure that none suffer a loss, that every one must gain without gross inequalities.

Existing attempts at integration illustrate the importance of these issues. Although the Central American integration scheme provides that one partner country may not establish a second industry or a second plant in a given industry until every other partner country has at least one such industry or plant, negotiations for sharing regional "integration industries" have been difficult and slow. In East Africa, the problem of distributing one steel mill among three participating countries proved an almost impossible task.

An Asian example of the problems associated with the distribution of benefits is the RCD, consisting of Pakistan, Turkey, and Iran. This experience shows that, in order to create the conditions for each member country to share equitably in the gains from establishing joint industrial ventures, it was necessary to generate a sufficiently large portfolio of potential joint-purpose regional industries, so that there would be a sufficient degree of freedom for bargaining for the distribution of the industries.

The next problem was to decide on the distribution and location of each of these industries among the participating countries. While each country was to be in charge of feasibility studies for approximately an equal number of industries, the RCD provided that the other member countries should also contribute to, and participate in, these feasibility studies by providing data on cost and demand in individual countries.

Another decision was that, once the location of joint-purpose industries had been agreed on, there should be a pooling of equity capital by the three countries, as well as joint participation in management, so that the industries would belong in a real sense to all of them. The establishment of joint-purpose industries has been initiated in the first stage mainly in the public and the semipublic sectors. The latter allows private-capital participation under the aegis of the public sector. Moreover, the joint-purpose industries are to be matched or accompanied by long-term agreements for the exchange of the products of these industries among the participating countries.

Most of the industries selected for regional specialization are new industries, mainly intermediate- and capital-goods industries which require large markets. There is a danger that monopolies may result, insofar as there may be only one firm or plant in the three countries. Over time, however, there would probably be other plants in the same country as the market expanded or, if the comparative cost situation changes, there will be plants in other countries. Thus, it is necessary to provide for a periodic reassessment of the commitments on the joint-purpose industries as conditions change on the side of either costs or demand.

Existing industries, mainly consumer goods, have been excluded from the program of regional specialization. Some of these industries, such as textiles, sugar, and matches, have been in existence for many years; they should be beyond the infant-industry stage and should, in all probability, have developed competitive strength. For these sectors, increased intraregional competition could contribute considerably to an increase in efficiency.

Sectoral integration may create distortions in the rest of the national plan. Specialization in closely interdependent industries or industrial complexes which generate external economies and reduce cost for each of the partner countries may minimize the impact of these distortions.

While trade liberalization independent of the sectoral-integration programs has limited possibilities (as shown by the experience of the Latin American and Central American countries), even these limited possibilities have not been entirely exhausted in the countries of Southeast Asia. The established trade connections of developing countries of the region with the metropolitan centers in the developed world, as well as the existing shipping, insurance, and banking facilities relevant to the exports and imports of the region, tend to favor extraregional, rather than intraregional, trade.

To some extent, information about sources of supply and demand for regional products within the individual countries is inadequate. In the RCD, for example, the establishment of joint chambers of commerce is intended to remedy the lack of information on trade and investment opportunities in the member countries. An exchange of the lists of commodities for which either free trade or regional quotas can be instituted, as has been done in the RCD, is not without value. The objective of the lists is to find markets within the RCD countries for products in which excess capacity exists but for which it is difficult to find markets or outlets outside the RCD countries. Progress to date in the RCD has been in the direction of increased bilateral quotas, however, rather than of regional quotas.

Trade liberalization between developing countries has a number of other aspects which deserve serious consideration. For example, there is wide diversity in the techniques of commercial policy followed in different countries. Some countries follow liberal trade policies relying mainly on tariffs; others follow quantitative exchange- and import-control policies. The problem of achieving reciprocity in tariff reductions is difficult enough because of differences in demand and supply elasticities between commodities. The difficulty is compounded if tariff concessions by one country have to be reciprocated through quota increases by another.

There is a broader problem of trade liberalization on a regional basis among developing countries. Groups of such countries in each region may enter into preferential arrangements that discriminate not only against the developed countries but also against the other developing countries. The problem in this case is how best to liberalize trade among developing countries or groups of developing countries in a region without sacrificing possibilities of gains from enhanced extraregional trade.

II

Evidence on
Trade Policy and
Economic Development

CHAPTER 3

TARIFF PROTECTION, COMPARATIVE COSTS, AND INDUSTRIALIZATION IN PAKISTAN

NURUL ISLAM

This paper analyzes the comparative costs of a number of manufacturing industries in Pakistan vis-à-vis the prices of competing imports over the sixteen-year period 1951–66. Earlier studies[1] have estimated the effective rates of protection for major industry groups in Pakistan, based on tariff rates aggregated or averaged for the constituent industries within each group. This method does not measure the extent of protection implied by quantitative restrictions, however, in the absence of direct evidence on the differentials between domestic and foreign prices of inputs and outputs. Some studies have used domestic prices of a number of imported goods in order to measure the extent of scarcity margins on the tax-paid value of these goods, but there has been no direct comparison of the domestic prices of narrowly defined and clearly identifiable goods with the c.i.f. prices of closely competing and comparable imports.

The present paper attempts to provide empirical evidence on the comparative costs of domestic industries. It also will analyze additional evidence in order to identify and examine the nature of cost disabilities of the manufacturing industries in Pakistan, as well as the rationale underlying the protective tariff rates determined by the Tariff Commission for specific industries.

This study attempts to test two hypotheses regarding the comparative costs and the competitive strength of the manufacturing industries that have developed under tariff protection. First, it investigates the changes, if any, in the comparative-cost situation over the years. The expectation is that, with the passage of time and the accumulation of experience in techniques of production and training of labor and management, the cost disabilities of the manufacturing industries may have declined and prices will become more competitive. Second, it is expected that cost disabilities would differ between different industries, especially between consumption-goods manufactures and intermediate-goods and investment-and-related-goods industries.[2]

THE PATTERN OF INDUSTRIAL GROWTH AND ITS PRINCIPAL DETERMINANTS

Industrial output expanded at the rate of 19 percent per annum during 1954/55–1959/60 and at about 15 percent per annum during 1959/60–1963/64. (See Table 3.1) Industrial structure has become increasingly more diversified. The preponderance of textile, food, and related industries declined from 68 percent to 58 percent of total industrial output.[3] The spurt in industrial development in Pakistan was initiated by the foreign-exchange crisis following the Korean War boom. Import restrictions provided a sheltered market for the development of those industries that were based on domestic raw materials and that were judged to be essential consumption-goods industries. Industries considered essential for defense purposes also received protection.

The pattern of growth of manufacturing industries in Pakistan is the result of a set of interrelated factors including tariffs, quantitative restrictions, industrial licensing, and credit policies. Priorities in the field of industrial investment were not clearly formulated in the early years but were articulated in the course of time as a part of an integrated, overall plan. These priorities were implemented by credit and licensing policies and by direct investment on the part of the government or of government-sponsored public corporations. These controls and policies did not operate without serious limitations. There were significant deviations from the government-determined investment schedule on the part of private investors, because they were more apt to be guided by opportunities for profit than by the priorities set by the government.

Only in a few cases are tariff rates set and changed because of recommendations by the Tariff Commission. Until 1964, protection was more often provided by quantitative restrictions on imports. Then a relaxation of quantitative restrictions took place, and tariffs played a more important role.

TABLE 3.1—Rates of growth in large-scale manufacturing industries in Pakistan, 1954–64
(Percent)

Major commodity group	Gross value of output Share in total industrial output			Rates of growth		Gross-value-added rates of growth	
	1954/55	1959/60	1963/64	1954/55–1959/60	1959/60–1963/64	1954/55–1959/60	1959/60–1963/64
All manufacturing	100.00%	100.00%	100.00%	19.3%	14.5%	19.5%	15.7%
Consumption goods	72.69	64.38	59.05	16.1	12.8	15.6	12.8
Intermediate goods	15.89	20.94	21.54	39.0	12.8	27.0	13.7
Investment and related goods	11.42	14.68	19.41	25.0	23.0	28.0	26.0

Sources: Stephen R. Lewis, "Economic Policy and Industrial Growth in Pakistan," Williams College, Research Memorandum no. 18 (Williamstown, Mass., 1966), p. 5, table 1; and Stephen R. Lewis and Ronald Soligo, "Growth and Structural Change in Pakistan's Manufacturing Industry, 1954–64," *Pakistan Development Review*, 5, no. 1 (1965): appendix A, pp. 115–20, and table A-1, p. 121.

It may be asked why, in spite of strict quantitative restrictions, the manufacturing industries also sought tariff protection. First, the price differential resulting from quantitative restrictions may have been insufficient in a few cases to provide adequate protection to the high-cost domestic industry. Second, quantitative restrictions have multiple purposes. The extent of quantitative restrictions on imports is geared more often to considerations of general balance of payments than to the needs of specific industries. Accordingly, individual industries may be faced, in a period of liberal imports, with severe competition from abroad. Protective tariffs are a second line of defense that becomes effective when quantitative restrictions are relaxed. Third, revenue duties are not fixed on the basis of the costs of specific industries but rather are adjusted in response to budgetary considerations. A revenue duty may be converted to a protective duty without any change in the level of duty and without an examination by the Tariff Commission.

The tariff structure of Pakistan, including both revenue and protective tariffs, imposes a lower rate of tariffs on intermediate goods and on investment and related goods than on consumption goods. The

TABLE 3.2—Unweighted and weighted nominal tariff rates for
large manufacturing industries in Pakistan by
major commodity group, selected years

Major commodity group	1954/55	1959/60	1963/64
Consumption goods			
Unweighted	65	68	88
Gross domestic output as weights	65	68	101
Total domestic absorption as weights	68	70	114
Intermediate goods			
Unweighted	40	40	54
Gross domestic output as weights	46	47	61
Total domestic absorption as weights	40	39	50
Investment and related goods			
Unweighted	39	40	46
Gross domestic output as weights	45	45	43
Total domestic absorption as weights	32	36	40

Sources: The rates for individual industries are taken from Stephen R. Lewis, "Economic Policy and Industrial Growth in Pakistan," Williams College, Research Memorandum no. 18 (Williamstown, Mass., 1966), p. 16. Weights are taken from Stephen R. Lewis and Ronald Soligo, "Growth and Structural Change in Pakistan's Manufacturing Industry, 1954–64," *Pakistan Development Review*, 5, no. 1 (1965): appendix A.

unweighted and the weighted nominal tariff rates for the three major groups of commodities for three different years are given in Table 3.2. The effective rates of protection are compared with nominal tariff rates for three classes of goods for the year 1963/64 in Table 3.3.

TABLE 3.3—Unweighted and weighted nominal
and effective tariff rates in Pakistan
by major commodity group,
1963-64

Major commodity group	Simple averages of rates		Weighted averages of rates[a]	
	Nominal rates	Effective rates	Nominal rates	Effective rates
Consumption goods	108.30	91.78	116.33	104.00
Intermediate goods	61.00	61.18	60.86	33.51
Investment and related goods	64.96	110.50	56.95	125.57

[a] Weights are the total domestic availability in value terms of each of the commodities.

Sources: Data on nominal and effective protection rates were obtained from Stephen R. Lewis, "Economic Policy and Industrial Growth in Pakistan," Williams College, Research Memorandum no. 18 (Williamstown, Mass., 1966), p. 5, table 1; and Stephen R. Lewis and S. E. Guisuiger, "Measuring Protection in a Developing Country: The Case of Pakistan," Williams College, Research Memorandum no. 6 (Williamstown, Mass., 1966), p. 16, table 1. The classification of industries has been changed slightly; metal furniture, electrical goods, motor vehicles, and cycles are treated as consumption goods in that publication but we treat them as investment and related goods. Data on availability are from Government of Pakistan, Planning Commission, "The Methodology of Estimating Import Requirements," mimeographed, March, 1965.

The nominal rates of tariffs on intermediate goods and on investment and related goods are roughly similar, whether weighted or unweighted, and both are lower than the rates on consumption goods. The effective rates, however, both weighted and unweighted, are higher for investment and related goods than for intermediate goods or for consumption goods. Thus, the incentive structure implicit in the tariff system tended to shift resources to the investment-and-related-goods industries in 1963/64. The rank correlation coefficient is high, however, between effective and nominal rates of protection for twenty-eight or more major groups of industries, indicating that the relative levels of protection for different industries are not affected by the choice of rates.

COMPARATIVE COSTS
OF PAKISTANI INDUSTRIES

There are two ways of estimating the comparative costs of Pakistani industries. The indirect method is to estimate the domestic prices of imported goods on the assumption that they can be compared validly with the wholesale prices of locally-produced close substitutes. This procedure was used in a number of previous studies. Depending upon such variables as the domestic market structure and margins of profits, however, domestic ex-factory prices may differ from the prices in the domestic market of the competing imported goods.

The second method is to estimate directly the ex-factory prices of local products and to compare them with the c.i.f. prices of closely competing import products. The advantage of this method is that the ex-factory prices of the domestic products often are based on the examination of the cost of production of the domestic industry plus some allowance for profit, as reported and analyzed in the reports of the Tariff Commission. In a number of cases, the Tariff Commission has modified or adjusted cost figures as well as profit margins and so has used its own estimate of "fair" prices in place of prevailing prices quoted by the producers. Therefore, the second method attempts to compare domestic *costs* with foreign prices, rather than domestic *prices* with foreign prices.

The present study follows the second method and compares the ex-factory prices of domestic manufactures with the prices of the closely competing or identical products from abroad. Unless otherwise specified, the data for the present study have been derived entirely from various reports of the Tariff Commission.

A comparison of the ex-factory price with the c.i.f. price of the competing product is intended to reveal the extent of cost disabilities of domestic industries. Tariff rates are sometimes used as an indicator of cost disabilities of particular groups of industries, on the assumption that tariffs completely account for the difference between domestic and world prices.[4] But tariffs do not account completely for the difference between the world price and the domestic price of similar articles, not only because of the existence of quantitative restrictions, but for other reasons as well. There is usually a consumers' preference for the established brand names of foreign products with which the consumers have been familiar for a long period. For this reason, tariffs or quantitative restrictions, to be effective, must create a greater price divergence than is warranted by the difference between the ex-factory price and the c.i.f. price of competing imports.

Furthermore, the difference between the c.i.f. price and the ex-factory price (excluding indirect taxes such as sales taxes) is greater than the amount of tariffs and sales taxes on imports because there are additional elements of costs which are incurred on entry of imports into local markets. There are (a) costs of insurance, around 1 percent; (b) landing charges at the port, around 1 percent; (c) handling charges, 2 percent; and (d) import license fee, around 0.5 percent—which account for an additional impost of 4.5 percent. If the domestic prices of competing products are to be compared with export prices of domestic products, then the comparison must be with f.o.b. prices and *not* with c.i.f. prices. Usually, the former are taken to be 5 percent less than the latter in the cost calculations of the Tariff Commission.

The above analysis suggests a number of factors that can account for a divergence between ex-factory prices and c.i.f. prices in excess of the sum of tariffs plus sales tax. If this disparity occurs in the cases intensively investigated by the Tariff Commission, it seems even more likely that it would occur for the rest of the tariffs, which were fixed without exhaustive examination of costs and prices. Our assumption is that, in the absence of quantitative restrictions, or with relatively free imports, tariffs are likely to be excessive for fear of hurting the domestic industry through inadequate protection.

The comparative cost ratios—i.e., the ratios of ex-factory prices (without indirect taxes) to c.i.f. prices—for a large number of industries that have been investigated by the Tariff Commission are given in Table 3.4. These investigations by the Tariff Commission cover the years 1951–66. Out of 115 industries, 10 had ex-factory prices below the c.i.f. prices, whereas 46 industries had ex-factory prices up to 50 percent higher than the c.i.f. prices. Forty-three percent of the industries had ex-factory prices from 50 percent to 150 percent higher than the corresponding c.i.f. prices.

Over the years, there does not seem to have been any significant change in the pattern of comparative costs. The industries were analyzed in terms of three time periods corresponding to the pre-plan, first-plan, and second-plan periods.[5] In all periods, the greatest number of industries had ex-factory prices varying between 1.00 and 1.50 times the corresponding c.i.f. prices. The second largest number of industries had price differentials between 1.51 and 2.00. The average

TABLE 3.4—Frequency distribution of individual Pakistani industries by
comparative cost ratios (without indirect taxes)

Comparative cost ratio	Midpoint	1951–66		1951–55		1956–60		1961–66	
		Frequencies	Distribution %	Frequencies	Distribution %	Frequencies	Distribution %	Frequencies	Distribution %
0.50–0.99	0.75	10	8.70	2	6.90	5	20.83	3	4.84
1.00–1.50	1.25	46	40.00	14	48.28	9	37.50	23	37.10
1.51–2.00	1.75	36	31.30	9	31.03	8	33.33	19	30.65
2.01–2.50	2.25	14	12.17	3	10.34	1	4.17	10	16.13
2.51–3.00	2.75	4	3.48	0	0.00	1	4.17	3	4.84
3.01–3.50	3.25	0	0.00	0	0.00	0	0.00	0	0.00
3.51–4.00	3.75	3	2.61	1	3.45	0	0.00	2	3.22
4.01–4.50	4.25	1	0.87	0	0.00	0	0.00	1	1.61
4.51–5.00	4.75	0	0.00	0	0.00	0	0.00	0	0.00
5.01–5.50	5.25	0	0.00	0	0.00	0	0.00	0	0.00
5.51–6.00	5.75	1	0.87	0	0.00	0	0.00	1	1.61
Total	—	115	100.00	29	100.00	24	100.00	62	100.00

Sources: Government of Pakistan, reports of the Tariff Commission, various years, 1951–66; Nurul Islam and J. O. Malik, *Comparative Costs of the Manufacturing Industries in Pakistan—A Statistical Study*, Pakistan Institute of Development Economics, Research Report 58 (Karachi, 1967).

price differentials were 1.56, 1.44, and 1.83 respectively for the periods 1951–55, 1956–60, and 1961–66. The price differentials, including indirect taxes on domestic output, were 1.76, 1.54, and 2.12 respectively.[6] These ratios do not indicate any improvement over time in the comparative position of Pakistani manufacturing industries. In each case, the differential drops for the years 1956–60 and rises again for the years 1961–66. A comparison over time is limited, however, because the composition of industries in the three time periods is very different.

The comparative cost ratios in these three periods for the major commodity groups (as defined in note 2) are:

	1951–55	1956–60	1961–66
Consumption goods	1.44 (10)	1.27 (8)	1.79 (6)
Intermediate goods	2.19 (4)	1.76 (3)	2.04 (21)
Investment and related goods	1.48 (15)	1.46 (13)	1.71 (35)

The figures in parentheses are the number of industries in each group.

When this classification of industries is used, all rubber products, pharmaceuticals, and paper products are considered to be intermediate goods; and all metal products, nonmetallic minerals, electrical products, and transport equipment are classified as investment and related goods. Depending on their use, however, some specific items within each of these subgroups might just as logically be assigned to one of the other two main groups. But the movements in the relative cost ratios for the three categories are still similar after such a reclassification has been made. One exception is the pattern followed by intermediate goods in the first two periods; the number of observations for this category is small for those periods, however.

	1951–55	1956–60	1961–66
Consumption goods	1.61 (16)	1.27 (13)	1.86 (14)
Intermediate goods	1.32 (3)	1.64 (3)	1.83 (33)
Investment and related goods	1.57 (10)	1.64 (8)	1.81 (15)

Intertemporal comparisons are unsatisfactory, however, because the number of industries covered in each category of commodities is much

TABLE 3.5—Comparative cost ratios (without indirect taxes)[a]
of selected Pakistani industries
for selected years[b]

Industry	Cost ratio	
	First period	Second period
Vermicelli, macaroni, and		
spaghetti	1.29(1952)	0.67(1963)
Slate and slate pencils	1.77(1957)	1.22(1962)
Washing soap	1.43(1952)	1.07(1960)
Sodium bichromate	1.73(1960)	1.65(1965)
Umbrellas	3.58(1952)	1.42(1963)
Iron safes and almirah	1.76(1953)	1.67(1960)
Safety-razor blades		
Average quality	.96(1958)	.78(1964)
High quality	2.15(1958)	1.39(1964)
Hurricane lanterns	.96(1953)	.73(1964)
Transformers		
Type 1	1.97(1960)	1.74(1963)
Type 2	1.27(1960)	1.13(1963)
Electric bulbs		
Type 1	1.68(1954)	1.51(1963)
Type 2	1.47(1954)	1.34(1963)
Fire bricks	1.32(1954)	.90(1960)
Grinding wheels	2.26(1951)	1.06(1958)
Matches	1.80(1952)	1.55(1963)
Fruit preserving		
Squashes (orange and lemon)		
Type 1	n.a. (1952)	1.42(1959)
Type 2	1.91(1952)	1.63(1959)
Fruit syrup or lime juice	1.55(1952)	1.13(1959)
All products	1.41(1952)	1.42(1959)
Diesel-oil engines		
Type 1	1.57(1953)	1.52(1960)
Type 2	1.81(1953)	1.38(1960)

n.a.: Not available.

[a] Ratios of ex-factory prices (excluding indirect taxes) to c.i.f. prices.

[b] The year indicates approximately the period for which the cost comparison was made, rather than the time when the Tariff Commission report was either submitted to the government (without being published) or published by the government. There are a few other industries, including plastic products, industrial-type power switchboards, and wire netting, on which reviews are available but for which the product mix has changed too radically to allow any comparison.

Sources: See Table 3.4.

smaller in the earlier periods for both intermediate goods and investment and related goods and because the composition of categories is changing.

From our sample of 115 industries, it is possible to identify a

TABLE 3.6—Comparative cost ratios (without indirect taxes)
of major groups of Pakistani industries and weighted
indices for each period

1951–55		1956–60		1961–66	
Industry group	Ratio	Industry group	Ratio	Industry group	Ratio
Basic metal (2)	1.00	Matches (1)	0.96	Food manufacturing (3)	1.25
Transport equipment (1)	1.31	Nonmetallic minerals (2)	0.98	Nonelectrical machinery (1)	1.30
Food manufacturing (3)	1.34	Miscellaneous (4)	1.03	Petroleum products (1)	1.40
Chemicals and pharmaceuticals (2)	1.39	Soap and cosmetics (1)	1.07	Miscellaneous (3)	1.46
Soap and cosmetics (1)	1.43	Food manufacturing (2)	1.43	Matches (1)	1.55
Metal products (5)	1.48	Electrical machinery and		Nonmetallic minerals (7)	1.59
Tobacco (bidi) (1)	1.51	equipment (4)	1.43	Electrical machinery and	
Electrical machinery and		Metal products (6)	1.57	equipment (7)	1.62
equipment (3)	1.53	Chemicals and pharmaceuticals (2)	1.60	Metal products (17)	1.65
Footwear (2)	1.54	Nonelectrical machinery (1)	1.88	Paper (2)	1.69
Nonelectrical machinery (1)	1.69	Paper (1)	2.08	Rubber products (3)	1.87
Nonmetallic minerals (2)	1.79			Chemicals and pharmaceuticals (14)	2.20
Matches (1)	1.80			Transport equipment (2)	2.94
Miscellaneous (4)	1.97			Sugar (1)	3.63
Rubber products (1)	2.39				
Weighted average	1.52	Weighted average	1.41	Weighted average	2.02
				Without sugar	1.72

Note: The figures in parentheses indicate the number of firms in each industry group.
Sources: See Table 3.4.

number of specific industries on which comparative-cost data are available and for which the comparability of products, over time, is reasonably satisfactory. The evidence (see Table 3.5) indicates that, where specific industries can be narrowly defined, there has been a consistent improvement in comparative costs. Considering the short period covered—barely fourteen years—the improvement in the com-

TABLE 3.7—Comparative cost ratios (without indirect taxes) of major groups of Pakistani industries, 1951–66

Industry group	Ratio
Basic metal	1.000
Soap and cosmetics	1.125
Food manufacturing	1.340
Petroleum products	1.400
Matches	1.437
Nonmetallic minerals	1.453
Miscellaneous	1.487
Tobacco	1.510
Electrical machinery and equipment	1.527
Footwear	1.540
Metal products	1.567
Nonelectrical machinery	1.623
Chemicals and pharmaceuticals	1.730
Transport equipment	2.125
Rubber products	2.130
Paper	2.385
Sugar	3.630
Weighted average	1.820

Sources: See Table 3.4.

petitive strength of these specific industries deserves recognition. The industries concerned are relatively simple from the point of view of production technique, however, so that costs could be reduced rather quickly.

We have also grouped our sample of 115 industries into major industry groups and computed their comparative cost ratios (Table 3.6). Weighted average cost ratios for the three time periods were computed by weighting the cost ratios of each group by the value of output of that group for the years 1954/55, 1959/60, and 1963/64. The resulting weighted averages were 1.52, 1.41, and 2.02 respectively. The cost ratio for the last period drops to 1.72 if sugar, which has a very large cost ratio, is excluded. Weighted cost ratios show no more significant change over time than do unweighted cost ratios. The decline in cost ratio in 1959/60 (as compared with 1954/55) and a subsequent rise by 1963/64 are partly explained by the devaluation at the end of 1955. Comparative cost ratios are the obverse of scarcity prices of foreign exchange: their appropriately weighted averages indicate the extent of overvaluation of the Pakistani rupee.

The cost ratios for the major groups of industries over the whole period appear in Table 3.7, ranked in order of their magnitude. The two consumption-goods groups, paper and sugar, appear to have the highest cost ratios, and those for the transport equipment and the rubber products groups follow closely. These four groups of industries have cost ratios above the weighted averages for all the groups (1.82).

The estimates of ex-factory price used in the comparisons in Table 3.7 do not include indirect taxes, such as sales taxes. When indirect domestic taxes are included, the cost ratios are of course higher. The average comparative cost ratio for all industries is as follows (see also Table 3.10):

1951–55	1956–60	1961–66
1.76	1.54	2.12
(0.64)	(0.51)	(0.98)

Furthermore, our estimate is, in many cases, a "fair price" estimated by the Tariff Commission, rather than the actual or prevailing ex-factory price. To the extent that the actual or prevailing ex-factory price is above the fair price, the cost ratios computed on the basis of "fair price" underestimate the actual price ratios between the domestic product and its competing import.

THE LOGIC OF TARIFFMAKING IN PAKISTAN

When examining a claim for tariff protection, the Tariff Commission must satisfy itself that:

a) the industry is established on sound lines and conducted with reasonable efficiency;

b) (*1*) the industry is likely to be able to dispense with the necessity of protection by, or assistance from, government within a reasonable time period, during which the additional cost to the consumer or government is not excessive, or (2) the establishment of the industry is essential to the security or economy of Pakistan;

c) the protection of the industry is not inconsistent with any treaty obligations undertaken by government.

After satisfying itself that the claim for protection is justified, the Commission recommends the rate of protection to be imposed upon any article or class of articles that may compete with the products of the industry concerned. It may, in addition or alternatively, recommend any other forms of assistance which may be given to the industry by the central and/or provincial government, and it may also specify the period for which protective duties and/or other forms of assistance should be applicable. In making its recommendations, the Commission must take into consideration the interests of the consumers and must also give due weight to the interests of those industries that may use the articles for which protection is to be granted.

In order to qualify for protection, a firm has to be well enough established to supply cost data to the Tariff Commission. Protection is seldom given to an industry before it is established. This implies that, once the first firm has established its case for protection, a firm entering the industry subsequently enjoys the external economy of tariff protection automatically. During the sixties, the Tariff Commission has also considered the foreign-exchange saving or earning capacity of the industry concerned and promotes those industries which tend to save foreign exchange either through import substitution or through export expansion.

The Tariff Commission examines and suggests tariff rates for one industry at a time, as different industries apply for protection. The government refers each case to the Commission for examination. Determination of industrial priorities belongs to different policymaking organizations, such as the industrial licensing authorities and the Planning Commission. The Tariff Commission only comes into the picture at a later stage, when the industry has already been sanctioned by the appropriate authorities and has been functioning for some time. If an examination of the relative cost structure has already been made at earlier stages of industrial programming, the Tariff Commission's task becomes a very simple one: merely to provide temporary relief for the estimated cost disadvantage of a particular industry.

The Tariff Commission does not undertake general comparative cost studies of various industries. Admittedly, in a nascent economy like Pakistan the relevant question is the relative inefficiency of different industries. The optimum industrialization program will yield the least inefficient group, or the potentially most efficient group, of industries in terms of their cost vis-à-vis international prices.

A comprehensive exercise in industrial programming was not done even nominally, however, during the First Five-Year Plan. After the Second Five-Year Plan and the introduction of the investment schedule, it was done rather imperfectly, particularly in relation to industrial investment undertaken by the private sector. The major considerations governing industrial priorities in the early fifties were "(a) use of domestic raw materials such as jute, cotton, sugar cane, wool, hides and skins, cereal straws, oilseeds, limestone, gypsum, etc.; (b) reduction of imports, particularly essential items, in which the country should have certain minimum indigenous productive capacity; (c) maximum productivity in relation to capital invested and maximum employment; and (d) net social and economic advantage to the country."[7] Even if capital costs were high in relation to the value of output, it was felt that there were certain articles in which Pakistan should become self-sufficient, such as essential medicines, pharmaceutical products, insecticides and disinfectants, refined petroleum and allied products, chemical fertilizers, certain heavy chemicals, materials on which other industries were dependent, and industries which met essential defense requirements. The development of light and medium engineering industries—such as motor trucks, cycles, light and heavy electrical equipment, and machine tools—was considered important not only to reduce imports but also to provide the nucleus for building up more complete plants in Pakistan.

When deciding on the need for tariff protection in a particular industry, the Tariff Commission does pay careful attention to domestic demand for the product and to installed capacity, including possible plans for expansion of the industry. In order to qualify for protection, an industry must have sufficient capacity to meet domestic demand or at least a major part of domestic demand. This requirement is important in case a ban on imports is requested by the industry in question. Protection is intended to substitute domestic production for imports and not simply to curtail imports. Successful protective tariffs, therefore, must enable an expansion of domestic supply. Demand for imports must be price elastic and the elasticity of supply of domestic substitutes must also be high. The former restricts the demand for imports, and the latter ensures an expansion in supply in response to a high price and the availability of an assured market. The Tariff Commission, accordingly, pays considerable attention, both in its analysis and in its recommendations, to removing bottlenecks to increased production. The need to expand productive capacity has not been felt in most Pakistani manufacturing industries under investigation by the Tariff Commission, because there is almost universal excess capacity in the manufacturing sector. Protection has, in fact, facilitated the utilization of already existing excess capacity.

If domestic demand is inadequate, the Tariff Commission usually is reluctant to recommend tariff protection unless export prospects are good. Given excess capacity in an already established industry, one may argue that tariff protection may reduce costs in the long run by enabling economies of scale through greater utilization of capacity. Ideally, if excess capacity is the only reason for high cost, and if a greater output reduces costs below the prices of competing imports, then the industry in question may incur temporary losses which would be offset by profits later on. On the other hand, attainment of a higher scale of output may itself involve a learning process and, therefore, the industry qualifies for protection on the basis of the infant-industry argument. In such a case, either temporary protection on a sliding scale or subsidies on a sliding scale are called for, on the condition that they will be withdrawn when an efficient scale of output is obtained. An export-bonus scheme may be justified in some instances because high costs and inability to compete abroad on the part of manufacturing industries are due to an inadequate scale of production. Once a foothold which enables a larger output on a permanent basis has been obtained, the bonus scheme may be withdrawn, since costs and prices then will be lower and competitive.

Excess capacity may be not merely the result of an inadequate market but may be also a function of an inadequate supply of key imported inputs as well as of inadequate managerial and supervisory capacity. If the latter is a matter of inadequate experience, one may consider the training and development of managerial and supervisory skills as a function of "learning by doing." In this case also, it has been argued that the losses of the early period are really investments needed to obtain the gains of a later period, for which the industry in question may borrow. Objections to this line of reasoning are twofold. First, even if private entrepreneurs visualize long-run gains, their evaluation will be based on a comparison of the uncertainty of future developments with the certainty of present losses and the present cost of investment. Their estimate is therefore likely to be less optimistic than the government's or society's estimation of future gains. Second, the capital market may be imperfect, with the result that capital for this type of investment may not be available or, if available, may only be obtained at a higher cost than for other types of investment.

The problem of excess capacity has other aspects. The question of why the expansion of existing capacity is sanctioned by the investment licensing authorities, while existing capacity is underutilized because of the shortage of imported raw materials, has often been raised. The answer is related to the existence of market imperfections and to the criteria that govern the allocation among competing uses of foreign-exchange resources derived both from foreign aid and from Pakistan's own earnings. Insofar as investment controls are not universally effective, the existence of high profits attracts the entry of new firms. In an imperfect market, with its characteristic features of product differentiation and selling costs, existing firms contract their scale of production and incur a rise in their average costs of production. Both costs and prices go up, and the excess profit per unit of output goes down.

In Pakistan, the licensing procedures for imports and industrial expansion cause additional complications. To a certain extent, the licensing authorities help generate the consequences of an imperfect market when new firms are licensed while existing firms operate with excess capacity. This is done on the doubtful assumption that increasing the number of firms necessarily increases the degree of competition. From the point of view of an efficient allocation of resources, an increase in the number of firms—each with excess capacity—involves a waste of resources. The licensing procedure is also motivated by the desire for a wider distribution of entrepreneurship and industrial profits—a motive which is based on equity rather than on efficiency. Moreover, new capacity may be sanctioned with a view to meeting future demand rather than present demand. Foreign aid is more readily available on a project basis for the creation of new capacity than for commodity imports for the utilization of existing capacity. Aid is lost, therefore, if it is not used for the establishment of new projects or capacity. Because of uncertainty about the future flow of foreign aid, it is difficult to pass up available project assistance. And there is, in addition, the hope that the installation of new capacity may eventually enlarge the flow of commodity aid to enable the utilization of excess capacity created with the initial injection of project aid. Once the new capacity is created, it becomes difficult to deny foreign exchange to all the firms in an industry. In fact, licenses for raw materials and spare parts are based on the assessed capacity of each firm and are usually for a certain percentage of the assessed requirements of that firm.

The Tariff Commission does not accept uncritically the ex-factory prices quoted by the manufacturers. Since costs and prices often vary among different firms in the same industry, the Commission undertakes detailed cost investigations of a few selected firms and decides on a representative firm in light of its general efficiency. The firms with costs lower than the representative firm chosen by the Commission end up earning excess profits. In many cases, the Commission estimates an ex-factory "fair price" with the result that costs of production and "a fair rate of return" on capital are determined by the effect of Tariff Commission estimates.

The Tariff Commission in some instances has attempted to work out the cost of production and the fair selling price, or fair ex-factory price, not only on the basis of existing capacity, but also on the basis of an increased utilization of capacity. Table 3.8 indicates the comparative cost ratios on the basis of fair selling prices (as against actual selling prices) and also indicates the ratios between fair selling prices based respectively on existing capacity and on a greater utilization of capacity. Such comparisons are possible only for a very limited number of industries. In four cases out of fifteen, increases in the utilization of capacity do not make any difference to costs and fair selling prices. In the rest of the cases, however, the ex-factory prices at the present capacity are 8 percent to 25 percent higher than the ex-factory prices would be at a fuller utilization of capacity.

The Tariff Commission also devotes considerable attention to the problem of the quality of indigenous products. It undertakes detailed technical investigations and makes inquiries among the users of the product. The Commission attempts to be satisfied with the quality of the product before it recommends protection, or it makes adoption of measures for quality improvement a condition for the grant of protection. This procedure is followed particularly in the case of intermediate-goods and investment-and-related-goods industries.

The Tariff Commission examines the specific causes of cost disabilities in a particular industry: the limited size of the market or the high costs of labor, of materials overhead, or of distribution. The Commission only compensates for these disabilities to the extent it thinks they can be overcome in time.

Among the specific causes of cost disabilities are those related to the size of the market and the possibilities of economies of scale. In a chemical firm, for example, efficiency and economical production depend on diversity of products. Often the output of the main product has to be less than the size of the market warrants because there is no

TABLE 3.8—Economies of scale in selected Pakistani industries

Industry	Comparative cost ratio (excluding indirect tax)	Ratio between fair ex-factory prices at present level of production to fair ex-factory price on a fuller utilization of capacity[a]
Brass ingots	1.15	1.00
Emery cloth and paper and sand-paper	1.17	1.16
Umbrellas	1.33	1.17
Grinding wheels	1.34	1.11
Electric motors	1.40	1.00
Cement	1.41	1.00
Transformers	1.44	1.10
Textile powerloom mfg.	1.51	1.19
Hydrogen peroxide	1.71	1.15
Shell lining plate	1.74	1.19
Caustic soda	1.84	1.00
Sodium hydrosulphate	1.89	1.08
Strawboard	2.00	1.25
Umbrella fittings	2.22	1.08
Dry cell batteries	2.50	1.10

[a] The estimates of fair ex-factory prices at existing capacity are not necessarily for the same year in every case but are each for the period during which the Tariff Commission was examining that particular industry. Indirect taxes are excluded.

Sources: See Table 3.4.

demand for the by-products. There is often a lack of integration between different branches of production, and a particular branch may be established mainly because of the availability of foreign technical knowledge.

The shortage of skilled labor adversely affects the electrical-machinery-and-equipment industry group in Pakistan. The inadequate development of ancillary and interdependent industries which supply semifinished inputs like castings, forgings, and standard hardware to the electrical-equipment industry raises the price of inputs and affects the quality of the final product in the latter industry. Moreover, the lack of competition in the electrical-equipment industry is an important factor in keeping domestic prices high. There is an agreement among domestic producers to share the market among themselves. This is particularly true in the switchgear, transformer, and electric-motor industries.

A disability that affects most industries relying heavily on imports for critical inputs is the need to hold large inventories because of the uncertainty of such things as foreign-exchange availability and administrative delays in obtaining permits. This raises current costs. In the electrical-equipment industry, the ratio of inventories to total sales is 100 percent to 120 percent—compared to 10 percent in West Germany.[8] In some industries, the excess employment of labor has been a problem, because of the employment of superfluous clerical and administrative staff and the overmanning of machines due to unskilled labor and poor management. Labor productivity in the electrical-equipment industry is 50 percent of that in Germany, while wages are only 15 percent lower.[9]

The number of firms in most of the manufacturing industries is small, and this, combined with excess demand, provides opportunities for manipulating prices and for realizing excessive profits. In about 41 percent of the 115 manufacturing industries in our sample, there are only one or two firms per industry, and, in another 16 percent, there are only three to five firms per industry.[10]

The Tariff Commission usually attempts to equalize landed cost (including tariffs) and the ex-factory price as accepted by the Commission. Not only do cost conditions vary between individual firms, but there is also usually more than one quotation of c.i.f. prices, depending upon the source of imports. The Commission attempts to identify the source of competing imports that provides the maximum competition to the indigenous industry. Usually it attempts to formulate tariff rates that will protect the industry against the cheaper sources of imports.

The differential tariff rates recommended by the Commission do not completely protect the high price of the domestic product if the high price is due to monopoly or excessive profits (excessive in the sense of being higher than normal profit as determined by the Commission). Moreover, the Commission attempts to fix tariff rates at levels that do not protect the obvious or gross inefficiency of the domestic producer. For twenty industries, the Commission has recommended conditional protection if the industry does not charge prices higher than those fixed or considered fair by the Commission. These are cases in which the industries are making excessive profits because of lack of competition, or in which, in the judgment of the Commission, there are opportunities for the reduction of cost. The Commission, on the whole, is averse to raising the price of an intermediate product or of capital equipment because of the effect such an increase would have on the cost structure of other industries. It is also wary of price-raising measures in the case of essential commodities like drugs, medicines, and educational equipment such as slate and slate pencils. In such cases, cost reduction is assisted by the reduction of duties and taxes imposed on raw materials and components.

In recent years, saving or earning of foreign exchange has become an important criterion in deciding eligibility for protection. In order to deserve protection, an industry is expected to have a net foreign-exchange saving. It is not clear from a perusal of the Tariff Commission reports, however, what level of foreign-exchange saving is necessary in order to qualify for protection. Nor is there any indication that an industry is necessarily preferred if it saves more foreign exchange than another. There has been no interindustry comparison to decide on the optimum group of industries deserving protection. The Commission has dealt with each case separately.

The calculation of foreign-exchange saving is based on the direct foreign-exchange requirements. In many cases, however, remittances of dividends and interest on foreign loans and investments are excluded from these calculations, as are royalties, fees for foreign patent rights, and salaries for foreign personnel. Nor, except in a few cases, is the foreign-exchange cost, or even the annual depreciation, of imported capital equipment included. Accordingly, even the direct foreign-exchange requirements are underestimated. The Tariff Commission reports provide data on foreign-exchange saving for only 38 of our 115 industries. Of these 38 industries, 86 percent yield foreign-exchange savings of 25 percent or more, and 64 percent yield foreign-exchange savings of more than 50 percent.

There is no correlation between the tariff rates and the extent of foreign-exchange saving, since a multiplicity of other considerations already discussed affect the determination of the rates.

The Commission seldom describes in detail its decisionmaking operations, but, in a few cases, it has spelled out the reasons for its action. In 1961, the Commission considered the synthetic-dyestuff-manufacturing industry eligible for protection. The ratio of ex-factory price to c.i.f. price of competing imports was 1.98. The Commission based its recommendation for protection on the following considerations: (*a*) substantial saving of foreign exchange; (*b*) establishment of an important intermediate-goods industry, i.e., initiation of an organized chemical industry in the country; (*c*) attainment of a high-quality product, training of technicians, and acquiring of advanced techniques as a result of collaboration with the foremost continental manufacturers of synthetic dyes; and (*d*) scope for the expansion of both variety and quantity of product. The price of the local product was falling, and protection was expected to facilitate cost and price reduction by stimulating full-capacity production.

The case of the transformer-manufacturing industry is even more illuminating. The ratio of the ex-factory price to the c.i.f. price was 1.62. The Commission considered the transformer-manufacturing industry eligible for protection in 1960 for these reasons: (*a*) adequate domestic demand, which was expected to increase with an increase in the use of electricity; (*b*) saving of 40–50 percent of foreign exchange involved in the importation of an equivalent amount of finished products; (*c*) good quality and satisfactory standard of performance in comparison with the imported product; (*d*) introduction of an advanced technology in the Pakistan manufacturing sectors; (*e*) its useful role in the electrical-equipment complex which was being established in Pakistan; (*f*) scope for external economies because of the external interdependence with the rest of the electrical-equipment industry; (*g*) temporary dumping by foreign suppliers in order to capture the Pakistani market; (*h*) duties and taxes on raw materials —a cost disadvantage from which foreign suppliers do not suffer; and (*i*) existing dependence mainly on purchases by government agencies and public-sector enterprises.

The Tariff Commission does not rank the industries by their relative cost disadvantages and then cut off those which exceed a certain level, nor does the Commission have a predetermined level of disadvantage that it feels should be offset. In the case of the transformer industry, the Commission felt that the following cost disabilities needed to be offset adequately: (*a*) high freight and clearance charges, as well as taxes and local duties on raw materials and components; (*b*) the need to keep large inventories, with consequent high packing, warehousing, and interest charges; (*c*) high cost of fuel; and (*d*) the possibility that foreign producers may manipulate prices by quoting especially low prices for exports.

The Commission in its analyses and recommendations is aware that import duties on the inputs of intermediate products constitute a tax on the finished product, that a duty on the import of finished products is a subsidy, and that the net protective effect on a particular industry is composed of both these elements. But the Tariff Commission does not formulate its ideas in a way that enables it to calculate the net value of protection to each industry. The concept of net or effective

TABLE 3.9—Import restrictions and tax
concessions on raw materials in
Pakistan, 1951–66

Period	Total number of cases	Number of cases		
		Ban on imports	Increased import restrictions	Rebates and exemptions on duties on raw materials and components
1951–55	29	1	6	13
1956–60	24	4	4	9
1961–66	62	13	8	9

Sources: See Table 3.4.

protection does not appear either in its analyses or its recommendations. In many cases, it recommends import duties on finished products and exemption from, or rebates on, customs duties on raw materials and components, in order to reduce the cost of domestic production on the one hand and to raise the price of the imported product in the domestic market on the other.

The Commission's recommendations relate not only to the level of protective duty but also to the restriction of, or a complete ban on, imports. The Commission often considers restriction of imports an effective method for dealing with foreign competition. A qualitative analysis of the Commission's recommendations is given in Table 3.9.

Throughout the whole period, quantitative restrictions have been in force in varying degrees on all imports, so that even in cases where the Commission does not recommend import restrictions they exist nonetheless. The outright ban on imports has become important only in the latter period, while concessions to raw materials have become relatively less important in the latter years.

CONCLUSION

The preceding pages throw some light on the comparative costs of Pakistani manufacturing industries on the basis of a direct investigation and an analysis of ex-factory prices of industrial products vis-à-vis the prices of the competing imports. In cases where c.i.f. prices are

TABLE 3.10—Average comparative cost ratios and
average implicit rates of exchange (PRs)
in Pakistan, 1956–66

	Average comparative cost ratios		Implicit rate of exchange (PRs)	
Period	Without indirect tax	With indirect tax	Without indirect tax	With indirect tax
1956–60	1.44	1.54	6.86	7.33
1961–66	1.83	2.12	8.51	10.09

Sources: See Table 3.4.

many and various, the ex-factory price is usually compared with all of them, and an average of these ratios has been used in this study to represent the price differential. Even though only 115 industries over a period of 16 years have been investigated, each frequently represents not *one* but a number of products, so that, in fact, over 351 products have been investigated.

Under conditions of equilibrium in the balance of payments and free trade, the average ratio of properly weighted domestic prices to foreign prices converted at the prevailing rate of exchange should be equal to one, if the rate of exchange is the equilibrium rate. The divergence of cost ratios from unity may be said to reflect the disequilibrium in the rate of exchange. Price differentials reflect the relative overvaluation of the official rate of exchange. The official rate of exchange since 1955 has been PRs4.76 to the United States dollar. Table 3.10 indicates the rates of exchange, implicit in the price differentials.

This set of implicit rates of exchange may be compared with the PRs6.19 and PRs6.91 implied in the export-bonus scheme under which exporters receive 20 percent and 30 percent respectively of their export earnings. These entitlements bring a 150 percent premium in the free market where they are traded.

The structure of multiple exchange rates which emerges from the above small sample indicates that import substitution receives a greater incentive than export expansion. We should remember, however, that the implicit rates for imports have been estimated from a relatively small sample of direct comparisons between ex-factory prices and c.i.f. prices.

One may ask whether the multiple import rates which now exist tend to promote an efficient group of industries from the point of view of demand and comparative costs in Pakistan. The advantage of a uniform tariff, which implies a uniform effective rate of protection, would be that those industries benefit the most that produce the lowest-cost import substitutes. The most efficient industries will thus develop and expand the fastest. It may be argued that only a uniform level of protection—determined on the basis of general economic and industrial policy—is necessary in young, rather inefficient economies such as Pakistan. Deviations from uniform protection can be justified, however, by economic, social, and strategic factors. Tariffs cannot be drawn up in a vacuum, and the existence of vested interests and distortions cannot be ignored. In addition, the existence of differential external economies and of differential divergence between private and social costs justifies departures from uniform protection, although these differences are admittedly difficult to quantify. One can at least hope that deviations for noneconomic reasons will be kept to a minimum.

One may legitimately ask whether the high costs in most industries provide any basis for judgment as to the selection of industries, i.e., for an optimum pattern or strategy of industrialization. There may well be a limit to the excess of domestic costs over the prices of competing imports which should be borne as a cost of industrialization in a developing economy. For example, the limit of the permissible cost differential may be set at 50 percent or 70 percent above the c.i.f. price of the competing imports. Once an appropriate and socially desirable rate of subsidy is determined, industries which suffer from a cost disadvantage higher than the permissible limit would be judged unsuitable for development in Pakistan.

The permissible limit of cost disability is affected by a number of other factors, such as distortions in domestic factor markets and divergence between social and private costs, some of which may arise from the external effects of industrialization. There may be noneconomic arguments, such as security and defense. A policy of domestic taxes and subsidies may be the ideal way to deal with these factors, but such a policy may not be feasible in an underdeveloped economy such as Pakistan, with inherent deficiencies in its fiscal system. The second-best method may still be to resort to tariffs.

The cost ratios of a genuine infant industry will be higher than the cost ratios of that industry at a later stage of development. For a number of Pakistani industries, the evidence suggests that cost ratios are on the decline, although data are limited. Detailed industry studies, each covering a considerable period of time, are needed to throw more light on the ability of the Pakistani industries to overcome their initial cost disadvantages. It would also be useful to examine the extent to which high costs are due to high wages, high profits, and high costs of purely domestic (nontraded) inputs such as power and transportation facilities. The best way to deal with the high cost of domestic inputs, as distinguished from traded inputs, may be to subsidize the cost of such inputs rather than to compensate with tariffs for industries using these inputs more intensively.

The present study does not describe or analyze differences in wage costs among different industries when such differences have been caused either by trade-union activities or by government wage policy. As to profits, in a number of cases the ex-factory prices estimated by the Tariff Commission are "fair" prices in the sense that high profits are not included in the prices nor, therefore, in the comparative cost ratios. The Tariff Commission has allowed rates of profits varying from 12 percent on invested capital in the earlier years to about 20 percent of the invested capital in the later years, however.

To plan and to implement an appropriate industrial program requires a number of policy instruments, only one of which is tariffs. Rational tariff policy has to be considered within the context of general economic programming. While it is true that the protective effects of tariffs have often been swamped by import restrictions, there have been occasions when they have been important. An increasing reliance on the market mechanism for the regulation of imports—a policy which Pakistan professes to follow—will mean a more important role for tariffs. Pakistan's differential tariff structure is only partly a result of the recommendations of the Tariff Commission. A large majority of tariffs that have serious protective effects have been determined by administrative, revenue, and balance-of-payments consider-ations. So long as quantitative restrictions remain, it is important to have a proper balance between the two. Indeed, there should be coordination among all three instruments—tariffs, import restrictions that may persist, and exchange-rate policy. These measures all have the common aim of promoting an optimum and efficient pattern of import substitution in Pakistan, although each has other objectives as well.

One way of evaluating the relative efficiency of Pakistani manufacturing industries is to analyze their performance in competitive export markets. For a number of years, the manufactured exports of Pakistan have been receiving various kinds of incentives such as exemptions from excise and sales taxes, rebates on income tax on profits earned from exports, special and additional import licensing to industries on the basis of their export performance, and, above all, the export-bonus scheme begun in 1959. The combined significance of all these export incentives is not known. The most important of them is the export-bonus scheme, which has undergone changes since its inception in the bonus rates and in the commodities covered. By 1963/64, the bonus system was considerably simplified by the establishment of only two rates. A few manufactured-goods exports are given bonuses of 20 percent; the vast majority receive a bonus of 30 percent. Industries that obtain the same rate of export bonus have widely different tariff protection, implying wide differences in their comparative cost positions. Among the industries analyzed here that receive a 30 percent bonus rate, nominal tariff rates vary from 14 percent to 200 percent, and the effective rates vary from 15 percent to 240 percent. This excludes four negative rates ranging from − 10 to − 60. (See Table 3.11.) The contrast between uniform export subsidy and widely varying import tariffs seems paradoxical.

The logic of uniform tariffs to overcome the general cost disabilities of young industrializing economies seems to have been accepted by the framers of the export-bonus scheme. In the recent revisions of the import tariff schedule of Pakistan, a considerable simplification has also been attempted. The multiplicity of tariff rates has been reduced, but the number is still greater than the two rates of the export bonus.

The relative export performance between 1954/55 and 1963/64 of the different manufacturing industries in Pakistan can be seen in Table 3.12. The most important manufactured exports of Pakistan are jute textiles, cotton textiles, and leather manufactures, in that order of importance. The effective rates of protection received by them are 92 percent, 147 percent, and 80 percent respectively, whereas the export subsidy received by them is 30 percent, 45 percent, and 45 percent of the f.o.b. value of their exports.[11] The effective rate of protection is higher than the export subsidy. Jute textiles are in a separate category, since Pakistan does not face any competition in the home market from imports of jute textiles from abroad, and the tariff rate has no protective significance. The export items that were of growing importance (as a percentage of exports in 1963/64) are

TABLE 3.11—Rates of export bonus and nominal
and effective tariff rates in Pakistan

(Percent)

Bonus	Range of nominal rates	Range of effective rates
0%	0, 14, 57, 100%	$- 60, - 55, 28, 40\%$
20	62, 70, 130	20, 92, 109
30[a]	$14^5, 44^5, 79^{15}, 110^7, 200^6$	$- 13, - 10, 15^6, 39^5, 78^{11}, 123^6, 240^8$

[a] For the 30 percent bonus rate, we show the averages of individual rates grouped as follows: 0–30, 30–50, 50–100, 100–150, and 150 and above. The superscript figures indicate the number of observations on which the average is based; if no superscript figure is given, the tariff rate is based on one observation.

Source: Ronald Soligo and J. J. Stern, "Some Comments on the Export Bonus, Export Promotion and Investment Criteria," *Pakistan Development Review*, 6, no. 1 (1966): 38–56.

chemicals and pharmaceuticals (2.42 percent), footwear (1.75 percent), edible oils (1.56 percent), transport equipment (1.64 percent), soap and cosmetics (1.34 percent), food manufacturing n.e.s. (1.33 percent), and metal products (1.20 percent). The effective rates of protection for chemicals and pharmaceuticals and for soap and cosmetics are negative or unity; the effective rates for the other items vary widely, to a maximum of 269 percent.

Where tariff rates are much higher than the export subsidy, one may judge that the industries are over-protected: either the tariff rates overestimate the price differential between foreign and domestic products, or else the exporters practice price discrimination between the home and export markets.

The rest of the complex system of export incentives constitutes a subsidy in addition to that implied in the bonus. Even apart from export-performance licensing (one estimate puts the premium on export-performance licenses at 50 percent), there are other gains re-

TABLE 3.12—Export performance of manufacturing industries in Pakistan, various years

Industry	F.o.b. value of exports, 1954/55 (thousand PRs)	Increase 1955–60 (%)	F.o.b. value of exports, 1959/60 (thousand PRs)	Increase 1960–64 (%)	F.o.b value of exports, 1963/64 (thousand PRs)	Distribution of exports 1963/64 (%)	Export subsidy by bonus scheme 1963/64 (%)	Effective rate of protection, 1963/64 (%)
Sugar manufacturing	n.a.	n.a.	4,496	137	10,636	0.96	45	109
Edible oils	n.a.	n.a.	n.a.	n.a.	17,321	1.56	45	100
Tea manufacturing	40,547	– 13	35,490	n.a.	22	0.00	0	– 60
Food manufacturing n.e.s.	809	1,321	11,493	291	14,781	1.33	45	n.a.
Beverages	3	n.a.	3	4,733	145	0.01	45	90
Tobacco manufacturing	11	1,390	175	1,914	3,524	0.32	45	106
Cotton and other textiles	6,126	4,966	310,341	– 20	249,609	22.52	45	147
Jute textiles	49,020	513	300,311	54	461,480	41.62	30	92
Silk and art-silk textiles	n.a.	n.a.	7	900	245	0.02	45	121
Footwear	n.a.	n.a.	n.a.	n.a.	19,445	1.75	45	76
Wood and furniture	273	2	277	69	468	0.04	45	269
Paper manufacturing	30	3,113	964	920	9,838	0.89	45	83
Printing and publishing	208	420	1,081	– 46	583	0.05	45	– 13
Leather manufacturing	32,366	398	161,045	– 8	147,442	13.30	45	80
Rubber and rubber goods	9	3,955	365	1,225	4,835	0.44	45	39
Soap and cosmetics	23	3,713	877	1,594	14,852	1.34	45	1
Matches	n.a.	n.a.	n.a.	n.a.	n.a.	n.a.	45	n.a.
Chemicals and pharmaceuticals	3,974	250	13,909	93	26,800	2.42	45	– 10
Petroleum and coal manufacturing	10,326	69	17,423	57	7,503	0.68	0	– 55
Nonmetallic-minerals manufacturing	427	119	935	484	5,462	0.49	45	46
Basic-metal industries	45	2,642	1,234	60	13,275	1.20	45	3
Metal products	1,808	292	7,094	n.a.	n.a.	n.a.	45	247
Machinery except electrical	1,201	– 7	1,114	664	8,514	0.77	45	14
Electrical machinery and equipment	161	– 62	61	11,788	7,252	0.65	45	20 to 75
Transport equipment	1,187	1,008	11,963	52	18,133	1.64	45	26 to 292
Miscellaneous	5,802	430	30,791	116	66,578	6.00	—	—
Total						100.00		

n.a.: Not available.
Source: Data on exports by industry are from Stephen R. Lewis and Ronald Soligo, "Growth and Structural Change in Pakistan's Manufacturing Industry, 1954–64," *Pakistan Development Review*, 5, no. 1 (1965): 122–26.

ceived by manufacturers who are successful in export markets: help toward their goals of expansion, the modernization and balancing of equipment, and the benefits of speedy action in regard to government controls and patronage.

A more satisfactory analysis of export performance of the protected industries, and a judgment as to whether the protective rates are redundant or inadequate, is possible only after a much more detailed and disaggregative analysis of exports and tariff rates has been made. The aggregate nature of the above data—which is based on early studies—precludes a definite answer now. But the results raise questions that a subsequent study of the interrelation between commercial policy and industrialization can usefully explore.

NOTES

1. Mati Lal Pal, "The Determinants of Domestic Prices of Imports," *Pakistan Development Review*, 4, no. 4 (1964): 597–622; Ronald Soligo and J. J. Stern, "Tariff Protection, Import Substitution and Investment Efficiency," *Pakistan Development Review*, 5, no. 2 (1965): 249–70; Mati Lal Pal, "Domestic Prices of Imports in Pakistan: Extension of Empirical Findings," *Pakistan Development Review*, 5, no. 4 (1965): 457–585; Ronald Soligo and J. J. Stern, "Some Comments on the Export Bonus, Export Promotion and Investment Criteria," *Pakistan Development Review*, 6, no. 1 (1966): 38–56; Gustav F. Papanek, Ronald Soligo, and J. J. Stern, "Tariff Protection, Import Substitution, and Investment Efficiency: A Comment," *Pakistan Development Review*, 6, no. 1 (1966): 105–19; and P. T. Ellsworth, "Import Substitution in Pakistan: Some Comments," *Pakistan Development Review*, 6, no. 3 (1966): 395–407.

2. Consumption goods include sugar, edible oils, tea, other food and beverages, tobacco, cotton and other textiles, silk and art-silk textiles, footwear, wood and furniture, printing and publishing, soap, cosmetics, matches, and miscellaneous manufactures. Intermediate goods include jute textiles, paper, leather, rubber and rubber products, fertilizer, chemicals and pharmaceuticals, and petroleum and coal products. Investment and related goods include nonmetallic mineral products, basic metals, metal products, machines except electrical, electrical machinery and equipment, and transport equipment.

3. Stephen R. Lewis, "Economic Policy and Industrial Growth in Pakistan," Williams College, Research Memorandum no. 18 (Williamstown, Mass., 1966), p. 5, table 1; Stephen R. Lewis and Ronald Soligo, "Growth and Structural Change in Pakistan's Manufacturing Industry, 1954–64," *Pakistan Development Review*, 5, no. 1 (1965): appendix A.

4. An example of such analysis is the measurement of implicit protection by

Soligo and Stern in their article "Tariff Protection," in which a simple average of the tariff rates on groups of industries is used to derive both nominal and effective rates of protection. Such an analysis by groups of industries has the disadvantage of aggregation, which hides significant differences within the subgroups, especially since the tariff rates for the groups are unweighted averages of the tariff rates on the subgroups or on the individual industries in each group. A disaggregative analysis at a particular industry level, therefore, is expected to yield a more accurate picture.

5. The pre-plan period refers to years before 1955; the first-plan period to 1955–60; and the second-plan period to 1960–65.

6. The standard deviations of these three averages are 0.64, 0.51, and 0.98 respectively.

7. Government of Pakistan, Ministry of Economic Affairs, *Report of the Economic Appraisal Committee* (Karachi, 1953), pp. 104–5.

8. International Bank for Reconstruction and Development, "The Industrial Development of Pakistan" (report for restricted circulation, Washington, D.C., June 1966), p. 108.

9. *Ibid.*

10. Nurul Islam and J. O. Malik, *Comparative Costs of the Manufacturing Industries in Pakistan—A Statistical Study,* Pakistan Institute of Development Economics, Research Report 58 (Karachi, 1967).

11. The rate of subsidy is a function of the rate of bonus and the premium on the sale of bonus vouchers. An exporter receives a certain percentage of his export earnings in the form of entitlements to import, called bonus vouchers, which are freely bought and sold at a premium of about 150–160 percent.

COMMENT ON CHAPTER 3

JOHN H. POWER

Professor Nurul Islam's skillful exploitation of the data from sixteen years of comparative-cost studies by the Tariff Commission is a valuable addition to prior studies which have tried to estimate implicit exchange rates from the tariff structure and/or price data. His approach has the prime advantage of attacking directly the key question —comparative costs. Moreover, his study uses data from well-defined industries rather than from larger groupings where problems of weighting and comparability with imports loom large.

On the other hand, the sample of industries studied by the Tariff Commission is a changing one, and this makes comparisons over time difficult. The sample is probably a biased one also, although the direction of bias is not immediately clear.

If we can take this sample as representative of Pakistani manufacturing, what are some of the conclusions we could draw? First, while there is no evidence of an improving competitive position when averages for the three subperiods are compared, the fifteen specific industries appearing in Table 3.5 showed an almost uniform picture of improvement. (This is more significant for the second half of the period. The change in the first half includes the effects of devaluation.) While the sample is very small, the uniformity of the result is mildly encouraging to the infant-industry thesis.

Second, there is a wide variation in cost ratios among the major groups of industries studied: the average for the entire period ranged from 1.00 (basic metals) to 3.63 (sugar). (See Table 3.7.) Classifying the industries as consumption goods, intermediate goods, and investment-and-related goods turns up no significant differences among the major commodity groups, however, especially when the usual classification is modified to eliminate some of the ambiguities pertaining to durable goods (as Professor Islam has commendably done).

For just the most recent period, 1961–66, in which almost half of the studies occurred, Table 3.10 shows an average cost ratio of 1.83, implying an implicit rate of PRs8.5 per United States dollar (as against an official rate of PRs4.76). As Professor Islam points out, however, these industries earn, under the export-bonus scheme, about PRs6.91 per dollar of exports. And, as he argues, the various other advantages accorded to exports may bring the average rates for export expansion and import substitution even closer together, leaving a net difference that might conceivably be justified by terms-of-trade considerations.

These findings indicate a strong element of rationality in Pakistani economic policy that is not found in the policies of some other countries that have encouraged manufacturing behind protection. As Professor Islam indicates, it makes little sense to give a substantially greater subsidy for sale in the home market than for sale in the world market to this range of products, for which world-demand elasticities must be very high. It is for just this reason, however, that he also criticizes the existence side by side of a generally uniform set of implicit rates for manufactured exports and a wide range of differences in rates for the same products as import substitutes. If these differences can be justified in some manner, they should be matched by differential subsidies for export. If they cannot (as seems more likely), the structure of protection should be brought more into line with the structure of subsidies to exports, as Professor Islam suggests.

The Tariff Commission in recommending rates of protection considers various cost disadvantages as valid reasons for compensating tariff protection. At worst, this could be naive "scientific" tariffmaking, the effect of which would be simply to eliminate any gains from comparative advantage. At best, it would pertain only to cost disadvantages—either temporary or representing a market cost greater than social-opportunity cost. Even in the latter cases, subsidies are ideally superior to tariffs, since the latter create new distortions even as they correct existing market failures. Subsidies require taxes, however, and there is no assurance that these taxes would create less distortion than tariffs.

CHAPTER 4

TRADE POLICIES AND ECONOMIC DEVELOPMENT IN TAIWAN

I-SHUAN SUN

GENERAL BACKGROUND OF TAIWAN'S ECONOMY

Taiwan is an island with limited natural resources. Its arable land has been fully utilized. During the early years of Japanese occupation,[1] Taiwan's economy remained almost exclusively agricultural, complemented by small-scale handicraft industries. Large-scale manufacturing started around 1910, when mechanized sugar plants were established; later there was development of a chemical-fertilizer industry, a canning industry, and a cement industry. Due to Japanese colonial policy, however, industrial development during the period before the Second World War was limited mainly to the processing of agricultural products. Exports were heavily concentrated on agricultural products and were exclusively destined for Japanese markets. In return, Taiwan imported manufactured goods from Japan. In short, Taiwan's economic development during this period followed the direction of increasing dependence upon Japan. The Taiwan economy became an agricultural component of the Japanese economy.

With the withdrawal of the Nationalist central government from the Chinese mainland to Taiwan in 1949 and the establishment of the Republic of China, attention was focused on the development of the island as an independent economy. The total dependence of Taiwan's economy on its agricultural sector was found to be a handicap to economic progress. Nevertheless, the steady growth of the economy during fifty years of Japanese occupation did lay some structural foundations for further development. According to an estimate made by the Joint Commission on Rural Reconstruction, the national product of Taiwan grew in real terms over the period 1911–40 at an average rate of 4 percent per year.[2] During this period, infrastructure and social capital began to take form, a modern educational system was popularized, and production technologies improved. These changes formed the basis for recovery from the physical devastation of the Second World War.

After 1949, technical, managerial, and administrative talents from mainland China supplied much-needed leadership in the reorganization of the economy. Helped by a continuous and sizeable inflow of United States aid, production levels recovered the prewar peak by 1952, and per capita income reached the prewar high in 1956. Industrial progress had led to a steady change in the structure of the economy in order to attain self-sustained growth.

Immediately after the war, the island needed large imports of chemical fertilizer to increase its agricultural production for domestic consumption and exports. Industrial goods were also scarce. At the same time, defense requirements put a heavy burden on the government budget. The result was serious inflationary pressure that suffocated development potentials. United States aid imports, however, provided foreign exchange to finance urgently needed imports, and the sales proceeds of the commodities financed by United States aid were used to meet budget deficits. In both ways, United States aid in those years helped stabilize the economy and therefore facilitated reconstruction.

Accelerated industrialization took place thereafter. First came the development of immediate import-substituting industries such as chemical fertilizer, cement, pulp and paper, leather, and textiles. With an increasing supply of fertilizer and the success of the "Land to the Tiller" program,[3] agricultural production recovered its prewar level. The revival of agricultural processing industries helped to expand export capacity to earn more foreign exchange. At this stage of development, however, the economy was neither able to yield domestic savings sufficient to meet investment requirements nor capable of earning enough foreign exchange to finance necessary imports. United States aid continued to play the double role of providing additional resources to fill both the savings-investment gap and the foreign-exchange gap. At the same time, monetary and trade policies rendered strong support to the accelerated growth of the economy. A high-interest-rate policy successfully channelled savings into financial organizations to be used for industrial development. A careful loan policy and a strict import-screening system succeeded in allocating the limited resources of capital and foreign exchange to the most desired uses. Export-promotion measures brought about a remarkable four-fold increase in exports from 1952 to 1964.

This stage of development extended to the early sixties, covering the period of the first three "Four-Year Plans for Economic Development."[4] Per capita real income increased at a rate of 4 percent per year, with the result that both the domestic market and domestic savings expanded tremendously. The structure of the economy was greatly changed. The production share of the agricultural sector fell from 35 percent in 1952 to 25.5 percent in 1964, while that of the industrial sector increased from 17.6 percent to nearly 30 percent during the same period. This structural change is reflected also in the composition of exports. In recent years, the relative share of industrial exports has increased very rapidly, while the share of agricultural products has declined substantially. Capital has become more intensively used in production, as indicated by a steady increase in the marginal capital coefficient of manufacturing industries. Capital-goods imports increased their share in total annual imports.

Near the end of the Third Plan for Economic Development (1961–64), Taiwan experienced a phenomenal expansion in the value of exports, which went up to nearly 19 percent of GNP, thus bringing that ratio close to the ratio of imports to GNP. Expansion of the volume of exports in 1963 and 1964, plus high sugar prices, gave high export values. If further export expansion can be achieved to compensate for the decline in the international sugar price, a positive trade balance is in sight.

With the termination of United States aid, there must be a shift in development policy from import substitution to export expansion. At the same time, a more ambitious plan might be established to undertake structural changes in the economy. To attain the goal of self-sustaining economic growth, it may be necessary to promote capital-intensive production in order to expand gradually the domestic supply of capital goods.

THE TRADE PATTERN OF TAIWAN'S ECONOMY SINCE 1950

Commodity Patterns

The exports of Taiwan before the end of the Second World War were composed mainly of rice, sugar, and other agricultural or processed agricultural products; imports were manufactured products such as cotton textiles and chemical fertilizers. Both the trade pattern inherited from the prewar period and the structure of the domestic economy have changed gradually. In 1950, exports of agricultural and processed agricultural products were as high as 90 percent of total exports, and imports of manufactured consumer goods were nearly 50

TABLE 4.1—Composition of Taiwan's imports, 1950–65

(Percent)

Year	Capital goods	Raw material	Consumer goods	Total
1950	12.46%	37.90%	49.64%	100.00%
1951	13.39	50.98	35.63	100.00
1952	12.14	54.00	33.86	100.00
1953	16.17	48.18	35.65	100.00
1954	17.97	51.46	30.57	100.00
1955	17.64	56.97	25.39	100.00
1956	22.90	57.44	19.66	100.00
1957	25.17	53.50	21.33	100.00
1958	24.26	50.99	24.75	100.00
1959	28.96	51.77	19.27	100.00
1960	25.55	49.27	25.18	100.00
1961	26.53	49.13	24.34	100.00
1962	23.79	54.11	22.10	100.00
1963	22.72	51.97	25.31	100.00
1964	22.99	54.04	22.97	100.00
1965	27.34	52.46	20.20	100.00

Sources: *Taiwan Export and Import Exchange Settlement Statistics 1950–1964* (includes U.S. aid imports and other imports), compiled and published by the Foreign Exchange and Trade Commission, Republic of China (Taipei, 1965), pp. 570–75; Bank of Taiwan, *Export and Import Exchange Settlements for the Year 1965* (includes U.S. aid import arrivals and other imports) (Taipei, 1966), p. 67.

percent of total imports. Japan still remained the most important trade partner, importing sugar, rice, and other agricultural products, and supplying textiles, medicines, and other manufactured goods. At this stage, the major development policy was to expand import-substitute industries for such consumer and capital goods as textiles, cement, fertilizers, and steel products. Reflecting this development policy, the import pattern gradually changed. During the period 1950–65, the percentage share of consumer-goods imports showed a decreasing trend, while that of capital-goods imports increased steadily (see Table 4.1).

Of particular interest is the share and composition of raw-materials imports. Development of import-substitute industries meant a decreased demand for semiprocessed raw materials and an increase in demand for crude raw materials. Since the country is poor in natural resources, crude raw materials still had to be imported. Imports of raw cotton increased to replace those of cotton yarns and other textile products; raw wools to replace wool yarns and fabrics; crude oil to

TABLE 4.2—Composition of Taiwan's exports, 1950–65

(Percent)

Year	Agricultural products	Processed agricultural products	Industrial products	Other products	Total
1950	4.84%	84.55%	6.21%	4.40%	100.00%
1951	22.58	65.52	8.33	3.57	100.00
1952	28.18	66.99	3.62	1.21	100.00
1953	13.64	78.98	6.39	0.99	100.00
1954	15.38	76.53	6.83	1.26	100.00
1955	30.04	62.08	6.19	1.69	100.00
1956	15.31	71.15	12.00	1.54	100.00
1957	17.14	73.98	7.30	1.58	100.00
1958	24.32	62.38	11.34	1.96	100.00
1959	24.59	52.90	20.91	1.60	100.00
1960	12.32	55.15	30.42	2.11	100.00
1961	15.75	42.00	39.70	2.55	100.00
1962	14.14	35.23	47.17	3.46	100.00
1963	14.66	42.54	39.48	3.32	100.00
1964	16.62	40.74	40.74	1.90	100.00
1965	27.51	29.03	41.32	2.14	100.00

Sources: *Taiwan Export and Import Exchange Settlement Statistics 1950–1964* (includes U.S. aid imports and other imports), compiled and published by the Foreign Exchange and Trade Commission, Republic of China (Taipei, 1965), pp. 2–3; Bank of Taiwan, *Export and Import Exchange Settlements for the Year 1965* (includes U.S. aid import arrivals and other imports) (Taipei, 1966), p. 5.

replace fuel oils and other petroleum products; chemicals to replace pharmaceuticals, chemical fertilizers, and other chemical products; and raw rubber to replace rubber products. But the establishment of new industries created a demand for other kinds of imported raw materials. For instance, synthetic-textile factories required the import of vinyl yarns, and the plywood industry required a large volume of *luan* timber imports. Thus, while the share of raw materials imports has remained constant, the composition has changed substantially.

The change in the structure of the economy also had a quite remarkable effect on exports (see Table 4.2). Before 1956, exports of industrial products were below 9 percent of total exports. After that year, the percentage share increased (except in 1957) steadily and rapidly every year up to 1962. It achieved a level of about 40 percent after 1962. During approximately the same period, the percentage share of annual exports of agricultural and processed agricultural products declined from a high of 92 percent in 1955 to 56 percent in 1965. There have been only a few new kinds of canned-food products in recent years, and the export of sugar, the most important agricultural item, has not increased. Several new varieties of raw agricultural products, such as bananas, other fresh fruits, bamboo shoots, ramie, sisal, and hogs have entered the export trade, however, and have increased in volume very quickly.

Concentration Patterns

Efforts during the period 1950–65 to industrialize Taiwan have involved a gradual change in the agricultural production pattern inherited from the period of Japanese occupation. However, Japan will remain the most important country in Taiwan's export trade as long as exports of agricultural and processed agricultural products remain over 50 percent of total exports, and as long as sugar and rice, which were the two main exports from Taiwan to Japan during the prewar period, maintain an important position in the total exports of Taiwan (see Table 4.3 for Japan's total share). This pattern is reenforced by the newly developed banana exports, the sole market for which is Japan.

Japan has also been a major source of Taiwan's imports (see Table 4.4), and it is probable that Japan will remain so in the near future. The causes are threefold: the former bilateral trade agreement between the two governments, the traditional market preference for Japanese products, and the geographic proximity of the two countries.

Relationships between Taiwan's trade pattern and its economic growth can be seen by calculating various coefficients of trade concentration. The coefficient of commodity concentration of exports, C_x, can be defined by the following formula:

$$C_x = 100 \sqrt{\sum_i (X_i/X_o)^2},$$

where

X_i = value of exports of commodity i to the rest of the world, and
X_o = total value of all exports to the rest of the world.

TABLE 4.3—Taiwan's exports by countries and areas of destination, 1954-65

(Percent)

| Year | Far East and Southeast Asian countries | | Middle and Near East | Africa | Europe | Australia and New Zealand | North America | South America | Total |
	Japan	Others							
1954	54.40%	27.17%	4.53%	1.33%	5.74%	0.33%	4.87%	1.63%	100.00%
1955	60.99	18.77	9.30	0.59	5.42	0.14	4.39	0.40	100.00
1956	35.89	32.12	14.81	6.08	5.61	0.11	4.92	0.46	100.00
1957	39.31	31.89	16.74	5.91	3.14	0.08	2.60	0.33	100.00
1958	44.76	25.12	15.82	2.89	4.69	0.08	6.22	0.42	100.00
1959	44.32	26.03	10.93	2.97	5.79	0.11	9.79	0.06	100.00
1960	39.03	28.53	10.12	2.33	6.36	0.24	13.33	0.06	100.00
1961	30.62	31.75	3.38	2.93	8.25	0.29	22.71	0.07	100.00
1962	26.26	34.11	2.30	1.63	8.55	0.38	26.65	0.12	100.00
1963	34.91	33.65	1.49	1.41	8.11	1.00	18.45	0.98	100.00
1964	31.53	28.70	5.70	3.40	8.46	1.01	20.44	0.76	100.00
1965	32.99	25.69	3.01	3.22	10.80	1.31	22.51	0.47	100.00

Sources: Taiwan Export and Import Exchange Settlement Statistics, 1950–1964 (includes U.S. aid imports and other imports), compiled and published by the Foreign Exchange and Trade Commission, Republic of China (Taipei, 1965), pp. 416–19; Bank of Taiwan, Export and Import Exchange Settlements for the Year 1965 (includes U.S. aid import arrivals and other imports) (Taipei, 1966), pp. 8–19.

TABLE 4.4—Taiwan's imports by countries of origin, 1954–65

(Percent)

Year	Far East and Southeast Asian countries		Middle and Near East	Africa	Europe	Australia and New Zealand	North America	South America	Total
	Japan	Others							
1954	56.09%	8.19%	2.08%	0.56%	11.59%	1.92%	19.24%	0.33%	100.00%
1955	40.90	4.63	4.16	0.37	10.70	1.70	37.08	0.46	100.00
1956	41.13	5.10	5.34	1.03	11.04	0.90	34.84	0.62	100.00
1957	38.31	5.23	6.86	0.23	9.46	1.08	38.63	0.20	100.00
1958	43.13	5.51	8.47	0.47	10.07	1.13	31.03	0.19	100.00
1959	43.37	6.73	6.26	0.53	13.30	1.55	28.03	0.23	100.00
1960	34.63	7.37	3.84	0.52	10.28	1.36	41.59	0.41	100.00
1961	32.16	8.57	2.05	0.38	10.29	1.87	44.11	0.57	100.00
1962	32.75	6.84	2.80	0.41	9.35	1.83	44.07	1.95	100.00
1963	28.91	8.65	3.64	0.87	9.30	1.89	46.24	0.50	100.00
1964	34.36	8.77	3.79	2.10	10.55	2.37	35.99	2.07	100.00
1965	37.10	8.35	3.56	1.15	9.76	2.24	35.42	3.33	100.00

Sources: *Taiwan Export and Import Exchange Settlement Statistics, 1950–1964* (includes U.S. aid imports and other imports), compiled and published by the Foreign Exchange and Trade Commission, Republic of China (Taipei, 1965), pp. 722–25; Foreign Exchange and Trade Commission, *Foreign Trade Quarterly*, June, 1966, pp. 42–45, statistical tables.

The more a country's exports are concentrated in a few commodities, the higher is the value of the coefficient. At the limit, when a country exports only one commodity, the value of the coefficient becomes exactly 100. The coefficient of commodity concentration of imports, C_m, can be defined by the same formula, with M_i as the value of imports of commodity i and M_o as the value of total imports.

TABLE 4.5—Coefficients of commodity concentration
in Taiwan's foreign trade, 1950–65

Year	C_x	C_m	C_x/C_m
1950	80.1	28.2	2.84
1951	56.9	22.5	2.53
1952	62.0	26.0	2.38
1953	70.5	24.6	2.87
1954	61.7	26.1	2.36
1955	57.0	26.7	2.13
1956	60.0	27.5	2.18
1957	67.2	28.2	2.38
1958	55.1	27.1	2.03
1959	45.4	28.1	1.62
1960	46.8	27.3	1.71
1961	35.0	27.3	1.28
1962	31.0	27.8	1.12
1963	35.8	26.6	1.35
1964	36.0	26.2	1.37
1965	28.9	27.9	1.04

C_x = Coefficient of commodity concentration of exports.
C_m = Coefficient of commodity concentration of imports.
Source: Calculated by the author on the basis of statistics provided in Tables 4.1 and 4.2.

Table 4.5 shows both coefficients of concentration and their ratio to each other for the period 1950–65. The ratio C_x/C_m was higher than unity for the entire period but declined sharply after 1959. Since the value of C_m remained very stable over the entire period, the sharp decline in the ratio was the result of a fall in C_x. The decreased concentration of Taiwan's exports coincided with an increasing share of industrial products in exports.

Two factors contributed to the stability of C_m: government control over allocation of foreign exchange helped prevent too much import concentration, and the development of import substitutes gave rise to increasing imports of raw materials and capital goods. Had development policies led to an acutely unbalanced industrialization, this ratio would have fluctuated noticeably during the period under study. Its stability therefore suggests a well-balanced industrialization process.

We can also calculate the coefficient of geographic concentration for Taiwan's exports and imports. The coefficient of geographic concentration of exports, G_x, is defined as

$$G_x = 100 \sqrt{\sum_s (X_s/X_o)^2},$$

where

$$X_s = \text{exports to country } s, \text{ and}$$
$$X_o = \text{total exports.}$$

The more evenly exports are distributed among many trading countries, the lower the coefficient. If all exports are destined to one country, the value will be 100. A coefficient of geographic concentration of imports, G_m, can be similarly defined. Table 4.6 shows these two coefficients, together with the ratio G_x/G_m, for the period 1954–65.

TABLE 4.6—Coefficients of geographic
concentration in Taiwan's
foreign trade, 1954–65

Year	G_x	G_m	G_x/G_m
1954	55.9	59.3	0.94
1955	61.9	55.2	1.12
1956	40.2	54.1	0.74
1957	43.2	54.5	0.79
1958	47.2	53.2	0.89
1959	46.4	52.1	0.89
1960	42.8	53.9	0.79
1961	38.8	54.2	0.72
1962	38.3	54.5	0.70
1963	40.1	53.8	0.75
1964	38.1	48.9	0.78
1965	39.7	50.8	0.78

G_x = Coefficient of geographic concentration of exports.

G_m = Coefficient of geographic concentration of imports.

Source: Calculated by the author on the basis of statistics provided in Tables 4.1 and 4.2.

The geographic concentration of exports, G_x, remained fairly stable, except for the first two years, 1954 and 1955. On the other hand, the geographic concentration of imports, G_m, was stable over the period 1955–63 but showed a slight drop in 1964 and 1965. The ratio G_x/G_m was less than unity, with the exception of the 1955 ratio

TABLE 4.7—Composition of Taiwan's exports
to developing ECAFE countries

(Percent)

Year	Agricultural products	Processed agricultural products	Industrial products	Other products	Total
1954	2.16%	74.44%	15.28%	8.12%	100.00%
1955	4.25	71.14	9.88	14.73	100.00
1956	3.62	74.57	20.61	1.20	100.00
1957	10.99	75.17	9.86	3.98	100.00
1958	6.23	57.35	26.90	9.52	100.00
1959	14.39	37.83	44.92	2.86	100.00
1960	10.36	31.73	56.82	1.09	100.00
1961	11.77	16.07	65.88	6.28	100.00
1962	14.46	10.48	70.13	4.93	100.00
1963	14.74	13.74	65.22	6.30	100.00
1964	7.43	19.88	67.66	5.03	100.00
1965	9.30	14.74	71.45	4.51	100.00

Sources: *Taiwan Export and Import Exchange Settlement Statistics, 1950–1964* (includes U.S. aid imports and other imports), compiled and published by the Foreign Exchange and Trade Commission, Republic of China (Taipei, 1965), pp. 420–90; Bank of Taiwan, *Export and Import Exchange Settlements for the Year 1965* (includes U.S. aid import arrivals and other imports) (Taipei, 1966), pp. 8–10.

—which reflects an exceptionally high degree of concentration of exports to Japan.

The high value of the coefficient G_m is explained by the fact that imports from Japan and the United States added up to more than 70 percent of total imports each year.

In his book *Concentration in International Trade*,[5] Michael Michaely made a study of the degree of trade concentration in several countries and correlated these figures with the size and the stage of development of those countries. This study shows that, by 1965, Taiwan's coefficient of geographic concentration was typical of small developed countries, and its coefficient of commodity concentration was considerably lower than the average of small developed countries.

Regarding the trade relationship of Taiwan with all Far East and Southeast Asian countries (excluding Japan), it can be seen from Table 4.3 that this region offered a large market for Taiwan's exports: the percentage share of this region fluctuated between 19 and 34

TABLE 4.8—Composition of Taiwan's imports
from developing ECAFE countries

(Percent)

Year	Capital goods	Raw materials	Consumer goods	Total
1954	1.89%	51.41%	46.70%	100.00%
1955	0.31	63.44	36.25	100.00
1956	0.99	72.42	26.59	100.00
1957	1.90	76.83	21.27	100.00
1958	0.37	79.17	20.46	100.00
1959	0.70	71.46	27.84	100.00
1960	0.61	58.65	40.74	100.00
1961	0.38	46.80	52.82	100.00
1962	0.61	78.12	21.27	100.00
1963	0.60	74.31	25.09	100.00
1964	0.94	72.97	26.09	100.00
1965	2.83	77.25	19.92	100.00

Sources: *Taiwan Export and Import Exchange Settlement Statistics, 1950–1964* (includes U.S. aid imports and other imports), compiled and published by the Foreign Exchange and Trade Commission, Republic of China (Taipei, 1965), pp. 726–39; Bank of Taiwan, *Export and Import Exchange Settlements for the Year 1965* (includes U.S. aid import arrivals and other imports) (Taipei, 1966), pp. 70–74.

percent of total exports. The composition of exports to this region has shown a noticeable shift. Industrial products gained rapidly and replaced the processed agricultural products that were the main exports to this region in the early 1950's. On the other hand, imports from this region remained lower than 9 percent of Taiwan's total imports throughout the period 1954–65 (Table 4.4) and were composed mainly of raw materials. The trade pattern with this region is a reflection of the fact that hitherto Taiwan has industrialized more rapidly than many of these countries. In Tables 4.7 and 4.8, we show the composition of Taiwan's exports to and imports from the developing ECAFE countries.

TRADE POLICIES AND ECONOMIC GROWTH

Our analysis of Taiwan's trade pattern suggests that foreign trade has furnished effective support for economic growth. It seems appropriate, therefore to review the trade policies followed by Taiwan, because, in my opinion, the remarkable results achieved could have been obtained only by sound trade policies.

The process of economic growth in Taiwan can be roughly divided into two stages. Economic stabilization and rehabilitation characterized the first stage, which ended in 1956, and a second stage of accelerated industrialization followed. Trade policies can also be divided into two stages, although the year dividing these stages was 1958 instead of 1956.

In the early 1950's, price inflation proceded vigorously—partly because of an acute shortage of consumer goods, particularly of necessary manufactured goods. At the same time, imports of capital goods and raw materials were urgently needed to rehabilitate war-damaged equipment and to restore production capacity. Faced with the serious problem of allocating the limited foreign exchange to meet urgent requirements, the government exercised strict control over imports by means of a quota system of foreign-exchange allocation. Goods from abroad were classified into three categories: prohibited, controlled, and permissible. Luxury consumer goods and goods that were deemed seriously competitive with domestic products belonged in the first category. Secondary necessities were included in the second category, and principal daily necessities and production goods in the third. This policy succeeded in limiting imports of consumer goods to a minimum and in allocating more foreign exchange to importing capital goods and raw materials. At the same time, a system of multiple exchange rates gave lower rates to producers' goods in order to accelerate industrial development. This system was necessary because, in the presence of import quotas, tariffs could not work effectively to influence trade patterns.

The development of import substitutes became the major policy guideline, and, following the transfer of four big government-owned enterprises to private ownership, the government established a policy of encouraging and protecting private enterprises. Trade policy was used, among other measures, to encourage industrial investment activities and to protect infant industries. Several goods produced by the emerging import-substitute industries have been shifted from the permissible-import category to the controlled category or directly to the prohibited category. For example, cotton yarn appeared on the permissible list until 1953, when it was shifted to the controlled list. Many other textile products, several kinds of paper products, small-capacity watt-hour meters, and polyvinyl chloride resins were also shifted to the prohibited list as soon as they were produced domestically.

It is interesting to consider at this point how far the policy of protection has been effective in promoting industrial development. To measure the protective effect of a tariff structure, Bela Balassa[6] has developed the formula

$$f_j = \frac{t_j - \sum_i a_{ij} t_i}{v_j},$$

where

f_j = rate of protection of value added in industry j;
v_j = value-added coefficient in industry j, at world prices;
t_j = tariff rate on the product of industry j;
a_{ij} = input coefficient of industry i to industry j, at world prices; and
t_i = tariff rate on the ith input to industry j.

This formula is designed to evaluate the extent to which primary factors of production are protected by a tariff on the final goods, after tariffs on imported intermediate inputs have been taken into account.

In the case of developing a new industry in an underdeveloped country, protection is often used to overcome the competition from advanced countries. Some of the important factors subjecting the new industry to severe competition are inferior technology, deficiencies in managerial experience, and a small volume of production due to a limited market size.

Protection of a new infant industry must be able to maintain the domestic price of the industry's products as high as required to provide entrepreneurs with incentives to organize the primary factors of low productivity into profitable production. The effective rate of protection is a useful guide in determining the extent to which the tariff structure provides these incentives.

Before turning to some rough estimates of the rate of protection of several industries in Taiwan, we feel obliged to give a short explanation of the data used and the necessary changes made in Balassa's formula. The basic data for the cost structure of each industry were obtained from a 55-sector input-output table prepared by the Council for International Economic Cooperation and Development (CIECD). The table itself is still in draft form and hence will be subject to change.

The input-output table does not divide input items into domestic and imported sources. For the present purpose, supplementary data were collected to make a preliminary division into domestic or imported inputs. Time did not permit further refinement of the data. Estimates based on the data should be considered nothing more than tentative, for which CIECD bears no responsibility.

Because Taiwan's imports have been more strongly influenced by the quota system of foreign-exchange allocation than by tariff policies, the domestic prices of several products are far higher than the international prices adjusted for the published tariff rates. When this happens, the rate of protection based on Balassa's formula gives an underestimation. The tariff rates on the products given in the formula should be replaced with the rates of actual differences between the domestic and the international prices, in order to obtain more accurate estimates of the protection rates.

Rough estimates of the rate of protection in thirty-seven major industrial groups of Taiwan are given in Table 4.9. The rates of effective protection shown in the table cover a very wide range, from as low as 6.3 percent for chemical fertilizers up to more than 400 percent for miscellaneous processed foods and beverages. As a general rule, there is heavy protection for the food-processing industries that use domestic agricultural products as the main raw materials, for the industries producing necessities, for the raw materials for these necessities, and for the basic capital-goods industries. Strong protection to the import-substitute industries is obviously aimed at the development of agriculture. Undoubtedly, the rapid growth of the food-processing industries (particularly the canning industries) has been of great help in bolstering agricultural production and in increasing the varieties of agricultural products. Consequently, it has contributed to the achievement of a balanced growth between the agricultural and nonagricultural sectors.

It is not correct, however, to deduce that the industry that is

TABLE 4.9—Rates of effective protection and output growth
for selected industries of Taiwan, 1954–65
(Percent)

Major industrial group	Rate of effective protection, 1965	Rate of growth, 1954–64
Metallic ores	13.31%	n.a.
Crude petroleum and natural gas	15.82	n.a.
Salt	111.36	n.a.
Nonmetallic minerals	32.38	n.a.
Sugar	218.81	6.60%
Canned pineapple	293.61	10.69
Canned mushrooms	264.38	16.13
Miscellaneous canned foods	368.31	32.64
Tobacco	131.95	6.33
Wine	129.16	6.59
Monosodium glutamate	74.00	4.67
Miscellaneous processed foods and beverages	423.45	7.10
Synthetic and artificial fibre	88.44	8.81
Textiles	248.79	9.76
Lumber and plywood	99.44	11.20
Furniture (wood, bamboo, and rattan)	148.46	n.a.
Pulp paper and paper products	155.22	16.89
Leather and leather products	228.62	19.18
Rubber products	112.48	14.56
Chemical fertilizers	6.29	20.63
Drugs	55.33	n.a.
Plastic products	197.91	15.75
Petroleum products	32.72	5.55
Miscellaneous chemicals	115.62	17.38
Cement	103.18	20.62
Cement products	15.52	18.70
Glass and glass manufactures	83.92	17.38
Miscellaneous nonmetallic products	36.60	13.52
Iron and steel	132.45	13.57
Iron and steel products	93.74	10.33
Aluminum	70.68	40.14
Aluminum products	91.01	8.50
Miscellaneous metal products	104.56	5.51
Machinery and instruments	40.55	33.61
Electrical machinery and equipment	80.93	29.29
Transportation equipment	68.21	13.55
Miscellaneous manufactures	134.00	12.18

n.a.: Not available.

Source: Data obtained from a draft input-output table prepared by the Third Department, Council for International Economic Cooperation and Development, Republic of China.

provided with greater protection will necessarily grow more rapidly than those industries that are less protected. Protection only provides a condition that will permit industries to grow at the rate warranted by factors such as available market size, potential shift of commercial tastes, and the potential advancement of production technologies. Table 4.9 indicates that there is a negligible correlation between the rate of protection and the average growth rate of several major industrial groups of Taiwan.

The chemical-fertilizers group grew very quickly with increasing domestic demand, yet its price had to be maintained low enough to help the development of agriculture. Fertilizer imports have been exclusively handled by government agencies. The aluminum industry is a monopolized industry owned by the government and has been protected by strict import control. Its high growth rate has been assured, however, by an enlarged market due to new uses of aluminum. High growth rates in the machinery-and-instruments group and the electrical-machinery-and-equipment group have been the result of growing domestic and foreign demand in recent years.

Industrialization of the economy accelerated after 1956, indicating remarkable progress. Internally, GNP grew, with remarkable price stability, on the average of 7–8 percent per year. Externally, annual exports have expanded very quickly since 1960. Since 1958, the government has set forth a new trade policy aimed at lessening controls on the one hand and at simplifying exchange rates on the other. The import-screening system has operated with greater flexibility, and, in 1963, a unified exchange rate was established. The phenomenal expansion of exports during the past few years has given rise to the prospect that trade can be gradually liberalized without damaging the balance of trade.

Because Taiwan is a small island economy, its further development depends heavily on external factors. Taiwan requires resources from abroad (capital goods and raw materials) for productive uses, and it needs foreign markets to sustain profitable production. At its present stage of economic development, Taiwan has enough domestic savings to finance investments which are considered necessary to sustain economic growth at a rate of 5–6 percent per year. Indeed, the marginal propensity to save in Taiwan in recent years has been as high as 30 percent; there is reason to believe that it will rise in the future. The key to channelling potential domestic savings into real investment rests on trade expansion. As modern technology continuously enlarges the economic scale of production, Taiwan's dependence on trade expansion becomes more and more significant. Taiwan has, at present, a trade-limited type of economy. Therefore, how quickly trade expansion can be accelerated will be the main concern of the Republic of China's trade policy, or, more accurately, of its development policies during the next stage of growth.

THE PROSPECT OF FOREIGN TRADE AND FURTHER ECONOMIC DEVELOPMENT

Taiwan's external trade during the sixteen-year period 1950–65 increased more than fourfold. Imports rose from US$125 million in 1950 to US$555 million in 1965 and exports went up from US$93 million in 1950 to US$488 million in 1965. Trade acted as a catalyst to rapid economic growth, accounting for over 30 percent of GNP. The key to Taiwan's economic development in the next stage lies in accelerated expansion of its external-trade sector.

Despite the steady growth of both exports and imports during the period under review, there has been a fairly large trade deficit, totaling about US$100 million each year. Ninety percent of this deficit was financed by United States concessional aid. The exceptional years were 1963 and 1964; they did not show a trade deficit, primarily because of the windfall profit from sugar exports sold at exceedingly high prices. Consequently, heavy foreign-exchange reserves were built up during those two years.

It is probable that with the discontinuation of United States aid, the trade gap will not be eliminated overnight. For the foreseeable future, other outside assistance will have to be solicited to help finance the trade gap. It was contended by the United States aid authorities that Taiwan had already established a credit worthiness able to attract needed capital from conventional foreign sources such as the United States and Japanese export-import banks, American banks and firms, and international institutions such as the International Bank for Reconstruction and Development (IBRD) and the Asian Development Bank (ADB). The Republic of China has passed a very liberal investment statute for foreign investment and has made great efforts to seek medium- and long-term capital flows from foreign investors. These efforts have proved quite successful, as exemplified by an amount of US$150 million credit in yen from Japan and the more than US$80 million loans from the IBRD and the Export-Import Bank of the United States.

A country with a large amount of foreign commercial debt will soon find, however, that its total debt service accelerates to a point where the gross capital inflow resulting from incurring new debts may be barely enough to finance the debt servicing charges, or may even reflect a net outflow. In order that Taiwan may depend less on foreign loans that will ultimately become a heavy drain on her foreign exchange, exports must increase at a faster rate than imports. For instance, if (as assumed in the Fifth Four-Year Plan for Economic Development) imports for the next ten years were to grow at an annual rate of 7 percent, the same growth rate as that projected for GNP, total imports would reach US$1,090 million by 1974 (slightly less than doubling the 1965 total of US$555 million). If total exports were to attain the same level as imports by 1974 so that the trade gap would then be closed, the annual export growth rate would have to be about 8.5 percent. A greater margin in the export surplus will help to increase Taiwan's external debt-servicing capacity.

In the Fourth Plan for Economic Development of Taiwan (1965–68), the excess of the annual average growth rate of exports over that of imports was much smaller than the above projection; the export growth rates for 1967 and 1968 were projected at less than the import growth rates. No attempt was made in the Plan to close the trade gap either within or beyond the planned period.

In the past, invisible imports have usually been greater than invisible exports. Anticipated receipts from the increases of tourism, shipping industries, and other activities among invisible exports will probably cover only the anticipated increases in service expenditures such as royalties, dividends, freight, and foreign travel. The projection of a surplus in invisibles to offset a portion of the visible trade deficit seems to be unrealistic.

Table 4.10 shows that, except in 1957, 1963, and 1964, there has been a protracted deterioration since 1953 in Taiwan's commodity terms of trade. The years that registered better terms of trade were those of high sugar export prices, while other years, which registered worsening terms of trade, corresponded to the low sugar prices. Thus, Taiwan's external sector is still dominated by sugar exports.

Had the index of the commodity terms of trade for Taiwan been kept at 100 percent during 1965, the total export value would have gone up from the actual US$488 million to US$575 million. The difference of US$87 million could have been used for additional imports of capital goods to help achieve a higher level of subsequent growth or to strengthen the balance-of-payments position. The annual loss sustained from the deterioration in terms of trade almost equals

TABLE 4.10—Index of Taiwan's
terms of trade[a]

(1952 = 100)

Year	Terms of trade
1952	100.0
1953	98.0
1954	95.0
1955	97.5
1956	97.2
1957	103.0
1958	92.2
1959	89.5
1960	83.6
1961	87.6
1962	87.1
1963	105.2
1964	111.1
1965	84.6

[a] The index is used to measure the change in the volume of imports that could be received, on the basis of price relations only, in exchange for a given volume of exports.

Sources: *Index Numbers of the Import and Export Trade of China*, March, April, 1965, no. 60, p. 2; *Statistics of Foreign Trade of China*, July, August, 1965, no. 1, p. 2. Both were published by the Department of Statistics, Ministry of Finance, Republic of China.

the present yearly capital inflow, or almost the entire trade gap. We may, therefore, draw the inference that, in planning the development of the external sector of Taiwan's economy, one priority should be improving the terms of trade.

Protracted deterioration in the terms of trade is very common among the underdeveloped countries, which import industrial products and export primary goods. Some economists contend that the accrual of the gains from trade is biased in favor of the advanced industrial countries.[7] The arguments are inconclusive, but Taiwan's own experience supports the above contention. The only way to alle-viate the bias favoring the advanced industrial countries seems to be to stress further development in the industrial sector. With the added weight of industrial products in Taiwan's exports, the high geographic and commodity concentrations in export trade patterns would be effectively reduced. Industrial growth would also end the buyers' market in some of Taiwan's export products.

The effort to bring about such a change in the trade pattern seems to be, at first sight, in conflict with the principle of international specialization. But countries can attempt specialization only in those items that will yield high returns in trade. Industrialization is not an inherent asset of a nation. For example, in the past twenty years, a pastoral economy like Australia's has had high achievements in indus-trialization.

The emphasis on industrialization by no means aims to minimize the past achievement of balanced development. A prosperous agricul-tural community is essential to the industrial sector, both as its raw-material supplier and as its market for finished products. A shift of emphasis to industrialization is appropriate, however, not only be-cause Taiwan's external trade requires further diversification, but also because of the high component of marginal capital in the agricultural sector. This high capital coefficient is the result of optimum use of the limited land; of the relatively high cost for developing marginal land; and of the low labor productivity on land, implying high underem-ployment for manpower.

Taiwan does not intend, however, to abandon its efforts to strive for continuing development in the agricultural sector. Technical innova-tions—such as developing plant and animal varieties, introduction of new cash crops, soil preservation, and better application of fertilizer—should be encouraged. On the other hand, development of marginal and tidal land should first undergo a thorough cost-benefit analysis. Development of a perishable crop product for a single foreign market—such as the very extensive increase in bananas destined for Japan—should be handled with extreme caution, since the inevitable result is to place the large crop at the mercy of a sole buyer.

The industrialization process during the years ahead may differ substantially from industrial development during the past. In the past, industries were import substitutes, characterized by low capital, lim-ited technical knowledge, high labor concentration, and heavy govern-ment protection. Most of the export industries developed at later dates are either an extension of those import-substituting industries, such as textiles, or industries making products containing a high labor-factor cost, such as plywood. Some of these export industries have been heavily subsidized in the past by domestic sales, but there are fewer profitable projects of this type at present. For future industrialization, large-scale and high-risk projects may eventually become the only alternatives. Numerous stumbling blocks will have to be removed before Taiwan can embark on the development of heavy industries.

Large-scale, capital-intensive industries require very extensive capitalization, calling for the mobilization of public savings. Taiwan will need enlightened entrepreneurship, the underwriting services of investment companies or stockbrokers, the establishment of public confidence by full and truthful disclosure of company financial statements, and rigid supervision of the listed stocks by the Securities Exchange Commission. These are but some of the many conditions essential to ensure the successful organization and operation of large enterprises. The society does not as yet provide all these facilities.

Another, equally important, condition is the technical knowledge associated with large-scale industries. Taiwan still lags far behind the advanced industrial countries in the technical field. The purchase of foreign patents is the most expedient way to make up this deficiency. Research personnel must be recruited and trained, however, and facilities must be acquired in order that technology may take roots in Taiwan's soil to provide for future growth.

Foreign investments are, of course, welcome to help accelerate economic growth. Taiwan's own capital resources must also be channelled into capital-intensive projects, however, so that there will not be complete foreign domination. At present, due to lack of a long-term capital market, there appears to be no effective method of pooling public savings to finance such large-scale projects. The nation needs the guidance of government and business leaders to bring about conceptual as well as structural changes that will induce a continuous high rate of growth through industrialization.

In implementing capital-intensive projects, careful preparation should be made to ensure their successful and uninterrupted operation. Necessary steps before launching these large-scale investments are preproject planning, feasibility studies, cost-benefit analysis, financing, construction and management plans, marketing research (particularly foreign-market potentials), analysis of the impact on other industries, and alternative-project studies.

In the meantime, labor-intensive projects should also be explored to alleviate the problem of the ever-increasing labor force. Projects that call for greater use of skilled labor are preferred, for they will not adversely affect the terms of trade. Labor quality should be improved through extension of compulsory education from six to nine years. Quantitative and qualitative improvements in the vocational-education system and installation of in-service training courses are required to increase labor productivity further.

In the Fourth Four-Year Plan (1965–1968), export growth was projected at an annual average rate of 9.1 percent. Table 4.11 shows

TABLE 4.11—Taiwan's actual and projected export composition, 1965–68

(Percent)

Year	Agricultural products	Processed agricultural products	Industrial products	Other	Total
1965 (actual)	27.5%	29.0%	41.3%	2.2%	100.0%
1965	22.3	27.5	47.3	2.9	100.0
1966	23.3	25.1	48.9	2.7	100.0
1967	22.5	24.0	50.9	2.6	100.0
1968	22.6	22.7	52.3	2.4	100.0

Source: *The Fourth Four-Year Plan for Economic Development*, published by the Council for International Economic Cooperation and Development, Republic of China (Taipei, 1965), pp. 262–63, table VI–1.

that actual industrial exports during 1965 lagged far behind the planned target (41.3 instead of 47.3 percent), and it seems doubtful that industrial exports reached 52.3 percent of total exports in 1968. This is disheartening because the rate of increase in industrial exports projected for the period 1965–68 was already extremely slow.

If we assume that there will be an average growth rate of 9.1 percent per annum in total exports for the ten-year period 1965–75, and that industrial exports will increase by 2.5 percent each year as a percentage of total exports, we can expect that industrial exports will constitute 66.3 percent of total exports by 1975, compared with 41.3 percent for 1965. Industrial exports will have to grow at a very fast rate, averaging 14.4 percent yearly to attain this goal. (See Table 4.12 for details.) If we recall that industrial exports rose from between 6 percent and 12 percent of total exports in the middle fifties to about 40 percent in the middle sixties (see Table 4.2), then the seemingly ambitious projection of a shift in the export pattern toward a larger industrial composition is not totally impossible.

With respect to the import composition, the Fourth Four-Year Plan estimated a fairly constant level of capital-goods imports at about 29 percent of total imports for the three years 1966 to 1968. This level is higher than the average of 25 percent for the ten preceding years (see Table 4.1). High capital-goods imports must be planned for the years ahead, however, in order to accelerate industrialization.

TABLE 4.12—Estimate of Taiwan's industrial exports, 1965–75

Year	Total exports (million US$)	Industrial exports as % of total exports	Industrial exports (million US$)	Growth rate of industrial exports (%)
1965	488	41.3	202	—
1966	532	43.8	233	15.3
1967	580	46.3	269	15.4
1968	633	48.8	309	14.9
1969	691	51.3	354	14.6
1970	754	53.8	406	14.7
1971	823	56.3	463	14.0
1972	898	58.8	528	14.0
1973	980	61.3	601	13.8
1974	1,069	63.8	682	13.5
1975	1,166	66.3	773	13.3

Source: Data obtained from a draft input-output table prepared by the Third Department, Council for International Economic Cooperation and Development, Republic of China.

Because the trade of the developed countries grows much faster than that of the underdeveloped countries, and because the underdeveloped countries trade more with developed countries than among themselves, a closer regional trade relationship among the ECAFE countries and the ultimate goal of establishing a common market for the region appear to be rather remote. Nevertheless, because of geographical proximity, the ECAFE countries are the best potential buyers of Taiwan's increasing industrial exports. With the ending of United States economic assistance, Taiwan's demand for certain agricultural commodities such as soybeans, corn, and coconut oil (as a substitute for beef tallow if the price is competitive) could be met by imports from Thailand and the Philippines. The aim of promoting regional trade would be furthered, and part of the increased exports of industrial products to these countries would be offset.

Increased exports of industrial and finished products will require active government support of aggressive marketing and advertising; timely commercial intelligence; a coordinated distribution system, including the best location of dealers; inventory control over the dealers; prompt transportation; improved packaging; and marketing research. The market potential in the new African countries and in Latin America should be explored and promoted, while the established markets in North America and Europe should be enlarged. Foreign trade in the future is the frontier of the economy and presents a major challenge to the people of the Republic of China.

NOTES

1. Taiwan was occupied by Japan after the Sino-Japanese War of 1894–95 and was recovered by the Republic of China after the Japanese surrender in 1945.
2. S. C. Hsieh and T. H. Lee, "Agricultural Development and Its Contributions to Economic Growth in Taiwan," mimeographed (Taipei: Joint Commission on Rural Reconstruction, 1966).
3. The Taiwan "Land to the Tiller" program was first instituted in 1954. The essence of this program was to limit ownership of land by absentee landlords and to sell their excess holdings to the farmers, with the government advancing funds. The farmers paid back capital and interest in ten yearly installments.
4. The Republic of China launched its First Four-Year Plan for Economic Development in 1953. The Fourth Four-Year Plan for Economic Development ended in 1968. The Fifth Plan runs 1969–73.
5. Michael Michaely, *Concentration in International Trade* (Amsterdam: North Holland Publishing Co., 1962).
6. Bela Balassa, "Tariff Protection in Industrial Countries: An Evaluation," *The Journal of Political Economy*, 73, no. 6 (1965): 576–77.
7. For example, Raul Prebisch, "The Economic Development of Latin America and its Principal Problems," *Economic Bulletin for Latin America*, 7, no. 1 (1962); and Gunnar Myrdal, *Development and Underdevelopment*, National Bank of Egypt Fiftieth Anniversary Commemoration Lectures (Cairo, 1956).

COMMENT ON CHAPTER 4

D. V. RAMANA

The export performance of Taiwan has improved phenomenally since 1956. Although Taiwan has been doing very well in the export sector, several studies indicate that the exchange-control system there has been very restrictive in its operation. Exchange control has been liberalized lately, but it is still quite restrictive. Taiwan's exports may show even better performance as further liberalization takes place.

In the recent Fourth Four-Year Plan for Economic Development, there are some proposals for more vigorous import-substitution programs. Hitherto, Taiwan has been producing consumer goods and diversifying its agriculture; it now seems to be on the point of embarking on the production of capital goods. The production of capital goods has to be taken up at some stage, but whether the program of producing capital goods should be undertaken just now is open to question. A steel mill in Taiwan, for example, could be very expensive at this stage.

Import substitution is perhaps given too much importance in our discussions. With or without planning, import substitution has been going on for ages. Without planning, the import-substitution policy will be determined by the response to changes in relative prices. With planning, the production of import substitutes will be accelerated. What is at issue is not the scale of import substitution as such, but the choice of commodities. Import substitution on a planned basis should be undertaken only if the cost of production of import substitutes is more or less in accordance with prices in the market. The choice of import substitutes will have to be made on the basis of their eventually being exportable. We should insist upon the exportability of import substitutes; not that we have to export them, but that we could. Otherwise, the cost of import substitutes will keep going up.

CHAPTER 5

SOME SALIENT ASPECTS OF THAILAND'S TRADE, 1955–64

SUPARB YOSSUNDARA AND YUNE HUNTRAKOON

GENERAL CHARACTERISTICS

During the ten-year period from 1955 to 1964, Thailand's trade increased at an annual compound rate of 7.4 percent. This compares with the growth rates of 6.9 percent in world trade and 7.7 percent in the trade of developed countries. Developing countries as a whole did less well, their trade expanding at a rate of only 4.3 percent. If we divide the decade under review into two periods, 1955 to 1960 and 1960 to 1964, the second period shows—with the exception of the group of less-developed countries in the ECAFE area—a general acceleration in the rate of trade expansion throughout the world. Thailand also had marked improvement, its annual growth rate doubling from 5.2 percent in the first period to 10.3 percent in the second.

The role of quantity expansion was significant in the trade of Thailand, especially during the second period. Table 5.1 shows that, while in the first period the quantities of exports and imports increased at annual rates of 3.5 percent and 5.1 percent respectively, in the second period they grew at the rates of 10.9 percent and 11.9 percent. The rate of increase in the export quantity trebled, while the import quantity only slightly more than doubled. In relation to the quantity expansion of both developed and developing countries as a whole, Thailand's rate of quantity increase during 1960–64 was outstanding, especially for exports.

The most important causes were the emergence of a vigorous external demand and the existence in the country of conditions favorable for the expansion and diversification of domestic production. Since

TABLE 5.1—Annual growth rates of trade: Thailand and all developed and developing countries, 1955–64

(Percent)

Period and country	Exports			Imports			Terms of trade
	Quantity	Unit value	Value	Quantity	Unit value	Value	
1955–60							
Developed countries	6.70%	0.60%	7.40%	7.10%	− 0.60%	6.40%	1.20%
Developing countries	4.40	− 1.30	2.90	4.10	− 0.20	4.30	− 1.10
Thailand	3.50	0.30	3.80	5.10	− 0.05	5.05	0.35
1960–64							
Developed countries	7.20	1.00	8.30	8.50	0.30	8.80	0.70
Developing countries	5.80	− 0.20	5.60	3.30	0.00	3.30	− 0.20
Thailand	10.90	− 1.30	9.40	11.90	− 1.50	10.30	0.20
1955–64							
Thailand	6.70	− 0.40	6.20	8.00	− 0.70	7.40	0.30

Sources: Data for the developed and developing countries are from United Nations, Economic and Social Council, "World Economic Trends: Economic Progress During Initial Years of Development Decade: Major Economic Indicators for Developing Countries," mimeographed (E/4059), June 29, 1965, table 14; the figures for Thailand were prepared by the Bank of Thailand for the present study.

1960, the industrialized countries have experienced a rapid rate of income growth, especially the European Common Market countries and Japan. Domestic production in Thailand, unhampered by the internal difficulties that prevailed in most of her neighbors, reacted most favorably to the rising demand of the industrialized countries. Expansion took place, not only in the sales of traditional exports such as rubber and tin, but also in the sales of such new exports as maize, tapioca products (cassava), and kenaf (see Table 5.10). On the other hand, the quantity of Thailand's imports increased by even greater amounts than did that of exports. The increase was made possible partly by higher income from primary exports and partly by a greater inflow of aid goods and foreign capital, both private and official. Thus, in spite of relatively large annual trade deficits, Thailand's foreign-exchange reserves continued to grow steadily. Unlike most developing countries, which have had to enforce stringent import restrictions, Thailand could afford to allow a relatively free flow of imported goods needed for development projects as well as for the maintenance of a stable domestic price level.

Unit value appears to have played a smaller role in Thailand's trade picture. In the first period, the unit value of both exports and imports improved, the former at a much faster rate than the latter. In the second period, the unit value of exports deteriorated at an annual rate of 1.3 percent. The fall in export prices was more than offset, however, by the fall in the unit value of imports at an annual rate of 1.5 percent. The favorable trend in import prices in the second period could be attributed in part to a substantial increase in Thailand's imports of Japanese goods, for which the prices were generally lower than those of other industrialized countries. Apart from certain cases of protection for local industry, Thai import tariffs have been relatively low. The liberal import policy adopted by the government has made Thailand an intensely competitive market and has thus contributed to a lower overall domestic price level for imports than would otherwise have existed.

Thailand's favorable terms of trade between 1959 and 1964 would seem at first glance to run counter to the general trend of most developing countries. The fact is that, although the quantity and value of her exports were expanding at a remarkable rate during that period, the unit value of exports was declining most of the time (see Table 5.2). The prices of Thailand's individual export commodities, like those of other countries exporting primary products, fluctuated widely

TABLE 5.2—Thailand: trade indices and terms of trade

(1958 = 100)

| Year | Exports | | | Imports | | | Terms of trade |
	Quantity	Unit value	Value	Quantity	Unit value	Value	
1955	103.39	107.45	111.09	90.72	100.67	91.34	106.73
1956	109.27	98.16	107.26	92.94	100.68	92.94	97.49
1957	119.78	97.52	116.81	100.29	103.34	103.64	94.37
1958	100.00	100.00	100.00	100.00	100.00	100.00	100.00
1959	110.86	105.85	117.34	110.54	98.72	109.13	107.22
1960	122.58	109.08	133.71	116.34	100.40	116.81	108.65
1961	146.30	106.07	155.17	122.80	101.70	124.89	104.30
1962	141.80	104.31	147.91	146.17	95.54	139.65	109.18
1963	146.41	102.59	150.20	164.51	94.47	155.42	108.59
1964	185.18	103.43	191.53	182.82	94.63	173.01	109.30

Source: Bank of Thailand.

from year to year. Between 1959 and 1964, the terms of trade moved within narrow limits—between 107 and 109 except for the decline in 1961—as a result of export diversification.

Another salient feature of Thailand's commerce in the postwar period was the continuous deficit in its trade balance. This deficit increased between 1955 and 1964—in striking contrast to the prewar period, when every year produced a surplus. From 1929 to 1938, trade surpluses for the entire period amounted to Bht500 million (US$217 million), at current prices, the equivalent of over four years' imports at that time; from 1955 to 1964, trade deficits totalled Bht13,600 million (US$648 million), or the equivalent of about a year's imports at the 1964 rate.[1] The volume of imports increased more rapidly than did the volume of exports, because of a much higher level of economic activity in the postwar years than before the war, which, in turn, was a direct result of acceleration in domestic development expenditures and the consequent substantial increase in aggregate demand. On the other hand, these large trade deficits, associated with the growth of imported capital goods, indicate that Thailand's economy was entering a phase of capital goods accumulation that should enable her to advance at a quicker pace.

IMPORTS

The Composition of Imports

Grouped according to the Standard International Trade Classification (SITC), Thailand's imports reveal different rates of growth. For all but two groups, food and chemicals, the rate of increase was faster during the second period (1959–60 to 1963–64) than during the first period (1955–56 to 1959–60). In fact, some groups showed declining rates during the first period, due to the recession in 1958; in the second period, however, all groups, without exception, were expanding. As shown in Table 5.3, expansion during the second period was fastest for crude materials and for machinery and transport equipment, with annual rates of 24.0 percent and 16.4 percent respectively. Other groups rose by less than the overall rate of 9.8 percent a year.

The changing structure of imports through time is shown in Table 5.4. Imports of manufactured goods (Sections 6 and 8), which com-

TABLE 5.3—Annual growth rates of Thai imports, 1955–64

(Percent)

	SITC Section	1955–56 to 1959–60	1959–60 to 1963–64
0	Food	5.8%	1.4%
1	Beverages and tobacco	− 4.0	4.2
2	Crude materials	8.2	24.0
3	Mineral fuels and lubricants	7.6	8.0
4	Animal and vegetable oils and fats	− 1.9	0.9
5	Chemicals	11.3	9.5
6	Manufactured goods	2.8	7.4
7	Machinery and transport equipment	12.2	16.4
8	Miscellaneous manufactured goods	− 8.9	8.0
9	Miscellaneous transactions	3.2	5.5
	Overall growth rate	5.3	9.8

Source: Bank of Thailand.

prised nearly half the total imports in 1955–56, dropped to a little over one-third in 1963–64. The shares of food and of beverages and tobacco were considerably reduced. In contrast, the share of machinery and transport equipment rose from less than one-fifth to less than one-third. The very small portion of crude materials almost doubled, from 1.0 percent to 1.9 percent. Mineral fuels and lubricants more or less maintained their share, while that of chemicals grew fairly fast up to 1959–60 and remained unchanged during the second period.

TABLE 5.4—Share of Thailand's imports by SITC Section

(Percent)

	SITC Section	1955–56	1959–60	1963–64
0	Food	8.4%	8.6%	6.2%
1	Beverages and tobacco	2.2	1.5	1.2
2	Crude materials	1.0	1.1	1.9
3	Mineral fuels and lubricants	9.7	10.6	9.9
4	Animal and vegetable oils and fats	0.4	0.3	0.2
5	Chemicals	8.1	10.2	10.1
6,8	Manufactured goods and miscellaneous manufactured goods	47.5	39.8	36.6
7	Machinery and transport equipment	19.2	24.7	31.1
9	Miscellaneous transactions	3.5	3.2	2.8
	Total	100.0	100.0	100.0

Source: Bank of Thailand.

As a group, chemical imports were third in importance by 1964—following manufactured goods, and machinery and transport equipment. Their share rose from 8.1 percent in 1955–56 to 10.1 percent in 1963–64, their value from Bht600 million to Bht1,500 million. Among the fastest rising items in the chemical group were fertilizers, organic chemical products, and synthetic plastic materials, the imports of these items increasing 7 to 9 times between 1955 and 1964.

About equal in importance to the import total for chemicals was that for mineral fuels and lubricants. The rapid increase in the number of road motor vehicles and the growth of industries after the end of the war caused fuel consumption to rise almost as rapidly as did total imports.

Another change that deserves attention was the doubling in the proportion of crude-materials imports, due mainly to the sharp increase in purchases from the United States of raw cotton of the long-staple type required by the rapidly expanding textile industry.

The most striking change was the declining share of manufactured goods and the rapid rise in the share of machinery and transport equipment. In 1955–56, the share of manufactured goods (47.5 percent) was about two-and-a-half times as large as that of machinery and transport equipment (19.2 percent). By 1963–64, the shares were almost equal (36.6 percent and 31.1 percent, respectively). That the combined share of manufactured goods and of machinery and transport equipment remained practically unchanged (around 67 percent in 1963–64 as in 1955–56) means that, during the ten-year period under study, machinery and transport equipment was steadily replacing manufactured goods.

This shift away from "manufactured goods" to capital goods specifically is common to all countries undergoing economic development. In Thailand, the acceleration in this shift from 1960 to 1964 was due to the heavy public spending on development projects—power and irrigation, roads, railways, harbors, telecommunications, water supply, and sewerage—all of which had relatively high import content. During this same period, there was also a considerable expansion of investment in the private sector under the Promotion of Industrial Investment Act of 1962.[2]

On the other hand, imports of some manufactured goods were held back by the policy of encouraging their domestic production through quantitative controls and tariff increases. In the four years between 1960 and 1964, over 130 large and small industrial plants were established;[3] hence, some degree of import substitution has taken place in the postwar years, although still on a very small scale. A recent Bank of Thailand survey of import substitution has shown that savings on imports in about twenty new industrial plants were Bht190 million in 1962, Bht250 million in 1963, and Bht360 mil-

TABLE 5.5—Thailand: import substitution of
selected manufactured products,
1962 and 1964

Product	Production as % of total supplies	
	1962	1964
Weaving, spinning, bleaching, and dyeing	17.5	18.8
Electric appliances	12.5	59.3
Motor-car and tractor assembling	32.5	46.7
Tinplate, galvanized iron, and barbed wire	97.4	96.7
Flour (including wheat flour)	77.7	84.0
Dry cell batteries	84.2	83.7
Chemicals	19.4	23.6
Milk products	4.0	6.2
Aluminum products	14.1	15.6
Pharmaceutical products	10.8	12.6
Zippers	45.5	77.3
Vacuum flasks	54.5	75.9
Tin and gasoline drums	61.3	33.3
Cement fibers	85.6	88.5

Source: Bank of Thailand.

lion in 1964, compared with the total import figure of Bht12,000 million–14,000 million each year.[4] Thailand has now become self-sufficient, or virtually so, in a number of products, including cigarettes, matches, sugar, cement, soft drinks, beer, gunny-bags, plywood and shaving board, gourmet powder, rubber-soled canvas shoes, and certain types of textile goods. These new industries have also given rise to no small increase in imports of other manufactured goods, however, since many are only assembly and packaging plants that require a high proportion of finished or semifinished manufactured parts or products from abroad. Data on industrial production are not available to permit a full assessment of the extent of import replacement.

Table 5.5 gives some idea of import substitution in 1962 and in 1964 for a few selected products. The percentage of production to total supply was fairly high for such products as electric appliances; motor-car and tractor assembling; tinplate, galvanized iron, and barbed wire; flour; dry cell batteries; zippers; vacuum flasks; and cement fibers. Many of these products enjoy tariff protection.

The Source of Imports

Unlike the structure of imports, which was largely determined by the requirements of economic development and industrialization, the source of imports was also influenced by other factors such as competitiveness among the sources of supply, cost of transportation, conditions of loans and grants, and suppliers' credit terms. In the case of capital goods, the most important factor was that only developed countries could produce and supply the machinery and transport equipment required for development and industrialization. The rate of increase in Thailand's imports from the developed countries has been spectacular, as is evident in Table 5.6. Before the war (1937–38), one-half of Thailand's total import requirements came from developed countries. In the postwar years, the proportion increased sharply to over two-thirds in 1955–56, then to three-fourths in 1959–60, and finally to over four-fifths in 1963–64. Conversely, the share of devel-

TABLE 5.6—Share of Thailand's imports by country group

(Percentage of total value)

Country group	1937–38	1955–56	1959–60	1963–64
Developed countries	49.7%	67.6%	74.8%	82.3%
EEC	10.6	16.4	17.1	16.5
Other Europe	16.0	15.0	13.9	14.0
North America	4.9	17.7	17.1	17.2
Japan	17.1	17.4	25.4	32.4
Others	1.1	1.1	1.3	2.2
Developing countries	50.0	32.0	24.2	16.6
Middle East	0.3	0.9	0.4	2.4
Other Asia	49.7	30.8	22.8	13.8
Africa	0.0	0.0	0.1	0.1
Latin America	0.0	0.2	0.9	0.2
Others	0.0	0.1	0.0	0.1
Centrally planned economies	0.3	0.4	1.0	1.1

Source: International Monetary Fund, *International Financial Statistics*, various issues.

oping countries dropped steadily, from one-half before the war to only one-sixth in 1963–64.

The breakdown by groups of countries shows that, by 1963–64, Japan had become the largest supplier of goods to Thailand. Her share in Thailand's total imports averaged 17.1 percent in 1937–38, 17.4 percent in 1955–56, 25.4 percent in 1959–60, and 32.4 percent in 1963–64. Throughout the postwar period, North America (mainly the United States) and Western Europe (EEC and Other Europe) managed to keep their shares practically unchanged at 17 percent and 31 percent, respectively. North America's position improved substantially from the prewar years. Japan's gains appeared to have been made entirely at the expense of the developing countries, mainly Other Asia (mostly ECAFE countries, excluding Japan). Thailand's imports from Other Asia fell steadily from 49.7 percent before the war to 30.8 percent in 1955–56, to 22.8 percent in 1959–60, and then to only 13.8 percent in 1963–64.

A further breakdown by country group and by SITC Section shows some interesting points (see Table 5.7). The share of the developed countries increased in every group save two: animal and vegetable oils and fats, and miscellaneous transactions. By 1963–64 (average), the developed regions' share in Thailand's total imports of most groups reached exceedingly high levels—98.8 percent for beverages and tobacco, 83.9 percent for food, 84.4 percent for manufactured goods (Sections 6 and 8), and 70.4 percent for crude materials. In only one group, mineral fuels and lubricants, did the developing regions retain a major share—81.7 percent.

The high percentages for imports of beverages and tobacco, food, and crude materials call for immediate explanation. The major product imported under beverages and tobacco was tobacco leaf, 99 percent of which was purchased from the United States. The most important single item under crude materials was raw cotton of the long-staple type, which Thailand has not as yet been able to produce in sufficient quantity and which must, therefore, be imported—again, mainly from the United States. Milk products were the major component of the food group (55 percent of total food imports in 1964); they were supplied by developed western countries, especially the Netherlands. In most groups, Japan very often led the field, followed usually by the United States, West Germany, or the United Kingdom.

One item, tractors, under the heading of machinery and transport equipment, deserves special mention: the value of tractor imports rose

TABLE 5.7—Thailand's imports by SITC Section and by country group

(Percentage of total value)

Country group	Section 0 Food			Section 1 Beverages and tobacco			Section 2 Crude materials[a]		
	1955–56	1959–60	1963–64	1955–56	1959–60	1963–64	1955–56	1959–60	1963–64
Developed countries	58.2%	68.3%	83.9%	93.9%	97.1%	98.8%	20.5%	60.7%	70.4%
EEC	31.1	33.7	45.0	4.2	3.6	4.9	3.9	5.6	3.6
Other Europe	10.7	12.5	14.8	5.5	5.0	6.1	5.1	17.8	2.0
North America	6.9	7.8	9.5	84.2	88.5	87.8	5.1	29.9	47.0
Japan	2.0	6.5	3.1	0.0	0.0	0.0	5.1	5.6	13.8
Others	7.5	7.8	11.5	0.0	0.0	0.0	1.3	1.8	4.0
Developing countries	41.5	31.2	15.7	6.1	2.9	1.2	79.5	39.3	29.6
Middle East	0.0	0.0	0.0	0.0	0.0	0.0	3.9	0.0	4.7
Other Asia	39.7	27.8	15.0	6.1	2.9	1.2	75.6	37.4	13.4
Africa	0.0	0.0	0.5	0.0	0.0	0.0	0.0	0.9	0.8
Latin America	1.7	0.0	0.2	0.0	0.0	0.0	0.0	1.0	10.7
Others	0.1	0.0	0.0	0.0	0.0	0.0	0.0	0.0	0.0
Centrally planned economies	0.3	0.5	0.4	0.0	0.0	0.0	0.0	0.0	0.0

[a] Tin and rubber were exported to Malaysia and Singapore, not as final destinations, but for reexport to other countries. To give a true direction of Thailand's export trade, we have reallocated to other, final-destination countries her tin and rubber exports to Malaysia and Singapore.

(Table continued on following page)

TABLE 5.7 (continued)

Country group	Section 3 Mineral fuels and lubricants			Section 4 Animal and vegetable oils and fats			Section 5 Chemicals		
	1955–56	1959–60	1963–64	1955–56	1959–60	1963–64	1955–56	1959–60	1963–64
Developed countries	14.3%	14.3%	18.3%	78.6%	69.2%	74.1%	77.7%	83.9%	88.3%
EEC	2.7	4.5	1.5	3.6	3.8	7.4	19.9	23.5	27.3
Other Europe	2.2	3.6	5.0	17.8	19.2	22.3	21.9	19.1	17.7
North America	9.0	5.7	6.7	53.6	3.9	3.7	28.6	27.3	19.0
Japan	0.4	0.5	4.6	3.6	3.8	3.7	5.0	13.1	23.1
Others	0.0	0.0	0.5	0.0	38.5	37.0	2.3	0.9	1.2
Developing countries	85.6	85.7	81.7	21.4	30.8	25.9	22.1	16.0	11.0
Middle East	8.9	3.7	22.1	0.0	0.0	0.0	0.0	0.1	0.2
Other Asia	76.6	77.3	59.5	21.4	30.8	25.9	21.8	15.3	10.2
Africa	0.1	0.0	0.0	0.0	0.0	0.0	0.1	0.4	0.5
Latin America	0.0	4.7	0.1	0.0	0.0	0.0	0.2	0.2	0.1
Others	0.0	0.0	0.0	0.0	0.0	0.0	0.0	0.0	0.0
Centrally planned economies	0.1	0.0	0.0	0.0	0.0	0.0	0.2	0.1	0.7

(Table continued on following page)

TABLE 5.7 (continued)

Country group	Sections 6 and 8 Manufactured goods and miscellaneous manufactured goods			Section 7 Machinery and transport equipment			Section 9 Miscellaneous transactions		
	1955–56	1959–60	1963–64	1955–56	1959–60	1963–64	1955–56	1959–60	1963–64
Developed countries	68.1%	77.5%	84.4%	88.6%	93.0%	97.6%	89.4%	85.0%	87.4%
EEC	12.5	11.3	11.8	20.8	24.1	19.7	51.7	23.3	5.9
Other Europe	12.9	10.6	11.1	27.7	21.1	17.6	12.5	24.7	41.1
North America	12.5	10.6	11.3	27.4	25.6	22.9	21.1	26.3	29.7
Japan	30.0	44.7	48.5	12.4	21.6	36.1	1.1	6.3	6.7
Others	0.2	0.3	1.7	0.3	0.6	1.3	3.0	4.4	4.0
Developing countries	31.2	20.5	13.3	11.1	6.5	2.0	10.6	15.0	12.6
Middle East	0.0	0.1	0.3	0.0	0.0	0.0	0.0	0.3	0.3
Other Asia	31.2	20.4	13.0	11.1	6.4	2.0	10.2	14.7	8.6
Africa	0.0	0.0	0.0	0.0	0.0	0.0	0.0	0.0	0.0
Latin America	0.0	0.0	0.0	0.0	0.1	0.0	0.0	0.0	0.0
Others	0.0	0.0	0.0	0.0	0.0	0.0	0.4	0.0	3.7
Centrally planned economies	0.7	2.0	2.3	0.3	0.5	0.4	0.0	0.0	0.0

Source: Bank of Thailand.

ten times in ten years, the United States and United Kingdom being the principal suppliers, but with Japan rapidly increasing its share.

THE PATTERN OF EXPORTS

The Structure of Exports

The structure of exports in Table 5.8 presents some contrasts to that of imports for the period under study. First, while the pattern of imports changed, the export pattern was relatively static. Second, exports were highly concentrated in two main groups, food and crude materials, whereas imports were more widely distributed among the groups. On the average, food accounted for about 51 percent and crude materials for about 44 percent of Thailand's total exports.

Of the approximately 5 percent remaining, only 2.0 percent was manufactured goods (Sections 6 and 8) in 1963–64. During the preceding ten years, the share had risen only 0.5 percent. Corresponding manufactured-exports shares for 1964 were 6 percent for the Philippines, 25 percent for Pakistan, and over 30 percent for Taiwan. The share for India was around 45 percent, and so was that for the Republic of Korea. Thailand's first tin-smelting plant, which started

TABLE 5.8—Share of Thailand's exports by SITC Section

(Percentage of total value)

	SITC Section	1955–56	1959–60	1963–64
0	Food	50.7%	45.5%	56.4%
1	Beverages and tobacco	0.5	0.3	0.6
2	Crude materials	44.4	49.1	37.2
3	Mineral fuels and lubricants	0.0	0.0	0.0
4	Animal and vegetable oils and fats	0.1	0.1	0.1
5	Chemicals	0.2	0.1	0.1
6	Manufactured goods	1.1	1.1	1.7
7	Machinery and transport equipment	0.0	0.0	0.0
8	Miscellaneous manufactured goods	0.4	0.1	0.3
9	Miscellaneous transactions	0.3	0.7	0.8
	Reexports	2.3	3.0	2.8
	Total	100.0	100.0	100.0

Source: Bank of Thailand.

operation in mid-1956, will raise substantially the share of manufactured-goods exports; tin-metal exports will be classed as manufactured goods, whereas the tin concentrates exported in past years were classified as crude materials.

Manufacturing industries made a comparatively late start in Thailand. In 1960, a population census indicated that, out of a total of 13,800,000 workers, only 3 percent were engaged in manufacturing. The government's industrial-promotion policy has given industry an impetus to expand, but most of the newly established industries are small and tend to cater more to the local market. Among the industries that have a surplus for export are raw and unrefined sugar, cement, Thai silk, ready-made clothing, and gunny-bags.

In 1959–60, the marked expansion in the proportion of crude materials was caused by the high volume of rubber exports relative to rice exports. In 1963–64, on the other hand, the volume of rice, maize, and sugar exports reached record levels and, consequently, carried the proportion of food to over 56 percent.

In order to probe deeper into the underlying structure of these major exports, it is necessary to combine food and crude materials and to reclassify them into three new subgroups, namely, traditional exports, new exports, and others, as shown in Table 5.9. This rearrange-

TABLE 5.9—Share of Thailand's exports by commodity

(Percentage of total value)

Commodity	1955–56	1959–60	1963–64
Traditional exports	77.2%	71.9%	62.7%
Rice	42.7	31.8	35.5
Rubber	23.7	30.4	18.0
Tin	6.7	6.0	7.8
Teak	4.1	3.7	1.4
New exports	2.8	10.1	18.7
Maize	1.3	4.9	9.9
Kenaf	0.2	2.0	3.9
Tapioca products	1.3	3.2	4.9
Others	20.0	18.0	18.6
Total exports[a]	100.0	100.0	100.0
	(7,022)	(8,087)	(11,008)

[a] Figures in parentheses represent total value of exports in millions of baht.

Source: Bank of Thailand.

ment reveals some very significant features. Between 1955–56 and 1963–64, Thailand achieved a remarkable degree of diversification in primary-product exports. In absolute terms, the combined value of traditional exports increased substantially from 1955–56 to 1963–64—by 27.3 percent—but their share in total exports fell steadily: from 77.2 percent in 1955–56 to 71.9 percent in 1959–60, and then precipitously to 62.7 percent in 1963–64. By 1963–64, rice, rubber, and teak were all of substantially less importance than in 1955–56, while tin gained about 1 percentage point. By contrast, the new exports

TABLE 5.10—Indices of Thailand's principal
exports by commodity
(1955–59 = 100)

Commodity	1960–64		
	Quantity	Unit value	Value
Traditional exports	121	100	121
Rice	117	97	114
Rubber	133	96	128
Tin	133	122	163
Teak	69	120	83
New exports	529	96	505
Maize	556	101	563
Kenaf	822	118	974
Tapioca products	389	78	304

Source: Bank of Thailand.

made spectacular gains, both in proportion to total exports and in absolute value. In terms of current values, maize exports expanded twelve times during the ten-year period, kenaf over twenty-six times, and tapioca products six times. The share of all the new exports rose from 2.8 percent to 18.7 percent between 1955–56 and 1963–64.

Table 5.10 gives five-year average indices of quantity and unit value, with 1955–59 as base. Of the seven main exports, there was a substantial improvement in the unit value of tin, teak, and kenaf, but there was a deterioration in that of rice, rubber, and tapioca products. The fall in the unit value of tapioca products was severe, but the composition of products under tapioca exports has been changing continuously. Only the unit value of maize was virtually unchanged. For rice and rubber, higher quantities more than offset a modest price decline, so that the export earnings rose substantially.

The Direction of Exports

Table 5.11 gives an overall picture of the direction of exports by country group. The direction of exports was different from that of imports in two respects. First, the total exports of Thailand were more equally distributed between the developed and the developing regions than were the total imports. Second, there was a declining trend in the

TABLE 5.11—Share of Thailand's exports[a] by country group
(Percentage of total value)

Country group	1955	1960	1964
Developed countries	59.7%	55.7%	52.3%
Developing countries	40.3	41.4	46.7
Centrally planned economies	0.0	2.9	1.0
Total exports	100.0	100.0	100.0

[a] Tin and rubber were exported to Malaysia and Singapore, not as final destinations, but for reexport to other countries. To give a true direction of Thailand's export trade, we have reallocated to other, final-destination countries her tin and rubber exports to Malaysia and Singapore.
Source: Bank of Thailand.

proportion of exports going to developed countries, but for imports the trend was upward. This second difference resulted mainly from the sudden shift in Japan's rice policy after 1957. Prior to that year, Japan used to buy as much as one-third of Thai rice exports. By 1960, Japan had cut her share to 5.8 percent (see Table 5.12). On the other hand, several countries in the Middle East and Africa increased appreciably their purchases of Thai rice. Thus, the share of the developed countries in Thailand's total rice exports was reduced from almost two-fifths in 1955 to about one-tenth after 1960. This new pattern in the direction of rice exports is likely to continue. Japan —with her high level of rice production under strong domestic price-support policy and her preference for Japonica rice—is not likely to buy Thai rice in as large quantities as during the early postwar period. In the European market, Thai rice also faces very strong competition from both United States and EEC sources. The market for Thai rice has therefore become more concentrated in developing regions, with these areas taking 88.3 percent of the total by 1964. Malaysia, Hong

Kong, and Indonesia together accounted for 63 percent of this total (according to Bank of Thailand estimates). In more recent years, Ceylon and India have also become important buyers.

Because of the dominant place of rice in Thailand's total exports, rice needs to be considered separately from the other major Thai

TABLE 5.12—Share of Thailand's rice exports by country group

(Percentage of total value)

Country group	1955	1960	1964
Developed countries	39.0%	10.9%	11.7%
EEC	3.7	1.7	2.4
Other Europe	1.5	2.0	2.6
North America	0.1	0.0	0.0
Japan	33.7	5.8	6.4
Others	0.0	1.4	0.3
Developing countries	61.0	89.1	88.3
Middle East	0.6	10.2	7.1
Other Asia	59.1	77.0	75.8
Africa	1.3	1.9	5.4
Latin America	0.0	0.0	0.0
Others	0.0	0.0	0.0
Centrally planned economies	0.0	0.0	0.0
Total rice exports[a]	100.0	100.0	100.0
	(3,133)	(2,570)	(4,389)

[a] Figures in parentheses represent total value of rice exports in millions of baht.
Source: Bank of Thailand.

exports if a clear indication of their pattern is to be given. In Table 5.13, rice is left out; the totals for the remaining six main crops are given. On the average, the developed regions took over 88 percent of these six products, and about 9 percent went to the developing countries. Japan enlarged its share enormously, from 3.5 percent in 1955 to 37.5 percent in 1964. The EEC share increased from 5.2 percent to 25.7 percent and that of Other Europe from 5.6 percent to 11.6 percent, while the North American (mainly the United States) share fell sharply from 75.2 percent to 11 percent. By 1964, Japan and Western Europe (EEC and Other Europe) accounted for about three-fourths of the total value of the six principal exports.

TABLE 5.13—Share of Thailand's principal exports,[a]
excluding rice, by country group

(Percentage of total value)

Country group	1955	1960	1964
Developed countries	90.2%	87.4%	87.0%
EEC	5.2	16.7	25.7
Other Europe	5.6	11.4	11.6
North America	75.2	29.1	11.0
Japan	3.5	28.9	37.5
Others	0.7	1.3	1.2
Developing countries	9.8	7.1	10.9
Centrally planned economies	0.0	5.5	2.1
Total principal exports[b]	100.0	100.0	100.0
	(2,664)	(4,542)	(5,694)

[a] Includes rubber, tin, teak, maize, kenaf, and tapioca products. Tin
and rubber were exported to Malaysia and Singapore, not as final destinations, but for reexport to other countries. To give a true direction of
Thailand's export trade, we have reallocated to other, final-destination
countries tin and rubber exports to Malaysia and Singapore.

[b] Figures in parentheses represent total value of principal exports in
millions of baht.

Source: Bank of Thailand.

WHY AND WHEREFORE

The expansion and the current pattern of Thailand's foreign trade can
be largely attributed to the major financial reforms that took place in
1955. In that year, Thailand abolished multiple exchange rates and
reverted to the use of taxation to absorb excess purchasing power. The
most important tax imposed in that year was the rice premium, which
played a dual role: one, preventing excessive exports and keeping the
price of rice low for local consumers and, two, absorbing the excess
purchasing power that would have accrued to the exporter while the
world demand for rice was very high. In addition, collection of taxes
at the export point was simpler to administer than personal or corporation income taxes. As rice was by far the largest export, the premium could also bring in revenue badly needed for public development. Because rice was subject to heavy taxation, however, it became
financially attractive for traders to develop other exports, and the

emergence of maize, tapioca products, and kenaf as important exports can be attributed in part to this fact. Both development of highways that provided access to markets and the presence of external demand stimulated the process of export diversification after 1960. Even the drafters of the Six-Year Plan (for 1961–66)[5] could not foresee such rapid growth in these new crops. Early in the Plan period, production and export of these crops already far exceeded expectations.

When foreign exchange had to be surrendered to the Bank of Thailand under the regulations prior to 1955, the prescribed currencies were United States dollars and sterling, with the emphasis on United States dollars. Naturally, commodities such as rubber and tin were directed toward dollar markets. With the end of currency prescriptions in 1955, exporters began to sell in the markets that would earn them the most money. Through the efforts of the Central Bank and a Japanese commercial bank operating in Thailand, Japanese importers were persuaded to buy rubber directly from Thailand instead of via Singapore. Thus we see an increase in rubber exports to countries other than the United States in more recent years.

In late 1948, the first Open Account Arrangement was concluded with Japan.[6] The question in the mind of the Thai authorities was what commodity should be imported to compensate for the rice sold to Japan in exchange for Open Account dollars, since the funds could not be used until swing limits were exceeded or settlements were made. Negotiations were undertaken for the purchase of locomotives and rolling stock from Japan. Imports of various machinery and heavy equipment under Open Account were thus "seed" for the import in recent years of capital goods from Japan.

The situation then was far different from now, when Japan holds an exceptionally high proportion of the export market of many Thai commodities and is the main supplier of Thai imports. In the early fifties, Japan was sixth or seventh or a very insignificant supplier of any import commodity; in the sixties, that country leads in most commodities. Japan's nearness, salesmanship, and, above all, credit terms have enabled it to outpace all other suppliers.

One factor that partly explains the declining importance of developed countries as markets for Thai exports is the loss of the European market for rice. Unpublished Bank of Thailand data indicate that, in the fifties, Thailand exported about 74,600 tons of rice annually to Western Europe. This declined to 59,900 metric tons in the early sixties, as American competition became keener. The lowest figure in any one year (1960) was 41,000 metric tons. Exports to Western Europe improved a little in recent years (and even went up to 88,800 metric tons in 1965). Thai exporters blamed the decline of this market on the various incentives the United States gives to its grain exporters, but there is a lot to be said for modern techniques in packaging and presentation. Fortunately, some West Europeans still prefer long-grain rice—otherwise, the special levy imposed by the EEC on rice from nonmember countries would have wiped out Thailand's business entirely.

Another commodity that should be singled out is sugar. At the start, government policy was directed toward utilization of local materials and import substitution. It was known that Thailand could grow cane, although the sugar content of this cane is much lower than that of cane from other countries. At first, imports were subject to quotas; then they were prohibited entirely. Since most of the mills in operation were of the old type and even the modern ones had high costs, consumers were buying sugar at prices far above world prices. But the import ban provided enough incentive for manufacturers to expand their production. By 1961, production rose to 150,000 metric tons a year, while internal consumption was estimated at 120,000 metric tons. Means had to be found to get rid of this surplus. Beginning in 1962, a subsidy, based on a bidding system, was granted to exporters of sugar. The method proved unsatisfactory, and the subsidy ended in October, 1966. More recently, domestic prices of sugar have declined almost to the world level.

Similar trends seem to be developing in the gunny-bag industry. Until 1960, Thailand used to import about 20,000,000 bags a year, both new and old, at world prices. For a while, importers were compelled to buy one bag produced by the government factories for every three bags imported. This proportion was later changed to one to four. In 1962, it was decided that imports should be channelled through a government-owned corporation, and there were occasions when rice exporters had to buy bags at very much above world prices. On those occasions, and when shortages were evident, exporters' associations would be allowed to bring in certain amounts of imported bags to ease the situation. Nevertheless, it soon became apparent that gunny-bag manufacturing is a highly profitable business. Government factories expanded their capacities, and new private enterprises started up, some even without privileges granted under the Promotion of

Industrial Investment Act of 1962. In 1965, some 40,000,000 gunny bags were produced, and 153,600 bags were exported. Surpluses will probably be available for export in the coming years also. With new equipment and more active local competition, domestic costs can now more or less stand the test of competition abroad.

There is still a long way to go before some of the import-substitute products can stand overseas competition. Many of the new industries are very much tied up with the old supplier and have a high import content. The capital structure of the new enterprises also tends to promote high costs, because the equity proportion is small and foreign suppliers provide medium-term credit for plant and machinery. Domestic bank credit provides working capital.

WHERE DO WE GO FROM HERE?

Thailand's foreign trade enjoyed a very satisfactory rate of growth from 1958 to 1967. In spite of sizeable trade deficits each year,[7] there was also an overall surplus in balance of payments (except in 1958), made possible through capital inflows in the form of aid and loans—principally from the World Bank and the United States government. Two questions therefore come to mind—one: whether this inflow of capital can be kept up, and, two: whether Thailand will be able to maintain a level of export income adequate to pay for future import needs as well as for debt service.

Thailand's international reserves are now equivalent to about one year's imports at the current rate. This, coupled with its export potential and financial stability, has greatly enhanced the country's creditworthiness abroad. With proper programming, there should be no problem, therefore, in obtaining foreign financing on reasonable terms for development efforts. There are, however, many factors on both the supply and the demand side of exports that forbid complacency.

The population is growing at an annual rate of over 3 percent. Thailand has to produce enough rice to feed this growing population, as well as to leave some for export. Although rice has been declining in percentage of total exports, in tonnage terms, it has been increasing. The supply of good rice land is limited. Experiments are still being made to determine whether a second annual rice crop is possible. Increases in yield will require better irrigation, as well as the use of fertilizers. In order to achieve more use of fertilizers, the government's present policies on taxation of rice exports and on the price of rice for farmers and consumers in the urban areas will have to be reconsidered. There should be scope for farmers to get better prices for their product and to invest more on their land. There is need for distribution of fertilizers at subsidized prices. Other cash crops also have to be found if two rice crops in one year should prove uneconomical.

The government's policy of concentrating on providing the basic facilities for development should continue. Past experience shows that Thais do not lack enterprise. Give them the market, and the natural response to price incentives is ever present. Until recently, the government has allowed exporters to sell wherever they wish and at whatever price they can get. In recent negotiations with Japanese maize importers, exporters have been looking to the government to negotiate prices and deliveries on their behalf, because they fear cutthroat competition among themselves. Statistics on production are either lacking or unreliable, and exporters sometimes find they do not have the supplies for their overseas customers when delivery time arrives. The time may now have come for stepping up efforts toward modernization of the distribution system. Exporters may have to learn from experience, whether bitter or pleasant, how to conduct their own trade and how to maintain their position in the world market.

The fact that the market for some of Thailand's agricultural exports is concentrated in Japan, and the fact that Japan is the main supplier of imported goods, means that its bargaining position is very strong. There is need not only to diversify products but also to diversify markets.

In the preparation of the new Five-Year Plan (for 1967–71),[8] the National Development Board, for the first time, brought in members of the private sector for consultation. An exchange of views of this type is very useful. Although the Plan is only a public-sector plan and is only intended to give guidelines on the government's policy of development, the private sector should know what role it is expected to play in the country's development.

Regional cooperation in trade can be promoted by simplification of customs procedures, by the conclusion of commercial treaties, and by the lowering of tariffs, but further steps may also be necessary. Planners of the countries concerned can meet to compare notes on their respective plans and so get to know what others are doing, in both the public and the private sectors, to avoid waste and misuse of resources from duplication. A process of giving instead of taking may have to evolve, so that economies of scale and the advantages of a wider market can be achieved. Thailand, like other countries, will have to play her part in this move towards closer cooperation, not only as a good neighbor, but also for her own balanced growth.

NOTES

1. From 1929 to 1938, the free market rate was 2.3 baht to the United States dollar. From 1955 to 1964, it was about 21 baht to the United States dollar.
2. *Government of Thailand Gazette,* 79, part 12 (Special Issue, February 9, 1962).
3. These data are based on unpublished research by the Bank of Thailand.
4. This survey was made by the research staff of the Bank of Thailand and was not published.
5. National Economic Development Plan for the period B.E. 2504 (A.D. 1961) to B.E. 2509 (A.D. 1966), *Government of Thailand Gazette,* 77, part 85 (October 20, 1960).
6. The first Thai-Japanese bilateral trade agreement was made with the Supreme Commander of the Allied Powers (SCAP) in December, 1948, and became operative on March 1, 1949. A second bilateral trade agreement, this time concluded directly with the Japanese government on December 21, 1951, was terminated on April 16, 1956.
7. These deficits are apparent from trade statistics. It is possible to argue that, with illicit exports taken into account, the true deficits may not be substantial, and, in some years, they may even turn out to be surpluses.
8. National Economic and Social Development Plan for the period B.E. 2510 (A.D. 1967) to B.E. 2514 (A.D. 1971), *Government of Thailand Gazette,* 84, part 24 (Special Issue, March 8, 1967).

COMMENT ON PART II

GERARDO P. SICAT

Among the three countries whose trade and industrialization policies are under review, Pakistan and Taiwan present contrasting results. Because Thailand has followed somewhat less comprehensive policies up to now, a comparison of the experiences of Pakistan and Taiwan may be very useful for Thailand.

Professor Islam's discussion of tariff protection, comparative costs, and industrialization in Pakistan deals with a very important problem of general interest to all countries that have adopted policies for rapid import substitution. The evidence he presents tells us that protection plus industrialization are a very costly prescription. Even a superficial comparison with Taiwan suggests, however, that it is the particular economic policies designed to promote industrialization that may lead to specific costly results.

Economic development in the long run involves industrial import substitution and export creation. The problem with most countries that have adopted a conscious policy of import substitution is that of telescoping long-run adjustments. The devices used are: foreign exchange and import controls, tariff protection, and subsidies such as tax exemption. One effect of these measures, however, is that an import-dependent type of import substitution often takes place. This appears to be the case for some Pakistani industries that depend on imported raw materials.

Professor Islam makes a very fresh contribution to discussion of industrialization policies in the less-developed regions by emphasizing the quantitative aspects. The comparative cost ratios of many manufacturing industries studied show relative cost inefficiency measured by world prices. Moreover, data on excess-capacity utilization in the same industries give an appalling picture of how a very scarce resource—capital—has been misallocated.

151

It is interesting to note that the export-bonus scheme in Pakistan seems to show promise. This policy reflects the positive response to profit incentives that has been noted in other countries. For example, a study on investment demand in Philippine manufacturing[1] concludes that a great deal of the investment demand is a response either to profits or to sales. Putting together the lessons learned in all the countries in the ECAFE region that have adopted import-substitution policies, we have findings with broad policy implications.

There is no denying that Taiwan is today a success story of development. But let us not forget that at least two major fortuitous factors contributed to Taiwan's success. First, a tremendous inflow of immigrants from the mainland provided skills and, most important of all, entrepreneurial talents. Second, American aid has flowed into Taiwan in sizable magnitudes. But Taiwan also had appropriate economic policies which supplemented these factors. These policies included: (*a*) appropriate pricing of capital (a high interest rate policy); (*b*) an attempt to institute agricultural reform and to integrate agriculture with industry; and (*c*), most important, at least in the industrial sector, an export-oriented policy of industrialization. For these reasons, despite the high effective rates of protection for Taiwan's industries, these industries are not afflicted with the same kinds of problems as exist in Pakistan.

NOTE

1. R. W. Hooley and G. P. Sicat, *Investment Demand in Philippine Manufacturing*, University of the Philippines, Institute of Economic Development and Research (Manila, 1967).

III

Export Performance in New and Traditional Products and Markets

CHAPTER 6

HONG KONG'S CHANGING PATTERN OF
TRADE AND ECONOMIC INTERDEPENDENCE
IN SOUTHEAST ASIA

K. R. CHOU

The papers included in this book deal with Southeast Asia broadly defined. By the conventional definition, Hong Kong should be placed on the fringe of the region, instead of being taken as a component country. Hong Kong is undoubtedly the most industrialized area among the countries under discussion. It also leads the constituent countries in per capita income. In absolute size of industrial sector, however, Hong Kong can hardly compare with countries like India and Pakistan, or even with medium-sized countries such as the Philippines, Thailand, and Taiwan.

Hong Kong has, however, its own distinct advantages. First, it has a financial market without parallel in the region. Second, its industries often embody the most advanced techniques and equipment. Third, the potential for growth appears very promising in this city-state, which has a high proportion of managerial and technical staff and a large pool of skilled labor within its working population. Finally, the government and people are generally more conscious of the role of their industries and foreign markets in the promotion of their welfare than in most other countries.

Hong Kong looks to the advanced countries for the markets for its products. Those countries have provided rapidly expanding markets for its few special lines of industrial exports, such as manufactured garments, plastics, electronics, and some types of scientific instruments. These products are geared to the specifications of the Western markets; in most cases, they are either too expensive or too sophisticated for the domestic market in Hong Kong, in spite of the relatively high standard of living of its people, and they are even less suited for other Southeast Asian markets. Complementarity for Hong Kong products within the region is therefore out of the question at the moment.

Asian countries, both large and small, are currently engaged, however, in a process of rapid industrialization. Meanwhile, Hong Kong is acutely aware of the restrictions placed abroad on its most important group of exports, that is, textiles and textile manufactures. With this background, the consciousness of a regional entity will awaken when opportunities for selling Hong Kong's products outside appear less promising. Opportunities within the region will grow as more of the constituent countries have industrial goods to export in exchange for similar goods from within the region.

An "inward-looking"[1] phase may arrive in Hong Kong slightly later than in other countries, owing to the highly competitive position of Hong Kong's industrial exports. That stage of development has certainly appeared on the horizon, however. It is in this context that the following analysis of recent trade development of this British colony is presented.

THE CHANGING PATTERN OF FOREIGN TRADE

Before the Second World War, Hong Kong's main economic interests were to serve as an entrepôt for Southeast Asia and the Pearl River Basin and, at the same time, to act as a trading link between Europe and China. Immediately after the war, the balance of economic power in this part of Asia underwent some changes, but the basic features of Hong Kong's economy remained the same during the early years of postwar recovery.

Because of the Communist revolution in China, Hong Kong's trade pattern changed drastically. The change was due mainly to external forces, largely of a political nature, and was beyond the control of the Hong Kong government or its people. Fortunately, Hong Kong seems to have been able to face the changing situation with achievements very much to its own advantage, although it has suffered short periods of relapse.

The fundamental change was the transformation from an entrepôt economy to an industrialized economy. The transformation was brought about largely through changes in the trade policies of major world powers, in the context of their political conflicts in this part of the world. Hong Kong survived this turmoil because of coincidental developments that facilitated its industrial growth.

Changes in the trade pattern of this colony can be summarized as follows:

a) The volume of foreign trade was reduced considerably with the loss of the Chinese hinterland for entrepôt trade—particularly after the imposition of the trade embargo against China during and after the Korean War. But Hong Kong rapidly replaced mainland China as the main source of traditional Chinese goods for the non-Communist world.

b) There was an influx of capital and skill from predominantly Chinese sources for expansion of industrial exports during the 1950's. Recently, however, Hong Kong seems to have attracted more capital and technology from the industrially advanced countries, while the flow of capital and human resources from China (including capital inflow from overseas Chinese sources) has diminished somewhat.

c) There has been a rapid expansion of markets for Hong Kong products in advanced countries.

d) Hong Kong exports have become increasingly sophisticated as the colony has engaged more and more in the fabrication of special types of skill-intensive products.

e) The proportion of domestic Hong Kong products in total exports has increased and as of 1969 averaged about 80 percent. Before 1958, the proportion was less than 40 percent.

f) Hong Kong has neglected the production of foodstuffs and raw materials and has imported cheap food products from other countries, notably the traditional supplier, mainland China. Cotton is the only important item not supplied by China.

These changes in the pattern of trade will be discussed in detail in the sections that follow, but two important aspects of Hong Kong's foreign economic relations need to be emphasized at the outset. First, Hong Kong is one of the few remaining free ports in the world: it imposes tariff duties on only a few imported items, such as tobacco, liquor, petroleum, and motorcars. All other commodities are admitted free. Therefore, the only protection for Hong Kong's export industries, or in fact for all industries, is their own productivity. Second, the Hong Kong currency is one of the subsidiary currencies within the sterling bloc. Every Hong Kong dollar issued has a 100 percent reserve in sterling at 16*d*. per dollar.[2] The free-exchange market operating in Hong Kong serves as a safety valve, not only for the Hong

Kong dollar itself against nonsterling currencies, but also for all sterling currencies convertible into the Hong Kong dollar.

TOTAL TRADE

Hong Kong's economy has always been trade-oriented. Substitution of industrial activities for entrepôt businesses during the last decade has not changed this fundamental trade orientation as the mainstay of the

TABLE 6.1—Value of Hong Kong's commodity trade, 1946–65

(Million HK$)

Year	Total exports	Total imports	Domestic[a] exports	Retained[b] imports 1	Retained[b] imports 2	Trade balance
1946	766	934	n.a.	n.a.	n.a.	− 168
1947	1217	1550	n.a.	n.a.	n.a.	− 333
1948	1583	2078	n.a.	n.a.	n.a.	− 495
1949	2319	2750	n.a.	n.a.	n.a.	− 431
1950	3716	3788	n.a.	n.a.	n.a.	− 72
1951	4433	4870	n.a.	n.a.	n.a.	− 437
1952	2899	3779	486	1367	n.a.	− 880
1953	2734	3873	635	1775	n.a.	− 1139
1954	2417	3435	864	1881	n.a.	− 1018
1955	2534	3719	1003	2188	n.a.	− 1185
1956	3210	4566	1115	2471	n.a.	− 1356
1957	3016	5149	1202	3336	n.a.	− 2133
1958	2989	4594	1260	2865	n.a.	− 1605
1959	3278	4949	2282	3954	3940	− 1671
1960	3938	5864	2867	4793	4769	− 1926
1961	3930	5970	2939	4979	4966	− 2040
1962	4387	6657	3317	5587	5568	− 2270
1963	4991	7412	3831	6252	6321	− 2421
1964	5784	8551	4428	7195	n.a.	− 2767
1965	6530	8965	5027	7462	n.a.	− 2435

n.a.: Not available.

[a] Trade classification for "reexports" started in 1959. Figures for earlier years are therefore not strictly comparable with those for 1959 and after.

[b] Retained imports *1* were derived by subtracting reexports from total imports, according to *Trade Statistics* (after 1959) and the *Annual Reports* (up to 1959). Retained imports *2* are according to figures extracted from the *Annual Reports*.

Sources: Various issues of *Trade Statistics*, *Annual Reports*, and *Directory of Commerce, Industry, and Finance*, all published by the Department of Commerce and Industry, Government of Hong Kong.

economy. Before the past decade of rapid industrialization, the total
trade of Hong Kong was two to three times that of the total output of
the colony, because of the extensive scale of entrepôt trade. Value
added by handling charges in entrepôt trade was, nevertheless, much
smaller than that derived from fabricating imported materials, partic-

TABLE 6.2—Growth rates of Hong Kong's commodity trade, 1947–65

(Percent)

Year	Total exports	Total imports	Domestic[a] exports	Retained[b] imports 1	Retained[b] imports 2	Domestic[a] exports as % of total exports	Trade balance as % of total exports
1947	59%*	66%*	n.a.	n.a.	n.a.	n.a.	− 27%
1948	30*	34*	n.a.	n.a.	n.a.	n.a.	− 31
1949	47*	32*	n.a.	n.a.	n.a.	n.a.	− 19
1950	60*	38*	n.a.	n.a.	n.a.	n.a.	− 2
1951	19*	29*	n.a.	n.a.	n.a.	n.a.	− 10
1952	− 35	− 22	n.a.	n.a.	n.a.	17%	− 30
1953	− 6	3	31%*	30%*	n.a.	23	− 42
1954	− 12	− 11	36*	6	n.a.	36	− 42
1955	5	8	16*	16*	n.a.	40	− 47
1956	27*	23*	11*	13*	n.a.	35	− 42
1957	− 6	13*	8	35*	n.a.	40	− 71
1958	− 1	− 11	5	− 14	n.a.	42	− 54
1959	10*	8	n.a.	n.a.	n.a.	70	− 51
1960	20*	19*	26*	21*	21%*	73	− 49
1961	0	2	3	4	4	75	− 52
1962	12*	12*	13*	12*	12*	76	− 52
1963	14*	11*	16*	12*	14*	77	− 49
1964	16*	15*	16*	15*	14*	77	− 48
1965	13*	5	14*	4	n.a.	77	− 37
Average, 1947–65	14	15	16	13	13	n.a.	− 40
Average, 1960–65	13	11	15	11	13	75.8	− 50

* Annual growth rate 10 percent or above.

n.a.: Not available.

[a] Trade classification for "reexports" started in 1959. Figures for earlier years are therefore not strictly comparable with those for 1959 and after.

[b] Retained imports 1 were derived by subtracting reexports from total imports, according
to *Trade Statistics* (after 1959) and the *Annual Reports* (up to 1959). Retained imports 2 are
according to figures extracted from the *Annual Reports*.

Sources: Various issues of *Trade Statistics*, *Annual Reports*, and *Directory of Commerce,
Industry, and Finance*, all published by the Department of Commerce and Industry, Government of Hong Kong.

TABLE 6.3—Hong Kong's domestic exports, 1959–65

Value in million HK$[a]

SITC Section	1965	1964	1963	1962	1961	1960	1959
0 Food	135.1	160.4	156.3	120.4	114.3	130.0	119.6
1 Beverages and tobacco	66.4	58.6	60.3	47.4	26.8	13.5	14.0
2 Crude materials, inedible, except fuels	108.2	102.4	85.0	84.8	130.6	137.9	115.9
3 Mineral fuels, lubricants and related material	0.1	0.9	0.0	0.0	n.a.	0.0	0.0
4 Animal and vegetable oils and fats	4.2	3.9	4.1	3.9	4.0	3.6	2.3
5 Chemicals	54.7	51.6	52.1	56.9	55.8	51.1	42.9
6 Manufactured goods classified chiefly by material	1,104.3	952.2	941.4	861.6	908.5	769.6	602.9
7 Machinery and transport equipment	343.8	225.6	196.0	151.2	100.4	76.8	73.8
8 Miscellaneous manufactured articles	3,191.0	2,856.7	2,317.1	1,968.4	1,571.5	1,672.8	1,299.4
9 Miscellaneous transactions and commodities, n.e.s.	19.3	16.3	18.8	22.8	27.2	12.3	12.6
Total	5,027.1	4,427.7	3,831.0	3,317.4	2,939.0	2,867.5	2,283.3

Percentage distribution[a]

SITC Section	1965	1964	1963	1962	1961	1960	1959
0 Food	2.7%	3.6%	4.1%	3.6%	3.9%	4.5%	5.2%
1 Beverages and tobacco	1.3	1.3	1.6	1.4	0.9	0.5	0.6
2 Crude materials, inedible, except fuels	2.2	2.3	2.2	2.6	4.4	4.8	5.1
3 Mineral fuels, lubricants and related material	0.0	0.0	0.0	0.0	n.a.	0.0	0.0
4 Animal and vegetable oils and fats	0.1	0.1	0.1	0.1	0.1	0.1	0.1
5 Chemicals	1.1	1.2	1.4	1.7	1.9	1.8	1.9
6 Manufactured goods classified chiefly by material	22.0	21.5	24.6	26.0	30.9	26.8	26.4
7 Machinery and transport equipment	6.8	5.1	5.1	4.6	3.4	2.7	3.2
8 Miscellaneous manufactured articles	63.5	64.5	60.5	59.3	53.5	58.3	56.9
9 Miscellaneous transactions and commodities, n.e.s.	0.4	0.4	0.5	0.7	0.9	0.4	0.6
Total	100.0	100.0	100.0	100.0	100.0	100.0	100.0

(Table continues on following page)

TABLE 6.3 (continued)

SITC Section	1965	1964	1963	1962	1961	1960	Average, 1960–65
Year-to-year percentage changes							
0 Food	−15.8%	2.6%	29.8%	5.3%	−12.1%	8.7%	3.1%
1 Beverages and tobacco	13.3	−2.8	27.2	76.9	98.5	−3.6	34.9
2 Crude materials, inedible, except fuels	5.7	20.5	0.2	−35.1	−5.3	19.0	0.8
3 Mineral fuels, lubricants and related materials	—	—	—	—	—	—	—
4 Animal and vegetable oils and fats	7.7	−4.9	5.1	−2.5	11.1	56.5	12.2
5 Chemicals	6.0	−1.0	−8.4	2.0	9.2	19.1	4.5
6 Manufactured goods classified chiefly by material	15.9	1.1	9.3	−5.2	18.0	27.6	11.1
7 Machinery and transport equipment	52.4	15.1	29.6	50.6	30.7	4.1	30.4
8 Miscellaneous manufactured articles	11.7	23.3	17.7	25.3	−6.1	28.7	16.8
9 Miscellaneous transactions and commodities, n.e.s.	—	—	—	—	—	—	—

n.a.: Not available.

^a Components may not add up to totals because of rounding.

Sources: Various issues of *Trade Statistics*, *Annual Reports*, and *Directory of Commerce, Industry, and Finance*, all published by the Department of Commerce and Industry, Government of Hong Kong.

TABLE 6.4—Hong Kong's domestic exports: details for SITC Section 6, 1959–65

Value in million HK$[a]

Manufactured goods classified chiefly by material	1965	1964	1963	1962	1961	1960	1959
Leather, leather manufactures and dress furs	4.8	1.6	1.6	1.2	1.6	1.3	1.4
Rubber manufactures	1.4	1.0	1.2	1.1	1.2	1.1	0.9
Wood and cork manufactures (excluding furniture)	11.8	11.7	13.9	7.6	5.8	4.4	3.7
Paper, paperboard and manufactures thereof	7.9	8.7	10.1	11.4	8.3	7.8	6.3
Textile yarn, fabrics and made-up articles	834.5	706.7	648.3	590.3	669.0	554.2	413.9
Nonmetallic mineral manufactures	{ 86.5 }	{ 76.6 }	13.6	14.5	13.5	14.9	16.2
Silver, platinum, gems and jewelry			76.1	69.4	54.8	34.4	24.9
Base metals			35.7	30.7	33.5	33.7	15.4
Manufactures of metals	157.4	145.9	140.9	135.4	120.8	117.8	120.1
Total	1,104.3	952.2	941.4	861.6	908.5	769.5	602.9

Percentage distribution[a]

Manufactured goods classified chiefly by material	1965	1964	1963	1962	1961	1960	1959
Leather, leather manufactures and dress furs	0.4%	0.2%	0.2%	0.1%	0.2%	0.2%	0.2%
Rubber manufactures	0.1	0.1	0.1	0.1	0.1	0.1	0.1
Wood and cork manufactures (excluding furniture)	1.1	1.2	1.5	0.9	0.6	0.6	0.6
Paper, paperboard and manufactures thereof	0.7	0.9	1.1	1.3	0.9	1.0	1.0
Textile yarn, fabrics and made-up articles	75.6	74.2	68.9	68.5	73.6	72.0	68.7
Nonmetallic mineral manufactures	{ 7.8 }	{ 8.0 }	1.4	1.7	1.5	1.9	2.7
Silver, platinum, gems and jewelry			8.1	8.1	6.0	4.5	4.1
Base metals			3.8	3.6	3.7	4.4	2.6
Manufactures of metals	14.3	15.3	15.0	15.7	13.3	15.3	19.9
Total	100.0	100.0	100.0	100.0	100.0	100.0	100.0

(Table continued on following page)

TABLE 6.4 (continued)

Manufactured goods classified chiefly by material	1965	1964	1963	1962	1961	1960	Average, 1960–65
	Year-to-year percentage changes						
Leather, leather manufactures and dress furs	200.0%	0.0%	33.3%	− 25.0%	23.1%	− 7.2%	37.4%
Rubber manufactures	40.0	− 16.7	9.1	− 8.3	9.1	22.2	9.2
Wood and cork manufactures (excluding furniture)	0.9	− 15.8	82.9	31.0	31.8	18.9	25.0
Paper, paperboard and manufactures thereof	− 9.2	− 13.9	− 11.4	37.3	6.4	23.8	5.5
Textile yarn, fabrics and made-up articles	18.1	9.0	9.8	− 11.8	20.7	33.9	13.3
Nonmetallic mineral manufactures	12.9	− 38.9	− 6.2	7.4	− 9.4	− 8.0	10.9
Silver, platinum, gems and jewelry			9.7	26.6	59.3	38.2	
Base metals			16.3	− 8.4	− 0.6	118.8	
Manufactures of metals	7.9	3.5	4.1	12.1	2.5	− 1.9	4.7
All items under SITC Section 6	16.0	1.1	9.3	− 5.2	18.1	27.6	11.2

a Components may not add up to totals because of rounding.
Sources: Various issues of *Trade Statistics*, *Annual Reports*, and *Directory of Commerce, Industry, and Finance*, all published by the Department of Commerce and Industry, Government of Hong Kong.

TABLE 6.5—Hong Kong's domestic exports: details for SITC Section 8, 1959-65

Miscellaneous manufactured articles	1959	1960	1961	1962	1963	1964	1965
Value in million HK$[a]							
Prefabricated buildings; plumbing, heating and lighting fittings	60.9	70.0	77.4	68.5	75.5	94.8	111.6
Furniture and fixtures	43.0	49.2	42.8	45.9	41.4	39.8	44.9
Travel goods	15.8	20.2	19.4	31.5	29.1	38.7	46.5
Clothing	793.3	1,010.4	862.1	1,147.4	1,382.9	1,619.7	1,772.6
Footwear	109.0	114.5	103.7	129.5	146.3	174.6	152.7
Scientific and controlling instruments; photographic and optical goods; watches and clocks	14.4	15.8	20.2	26.4	29.5	24.2	38.6
Miscellaneous manufactured articles, n.e.s.	262.9	392.7	445.9	519.3	612.4	864.9	1,024.1
Total	1,299.4	1,672.8	1,571.5	1,968.4	2,317.1	2,856.7	3,191.0
Percentage distribution[a]							
Prefabricated buildings; plumbing, heating and lighting fittings	4.7%	4.2%	4.9%	3.5%	3.3%	3.3%	3.5%
Furniture and fixtures	3.3	2.9	2.7	2.3	1.8	1.4	1.4
Travel goods	1.2	1.2	1.2	1.6	1.3	1.4	1.5
Clothing	61.1	60.4	54.9	58.3	59.7	56.7	55.5
Footwear	8.4	6.8	6.6	6.6	6.3	6.1	4.8
Scientific and controlling instruments; photographic and optical goods; watches and clocks	1.1	0.9	1.3	1.3	1.3	0.8	1.2
Miscellaneous manufactured articles, n.e.s.	20.2	23.5	28.4	26.4	26.4	30.3	32.1
Total	100.0	100.0	100.0	100.0	100.0	100.0	100.0

(Table continued on following page)

TABLE 6.5 (continued)

Miscellaneous manufactured articles	1965	1964	1963	1962	1961	1960	Average, 1960–65
	Year-to-year percentage changes						
Prefabricated buildings; plumbing, heating and lighting fittings	17.7%	25.6%	10.2%	− 11.5%	10.6%	14.9%	11.3%
Furniture and fixtures	12.8	− 3.9	− 9.8	7.2	− 13.0	14.4	1.3
Travel goods	20.2	33.0	− 7.6	62.4	− 4.0	27.8	22.0
Clothing	9.4	17.1	20.5	33.1	− 14.7	27.4	15.5
Footwear	− 12.6	19.3	13.0	24.9	− 9.4	5.0	6.7
Scientific and controlling instruments; photographic and optical goods; watches and clocks	59.5	− 18.0	11.7	30.7	27.8	9.7	20.2
Miscellaneous manufactured articles, n.e.s.	18.4	41.2	17.9	16.5	13.5	49.4	26.2
All items under SITC Section 8	11.7	23.3	17.7	25.3	− 6.1	28.7	16.8

a Components may not add up to totals because of rounding.
Sources: Various issues of *Trade Statistics*, *Annual Reports*, and *Directory of Commerce, Industry, and Finance*, all published by the Department of Commerce and Industry, Government of Hong Kong.

ularly chemical products. Therefore, the gains from entrepôt trade per unit of trade volume contribute much less to the economy than the same value of domestic exports.

In most other developing countries there are two common approaches to industrialization: import substitution and processing of domestically produced raw materials. In Hong Kong, the approach has been quite different. In the first place, Hong Kong does not produce any significant amount of raw materials for local processing. Second, industrial development in Hong Kong, during the last decade or so, has been mainly for the export market, or, in the earlier years, for replacing the supply of Chinese goods to the non-Communist world.

Although the increase in domestic exports during the last decade has reduced the ratio of foreign trade to total output, total trade is still about one and one-half times gross domestic product. This unusually high ratio is rarely seen in territories with similar sizes of population. International trade remains the leading factor in the economic growth of this colony.

Tables 6.1 and 6.2 give the postwar value and growth of Hong Kong's total exports and imports and of its domestic exports and retained imports. Although there were some years of trade depression following the Korean War, total exports and imports after 1959 grew, on the average, at the impressive rates of 13 percent and 11 percent respectively; the rates of growth for domestic exports and retained imports were 15 percent and 11 percent. The pace of industrialization has been reflected in the increasing share of domestic exports in total exports, reaching over 75 percent after 1961.

The last column in the table shows the annual deficits of commodity trade as percentages of total exports. Although trade deficits in recent years were usually about 50 percent as large as total exports, such deficits appear to have been amply compensated by income from invisible exports such as tourist trade, bunker services, and shipping and finance, as well as by net capital inflow. We do not propose, however, to go into the details of the colony's balance of payments in this paper.

Table 6.3 gives the absolute figures, the percentage distribution, and the growth rates for the main items of domestic exports for the years 1959–65, according to the Standard International Trade Classification (SITC). A few important features in this table should be noted. First, the huge concentration of exports classified under Sections 6, 7, and 8 shows the predominance of industrial exports in the total—around 90 percent during the last few years of our data. The other sections have never been significant. Second, among the three major groups, we can observe a decreasing proportion for Section 6, indicating the declining importance of textile yarn and metal manufactures. Third, we see a rapid growth of the share of Section 7 in total domestic exports, although that share is still small compared to those of Sections 6 and 8. This represents the rapid expansion of exports of electronic products. Fourth, Section 8 constituted roughly two-thirds of total domestic exports in 1965, largely because of the fivefold increase in clothing exports between 1955 and 1965. Optical instruments and photographic apparatus are the two newest kinds of industry in Section 8 that have enjoyed tremendous growth recently and that have very bright prospects for further development. The detailed distribution and changes in the composition of exports in Sections 6 and 8 are given in Tables 6.4 and 6.5.

EXPORTS AND EMPLOYMENT

Table 6.6 shows the growth rates of exports and of employment in the three industries that have been enjoying much higher rates of growth than other industries. Rates of growth for exports of clothing have recently been, on the average, twice as high as those for total exports; those for exports of plastic and electrical products have been three to four times higher. Growth in industrial employment has been strongly correlated with growth in these foreign exports. Year-to-year changes in the growth rates of employment and of exports do not correspond closely, both because of changes in domestic demand (for example, the plastic industries in the mid-1950's) and because of variations in productivity increases.

This table also indicates the distinctive growth periods for individual industries. Textiles and metal products took the lead during the early postwar years up to about the end of the Korean War. Then followed a period of intensive growth in the plastic and clothing industries. Clothing assumed the leading place in domestic exports beginning in the latter part of the last decade. The electrical industry started its intensive growth by about the mid-1950's, but the strong tendency upwards was evident only in the early 1960's. Phenomenal growth in the exports of binoculars, refracting telescopes, and photographic apparatus has also taken place during recent years, though the absolute value of such exports is still relatively small.

TABLE 6.6—Employment and exports: growth rates of selected Hong Kong industries, 1949–65

Year	Clothing		Plastic products		Electrical products	
	Employ-ment[a]	Exports	Employ-ment[a]	Exports	Employ-ment[a]	Exports
1949	13%	—	—	—	− 26%	—
1950	53	n.a.	450%	n.a.	23	n.a.
1951	9	n.a.	− 43	n.a.	27	n.a.
1952	− 16	n.a.	89	n.a.	3	n.a.
1953	36	n.a.	26	n.a.	14	n.a.
1954	38	n.a.	26	n.a.	− 10	n.a.
1955	38	25%	116	56%	83	28%
1956	67	21	154	46	− 25	− 11
1957	27	8	52	66	20	4
1958	79	13	70	21	16	5
1959	86	82	74	110	− 2	120
1960	45	27	54	73	21	34
1961	− 16	− 15	15	15	22	55
1962	12	33	55	18	63	45
1963	12	21	18	18	19	44
1964	21	17	34	31	62	22
1965	− 3	n.a.	0	n.a.	22	n.a.
Average, 1949–65	29	n.a.	49[b]	n.a.	20	n.a.
Average, 1959–65	22	28	36	44	30	53

n.a.: Not available.
[a] According to figures for March of each year.
[b] Figure for 1950 not included.
Sources: For figures on employment, see Commissioner of Labour, *Annual Departmental Reports*, various issues; for figures on exports, see Government of Hong Kong, Department of Commerce and Industry, *Directory of Commerce, Industry, and Finance*, 1954–65.

Manufacturing of garments, electrical products, and optical instruments requires considerable skill in production. The garment industry also has recently shown signs of increasing capital intensity. Thus, there has been some shift of employment and exports into the skill-intensive and capital-intensive industries, although such a tendency is noticeable in only a few lines of export production.

REEXPORTS AND RETAINED IMPORTS

In the earlier postwar years, well over half of Hong Kong's total imports were for reexport, which signified the importance of entrepôt trade to the economy. This proportion has been reduced quite rapidly during the last decade, and the share of reexports in total imports was reduced to about 15 percent in 1965, most of which is to developing countries in Asia and to Japan. The volume of entrepôt trade has, in fact, increased somewhat in absolute value during recent years, but its relative significance has been reduced considerably by the phenomenal expansion of domestic exports (see Tables 6.1, 6.2, and 6.8 and 6.9).

Within the total volume of retained imports (total imports minus reexports), a substantial portion is, in fact, reexported in another form —as tourists' purchases and as bunker services—and is, therefore, not recorded in official trade statistics. Estimates of the size of tourist purchases range from 500 to 1,000 million Hong Kong dollars a year. Over 400,000 tourists visited Hong Kong in 1965, not including military personnel and Chinese visitors. It can be quite safely assumed that the bulk of tourist purchases consists of commodities within sections 6, 7, and 8, with perhaps a predominance in Sections 6 and 7. Fragmentary surveys showed that many tourists buy products imported from their own countries. During recent years, an average of about 500 ocean vessels entered the port of Hong Kong every month. Hong Kong is a favorite port for offshore purchases of provision for crews and passengers, because of its free-port status.

Nevertheless, by far the largest portion of retained imports was for local consumption. Table 6.7 shows the distribution of the main items of retained imports, with indicators of their individual growth rates. Within each main group there have been some shifts from cheaper quality goods to more expensive products, although these shifts cannot be detected in this table.

The imbalance between Hong Kong's domestic exports and retained imports is still significant even after tourists' purchases have been taken into account. Nevertheless, the sales of Hong Kong's services to foreigners and the inflow of capital from abroad presumably have more than covered the deficits in the current account of Hong

TABLE 6.7—Hong Kong's retained imports, 1960–65

Value in million HK$[a]

SITC Section	1965	1964	1963	1962	1961	1960
0 Food	1,763.7	1,692.1	1,473.5	1,349.6	1,208.3	1,172.7
1 Beverages and tobacco	199.3	179.2	158.7	136.3	119.9	103.0
2 Crude materials, inedible, except fuels	767.6	746.5	693.0	601.6	586.9	515.7
3 Mineral fuels, lubricants and related materials	262.9	242.2	248.0	225.6	205.7	191.8
4 Animal and vegetable oils and fats	50.4	60.2	46.5	78.8	61.8	48.3
5 Chemicals	433.0	495.1	362.1	381.3	354.8	335.8
6 Manufactured goods classified chiefly by materials	2,223.0	2,232.8	1,985.1	1,720.8	1,497.3	1,551.6
7 Machinery and transport equipment	1,105.2	952.3	800.2	647.1	555.8	532.6
8 Miscellaneous manufactured articles	649.2	589.0	472.7	433.5	369.2	321.7
9 Miscellaneous transactions and commodities, n.e.s.	7.7	5.2	81.3	6.6	6.3	4.1
Total	7,462.0	7,194.6	6,321.2	5,567.9	4,966.0	4,769.2

Percentage distribution[a]

SITC Section	1965	1964	1963	1962	1961	1960
0 Food	23.6%	23.5%	23.3%	24.2%	24.3%	24.6%
1 Beverages and tobacco	2.7	2.5	2.5	2.4	2.4	2.2
2 Crude materials, inedible, except fuels	10.3	10.4	11.0	10.8	11.8	10.8
3 Mineral fuels, lubricants and related materials	3.5	3.4	3.9	4.1	4.1	4.0
4 Animal and vegetable oils and fats	0.7	0.8	0.7	1.4	1.2	1.0
5 Chemicals	5.8	6.9	5.7	6.8	7.1	7.0
6 Manufactured goods classified chiefly by material	29.8	31.0	31.4	30.9	30.2	32.5
7 Machinery and transport equipment	14.8	13.2	12.7	11.6	11.2	11.2
8 Miscellaneous manufactured articles	8.7	8.2	7.5	7.8	7.4	6.7
9 Miscellaneous transactions and commodities, n.e.s.	0.1	0.1	1.3	0.0	0.1	0.0
Total	100.0	100.0	100.0	100.0	100.0	100.0

(Table continued on following page)

TABLE 6.7 (continued)

Year-to-year percentage changes

SITC Section	1965	1964	1963	1962	1961	1960	Average, 1960–65
0 Food	4.2%	14.8%	9.2%	11.7%	3.0%	12.0%	9.2%
1 Beverages and tobacco	11.2	12.9	16.4	13.7	16.4	8.1	13.1
2 Crude materials, inedible except fuels	2.8	7.7	15.2	2.5	13.8	35.7	13.0
3 Mineral fuels, lubricants and related materials	8.5	− 2.3	9.9	9.7	7.2	2.5	5.9
4 Animal and vegetable oils and fats	− 16.3	29.5	− 41.0	27.5	28.0	3.6	5.2
5 Chemicals	− 12.6	36.7	− 5.0	7.5	5.7	32.5	10.8
6 Manufactured goods classified chiefly by material	− 0.4	12.5	15.4	14.9	− 3.5	20.3	9.9
7 Machinery and transport equipment	16.1	19.0	23.7	16.4	4.4	45.4	20.8
8 Miscellaneous manufactured articles	10.2	24.6	9.0	17.4	14.8	17.1	15.5

^a Components may not add up to totals because of rounding.

Source: Government of Hong Kong, Department of Commerce and Industry, *Annual Reports*, various years.

TABLE 6.8—Value and direction of Hong Kong's trade, selected years
(Million HK$)

| Area | 1965 | | |
	Imports	Domestic exports	Reexports
Developed areas			
United States and Canada	1,086.5	1,853.9	103.9
Western Europe	2,008.5	1,619.3	165.4
United Kingdom	961.6	860.7	47.0
Common Market	767.9	544.3	99.4
Other industrial Western Europe	264.1	182.4	16.1
Other Western Europe	14.9	31.9	2.9
Japan	1,550.9	133.0	255.5
Australia, New Zealand, and South Africa	299.4	276.2	48.3
Subtotal	4,945.3	3,882.4	573.1
Developing areas			
Other Asia	1,160.4	569.4	764.3
Middle East and other Africa	301.6	331.9	65.0
Latin America and other Western Hemisphere	162.3	116.6	15.8
Subtotal	1,624.3	1,017.9	845.1
Communist countries			
Mainland China	2,321.8	17.7	53.9
Other Communist countries	54.6	1.9	2.2
Subtotal	2,376.4	19.6	56.1
Miscellaneous	18.8	106.9	28.4
Total	8,964.8	5,026.8	1,502.7

Note: Components may not add up to totals because of rounding.

Source: Government of Hong Kong, Department of Commerce and Industry, *Hong Kong Trade Statistics*, various issues.

Kong's commodity trade. Hong Kong has become the financial center of the 15 million overseas Chinese in Southeast Asia, and the inflow of capital from Chinese sources may amount to several hundreds of millions of Hong Kong dollars a year.

HONG KONG'S DIRECTION OF TRADE

Tables 6.8 and 6.9 illustrate Hong Kong's changing direction of trade between 1965 and selected earlier years.

On the import side, the share of mainland China (as a chief supplier of food products and daily necessities) has remained rela-

TABLE 6.8 (continued)

| 1960 | | | 1955 | | 1952 | |
Imports	Domestic exports	Reexports	Imports	Total exports	Imports	Total exports
838.6	821.8	30.6	371.1	116.8	299.6	133.0
1,363.7	809.7	69.1	954.0	361.1	1,125.4	222.5
664.0	585.2	22.6	441.0	251.1	470.4	83.4
493.1	157.0	37.8	357.8	89.6	487.3	117.3
195.5	63.7	7.7	146.3	19.7	167.7	21.8
11.1	3.8	1.0	8.9	0.7	0.0	0.0
941.6	100.7	130.3	526.0	146.3	482.2	123.6
213.1	157.7	40.7	109.6	92.5	55.8	21.1
3,357.0	1,889.9	270.7	1,960.7	716.7	1,963.0	500.2
977.2	546.4	601.4	726.9	1,309.0	833.8	1,754.4
184.2	199.7	29.7	78.4	191.0	49.1	35.3
40.8	95.2	7.7	35.9	60.2	9.9	23.3
1,202.2	841.3	638.8	841.2	1,560.2	892.8	1,813.0
1,185.9	13.0	107.3	897.6	181.6	830.3	520.0
44.5	2.1	7.5	14.2	0.0	7.6	0.0
1,230.4	15.1	114.8	911.8	181.6	837.9	520.0
74.0	120.9	46.1	5.2	75.4	85.7	65.8
5,863.6	2,867.2	1,070.4	3,718.9	2,533.9	3,779.4	2,899.0

tively stable, fluctuating between about 20 percent and 26 percent of Hong Kong's total imports. The share of imports from Western Europe (including the United Kingdom) has been gradually reduced from about 30 percent to slightly over 22 percent. The shares of the United States and Canada and Japan have increased appreciably; their combined share in 1965 was about 30 percent. Imports from other less-developed countries in Asia have declined sharply in absolute value and more sharply in relative value. These countries now supply only about 13 percent of Hong Kong's total imports, including the important item of rice.

On the export side, changes in the market pattern have been even more striking. In 1952 the United States and Canada plus Western

TABLE 6.9—Distribution of Hong Kong's trade, selected years
(Percent)

Area	1965		
	Imports	Domestic exports	Reexports
Developed areas			
United States and Canada	12.1%	36.9%	6.9%
Western Europe	22.4	32.2	11.0
United Kingdom	10.7	17.1	3.1
Common Market	8.6	10.8	6.6
Other industrial Western Europe	2.9	3.6	1.1
Other Western Europe	0.2	0.6	0.2
Japan	17.3	2.6	17.0
Australia, New Zealand, and South Africa	3.3	5.5	3.2
Subtotal	55.2	77.2	38.1
Developing areas			
Other Asia	12.9	11.3	50.9
Middle East and other Africa	3.4	6.6	4.3
Latin America and other Western Hemisphere	1.8	2.3	1.1
Subtotal	18.1	20.2	56.2
Communist countries			
Mainland China	25.9	0.4	3.6
Other Communist countries	0.6	0.0	0.1
Subtotal	26.5	0.4	3.7
Miscellaneous	0.2	2.1	1.9
Total	100.0	100.0	100.0

Note: Components may not add up to totals because of rounding.
Source: Government of Hong Kong, Department of Commerce and Industry, *Hong Kong Trade Statistics*, various issues.

Europe took only about 12 percent of Hong Kong's *total* exports, but by 1965 they accounted for about 70 percent of *domestic* exports. Imports from Japan have increased moderately; total exports to Japan have increased sharply. Similarly, a decline in exports to China, while its share in imports remained relatively stable, has led to a severe imbalance, amounting to about HK$2,300 million in 1965.

In sum, the major markets for Hong Kong's domestic exports have now shifted from Asian countries to the United States and Canada; Western Europe; and Australia, New Zealand, and South Africa, which together took about 75 percent of Hong Kong's domestic exports in the year 1965. Only in the reexport trade do the Asian countries and Japan figure significantly.

TABLE 6.9 (continued)

	1960			1955		1952	
Imports	Domestic exports	Reexports	Imports	Total exports	Imports	Total exports
14.3%	28.7%	2.9%	10.0%	4.6%	7.9%	4.6%
23.3	28.2	6.5	25.7	14.3	29.8	7.7
11.3	20.4	2.1	11.9	9.9	12.4	2.9
8.4	5.5	3.5	9.6	3.5	12.9	4.0
3.3	2.2	0.7	3.9	0.8	4.4	0.8
0.2	0.1	0.1	0.2	0.0	0.0	0.0
16.1	3.5	12.2	14.1	5.8	12.8	4.3
3.6	5.5	3.8	2.9	3.7	1.5	0.7
57.3	65.9	25.3	52.7	28.3	51.9	17.3
16.7	19.1	56.2	19.5	51.7	22.1	60.5
3.1	7.0	2.8	2.1	7.5	1.3	1.2
0.7	3.3	0.7	1.0	2.4	0.3	0.8
20.5	29.3	59.7	22.6	61.6	23.6	62.5
20.2	0.5	10.0	24.1	7.2	22.0	17.9
0.8	0.1	0.7	0.4	0.0	0.2	0.0
21.0	0.5	10.7	24.5	7.2	22.2	17.9
1.3	4.2	4.3	0.1	3.0	2.3	2.3
100.0	100.0	100.0	100.0	100.0	100.0	100.0

PROSPECTS FOR INTRAREGIONAL TRADE

Data on the intraregional trade of Southeast Asian countries have been compiled by the Economic Research Center of the Chinese University of Hong Kong from statistics given in the *Direction of Trade* supplements to *International Financial Statistics*.[3] They show that the trade of the constituent countries has been conducted mostly outside of Southeast Asia, to the extent of over 95 percent for the Philippines and India and over 85 percent for Taiwan, Pakistan, and Hong Kong. Only one country in the region—Thailand—has important trade dealings with its fellow Southeast Asian countries, because of its important rice exports to them. Data on three important countries in the region—Indonesia, Malaysia, and Singapore—are missing from the *Direction of Trade* supplements, but, according to national data on the direction of trade for these countries, their patterns appear to be close to those of most other countries except Thailand. Details for the seven countries with data available are given in Table 6.10.

Certain characteristics must be pointed out concerning bilateral trade within the region. For example, Pakistan has had extensive trade

TABLE 6.10—Direction of trade in 1965[a]: seven Asian countries
(Percent)

| | Within the region | | Outside the region | |
Countries	Imports	Exports	Imports	Exports
Ceylon	15.4%	4.6%	84.6%	95.4%
Hong Kong	10.9	17.0	89.1	83.0
India	4.0	5.4	96.0	94.6
Pakistan	4.4	18.3	95.6	81.7
Philippines	6.4	2.3	93.5	97.7
Taiwan	6.3	15.6	93.7	84.4
Thailand	10.5	44.1	89.5	55.9

[a] For the first nine months only, except for the annual totals for Hong Kong.

Source: *Direction of Trade*, a supplement to *International Financial Statistics*, published monthly by the International Monetary Fund and the International Bank for Reconstruction and Development; republished in an annual compilation, 1962–66 (Washington, D.C., 1967), various pages.

with India, in spite of all their border incidents. This is partly because Pakistan produces the raw jute that is processed in India. Hong Kong's trade with Malaysia, particularly on the export side, partly reflects Hong Kong's entrepôt position between China and Malaysia. Malaysia is also the main customer for Thai rice.

These are three typical cases of regional complementarity, although the scale has been somewhat limited and trade is often confined to the exportation of a few commodities without a variety of exchanges in industrial goods. The first case is the export of raw materials for processing within the region. The second case is the provision of special services among constituent nations. The last case is that of providing goods for final consumption. Ultimately, it is the exchange of final goods that will provide a broad basis for continuing expansion of foreign trade. The prospects for developing the first two aspects are limited, especially because the constituent nations are at similar levels of industrial development and produce competing agricultural products in similar geographical and cultural environments.

Raw materials used in producing Hong Kong's industrial exports consist mainly of the products of highly advanced chemical industries, such as plastics and polyester fibers, which could not be supplied by Asian countries. Even the supply of cotton for Hong Kong's spinning mills is from non-Asian sources.

Specialization can only come about when each constituent nation develops its own lines of industries according to conditions specified by factor endowment, external economies, and marketing outlets. Until then, the direction of trade of Southeast Asian countries will be geared towards countries outside the region, particularly the developed countries of North America and Western Europe. The speed and the degree of industrialization in individual countries will decide, therefore, the prospects for expansion of intraregional trade.

NOTES

1. See Hla Myint, "The Inward and the Outward Looking Countries of Southeast Asia and the Economic Future of the Region," *Proceedings of the Kyoto Conference on Japan and the Future of Southeast Asia, Kyoto, 1965*, also available as Research Paper no. 7, AID—University of Wisconsin Research Project on Economic Interdependence in Southeast Asia, mimeographed, 1966.
2. After the devaluation of sterling in November, 1967, the exchange rate for the Hong Kong dollar was revalued to 17½ *d*. sterling, about 17½ United States cents.
3. Published monthly by the International Monetary Fund, Washington. D.C.

COMMENT ON CHAPTER 6

ROBERT J. LAMPMAN

In looking at the variety of experience concerning trade and growth among Asian countries, one would like a way of classifying the types of experience. I wonder if one classification is "inspiring versus relevant." Hong Kong's story is certainly inspiring but it may not be relevant, whereas some of the other stories we have heard about individual countries' export performances might be relevant, but not very inspiring.

What are the possibilities that other nations in this region could benefit from the experience of Hong Kong, by emphasizing exports rather than import substitution as a way to promote industrialization? Would this experience, if generalized, be self-cancelling? Does Hong Kong succeed in this area as a free-trade example precisely because the other nations have followed much more restrictive policies? In other words, is Hong Kong an illusory example for other nations to consider, or should we draw the lesson from Hong Kong that, if a country in a determined way emphasizes exports, and if the incentives of the free market are made clearly available to entrepreneurs, new markets can be found? And we should emphasize that Hong Kong found not only new markets in terms of new trading partners but also new products and new methods of producing old products. This is a basic kind of change that may be called for if exports are to succeed.

It would be interesting to know more about the process of industrialization in Hong Kong. The general story is one of industrialization going on under the aegis of free trade, or of longstanding open import and exchange policies. The industrialization was powered by an inflow of capital, largely from Chinese sources, but more recently from other sources as well. It appears that changes in the trade policies of Western nations were important in bringing about Hong Kong's industrialization. Little is said in the chapter about domestic governmental policies in Hong Kong that furthered this export performance, other than to say that the Hong Kong government is interested in promoting exports and is sympathetic to the trading community. It would be interesting to know more about entrepreneurship: how does a nation dominated by traders shift over to being one that attracts and produces outstanding industrial entrepreneurs? This is a question many countries in this region would like to comprehend more fully, and perhaps Hong Kong could give illustrations of this structural transformation.

Does Hong Kong's success suggest some basis for regional cooperation of different kinds from those emphasized here? For example, Hong Kong's highly developed capital market may be a basis for some new kinds of cooperation among countries in this region. What about the technical services that could be shared through some kind of regional cooperation device? Is Hong Kong's experience—like that of Japan—more immediately relevant to the developing countries of the region than that of some of the Western countries? Are there, in other words, certain patterns of cooperation into which Hong Kong's entrepreneurship, technical advice, and capital services can be drawn?

It seems to me that Hong Kong has a basis for wanting the economic growth of Southeast Asia. It is not clear that, up to this time, it has contributed significantly to the growth of other countries nearby, especially the less-developed countries in this region. But Hong Kong certainly does have a basis to hope that there will be more economic growth in this region and that this will, in turn, lead to greater economic interdependence between Hong Kong and Southeast Asia.

CHAPTER 7

PHILIPPINE EXPORT DEVELOPMENT, 1950–65

AMADO A. CASTRO

The story of Philippine foreign trade from 1950 through 1965 is in outline a simple one. Emerging from the war with a large part of its productive capacity destroyed,[1] the country was blessed with large foreign-exchange earnings from invisibles—chiefly United States military expenditures, pension payments, and war-damage benefits.[2] Earnings from commodity exports, however, were meager as the war-shattered economy struggled to rehabilitate itself. On the other hand, expenditures on imports were sizable due to reconstruction needs and pent-up consumer demand, abetted by a slight overvaluation of the currency. At the end of 1949, it was necessary to impose exchange controls, which became progressively more strict over the next twelve years, especially after 1958. Early in 1962, a bold decision was made to do away with all controls except some export controls. Before the end of 1965, the peso was officially devalued, and all foreign-exchange controls were removed.

The economy expanded during the period controls were in force, and its structure changed significantly. Real GNP in 1965 had grown to 2.2 times what it was in 1949, agriculture became less important as a source of income (40 percent of GNP in 1949, 33 percent in 1965), and industry achieved relative expansion (10 percent in 1949, 18 percent in 1965). Industrial output more than doubled in volume between 1949 and 1955, and by 1965 was twice again what it had been in 1955.[3] The striking growth of industry has been based on import substitution; the pattern of imports has changed from imports of finished consumer goods to import of semimanufactures, raw materials, and capital goods.

The behavior of exports is less well known abroad and even in the

Philippines, despite the fact that export earnings have been the main source of foreign exchange for economic development. Therefore, the experience of Philippine export trade between 1950 and 1965 will be examined in this paper.

There has been much controversy in the Philippines concerning the effects of currency overvaluation on exports. I have suggested elsewhere that overvaluation had a positive impact on the development of the economy because it led to import substitution.[4] Our concern here, however, is with its effect on exports.

The theses of this paper are, first, that because of circumstances peculiar to the Philippines exports did not stagnate despite restrictions and overvaluation; second, that the emerging Philippine export pattern differs in many ways from the export patterns of some of the other Asian underdeveloped nations; and, third, that, while Asian trade integration is still some way off, the trend toward export expansion in the Philippines can make it slightly easier for the Philippines to participate in regional economic cooperation.

THE PHILIPPINE TRADE PATTERN

Table 7.1 shows that in 1941, Philippine exports amounted to US$110.5 million. In 1948, when substantial but still incomplete postwar rehabilitation had been accomplished, exports were US$309.6 million. In 1950, the beginning of the period under study, exports amounted to US$331.0 million, and, in 1965, they were US$768.5 million. The compound annual rate of growth of export earnings between 1950 and 1965, using Central Bank data, was 5.8 percent (see Table 7.2).[5] Five-year averages were 3.9 percent in 1950–55, 6.9 percent in 1955–60, and 6.5 percent in 1960–65. With 1955 as base, the quantum index of exports was 70.6 in 1950 and 170.7 in 1965,[6] so that the compound annual rate of growth in volume of exports during the period 1950–65 was 6.1 percent (7.2 percent in 1950–55, 4.3 percent in 1955–60, and 6.7 percent in 1960–65).

Although decontrol began in 1962, the biggest jump in recorded exports was in 1963, when they rose by almost 31 percent—from US$556.0 million in 1962 to US$727.1 million in 1963. This increase is spurious, however, to the extent that items previously unrecorded were listed after decontrol had taken the profit from smuggling and from underdeclaration of exports. Estimates of Philippine exports, made by George Hicks for 1954–65 from the trade returns of the Philippines' trading partners, indicate the extent of the errors in estimation (see Table 7.1). After 1963, the official data and the Hicks estimates are closer than in most of the preceding years.

TABLE 7.1—Value of Philippine exports, 1941, 1946–65

Year	Central Bank (1)	Hicks esti-mates (2)	Difference (2) − (1)	1 as a % of 2
1941	110.5	—	—	—
1946	64.2	—	—	—
1947	263.4	—	—	—
1948	309.6	—	—	—
1949	247.9	—	—	—
1950	331.0	—	—	—
1951	427.4ᵃ	—	—	—
1952	345.7	—	—	—
1953	398.3	—	—	—
1954	400.5	424.4	23.9	94
1955	400.6	432.9	32.3	93
1956	453.2	496.6	43.4	91
1957	431.1	507.2	76.1	85
1958	492.8	486.8	− 6.0	101
1959	529.5	529.7	.2	100
1960	560.4	601.5	41.1	93
1961	499.5	582.8	83.3	86
1962	556.0	614.6	58.6	90
1963	727.1	701.7	− 25.4	104
1964	742.0	762.1	20.1	97
1965	768.5	784.5	17.2	98

ᵃ It will be recalled that 1951 was the height of the Korean War boom, when prices of raw materials were abnormally high. Therefore the export performance in that year was not typical.

Source: Central Bank of the Philippines, *Statistical Bulletin*, 19, no. 1(1967): 161; George Hicks, "Philippine Foreign Trade, 1950–65: Basic Data and Major Characteristics," and "Philippine Foreign Trade Statistics; Supplementary Data and Interpretations, 1954–66," mimeographed (Washington, D.C.: National Planning Association, Center for Development Planning, 1967).

The year 1950 was chosen as the beginning of the present study because it was the first year of more than nominal import and exchange controls. The terminal year is 1965 because on November 6 of that year devaluation was made official and the last vestige of controls was lifted.

The beginning of the period was abnormal since postwar rehabilitation was not yet complete. Not until the 1953/54 crop year, for instance, was the Philippines able to fill its quota for sugar in the United States market, even though the quota was the same as before the war.

Philippine trade still shows aspects of the traditional pattern in which raw materials or semiprocessed goods are exchanged for semi-manufactures or for finished goods.[7] This historical pattern did have economic justifications. As a plantation economy under Spanish, and more especially American, rule, the chief exports—sugar, coconut, abaca fiber, tobacco, pineapples, and similar products—were devel-

TABLE 7.2—Average annual rates of growth of Philippine
exports, 1947–65
(Percent)

	Value		
Years	Central Bank data	Hicks revision	Volume[a]
1947–50	7.9%	–	–
1950–55	3.9	5.5%[b]	7.2%
1955–60	6.9	6.8	4.3
1960–65	6.5	5.5	6.7
1950–65	5.8	5.9[b]	6.1
1955–65	6.7	6.1	5.5

[a] Using the Central Bank quantum index.
[b] Using Central Bank data for 1950, and Hicks' data for 1955 and 1965.
Source: Columns 2 and 3 computed from Table 7.1. Data for column 4 from Central Bank of the Philippines, *Statistical Bulletin*, 19, no. 1(1967): 162.

oped to a large degree by foreign investors to fill demand in the political suzerain. Admittedly sugar, when exported, is already a processed good with much value added. So are some other Philippine exports. Nevertheless, these commodities are classed as primary products that will be processed further in the importing country.

The ten most important export commodities accounted for 86.1 percent of Philippine exports in 1965, as against 87 percent in 1950 (see Table 7.3). In addition to this product concentration, which is typical of less-developed countries, there was also market concentration. The bulk of exports went to the developed industrial nations: the United States took 72.5 percent of all exports in 1950 and 45.4 percent in 1965; Japan purchased 6.6 percent of exports in 1950 and

28.3 percent in 1965; and Europe bought 13.4 percent in 1950 and 20.6 percent in 1965.[8] (In contrast, the import trade was less concentrated by commodity and source of supply. Whereas, previously, finished consumer goods had been the largest category of imports, since the mid 50's imports of raw materials, semimanufactures, and capital goods have become more important as domestic industrialization based on import substitution has proceeded.)

The export performance of the Philippines has been creditable

TABLE 7.3—Philippines: ten principal exports
(Thousand US$)

Exports	1950	1955	1960	1965
Copra	137,953	118,680	138,643	170,004
Sugar	45,906	106,295	133,484	132,439
Abaca	41,635	27,833	41,774	24,222
Logs and lumber	10,691	41,542	91,600	162,001
Desiccated coconut	24,157	12,810	18,837	20,447
Coconut oil	12,482	16,535	15,669	68,095
Copra meal or cakes	3,794	4,408	4,861	11,803
Canned pineapple	9,474	5,940	7,400	8,738
Plywood	59	923	6,482	17,579
Copper concentrates	1,730	7,391	29,589	46,518
Ten principal exports	287,881	342,357	488,339	661,846
Total exports	331,000	400,600	560,400	768,500

Source: Central Bank of the Philippines, *Statistical Bulletin*, 19, no. 1(1967): 161, 186–95.

among developing nations. In spite of the export instability to which primary products are subject, Philippine exports have grown consistently and at a respectable rate, doing better than the exports of many other primary-exporting countries.[9] This growth has taken place during a period in which the Philippine peso was continuously to some extent overvalued. What is the explanation? Philippine exports of primary products have risen in response to increased world demand for them, and the supply has increased because profits have been good notwithstanding overvaluation of the currency and deterioration in the terms of trade during most of the period.

The strength of the demand for Philippine exports can be judged from the volume and value of the exports of individual commodities. Table 7.3 indicates that there has been a steady increase in the value of almost all the ten principal commodities. Sugar exports have been especially large because of the guaranteed market in the United States. The Philippine Trade Act of 1946 provided for an annual quota of 952,000 short tons (the same quota set in the Philippine Independence Act of 1934). The quota was increased to 1,247,600 short tons in the 1962/63 crop year as a result of the Cuban situation.

Since the end of World War II, the Philippines has typically accounted for about half of the world's exports of copra. World demand for fats and oils has been increasing, and while Indonesia was and still is a large exporter of copra, its exports of coconut products were declining up to 1965. The Philippines has filled the widening gap. (There is also some reexportation of Indonesian copra, especially from the Celebes, through southern Philippine ports.) In the early postwar period and into the 1950's, there was a pronounced tendency to export more of low-value copra and less of high-value coconut oil. In the 1960's, however, exports of coconut oil have increased, in large part because of new methods of shipping coconut oil in bulk.

The category "logs and lumber" has achieved a spectacular rise in export earnings, reflecting the Philippine share of the worldwide increase in trade in forest products. The logs go to Japan, Korea, and Taiwan, where they are processed into plywood for sale, mainly to the United States.[10] Exports of base metals have also benefited from rising demand in the industrial countries: copper, chromite, and manganese go to the United States and to Japan; and iron ore is bought by Japan.[11]

Such strong demand could not have been filled if the supply had not been forthcoming to meet it. The physical supply would have to be easily expandable and the sellers responsive to price incentives. Despite an overvalued Philippine peso, the peso proceeds would have to be attractive.

Throughout the period of controls in the Philippines there was much clamor from the exporting sector about depressed conditions and lack of incentive for exports, and the complaints grew louder after 1955. The export record belies these complaints. If exporters were willing to expand their sales by 5.8 percent a year on the average— and by much more in some lines—then they were not really quite as exploited as they claimed.

To what extent was the Philippine peso overvalued? During the entire period of controls, the official parity was P2.00 to US$1.00. I would guess that until 1958 an equilibrium rate was in fact between

P2.50 and P2.75 to US$1.00. This estimate is based on the prevailing black-market rates, on purchasing-power comparisons, and on some appreciation of the degree of comprehensiveness of exchange controls. Through most of the 1950's the black-market rate for the peso in Hong Kong, the most prominent extralegal market, ranged between P2.75 and P3.00 to US$1.00. These rates would have been upper limits, since the relatively thin Hong Kong market covered only fringe transactions (those that could not be settled at the legal parity). The lower limit was probably P2.34, which was P2.00 plus the 17-percent foreign-exchange tax that was collected from 1950 to the end of 1955 on almost all purchases of foreign exchange.

Crude purchasing-power-parity comparisons are possible between the Philippines and the United States, the principal trading partner. In the first half of 1945, the Philippine cost-of-living index was about 800 (with 1941 as base year), but in the years 1954 and 1955, the index went down as low as 292.[12] Prices in the United States had risen to almost 200 and were still going up.[13] For a time, there was some chance that the two price indices would meet; unfortunately domestic money creation caused Philippine prices to rise again in the second half of 1955.

Finally, foreign exchange was relatively abundant up to 1958, and exchange controls were not stringent. International reserves fell below US$300 million but were still adequate to finance the equivalent of six months' imports. In the 1957 election year there was a marked liberalization of exchange allocations and a splurge in imports, so that international reserves dropped by US$100 million net.

The combination of internal monetary inflation and the fall of reserves in 1957 and 1958 drove up the black-market rate for the peso. By April, 1960, the Hong Kong rate had risen to P3.20 to US$1.00. Our previously calculated equilibrium rate of P2.50 clearly was no longer appropriate, but P2.75 or P3.00 probably could have been held.

Table 7.4 compares the behavior of export prices of the principal Philippine export commodities for the prewar year 1941 and for 1950–51, 1955–56, 1960–61 and 1964–65. Consumer price indices also appear in the same table. Wholesale price indices for export products and for domestic products from 1949 through 1965 are compared in Table 7.5.

Both tables show that in almost all cases the peso prices of export products moved more favorably than did Philippine prices generally.[14]

TABLE 7.4—Wholesale prices of major exports, Philippines, 1950–65
(Pesos)

		Price			
Commodity	1941	1950–51 (average)	1955–56 (average)	1960–61 (average)	1964–65 (average)
Consumer-price index[a]	*(100.00)*	*(368.70)*	*(342.70)*	*(379.90)*	*(468.90)*
Copra (100 kg.)	6.17	36.07	26.57	39.03	60.12
	(100.00)	*(584.60)*	*(430.60)*	*(632.60)*	*(974.40)*
Centrifugal sugar (picul)	4.81	13.86	13.88	18.84	27.84
	(100.00)	*(288.10)*	*(288.60)*	*(391.70)*	*(578.80)*
Unmanufactured abaca (picul)	8.09	57.95	33.24	59.82	62.04
	(100.00)	*(716.30)*	*(410.90)*	*(739.40)*	*(766.90)*
Desiccated coconut (kg.)	0.21	0.66	0.55	0.55	1.02
	(100.00)	*(314.30)*	*(261.90)*	*(261.90)*	*(485.70)*
Canned pineapple (kg.)	0.21	0.31	0.40	0.44	0.63[b]
	(100.00)	*(147.60)*	*(190.50)*	*(209.50)*	*(300.00)*
Copra meal (kg.)	0.02	0.12	0.12	0.15	0.25
	(100.00)	*(575.00)*	*(575.00)*	*(725.00)*	*(1250.00)*
Cordage (kg.)	0.37	1.05	0.72	0.93	0.82
	(100.00)	*(283.80)*	*(194.60)*	*(251.40)*	*(221.60)*
Coconut oil (kg.)	0.14	0.69	0.46	0.68	1.04
	(100.00)	*(492.90)*	*(328.60)*	*(485.70)*	*(742.90)*
Lumber (1000 bd. ft.)	66.38	225.58	242.60	274.87	330.72
	(100.00)	*(339.80)*	*(365.50)*	*(414.10)*	*(498.20)*
Logs (1000 bd. ft.)	31.21	144.44	167.27	200.55	280.84
	(100.00)	*(462.80)*	*(535.90)*	*(642.60)*	*(899.80)*
Leaf tobacco (11.5 kg.)	15.02	168.16	98.38	120.08	145.94
	(100.00)	*(1118.90)*	*(654.90)*	*(799.50)*	*(971.60)*
Iron ore (metric ton)	4.60[c]	14.56	16.45	21.34	33.35
	(100.00)	*(316.50)*	*(357.60)*	*(463.90)*	*(725.00)*
Chromite ore (metric ton)	14.58	25.04	35.92	50.24	66.26
	(100.00)	*(171.70)*	*(246.40)*	*(344.60)*	*(454.40)*
Copper ore (metric ton)	27.60[c]	100.44	122.28	105.37[d]	162.94[e]
	(100.00)	*(363.90)*	*(439.90)*	*(379.00)*	*(586.10)*

Note: Figures in parentheses show price as percent of 1941 price.

[a] Constructed by splicing the Central Bank consumer-price index for Manila (available from 1949) onto the Bureau of the Census and Statistics prewar and early postwar cost-of-living index.

[b] Peso prices not available; this estimate made by multiplying the average price of US $0.18 per kg. multiplied by P3.52, the composite rate arrived at when selling 20 percent of dollar proceeds to the Central Bank at the official parity of P2.00 to US$1.00 and the remaining 80 percent at the free-market rate of P3.90.

[c] Of somewhat doubtful reliability (taken by the Central Bank from old worksheets without explanatory footnotes).

[d] Peso price not available; this estimate made by multiplying the average price of US $42.15 per metric ton multiplied by P2.50, the effective rate at the middle of the period 1960–61. The effective rate moved gradually and fairly regularly from P2.30 on April 25, 1960, to P2.75 from March 2, 1961, up to the decontrol of January 21, 1962.

[e] Dollar price of US$46.29 per metric ton multiplied by P3.52.

Source: Central Bank of the Philippines, Department of Economic Research.

Evidently, increased demand for most Philippine exports caused dollar prices to rise to such an extent that even a 25-percent currency overvaluation was swamped. Prices of exports in peso terms already were favorable in 1955–56, and they improved further in 1960–61 and even more in 1964–65.

Profits are the final proof of the existence or absence of monetary

TABLE 7.5—Movements of peso wholesale prices in Manila, 1949–56
(1955 = 100)

Year	Wholesale-price index of export products (1)	Wholesale-price index of domestic products (2)	(1) as % of (2)
1949	112.1	115.9	96.7
1950	122.9	107.5	114.3
1951	126.7	117.4	107.9
1952	100.8	108.1	93.2
1953	123.5	108.3	114.0
1954	108.5	102.2	106.2
1955	100.0	100.0	100.0
1956	104.3	102.2	102.1
1957	109.2	106.4	102.6
1958	120.8	109.9	109.9
1959	136.5	109.9	124.2
1960	133.0	114.1	116.6
1961	138.1	119.7	115.4
1962	167.1	124.7	134.0
1963	200.0	137.7	145.2
1964	194.2	145.2	133.7
1965	199.6	149.0	134.0

Source: Central Bank of the Philippines, *Statistical Bulletin*, 19, no. 1 (1967): 281–82.

incentives, and Tables 7.6, 7.7, and 7.8 attempt to measure profit rates. The samples on which these data are based are somewhat incomplete, and the results can only be tentative. The data for agricultural corporations (for both domestic and export products) and for logs and plywood are influenced by the fact that a number of new establishments were not yet making profits in the early years. Nevertheless, as shown in Tables 7.7 and 7.8, average profit rates in almost all export lines have been decent even in bad years. At the worst, returns from exports have not been much below those in other areas of economic activity. They rose markedly after the unofficial devaluation, or "decontrol," of January, 1962, and again after the devaluation of November, 1965.

The Philippine case exemplifies the income-redistribution effect of a devaluation. The export sector gained windfall earnings, while the service and the domestic manufacturing sectors, which could not raise their prices as much as raw-material costs rose, found their profits being cut. It is no wonder that the export sector in the Philippines has been quite prosperous and that Philippine export performance has been creditable.

TABLE 7.6—Profit rates in mining, manufacturing,
and agriculture in the Philippines, 1955–62
(Percent)

	1955	1956	1957	1958	1959	1960	1961	1962
Net profit (after tax) to net worth								
Mining	15.1%	20.4%	14.9%	11.0%	15.4%	21.3%	23.0%	20.8%
Manufacturing	n.a.	15.5	18.3	20.9	19.3	14.8	15.8	11.7
Agricultural corporations	7.0	5.7	15.7	8.8	8.9	13.9	8.5	13.9
Net profit (after tax) to total assets								
Mining	11.4	15.0	10.6	8.0	11.1	15.8	17.4	15.4
Manufacturing	n.a.	9.2	11.0	12.3	11.2	7.8	7.7	6.0
Agricultural corporations	4.5	3.3	6.5	3.8	3.2	5.9	3.7	5.2
Net profit (after tax) to sales								
Mining	15.2	21.8	17.0	14.3	18.0	26.4	29.3	23.3
Manufacturing	n.a.	9.3	11.4	11.4	10.8	8.2	8.3	6.0
Agricultural corporations	5.4	5.0	7.4	4.1	5.7	10.0	7.0	8.4

n.a.: Not available.
Source: Sample data compiled by the School of Economics, University of the Philippines, from annual corporate financial reports in the Securities and Exchange Commission.

The general trend of the income redistribution is shown by preliminary studies, carried out by Joseph L. Tryon, of the terms of trade between the agricultural sector and the nonagricultural sector (see Table 7.9). The bulk of Philippine exports comes from the agricultural sector (which includes forestry and fishing). The agricultural sector, both the food-producing group and the export group, has gained at the expense of the nonagricultural sector in almost every year since 1949. The gain, as trade theory would lead us to expect, has been sizable since 1960.

How was it possible that export profits were so favorable in spite of

TABLE 7.7—Philippines: profit rates in selected export lines
and in all other manufacturing, 1956–62
(Percent)

	1956	1957	1958	1959	1960	1961	1962
Net profit (after tax) to net worth							
Agricultural corporations							
Copra	n.a.	n.a.	18.2%	14.6%	18.6%	14.5%	28.8%
Logging and forest products	n.a.	n.a.	13.4	15.0	32.0	15.3	22.7
Sugar	n.a.	n.a.	3.7	5.3	5.0	17.5	23.6
Manufacturing							
Sugar mills	9.6%	11.9%	14.8	11.3	11.5	16.3	23.6
Lumber and plywood	n.a.	− 4.0	− .1	21.7	− 7.1	7.8	14.1
Cordage	n.a.	17.1	13.9	4.4	24.2	28.2	21.0
Other manufacturing[a]	n.a.	18.8	21.4	19.8	15.1	15.8	11.3
Net profit (after tax) to total assets							
Agricultural corporations							
Copra	n.a.	n.a.	14.4	11.1	14.3	11.4	21.6
Logging and forest products	n.a.	n.a.	6.9	7.7	15.8	7.6	8.8
Sugar	n.a.	n.a.	1.7	2.7	2.7	9.3	10.5
Manufacturing							
Sugar mills	6.1	8.3	8.7	7.4	7.1	10.1	12.4
Lumber and plywood	n.a.	− 2.4	0.0	10.4	− 2.9	3.2	6.6
Cordage	n.a.	17.6	4.5	2.1	8.2	10.2	16.7
Other manufacturing[a]	n.a.	11.2	12.7	11.5	7.9	7.6	5.7
Net Profit (after tax) to sales							
Agricultural corporations							
Copra	n.a.	n.a.	22.2	18.3	20.6	16.8	28.3
Logging and forest products	n.a.	n.a.	6.6	7.0	13.7	8.9	11.5
Sugar	n.a.	n.a.	3.9	6.3	5.9	14.8	17.8
Manufacturing							
Sugar mills	7.8	9.7	10.7	9.3	9.4	12.0	15.2
Lumber and plywood	n.a.	− 4.9	0.0	10.3	− 4.0	3.6	5.6
Cordage	n.a.	12.5	6.9	2.4	8.2	10.1	8.3
Other manufacturing[a]	n.a.	11.6	11.5	10.9	8.3	8.2	5.7

n.a.: Not available.

[a] Includes all other manufacturing, both for export and for the domestic market.

Source: Sample data compiled by the School of Economics, University of the Philippines, from annual corporate financial reports in the Securities and Exchange Commission.

TABLE 7.8—Profit rates of agricultural corporations
in the Philippines, 1964, 1965
(Percent)

	1964	1965
Net profit (before tax) to net worth		
Sugar	29.38%	8.18%
Coconut	28.61	17.29
Timber and logging	15.36	10.25
Livestock	13.88	4.71
Rice and corn	8.15	1.56
Fishing	7.91	6.92
Unclassified	13.27	9.03
Net profit (before tax) to sales		
Sugar	31.84	12.06
Coconut	27.45	26.30
Livestock	18.59	7.94
Fishing	9.80	5.20
Timber and logging	8.44	2.66
Rice and corn	4.91	1.01
Unclassified	9.22	18.83

Source: Securities and Exchange Commission study published
in the *Manila Daily Bulletin*, October 8, 1966. The study covered
agricultural corporations filing financial statements with the
Commission. Corporations suffering losses or not operating
were excluded by the Commission from the study. (Tables 7.6
and 7.7 show the average of the profit rates of all firms in the
sample, whether or not they were making profits.)

controls and overvaluation? One answer is the generally favorable
dollar and peso prices of specific Philippine export products in the
postwar years; a second is the inventiveness of the businessman. Even
had the official prices been unfavorable, it was possible, especially
from 1955 on, to alter the exchange- and export-control systems or to
get around the regulations.

POLICY CHANGES, 1955–65

There were at least two schemes that made exports profitable during
the control era. The first export-incentive scheme was the no-dollar-
import or barter law (Republic Act 1410) that came into effect
(without the approval of the President) on September 10, 1955.
Under this law, so-called no-dollar imports were prohibited, except
that section (d) allowed for imports of "commodities in exchange for

TABLE 7.9—Gross product originating and gross product available in the agriculture and non-agriculture sectors of the Philippine economy, 1950–65
(Millions of pesos, 1955 prices)

Year	Gross product originating in agric. (1)	Gross product originating in non-agric. (2)	Gross national product (3)	Terms of trade between agriculture and non-agric. (4)	Goods and services flow from agriculture to non-agric. (5)	Internal terms of trade effect (6)	Gross product available in agriculture (7)	Gross product available in non-agric. (8)
1950	2,432	3,822	6,264	100	1,005	0	2,432	3,822
1951	2,717	3,832	6,548	103	1,539	46	2,763	3,786
1952	2,899	4,144	7,043	106	1,688	101	3,000	4,043
1953	3,212	4,409	7,621	103	1,814	54	3,266	4,355
1954	3,423	4,751	8,174	100	1,901	0	3,423	4,751
1955	3,540	5,199	8,739	100	1,824	0	3,540	5,199
1956	3,574	5,912	9,486	100	2,074	0	3,574	5,912
1957	3,649	6,157	9,806	103	2,195	66	3,715	6,091
1958	3,801	6,227	10,028	103	2,405	72	3,873	6,155
1959	3,619	6,988	10,607	98	1,989	− 40	3,579	7,028
1960	3,556	7,338	10,894	100	2,196	0	3,556	7,338
1961	3,755	7,891	11,646	103	2,595	78	3,833	7,813
1962	3,871	8,129	12,000	96	2,510	− 100	3,771	8,229
1963	4,072	8,579	12,651	98	2,713	− 54	4,018	8,633
1964	4,019	8,969	12,988	112	2,702	324	4,343	8,645
1965	4,257	9,563	13,820	106	2,891	173	4,430	9,390

Source: This table was prepared by Joseph L. Tryon and is reprinted here, with his permission, in essentially its original form, from his article, "Internal and External Terms of Trade in Postwar Philippines," *Philippine Economic Journal*, 6, no. 2(1967): table 4, p. 199.

goods exported by persons or firms making the importation on a straight barter basis when authorized by the Secretary of Commerce and Industry"; this was the "barter" provision of the bill. Under the regulations implementing the act, "no-dollar imports" meant "imported commodities, goods or merchandise for which no foreign exchange was remitted or provided in payment therefor." Persons engaged in "dollar producing or dollar saving" industries were allowed to bring in, on a no-dollar basis, machinery, equipment, accessories, and capital goods, irrespective of value. This provision was designed to take care of such cases as machinery imports in connection with foreign loans or equity investments. Other imports permitted were personal effects, gifts, goods of returning residents, and cloth to be embroidered and then reexported. Finally, exporters were allowed to barter their exports for imports.

Very soon, an active black market developed in barter rights to import goods. The dollar was being quoted at a premium. New exports began to appear, such as "rice bran" which went out in large quantities. But the trade returns of Hong Kong, their supposed destination, do not show large Philippine exports of rice bran; presumably the "rice bran," if there was any, got lost at sea.

The effect of the barter law was an increase in the prices of export products. "Barter" exports increased,[15] yet Philippine exports as a whole did not expand much more than they had previously, as the growth rates of exports show. The benefit to the country, if any, presumably was in the windfall profits to exporters, as well as in the monopoly profits to importers who used the barter licenses.

The abuses of the barter scheme were slowly curbed in response to criticism. The regulations were made tighter and on June 19, 1959, a new act (Republic Act 2261) repealed Republic Act 1410 and reduced the number of exports eligible for barter. The implementation of the law was transferred to the Central Bank and later to a Producers Incentive Board.

The next windfall, on top of the barter scheme, was the "decontrol" program put into effect in April, 1960. This was, in reality, a *de facto* devaluation through a multiple-exchange-rate system. At the beginning, exporters were allowed to sell 25 percent of their exports at the "free-market" rate, specified by the Central Bank at P3.20 to US$1.00, which meant an effective rate of P2.30 to US$1.00.[16] Subsequent revisions led to a maximum of eight different exchange rates (for both exports and imports). The effective exchange rate for exporters rose gradually and by March, 1961, it was P2.75 to US$1.00. The higher prices for exports in peso terms and the increased profits are generally reflected in the figures for 1960 and 1961 in Tables 7.4 and 7.7.

Although both the volume and value of exports fell rather than rose in 1961, the main reason was probably cyclical instability caused by the recession in the United States. Undoubtedly there was also increased underdeclaration or overshipment of exports. World-market forces appeared to be more important in determining the level of exports, however, than was the exchange rate.

On January 21, 1962, exchange controls were abolished and substantial freedom in exchange was decreed. A vestige of the multiple-exchange-rate system remained, however. Exporters were allowed to sell 80 percent of their export proceeds at a "free-market" rate, but were required to sell the remaining 20 percent to the Central Bank at the official parity of P2 to US$1. Importers could buy all they wanted at the "free-market" rate. Shortly after the middle of 1962, the free-market rate stabilized at about P3.90 to US$1.00, making a composite rate to exporters of P3.52 to US$1.00, which was appreciably better than the P2.75 they had been getting before the decontrol. On November 6, 1965, the peso was officially devalued to P3.90 to US$1.00, and the exchange rate was unified. The only trace of controls still remaining is that some capital transfers must be reported.

In summary, our position is that overvaluation did not hurt Philippine exports significantly. Overvaluation was not very severe in the early 1950's. The demand for exports was generally strong; prices and profit incentives through legal and extralegal methods were good and improved steadily through the years; and Philippine producers responded to these stimuli.

Since 1960 the devaluation has brought windfalls to exporters of traditional exports. There is no clear indication, however, that the rate of growth of exports has risen in comparison with the previous rate of growth; as a matter of fact, the annual rate of growth in value of exports declined from 6.9 percent in 1955–60 to 6.5 percent in 1960–65 (using Central Bank data).

The benefits from the controls of the 1950's and the early 1960's were the protection and monopoly profits that fostered import-substituting industries and laid the ground for Philippine industrialization. The 1950's should be looked upon as a period in which the structure of the Philippine economy was being changed away from a primary-producing economy towards a more industrialized one. Overvaluation and protection were the prices paid for industrialization. The pattern of industrial development set in the period of controls has implications for the future of Philippine foreign trade.

PHILIPPINE EXPORTS SINCE
DECONTROL (1962)

The changing composition of Philippine imports reflects industrial development. There has been some lag, however, in the effect of industrial development on the export pattern. The five major exports are still primary products: coconut products, logs and lumber, sugar, base metals (copper, iron ore, chromite, manganese, and other minor metals), and abaca. Where some primary-product exports have lagged, others have appeared to take their place. Logs and copper are examples of new exports which have developed as a response to profit incentives. The bulk of production of these new primary products is for export.

But new industrial goods are being exported, some of them in appreciable quantities. Many of these exports would not have been possible without the encouragement that controls gave to industrialization. This export pattern is consistent with the Linder hypothesis that internal demand determines the range of potential exportable articles.[17] Philippine experience seems to be consistent with that in Pakistan, and to some extent in South Korea. It differs from that in Hong Kong and, though to a lesser degree, Taiwan, where new products have been developed primarily for the export market. These latter countries are relatively small and therefore have limited markets for their industrial-goods production (and, in the case of Taiwan, for agricultural production as well). To some extent, they are also special cases: industrialization has been carried out in large part by immigrant entrepreneurs who brought with them accumulated experience from their former home countries.

Plywood and veneer are the biggest of the new Philippine industrial exports; these exports are built on substantial home demand. But other items now appear on the export list: drugs, beer, rum, cotton fabrics, cement, fertilizer, plate glass, bathroom fixtures, printing ink, etc. These commodities were first produced to fill home demand, often as import substitutes under the protection of controls, but they can now be sold abroad as production has increased and domestic efficiency has advanced.

Central Bank statistics show that exports of plywood and "other manufactured products" rose from $39.5 million in 1963 to $62.4 million in 1965, or from 5.4 percent to 8.1 percent of total exports.[18] This is not yet a large proportion, but the list of industrial articles being exported is expanding and the increase seems to be more marked since the devaluation of November, 1965. The unification of the exchange rate and the abolition of controls have probably been as important as the devaluation itself and the more favorable exchange rate. Businessmen are now free to devote their energies to problems of marketing their exports, without having to grapple with the red tape, the uncertainties, and the frustrations of bureaucratic interference and the distortion arising from exchange rates that were different for their raw-material imports and their exports of finished and processed articles. If it normally takes a lagged response of two or three years for industrial-goods exports to take full advantage of a changed market situation (and assuming Philippine exports are competitive), then we may expect an accelerating flow of industrial-goods exports some two years from now.

One lesson from the Philippine experience since 1962 (and much the same thing can probably be said of Taiwan) would seem to be that an export-incentive system, while not necessarily unimportant, is not as powerful in fostering new exports of industrial commodities as is a simple, unified exchange-rate system set at a realistic level. Another lesson is the importance of timing of policy changes: the Philippine "decontrol" of 1962 came at just the time that the gains from the import-substitution movement of the 1950's were tapering off.

PHILIPPINE TRADE WITH ASIA

Philippine exports of manufactured articles are becoming increasingly significant. It is worth noting, however, that the bulk of them still goes to the United States, the world's largest economy and the largest trading partner of the Philippines. Japan, the second most important trading relation, does not take Philippine manufactured goods, in spite of the fact that of all Asian countries the Philippines is Japan's largest trading partner and its second largest market in Asia. Other Asian countries purchase only small amounts of Philippine exports, although the Philippines does buy in large quantities from them, particularly petroleum products from Indonesia and rubber from Malaysia. What then are the prospects of Philippine trade with Asia?

That trade has been growing in both absolute and relative terms, but the statistical trend is largely the result of expanded primary-products exports to Japan. The answer to the question of the future of Philippine trade with Asia can probably be given only in general terms. One empirical regularity is that world trade grows fastest in industrial goods, and among industrial nations with high incomes and some similarity in economic structure. Among the less-developed nations of Asia, Malaysia, Thailand, and Indonesia seem to hold the most promise as trading partners for the Philippines, and, indeed, Philippine exports of manufactured goods are larger to these three nations than to other Asian countries. As incomes rise throughout Asia, and as the industrial sector grows in the Philippines, it can be expected that the Philippines will be in a better position to buy from her Asian neighbors. Conversely, it is to be hoped that she can sell more to Asia as well. This prospect is dependent not only on increased productive efficiency and vigorous promotion efforts in the Philippines, but also on whether incomes rise in the other Asian countries. It assumes the operation of normal competitive factors.

In the foreseeable future, however, the Philippines will probably remain a large exporter of primary products. The markets for Philippine primary products have remained firm through most of the postwar period, and the greatest absolute expansion has occurred in these products. Furthermore, new lines of primary products are developing, such as pineapples, which are being sent to the United States, and bananas, which are being sent to Japan. There seems no reason to expect greatly adverse developments in the trade in primary products (except for such possible unilateral actions as the Philippine government's controlling exports of logs in favor of those of plywood).

Nonetheless, growth in industrial-products exports can be expected to take place side by side with expansion in primary-products exports. The historical pattern of economic development is that of a rising share of manufactures in exports. The problem for the Philippines is to accelerate the natural course of events.

NOTES

1. The United States Survey Mission of 1950 (Bell Mission) estimated Philippine productive capacity after the war at only 20 percent of prewar levels.
2. The latter were advances by the United States government on reparations collections from Japan. The United States subsequently renounced all reparations claims in the treaty of peace with Japan in 1952.
3. Philippine National Economic Council, *Statistical Reporter* (Manila), various issues.
4. Amado A. Castro, "Economic Policy Revisited," *Philippine Economic Journal,* 1, no. 1(1962): 66–91.
5. For purposes of consistency, the official foreign trade statistics issued by the Bureau of the Census and Statistics, as quoted by the Central Bank, are used throughout this paper, except where otherwise noted. It might be useful to explain apparent discrepancies between Central Bank and Bureau of the Census and Statistics data on foreign trade. To meet its needs for as up-to-date data as possible, the Central Bank puts together preliminary figures on foreign trade based on customs manifests; thus within about six weeks it can publish rough estimates of exports and imports. The Bureau of the Census and Statistics on the other hand compiles its data when the transactions are completed; the process of compilation takes approximately six months. The Central Bank subsequently accepts the Bureau of the Census and Statistics figures as final.
6. Central Bank of the Philippines, *Statistical Bulletin,* 19, no. 1(1967): 162.
7. This pattern of development did, in fact, lead to relatively high levels of living in the prewar Philippines, second in Asia only to Japan. See M. K. Bennett, "International Disparities in Consumption Levels," *American Economic Review,* 41, no. 4(1951): 632–49. Professor Hla Myint has described colonial economic development in "The 'Classical Theory' of International Trade and the Underdeveloped Countries," *Economic Journal,* 68, no. 270(1958): 317–37.
8. Central Bank of the Philippines, *Statistical Bulletin,* 19, no. 1(1967): 166–85.
9. Castro, "Economic Policy Revisited," especially pp. 77–82. The Central Bank series on terms of trade starts with 1950; in any case, prices of Philippine exports were generally even better than in 1950. (Central Bank of the Philippines, *Statistical Bulletin,* 19, no. 1(1967): 162.)
10. Ironically, Taiwan is now the world's largest exporter of plywood, using Philippine logs to a great extent.
11. Central Bank of the Philippines, *Statistical Bulletin,* 19, no. 1(1967): 186–95.
12. The Philippine cost-of-living index referred to is that computed by the Bureau of the Census and Statistics. The Bureau of Commerce retail-price

index (with 1941 as base year) was as low as 212. Both indices are printed in *American Chamber of Commerce Journal,* February, 1956, p. 92, and subsequent issues.

13. United Nations, *Monthly Bulletin of Statistics* (citing the Bureau of Labor Statistics, *Index of Consumers Cost of Living*), various issues.

14. Table 7.4 also reveals the pattern of relative price movements. Export prices of commodities requiring some processing (such as sugar and, especially, coconut oil, lumber, and cordage) did not rise as much as the prices of raw materials (copra, logs, and abaca, respectively). This price squeeze explains, in part, the lag in exports of the former items through most of the period under review.

Canned pineapple was a special case. In the period of controls there was only one exporter of canned pineapple, a wholly-owned subsidiary of a United States-based parent company, so that it was a simple manipulation to get around controls and repatriate earnings by charging low prices for the exported pineapple.

15. Barter exports under Republic Acts 1410 and 2261 were as follows (in thousand US$):

Year	Barter exports	% of total exports
1955	745	.2
1956	27,774	6.1
1957	41,624	9.7
1958	35,384	7.2
1959	53,244	10.1
1960	36,729	6.6
1961	27,494	5.5
1962	5,903	1.1

Data are from the Central Bank of the Philippines, *Annual Reports,* various issues.

16. Central Bank of the Philippines, *Annual Report, 1960,* pp. 48–49.

17. Staffan Burenstam Linder, *A Theory of Trade and Transformation* (New York: John Wiley and Sons, 1961), chap. 3.

18. See Central Bank of the Philippines, *Annual Report, 1964,* p. 90, and also *Annual Report, 1965,* p. 95.

COMMENT ON CHAPTER 7

KEN'ICHI ODAWARA

The main focus of Professor Castro's paper is the effect of overvaluation of the peso on Philippine exports: he believes that overvaluation of the peso did not seriously hinder the growth of Philippine exports. Professor Castro lists the favorable prices for export products, which prevailed as a result of the strong demand abroad, and the responsiveness-to-opportunity of Philippine businessmen as the most important factors accounting for the increase in exports. He concludes that the unification of exchange rates and the abolition of controls were as important as the devaluation of November, 1965, or any export incentives.

But are the former really the reasons for the growth of exports? What is the relationship of the strong export sector plus a weak domestic sector to the exports of primary and manufactured goods and to the disparity between prices in the export and the domestic sectors? Perhaps the increase of exports came not only from the strong external demand, but also from inadequate domestic demand and continuing *de facto* devaluation.

CHAPTER 8

WEST MALAYSIAN EXTERNAL
TRADE, 1947–65

LIM CHONG YAH

Malaysia was formed in September, 1963; in August, 1965, Singapore withdrew from the union. West Malaysia is used here, following recent official practice, to refer to the former "States of Malaya" and the preceding "Federation of Malaya." Similarly, Sabah (former British North Borneo) and Sarawak are referred to as East Malaysia.[1]

"Malaya" has become an ambiguous concept. Before the Second World War and before the independence of the Federation of Malaya on August 31, 1957, the term was used to refer to the present West Malaysia together with Singapore. After independence, however, it was used at times to mean West Malaysia without Singapore, and at times to mean West Malaysia with Singapore. To avoid ambiguity, "Pan-Malaya," a concept with which the region is familiar, will be used in this chapter to refer to West Malaysia with Singapore.

All dollars (M$) refer to Malaysian dollars, which have remained equivalent to the British 2s. 4d. since 1906. Since 1949, after the devaluation of the British pound, the Malaysian dollar has been fixed at 32.6667 United States cents, or M$3.06 to one United States dollar.

Unless otherwise stated most of the statistics are from published and unpublished materials of the Statistics Department of the States of Malaya in Kuala Lumpur.[2] Some of the statistics are from the writer's own compilation in connection with previous studies on the Pan-Malayan economy. Efforts have been made, where necessary, to make the data comparable.

EXPORT PROCEEDS AND
NATIONAL INCOME

The following salient features become apparent from an examination of Table 8.1, which gives the 1947–65 West Malaysian statistics of

TABLE 8.1—West Malaysian gross domestic product, gross export proceeds, gross import expenditure, and gross export proceeds/gross domestic product ratio, yearly statistics, 1947–65

Year	Gross domestic product (million M$)	Gross export proceeds (million M$)	Gross import expenditure (million M$)	GEP/GDP (%)
1947	2,654	835	610	31.5
1948	2,494	1,117	847	44.8
1949	2,391	1,177	927	49.2
1950	4,137	2,608	1,311	63.0
1951	5,550	3,379	1,869	60.9
1952	4,693	2,134	1,660	45.5
1953	4,271	1,600	1,451	37.5
1954	4,208	1,626	1,319	38.6
1955	4,992	2,372	1,543	47.5
1956	5,060	2,262	1,751	44.7
1957	5,126	2,180	1,814	42.5
1958	4,896	1,882	1,658	38.4
1959	5,527	2,473	1,739	44.7
1960	6,134	2,924	2,151	47.7
1961	6,102	2,623	2,231	43.0
1962	6,367	2,621	2,447	41.2
1963	6,782	2,699	2,517	39.8
1964	7,272	2,774	2,521	38.1
1965	7,841	3,096	2,608	39.5

Note: Figures may differ slightly from one particular source to another due to rounding and to revisions of data from year to year.

Sources: *Malaysian Quarterly Statistics of External Trade*, various issues; States of Malaya, *Annual Statistics of External Trade*, various years; States of Malaya, *Monthly Statistics of External Trade*, various issues; States of Malaya, *Monthly Statistical Bulletin*, various issues; Federation of Malaya, *Official Yearbook* (Kuala Lumpur, 1962), statistical appendix.

gross export proceeds (GEP) and gross domestic product (GDP). First, the GEP/GDP ratios are large. Second, these ratios fluctuate. Third, they show a secular tendency to decline. Finally, there is a strong positive correlation between changes in GEP and GDP. Each of these features will be discussed below.[3]

The West Malaysian GEP/GDP ratio was approximately 40 percent in 1965 compared with about 27 percent for the Philippines, 17 percent for Burma, and 6 percent for Pakistan. Of the ten Southeast and Far East Asian countries and four Western nations shown in Table 8.2, West Malaysia has the greatest export orientation. Not all export-oriented countries are export-oriented to the same extent (compare West Malaysia with Thailand, for example), and some developing countries are not export-oriented at all (Pakistan and India are examples). Thailand, for instance, has a population about four times that of West Malaysia, but the former's export trade is only about 65 percent that of the latter. Pakistan has a population approximately thirteen times that of West Malaysia, but her export trade is only slightly more than half (54 percent) that of West Malaysia.

TABLE 8.2—Gross export proceeds and gross national product ratio of fourteen countries, 1965
(Percent)

Country	GEP/GDP ratio	Country	GEP/GDP ratio
West Malaysia	40%	United Kingdom	14%
New Zealand	33	Australia	14
Philippines	27	Japan	10
Ceylon	26	Pakistan	6
Taiwan	19	South Korea	5
Burma	17	India	4
Thailand	16	United States	4

Note: The figures for West Malaysia, Ceylon, Taiwan, Burma, Japan, Pakistan, and India refer to 1964 statistics. The denominator used is GNP, as GDP data cannot in all cases be easily obtained.
Source: International Monetary Fund, *International Financial Statistics*, 19, no. 8(1966).

The extent of export orientation can reveal a good deal about the nature of a country's economy. For one thing, it suggests a high degree of dependence on foreign markets, which leads in turn to the dependence of the country's economic welfare on foreign economic forces. Insofar as a country produces goods that have high foreign marginal income elasticities of demand, as do most West Malaysian exports, the prosperity of its export industries is directly correlated with the prosperity of the importing countries. West Malaysia, with a high GEP/GDP ratio and with high foreign marginal propensities to import for her main exports, is particularly susceptible to economic changes in countries that are her major importers.

The fluctuating nature of the GEP/GDP ratio is obvious from Figure 8.1. For the period 1947–65 as a whole, the highest ratio is

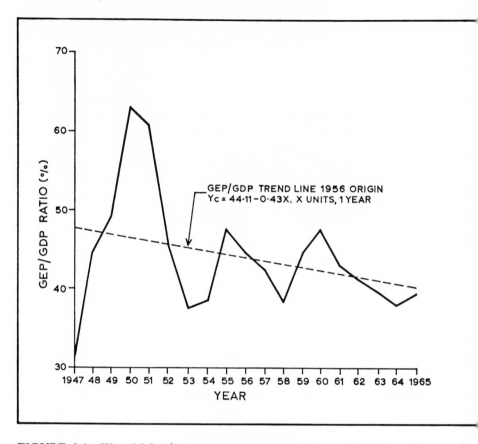

FIGURE 8.1—West Malaysian gross export proceeds/gross domestic product ratios 1947–65, with trend

63.0 percent in 1950, and the lowest, 31.5 percent in 1947. The standard deviation is 7.4 percent and the arithmetic mean of the yearly ratios is 44.1 percent, so that about 84 percent of the GEP/GDP ratios fall between 36.7 percent and 51.5 percent, reflecting again not only the importance of the export sector, but also its variability. In years of high export income the ratio is high, and in years of low export income the ratio is low.

There is a long-term tendency for the GEP/GDP ratio to decline. For the period 1947–65, the average decline was 0.43 points per year. The secular decline in the GEP/GDP ratio can also be seen from the average ratios for 1947–50, 1951–55, 1956–60, and 1961–65 which are 49.1, 46.9, 43.8, and 40.2 percent respectively. If we make a temporal comparison of years with high export income, the declining

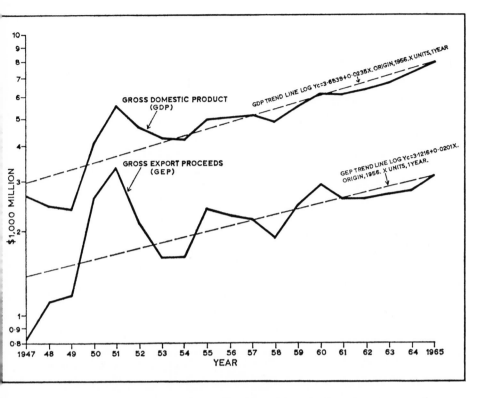

FIGURE 8.2—West Malaysian gross merchandise and gross domestic product changes, 1947–65, with trends

tendency can also be seen. The GEP/GDP ratio for the first boom period, 1950–51, was 62 percent; for the next boom period, 1955–57, it fell to 45 percent; for the third boom period, 1959–60, it was 46 percent; and for the latest boom period, 1962–65, it declined to 40 percent. For the period 1947–65 as a whole, GDP grew at a trend or compound rate of 5.5 percent per annum, whereas the corresponding growth in GEP was slower, at the trend rate of 4.7 percent per annum.

Gross domestic product had four upswings and three downswings for the period 1949–65[4] (see Figure 8.2) with peaks in 1951, 1957, and 1960. Gross export proceeds similarly had four upswings and three downswings, corresponding broadly to the GDP series. The correlation coefficient between the two series of yearly data for 1947–65 is + 0.84, indicating the close relationship between GDP and GEP changes.

Between 1947 and 1960, fluctuations were greater in the GEP

series than in the GDP series, indicating that the export sector was much more unstable than the economy as a whole. Due to the greater relative growth of the more stable non-export (domestic) sector of the economy, the effect of fluctuations of the GEP on the GDP became less severe. In each of the five periods between 1947 and 1960 the rates of change in GEP were greater than the corresponding rates of change in GDP (see Table 8.3). This greater variability of GEP characterized both the upswings and the downswings.

Beginning in 1961, this pattern was reversed. This export sector

TABLE 8.3—Comparison of rates of growth and fluctuations of
West Malaysian gross export proceeds and gross
domestic product, 1947–49 to 1962–65
(Percent)

| Period | Period-to-period changes | |
	Gross domestic product	Gross export proceeds
1947–49	—	—
1950–51	+ 93%	+ 187%
1952–54	− 9	− 40
1955–57	+ 15	+ 27
1958	− 3	− 17
1959–60	+ 19	+ 43
1961	+ 5	− 3
1962–65	+ 16	+ 7

Note: The grouping of years is based on yearly fluctuations of GDP.
Source: Computed from Table 8.1.

ceased to be the major force in GDP changes, although the correlation coefficient of yearly data between the two series for the five-year period beginning in 1960 was still positive.

The decline in the GEP/GDP ratio does not in itself indicate economic retrogression or progression, because a declining ratio can result from a faster rate of growth of GNP, as has been the case in Malaysia. But the growth of GDP alone is not an ideal measure of economic advance. In the West Malaysia case, the higher growth rate of the domestic sector was brought about by investments in the public sector, financed, significantly, from external borrowing and the use of accumulated reserves. Thus although the economy showed a rate of increase of GDP of 16 percent in the period 1962–65, when compared to 1961, or a simple average of 4 percent per year, this has entirely different significance from the growth of GDP, motivated mainly by a growth of GEP, in the 1950's.

Both the balance of payments and the government budget have

been very much affected by GEP changes. All the three major federal taxes (export taxes, income taxes, and import taxes) have been functions of GEP changes.[5] If the Malaysian government had not stepped up its development spending, thereby increasing its public debts and decreasing its accumulated reserves, to counteract the recent slow rate of growth of GEP, the GDP growth rate would have been considerably lower.[6]

EXPORTS: COMPOSITION, TRENDS, AND VARIABILITY

Composition of Exports

Rubber has been by far the most important export of West Malaysia. Tables 8.4 and 8.5 show the composition of West Malaysian gross exports from 1947–65, in absolute terms and by percentage. Of the nineteen years from 1947 to 1965, only in the last two did rubber account for less than 50 percent of total yearly exports. At its height in 1951 the percentage reached 72.3.

TABLE 8.4—Composition of West Malaysian exports, yearly statistics, 1947–65
(Million M$)

Year	Rubber	Tin	Iron ore	Timber	Palm oil	All exports
1947	587	114	0	7	19	835
1948	680	221	1	8	32	1,117
1949	590	292	7	13	36	1,177
1950	1,810	442	9	18	32	2,608
1951	2,445	564	17	21	39	3,379
1952	1,287	511	23	19	45	2,134
1953	896	383	21	20	31	1,600
1954	903	404	21	18	32	1,626
1955	1,584	434	33	26	36	2,372
1956	1,378	472	51	30	43	2,262
1957	1,304	439	66	29	46	2,180
1958	1,197	275	63	32	47	1,882
1959	1,722	299	100	33	52	2,473
1960	1,829	507	140	55	61	2,924
1961	1,442	533	164	42	61	2,622
1962	1,368	620	166	48	65	2,621
1963	1,374	642	176	65	69	2,699
1964	1,303	728	163	87	81	2,774
1965	1,368	872	161	92	106	3,096

Sources: See Table 8.1.

After 1959 rubber export income exhibited an alarming decline, from 69.6 percent of total export income to 44.2 percent in 1965. Although from 1960 to 1965 export volume increased from 767,000 metric tons to 887,000 metric tons, the rubber price fell from 108.08 cents per pound to 70.13 cents.

Tin exports also fluctuated a great deal from year to year. Tin exports reached their lowest percentage of total exports in 1959, their peak in 1965. In 1959, the tin price was low despite the operation of the International Tin Agreement whose provisions had necessitated the drastic curtailment of exports and therefore also of output in order

TABLE 8.5—Composition of West Malaysian gross exports,
1947–50 to 1961–65
(Percent)

Commodity	1947–50	1951–55	1956–60	1961–65
Rubber	64%	64%	63%	50%
Tin	19	21	17	25
Iron ore	0.3	1	4	6
Timber	1	1	2	2
Palm oil	2	2	2	3
All other	13.7	11	12	14
Total	100	100	100	100

Source: Computed from Table 8.4.

to stop the price level from falling further. The year 1965 saw high tin prices, averaging £1,413 per metric ton compared with £785 per metric ton in 1959.[7]

The rubber-growing industry recovered rapidly after the war and grew to be much more important than tin. It accounted for an average of 64 percent of total exports in the period 1947–50 compared with 19 percent for tin. Later, 1956 to 1960, because of the drastic curtailment of tin exports under the International Tin Agreement, the ratio of tin exports to total exports was only 17 percent, compared with 63 percent for rubber. But from 1961 to 1965 the rubber price declined relative to the price of tin, and rubber exports as a percentage of total exports fell to 50 percent. During those years tin increased to 25 percent of the total.

Iron ore ranked third in the export trade during this period and accounted for 6.5 percent of total exports at its height in 1963. During the immediate postwar period, iron ore was only 0.3 percent of total exports (average for 1947–50); and in 1951–55, the percentage was only 1.1. The rapid rise in percentage of total exports after 1955 was due almost entirely to increased production.

Palm oil, the fourth largest export of West Malaysia in the 1961–65 period has, like iron ore, been produced almost entirely for export. It formed 3 percent of total exports in this period. Close behind comes timber (2 percent), which is the fifth most important export of the country. Less significant exports have been pineapple, copra, coconut oil, and palm kernel, together forming only 2.6 percent of the total exports in 1965. The five major exports, on the other hand, constituted between 86 percent and 88 percent of total exports for the various periods.

Major Export Trends

Total export value increased at the rate of 4.7 percent per year between 1947 and 1965. Of the five major exports only rubber had a lower growth rate (3.2 percent) while the others exceeded the national growth rate in varying degrees (Table 8.6).

Of the five major exports for the period 1947–65, the rate of growth in the value of iron-ore exports was by far the highest, 21.1 percent per annum, raising it to the third most important export in the five years 1956–60 from its fifth position in 1947–50.

Although rubber showed a yearly rate of growth in value of 3.2

TABLE 8.6—Yearly trend rates of growth of
West Malaysian main exports, 1947–65
(Percent)

Commodity	Value	Quantity	Price
1947–65			
Rubber	3.2%	1.3%	1.8%
Tin	6.1	2.4	3.5
Timber	13.1	11.4	1.3
Palm oil	6.8	6.6	0.3
1956–65			
Rubber	− 0.2	4.5	− 3.9
Iron ore	15.3	13.6	1.5

Note: For 1947–65, the annual rate of growth in total export value was 4.7 percent, and for iron ore, 21.1 percent; for 1956–65, the annual rate of growth in tin export value was 10.3 percent, palm oil, 9.2 percent, and timber, 14.4 percent.
Sources: See Table 8.1.

percent during the period 1947–65, the rate dropped to a negative level (− 0.2 percent) in 1956–65. In the latter period the yearly growth rate in rubber export volume was high (4.5 percent) but export income went down because of the downward trend in rubber prices (− 3.9 percent per year). Because of the importance of rubber, this decline has had serious repercussions on the West Malaysian economy.[8]

The growth in West Malaysian output of natural rubber was due mainly to an increase in productivity per acre because of large-scale

TABLE 8.7—Prospects of Malaysian main exports, 1965 and 1970

	Price[a]		Quantity	Value		
			Annual growth	Annual growth	1965	1967
Commodity	1965	1970	rate (%)	rate (%)	(million M$)	
Rubber	69	55	+ 6.0	+ 1.7	1,454	1,584
Tin	11,760	11,760	− 4.0	− 4.0	823	670
Iron ore	25	20	− 14.3	− 18.1	163	60
Round timber	77	97	− .04	+ 4.2	225	277
Sawn timber	190	240	+ 2.4	+ 7.2	118	167
Palm oil	726	500	+ 14.1	+ 5.9	96	128
Total	—	—	—	—	2,879	2,886

[a] Rubber price is given in cents per pound; all other prices are in dollars per ton.

Source: Government of Malaysia, *First Malaysia Plan*, 1966–70 (Kuala Lumpur, 1965), table 3.2, p. 45.

replanting with new and higher-yielding rubber trees.[9] The decline in rubber price was due to synthetic rubber competition, and to a lesser extent, to the release of stockpiled rubber by the United States.[10]

The rapid rate of growth in the export value of iron ore, timber, and palm oil was due not so much to price increases as to a rise in the volume exported. In the case of tin, price also contributed to the growth in value.

The First Malaysia Plan, 1966–70, covering both West and East Malaysia, takes into consideration a probable fall in the prices of three out of the five major exports (see Table 8.7). Due to synthetic rubber competition, Malaysia has considered it prudent to diversify her agriculture by placing more emphasis on palm oil.

Rubber and palm oil export volumes are expected to follow an accelerated upward trend. Increased volume is expected by 1970 to slightly more than offset an anticipated fall in the rubber price, and much more than offset expected price decreases in palm oil. Altogether, the position of these five exports is expected to be about the same in 1970 as in 1965.

Measures of Fluctuation

Two measures of fluctuations will be used below: one is the five-year index, and the other is the coefficient of variation. The latter measure

TABLE 8.8—Five-year fluctuations and growth in West Malaysian major exports, 1947–50 to 1961–65

Period	Rubber	Tin	Iron ore	Timber	Palm oil
		Value indices (moving base)			
1947–50	100	100	100	100	100
1951–55	155	172	575	175	123
1956–60	104	87	365	171	135
1961–65	92	172	198	186	152
		Volume indices (moving base)			
1947–50	100	100	100	100	100
1951–55	86	114	311	133	100
1956–60	112	94	314	185	149
1961–65	117	126	189	189	158
		Price indices (moving base)			
1947–50	100	100	100	100	100
1951–55	182	145	140	140	124
1956–60	92	91	114	94	91
1961–65	78	139	108	97	96

Note: The corresponding indices for gross export proceeds are 100, 123, 105, and 118.
Source: See Table 8.1.

is obtained by dividing the standard deviation of the time series by the arithmetic mean of that series.

The five-year measure for the five main exports is given in Table 8.8. For rubber, the price index has fluctuated considerably without apparent effect on volume. In the two periods, 1951–55 and 1961–65, the quantity change moved in the opposite direction from the price and value index.

For palm oil, timber, and particularly iron ore, the quantity coefficient predominated (see Table 8.9). For tin, the price and quantity variations reinforced each other. The up-down-up value movements were, as can be seen clearly from Table 8.8, usually amplified by the same up-down-up movements in the quantity and price indices.

The total export value index fluctuated much less than each of the five indices in almost all five-year periods. In other words, the export sector as a whole was more stable than its component parts, because the greater individual fluctuations of the five main exports offset each other.

TABLE 8.9—Coefficients of variation of West
Malaysian exports: value, quantity, and price,
1947–65 and 1956–65
(Percent)

Commodity	Value	Quantity	Price
1947–65			
Rubber	34.8%	11.8%	37.0%
Tin	39.6	22.4	27.6
Timber	70.3	67.5	14.3
Palm oil	41.2	42.4	22.7
1956–65			
Rubber	12.3	10.6	16.0
Tin	34.1	n.a.	n.a.
Iron ore	39.7	36.8	1.3
Timber	45.4	n.a.	n.a.
Palm oil	30.3	n.a.	n.a.

Note: The coefficient of variation for the value of all exports, 1947–65, is 33.6.
Source: See Table 8.1.

TRADE POLICY AND DIRECTION OF EXPORTS

Trade Policy

From the earliest colonial days West Malaysia has followed a laissez faire policy of buying in the cheapest markets and selling in the dearest ones, both at home and abroad. Because of this policy, trade relationships have been developed with nearly every country, and West Malaysia has one of the highest standards of living in Asia.

However, restrictions have been placed on exports to specific countries, generally for political reasons. Following the outbreak of the Korean War, West Malaysia acted with other countries in accordance with a United Nations resolution to ban exports of strategic raw materials (including rubber and tin) to Communist China. The recent attempts of West Malaysia to reduce her exports and imports through Singapore are also basically political in nature, arising from competition between the top political leaders of the two states.

The ban on imports from the Union of South Africa as a protest against its apartheid policy, and the ban on imports from Indonesia during the period of the Indonesian Confrontation against Malaysia, 1963–66, are also departures from a laissez faire policy on political grounds.

There have also been exchange control restrictions on imports from the dollar area because of Malaysia's association with the sterling area bloc. Malaysia has always had a huge trading surplus with the dollar account countries, and consequently has been one of the most important net contributors to the sterling area dollar pool. However, restrictions on the dollar account countries have been progressively removed, particularly in the years immediately before and after independence.

Export and import duties have been increased enormously since the Second World War, but except for a number of recent exceptions applicable only to imports, the purpose of such increases has been primarily for revenue. Graduated export taxes have also been employed as anticyclical measures. The import tariff wall probably will be raised still further as pressures for increased revenue become stronger, and as more and more industries are brought under the umbrella of protection.

The Direction of Exports

The principal importers of West Malaysian products, and the value of the exports to these countries for the years 1958–65 are shown in Table 8.10. Table 8.11 shows the percentage of total exports going to the fourteen major importing countries. Singapore, the United States, Japan, the United Kingdom, the U.S.S.R., and West Germany have been the most important markets for West Malaysian exports. These six countries purchased 70.1 percent of all Malaysian exports in 1965 and 71.2 percent in 1958.

Between 1958 and 1965 Singapore was most important, although the percentage of total exports to Singapore declined from 23.8 percent in 1958 to 21.0 percent in 1965. More spectacular was the steady decline of the United Kingdom as an importer of West Malaysian products in both absolute and relative terms. In 1958, the year

TABLE 8.10—Direction of West Malaysian exports, yearly statistics, 1958–65
(Million M$)

Country	1958	1959	1960	1961	1962	1963	1964	1965
United Kingdom	349.7	330.5	382.4	315.1	245.7	223.5	263.2	251.5
U. of S. Africa	15.5	15.9	19.9	12.1	15.3	25.3	32.6	23.9
Canada	29.5	35.0	39.2	47.5	50.1	65.6	77.2	86.8
India	50.9	52.4	82.4	72.1	75.5	66.2	67.8	64.3
Australia	32.1	40.3	57.9	28.8	46.9	47.9	57.8	64.0
Czechoslovakia	9.9	8.8	36.3	19.9	1.7	8.0	8.9	3.9
France	49.0	79.6	113.4	100.9	98.4	77.3	83.8	82.6
West Germany	94.2	144.4	226.1	164.1	110.9	116.7	125.2	106.9
Italy	72.1	88.4	107.5	101.2	98.0	111.1	97.9	102.3
Netherlands	28.2	29.0	39.0	34.3	39.9	36.1	37.7	55.3
Poland	37.7	31.2	54.4	19.2	26.1	38.1	35.4	38.1
Spain	14.4	20.3	36.4	27.5	30.9	33.5	36.7	35.7
Sweden	8.2	17.4	27.1	16.7	15.2	15.8	17.3	16.7
U.S.S.R.	73.1	205.4	110.9	158.8	225.3	209.3	127.2	225.6
United States	200.6	285.1	303.1	333.7	382.5	390.1	407.9	547.9
Argentina	18.6	20.4	32.3	32.0	21.7	26.6	39.6	29.7
Burma	4.8	6.1	7.5	4.2	4.7	3.3	6.9	2.5
China (mainland)	53.8	22.3	8.0	0.8	0.0	2.0	0.0	2.1
Indonesia	11.5	12.3	23.1	37.7	26.5	6.0	2.9	0.1
Japan	177.2	317.9	370.0	383.0	363.9	396.6	413.7	394.1
Thailand	28.3	29.5	24.4	23.6	25.4	23.6	30.4	34.5
Singapore	447.8	571.4	631.8	521.4	521.3	540.8	568.6	650.0
Rest of world	77.9	112.4	194.2	171.6	200.0	241.2	242.2	284.4
Total	1,885.0	2,476.0	2,927.3	2,626.2	2,625.9	2,704.6	2,780.9	3,102.9

Source: See Table 8.1.

before Malayan (West Malaysian) independence, the United Kingdom was the second largest importer, taking 18.5 percent of all West Malaysian exports. The U.K. percentage had declined to 8.1 percent by 1965, and the U.K. had dropped to the position of the fourth largest importer.

TABLE 8.11—Main importers of West
Malaysian exports, 1958 and 1965
(Percentage of total imports)

Country	1958	1965
Singapore	23.8%	21.0%
United Kingdom	18.5	8.1
United States	10.6	17.6
Japan	9.4	12.7
West Germany	5.0	3.4
U.S.S.R.	3.9	7.3
Subtotal	71.2	70.1
Italy	3.8	3.3
Mainland China	2.9	0.1
India	2.7	2.1
France	2.6	2.7
Australia	1.7	2.1
Canada	1.6	1.8
Netherlands	1.5	1.8
Thailand	1.5	1.1
Total	89.5	85.1

Note: West Malaysian exports to Indonesia were only 0.6 percent in 1958, and 1.0 percent in 1962 (the year before Confrontation began).
Source: Computed from Table 8.10.

Offsetting the decline of the United Kingdom was the spectacular increase in demand from the United States, Japan, and the U.S.S.R. The United States replaced the United Kingdom as the second largest importer. The total percentage of exports to the three increased from 23.9 percent in 1958 to 37.6 percent in 1965.

The increase in West Malaysian exports to the U.S.S.R. was primarily due to rubber. The rise in West Malaysian exports to the United States was due mainly to tin, and to a lesser extent, rubber. The rise in West Malaysian exports to Japan was due primarily to iron ore and tin, while rubber exports decreased.

Of the less important export markets, eight should be noted here.

They are, in descending order (1965 figures), Italy, Canada, France, India, Australia, the Netherlands, Thailand, and Communist China. None of them accounted for more than 4 percent of West Malaysian exports in 1958 or 1965, and most of them considerably less. Together, the eight took 16.0 percent of West Malaysian exports in 1965, slightly less than the 17.6 percent of the United States alone in that year.

Of the six major importers, four are advanced Western industrial countries (the United States, the United Kingdom, the U.S.S.R., and West Germany) and one is an advanced Asian country (Japan). The last is a great trading center and international port, Singapore. There is an important difference between Singapore as a market for West Malaysian exports and the other five. Unlike the other five, who are final consumers of West Malaysian exports, Singapore mainly reexports West Malaysia's domestic products (sometimes referred to as Straits produce) to other countries.

Of the fourteen main importers of West Malaysian products listed in Table 8.10, only five are Asian. Of these, only Japanese imports increased between 1958 and 1965, while those of Singapore, India, Thailand, and Communist China declined. Thus, Malaysia was exporting very little to the underdeveloped countries of Asia or Africa and even this small quantity has shown signs of diminishing.

BALANCE-OF-MERCHANDISE TRADE

Export and Import Trends

Throughout the nineteen postwar years (1947–65), there was a significant, though fluctuating, surplus in the balance-of-merchandise trade. There was a tendency for the surplus to decrease (see Figure 8.3), since the rate of growth in export value for the period 1947–65, 4.7 percent per year, was slower than the corresponding growth rate of 6.4 percent for the import series.

Import expenditures followed the same pattern of upswing and downswing as export proceeds, except for the years 1955–57 and 1960–62, when import expenditures increased despite a decrease in export income (see Table 8.9). The correlation coefficient for the import and export series for 1947–65 is + 0.98, reflecting the im-

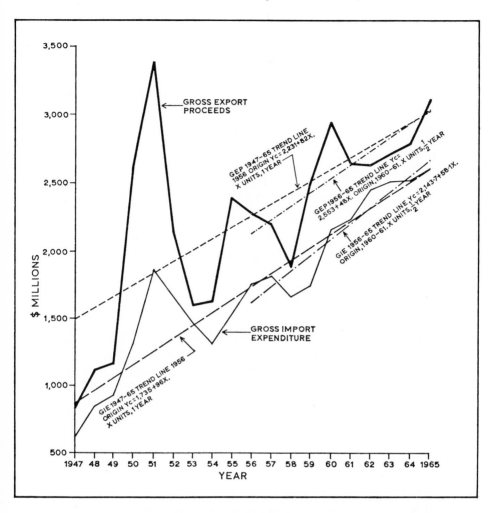

FIGURE 8.3—West Malaysian gross merchandise import and export and balance-of-trade surplus, 1947–65, with trends

portance of export income changes as a determinant not only of GDP changes, but also of changes in national import expenditures.

As can be observed from Table 8.12, in no five-year period[11] since 1947 was the growth of export income faster than the corresponding growth in import expenditure. This observation does not necessarily apply to yearly fluctuations. It holds good, however, whether the base period chosen is 1947–50 or whether a period-to-period comparison is made.

TABLE 8.12—Changes in value indices of West Malaysian imports and exports, five-year periods, 1947–65

	Imports		Exports	
Period	Value (1947–50 = 100)	Period-to-period changes	Value (1947–50 = 100)	Period-to-period changes
1947–50	100	100	100	100
1951–55	170	170	155	155
1956–60	197	116	163	105
1961–65	266	135	193	118

Note: Calculations are based on yearly averages. The period 1947 to 1950 is only four years.
Source: Computed from Table 8.1.

Trade Balance Prospects

In absolute terms, the average yearly trade surplus fell from M$654 million in 1951–55 to M$521 million in 1956–60, and still further to M$297 million in 1961–65 (Table 8.1).

When will this diminishing surplus be reduced to zero? From the experience of 1947–65, the surplus was reduced by an average of M$14 million per year from 1956, the base year used for deriving the trend equation. In 1956, the surplus was M$511 million, and so it would take 36.5 years from 1956, or to the middle of 1992, for the surplus to be reduced to zero. But, if the forecast is based on the performance of 1956–65, exports and imports would be equal ten years sooner, or by 1982.

The First Malaysia Plan is very pessimistic about the growth of merchandise exports in the foreseeable future, forecasting for Malaysia as a whole a growth rate of only 3 percent from 1965 to the end of the Plan period in 1970.[12] The Plan does not give a corresponding forecast of merchandise imports. If the 1956–65 experience is repeated, the average yearly increase in imports will be M$96 million per year in West Malaysia alone. At this rate it will take only about five years for the 1965 West Malaysian export surplus of M$488 million to be completely eliminated. The minor expected increase in export earnings would most probably be offset by an increase in import expenditures above M$96 million per year due to an expected rise in per capita income, an expected increase in population growth, and an anticipated acceleration in development expenditure, much of which would take the form of capital imports.

Pan-Malayan Trade Balance

The external trade balance of Pan-Malaya, that is, West Malaysia and Singapore combined, instead of showing a significant trade surplus every year, as was the case with West Malaysia, exhibits a substantial trade deficit in fourteen out of nineteen years in the postwar period. Only in exceptionally good years, namely, in 1950, 1951, 1955, 1959, and 1960 was there a Pan-Malayan trade surplus. A trade deficit persisted after 1961. In other words, a substantial West Malaysia trade surplus was reduced, and often even transformed into a deficit, by Singapore. This is significant to the extent that it affects each country's balance of payments and the exchange parity between the currencies of the two countries. (These two countries agreed to have their own currencies after June 12, 1967.)

Comparison of the postwar with the prewar Pan-Malayan trade position (separate prewar West Malaysian figures not being available) indicates that the trade balance deteriorated greatly. One of the main causes was the deterioration in the commodity terms of trade of Pan-Malayan exports and reexports after the war, particularly after 1960. The cessation of Indonesian trade with Malaysia and Singapore in 1963 also contributed significantly towards this deterioration.

COMPOSITION OF IMPORTS

While the main exports of West Malaysia are few and easily classified and analysed, imports are much more diverse (see Table 8.13). Seven sections out of the ten in the United Nations Standard International Trade Classification (SITC) are important in Malaysian import trade: food, beverages and tobacco, crude materials (except fuels), mineral fuels, chemicals, manufactured goods (classified by material), and machinery and transport equipment. In 1965, these seven sections constituted 87.5 percent of total West Malaysian imports. The three most important sections were food, manufactured goods, and machinery and transport equipment. They constituted 39.1, 17.0, and 11.0 percent respectively of total imports in 1953, the earliest year for which comparable data are available. In 1965 manufactured goods and machinery and equipment were 19.6 percent and

TABLE 8.13—Composition of imports, West Malaysia, yearly statistics, 1953–65
(Million M$)

SITC Section	1953	1954	1955	1956	1957	1958	1959	1960	1961	1962	1963	1964	1965
0 Food	568.2	421.4	477.7	525.0	528.6	525.8	510.2	558.1	564.2	562.7	656.9	695.2	613.9
1 Beverages and tobacco	83.6	76.0	79.7	83.1	88.5	80.5	80.3	82.3	88.2	71.8	60.8	57.5	60.1
2 Crude materials, inedible, except fuel	101.5	136.9	168.7	197.7	207.8	182.7	210.7	339.3	282.9	339.7	292.3	227.8	229.4
3 Mineral fuels	107.7	115.2	125.6	135.5	150.2	134.2	128.9	149.2	142.7	151.2	152.7	167.3	174.2
4 Animal and vegetable oils	4.8	3.8	5.7	7.7	9.6	10.0	12.8	13.1	13.5	13.6	11.7	12.4	14.8
5 Chemicals	62.1	72.9	88.0	103.4	111.9	105.5	119.5	143.2	158.7	152.5	168.1	177.0	208.3
6 Manufactured goods	246.4	244.3	295.0	312.2	320.1	260.0	289.3	366.2	395.5	471.9	469.3	464.7	510.2
7 Machinery and transport equipment	159.3	139.8	157.7	207.8	218.0	202.1	209.6	283.5	337.2	394.4	433.6	436.6	486.1
8 Misc. manufactured goods	103.3	98.9	128.0	154.9	152.8	135.0	145.1	168.7	192.4	201.6	204.5	203.0	216.6
9 Others	14.5	9.9	16.8	23.7	26.9	22.1	32.8	46.9	55.0	87.7	67.0	79.3	94.1
Total	1,451.4	1,319.1	1,542.9	1,751.0	1,814.4	1,657.9	1,739.2	2,150.5	2,230.3	2,447.1	2,516.9	2,520.8	2,607.7

Sources: See Table 8.1.

18.6 percent respectively, and their combined percentage exceeded the 23.5 percent for food. Using 1953 as the base year, the index for food in 1965 was 108, for manufactured goods, 207, and for machinery and transport equipment, 305.

Food imports have not increased much for two reasons. One is the relatively low marginal propensity to import food in West Malaysia. The other is the increasing substitution of local food for imported food, particularly rice. In 1953, rice imports constituted 14.1 percent of total West Malaysian imports, but in 1965 they had declined to 4.3 percent. The value of rice imports declined from M$203.8 million in 1953 to M$112.6 million in 1965, and the import volume from 353 thousand metric tons to 293 thousand metric tons.

The postwar growth in rice production in West Malaysia has been due primarily to increased productivity per acre, and, to a lesser extent, to an extension in planted acreage. With the increasing use of higher-yielding plants (such as the Malinja, Mashuri, and still better Padi Ria varieties), the increasing practice of double cropping, and the increase in newly planted acreage, rice production in West Malaysia will continue to accelerate, thus further cutting down the rice import bill. This will mean lower imports from Thailand from which West Malaysia has obtained the bulk of her rice supply.

Only beverages and tobacco imports exhibit an absolute and relative decline, from 5.8 percent of total imports in 1953 steadily down to 2.3 percent in 1965. The decline was caused particularly by import substitution in tobacco. Cigarette production in West Malaysia increased from 3.4 thousand pounds in 1954 to 13.1 thousand pounds in 1965, and imports dropped from 8.8 thousand pounds to 1.2 thousand pounds.

Chemicals registered the highest rate of increase, 235 percent, primarily accounted for by fertilizers and medical products. Fertilizer imports increased from M$5.6 million in 1953 to M$45.1 million in 1965, while the corresponding import bill for medical products increased from M$10.9 million to M$38.8 million. The enormous increase in fertilizer use has been partly responsible for the rise in agricultural productivity. The increasing spread and use of Western medicine and health services has been largely responsible for the increase in life expectancy, and the lowering of mortality rates, including the infant and child mortality rates.[13]

Crude materials imports increased by 126 percent, largely as a result of greater imports from Thailand of crude rubber and tin ore for processing and reexport from Penang. This increase would have been larger except for the banning of exports of crude rubber and tin ore and other exports from Indonesia to Malaysia in 1963. Total crude imports declined steadily from M$339.7 million in 1962, the year before Confrontation began, to M$229.4 million by 1965. With the end of Confrontation, crude materials imports can be expected to increase significantly, although the establishment of a tin-smelting plant in Thailand means that exports of tin ore to West Malaysia from that source may be drastically curtailed or stopped entirely.

Mineral fuels imports increased by 62 percent between 1953 and

TABLE 8.14—Changing composition of West Malaysian imports, 1953 and 1965
(Percent)

	SITC Section	1953	1965
0, 1	Food, beverages, and tobacco	44.9%	25.8%
2	Crude materials	7.0	8.8
3	Mineral fuels	7.4	6.7
4, 5, 6, 7, 8	Manufactured capital and consumer goods	39.7	55.1
9	Others	1.0	3.6
	Total	100.0	100.0

Source: Computed from Table 8.13.

1965, but their position as a percentage of total imports fell from fourth in 1953 to seventh in 1965.

In sum, West Malaysia was importing foodstuffs, manufactured consumer and capital goods of all kinds, raw materials which West Malaysia specializes in processing and which are mainly for reexport, and fuel (mainly petroleum) which she does not produce at all. As a percentage of imports, both foodstuffs and mineral fuel declined, particularly food. The increase in the import of capital and consumer manufactured goods, on the other hand, was particularly striking, as can be seen from Table 8.14.

SOURCES OF IMPORTS

Annual figures for imports from twenty-eight countries are given in Table 8.15. The origin of imports from thirteen main countries is shown in descending order of importance in Table 8.16 for 1958, 1962 (the year before Confrontation), and 1965.

Just as West Malaysian exports to the United Kingdom have been

TABLE 8.15—Sources of West Malaysian imports, yearly statistics, 1958–65
(Million M$)

Country	1958	1959	1960	1961	1962	1963	1964	1965
United Kingdom	414.8	386.1	462.4	505.2	533.6	534.2	486.9	532.3
U. of S. Africa	12.6	18.0	18.3	0.0	0.0	0.0	0.0	0.0
Canada	8.1	5.0	6.9	9.1	112.4	10.8	11.4	12.2
Hong Kong	59.2	70.8	81.6	84.5	84.8	84.7	86.7	75.3
India	41.8	43.5	45.2	72.1	51.0	68.0	58.7	52.6
Bahrein	6.8	3.9	4.0	3.7	3.0	4.2	4.9	7.6
Australia	89.2	85.6	99.9	95.5	114.7	130.4	148.0	159.5
New Zealand	4.6	4.0	4.5	8.3	7.8	12.0	11.5	15.0
Austria	2.1	2.5	3.0	5.2	5.9	3.5	2.4	3.1
Belgium	16.8	19.3	22.9	27.3	29.3	26.9	23.5	27.6
Denmark	9.9	10.4	10.2	11.4	10.5	11.5	11.3	11.2
France	13.4	16.2	23.0	26.7	28.6	29.7	29.6	34.6
West Germany	40.0	70.6	76.9	83.2	84.0	94.8	107.0	129.3
Italy	6.8	8.2	12.6	19.5	24.0	27.3	25.6	26.8
Luxemburg	0.7	1.1	1.2	1.9	negl.	negl.	negl.	negl.
Netherlands	28.1	39.1	48.2	56.6	65.2	59.4	59.0	56.7
Norway	2.0	2.5	4.4	3.4	4.4	3.5	3.1	2.9
Sweden	5.0	4.9	6.7	10.9	9.3	10.8	11.0	18.0
Switzerland	2.7	3.9	6.6	8.2	10.9	9.4	7.8	8.9
United States	41.1	50.6	89.1	112.4	144.2	133.1	131.5	139.6
Burma	47.7	49.3	30.0	29.9	45.3	53.8	27.7	16.5
China (mainland)	94.1	76.0	83.5	79.5	86.6	132.4	174.1	173.6
Formosa	7.5	5.8	9.0	7.9	9.9	21.4	30.9	26.6
Indonesia	228.4	213.0	324.6	250.0	293.3	212.5	42.8	7.0
Iran	2.3	8.9	6.5	8.7	11.7	26.0	22.9	5.0
Japan	95.1	124.3	172.3	182.1	214.2	252.3	266.6	300.3
Thailand	181.9	204.4	249.5	248.3	240.9	240.1	282.5	274.5
Singapore	139.1	180.5	192.2	205.2	242.7	236.0	247.9	274.2
Rest of world	55.4	30.9	55.4	73.8	79.2	105.2	206.0	217.4
Total	1,657.2	1,739.3	2,150.6	2,230.5	2,547.4	2,533.9	2,521.3	2,608.3

negl.: Negligible.
Sources: See Table 8.1.

reduced greatly in recent years, the percentage of West Malaysian imports from the United Kingdom has also declined noticeably. However, the United Kingdom still remains by far the most important supplier of goods to West Malaysia, although in all probability its importance will continue to decline.

Until Confrontation started, Indonesia was the second most important source of supply for West Malaysia, although Indonesia imported

TABLE 8.16—Main sources of West Malaysian
imports, 1958, 1962, and 1965
(Percentage of total imports)

Country	1958	1962	1965
United Kingdom	25.0%	21.8%	20.4%
Indonesia	13.8	12.0	0.3
Thailand	11.0	9.8	10.5
Singapore	8.4	9.8	10.5
Japan	5.7	8.8	11.5
Subtotal	63.9	62.2	53.2
Mainland China	5.7	3.5	6.7
Australia	5.4	4.7	6.1
Hong Kong	3.6	3.5	2.9
Burma	2.9	1.9	0.6
India	2.5	2.1	2.0
United States	2.5	5.9	5.4
West Germany	2.4	3.4	5.0
Netherlands	1.7	2.7	2.2
Total	90.6	89.9	84.1

Sources: Computed from Table 8.15.

little in return. Indonesia provided the primary raw materials for rubber and tin production, for which West Malaysia has been the world's largest supplier; and also materials for other less important West Malaysian exports, such as palm oil, copra, and coconut oil. The Indonesian exports came from the island of Sumatra opposite Penang in West Malaysia, and took advantage of the trading and entrepôt facilities that Penang has built up over the years. With the ending of Confrontation in 1966, this trade is expected to resume.

Thailand, West Malaysia's third most important source of imports, provides food (mainly rice), rubber (for reexport), and tin ore for smelting and eventual reexport. There is little that West Malaysia can export to Thailand, her northern neighbor, so there has always been an important trading surplus in favor of Thailand, much like the trade of

West Malaysia with her southern neighbor, Indonesia. The main exports to Thailand have been machinery and transport equipment, manufactured goods, and fuel, nearly all of which consisted of reexports.

Imports of rice and tin from Thailand can be expected to decrease with West Malaysia producing more rice for herself, and with the recently reported establishment of a tin-smelting plant in Thailand. On the other hand, when the Asian Highway between Thailand and West Malaysia is ready, and with further improvement in railway services between the two countries, the West Malaysian reexport trade to Thailand should benefit. Nonetheless, the outcome is still likely to be a reduction of trade between the two countries. The Association of Southeast Asia (ASA), in which Malaysia and Thailand are two of the three members, will probably not be able to reverse the tendency towards decreasing trade between the two countries.

Singapore's position improved somewhat between 1958 and 1965 as the fourth largest source of West Malaysian imports. West Malaysia sends her raw materials to Singapore for reexport, in return for foodstuffs and capital and consumer goods that Singapore has imported from the industrial nations. Throughout our discussion our statistics on West Malaysian trade with Singapore follow official practice in excluding trade through Singapore, as distinct from import from or export to Singapore. Exports direct to the United States from West Malaysia through Singapore are treated as exports of West Malaysia to the United States, whereas exports to Singapore with destination unknown, but which finally may find their way to the United States, are considered as exports to Singapore.

The vital economic and trading links between West Malaysia and Singapore, built up since Stamford Raffles founded Singapore in 1819, have been a subject of considerable interest in recent years in the Pan-Malayan region. From time to time Malaysia has expressed the intention to bypass Singapore as a port and entrepôt center as much as possible. The two countries have formally agreed to separate their currency systems.[14] The import tariff walls, particularly the protective ones put up in recent years by both countries, seem to have worked hardships on both sides, although the tariffs have been non-discriminatory, at least in the strict de jure sense.

Exports to and through Singapore have declined as a proportion of total exports (see Table 8.17). In the period 1947–50, West Malaysia exported as much as 44.2 percent of her exports to and through

Singapore. This percentage declined during 1961–65 to 28.1 percent.

On the other hand, imports from and through Singapore have remained a relatively stable percentage of total imports, so that the earlier trade surplus has been transformed into a deficit. The average yearly trade surplus in 1947–50 was M$239.6 million; this declined to M$55.4 million in 1956–60, and became a deficit of M$163.0 million in 1961–65. Since 1961, every year has shown a large trade deficit. A major factor was the shift in 1959 of the tin-smelting plant of the Straits Trading Company Ltd. from Pulau Brani, an island half a

TABLE 8.17—West Malaysian trade through and with Singapore, 1947–50 to 1961–65

Period	% of total imports from and via Singapore	% of total exports to and via Singapore	% of total trade through and with Singapore
1947–50	42.7	44.2	43.6
1951–55	38.6	41.9	40.5
1956–60	39.9	33.4	36.2
1961–65	38.2	28.1	32.9
1964	36.7	28.6	32.4
1965	36.0	28.6	32.0

Sources: See Table 8.1.

mile off Singapore and under Singapore's jurisdiction, to Butterworth, on the West Malaysian mainland opposite the island of Penang.

Imports from Japan have grown rapidly and are likely to continue to grow, especially since West Malaysia has removed imperial preference for a large number of imports. West Malaysia imports manufactured goods and machinery and equipment from Japan, and exports iron ore, rubber, and tin, as in its trade with other industrialized nations.

Table 8.18 shows the sources of West Malaysian imports by region. Although the percentage of imports from the United Kingdom has declined, that of West Europe as a whole has remained constant at 32.5 percent. On the whole, imports from Western nations have increased somewhat, whereas imports from Asia and Southeast Asia had declined significantly even before Confrontation began in 1963. Most of the Asian trade with West Malaysia has been transit trade, as the previous discussion indicated. Except for the import of foodstuffs from Thailand and Communist China, and of manufactured, capital, and consumer goods from Japan, most of the remainder comes from non-Asian industrial nations. Similarly, West Malaysian domestic exports are in fact almost all directly or indirectly to Western countries and Japan.

Although West Malaysia has followed a basically laissez-faire policy in international trade, her trading ties with Communist countries are not very important. Only Russia is a major importer from West Malaysia (Table 8.11), and Communist China an exporter to West Malaysia (Table 8.16). These figures, however, underestimate the

TABLE 8.18—West Malaysian imports by region,
1958, 1962, and 1965
(Percentage of total imports)

Region	1958	1962	1965
West Europe	32.5%	32.7%	32.5%
Asia	54.2	52.4	46.2
Australia and New Zealand	5.7	5.0	6.7
United States and Canada	3.0	6.4	5.9
Total	95.4	96.5	91.3
Western countries	41.2	44.1	45.1
Southeast Asia	36.1	33.6	21.9

Note: West Europe includes United Kingdom, Belgium, Denmark, France, West Germany, Italy, Luxemburg, Netherlands, Norway, and Sweden; Asia includes Hong Kong, Burma, Mainland China, Indonesia, Iran, Japan, Taiwan, Thailand, and Singapore; Western countries include West Europe, Canada, United States, Australia, New Zealand, and Austria; Southeast Asia includes Burma, Indonesia, Thailand, and Singapore.
Source: Computed from Table 8.16.

trading links with these countries, as an important part of their trade with West Malaysia is done indirectly by Singapore. However, trade with many of the non-Communist countries, such as the United Kingdom and the United States, is similarly underestimated because these countries also have important trading ties with Singapore.

Although West Malaysia has important trade links with many countries, trade with East Malaysia is limited. Both East and West Malaysia have stronger trading ties with Singapore than with each other (see Table 8.19). When the Malaysian Common Market comes into full operation, East and West Malaysia, as well as Sabah and Sarawak in East Malaysia, will undoubtedly draw closer to each other in trade matters although the scope is unlikely to be very large in the foreseeable future.

TABLE 8.19—Import and export relationships of West Malaysia,
Sarawak, Sabah, and Singapore, 1961
(Million M$)

Imports	Exports			
	West Malaysia	Sarawak	Sabah	Singapore
West Malaysia	–	3.4	3.5	723.6
Sarawak	0.2	–	0.8	159.9
Sabah	0.1	0.6	–	18.0
Singapore	886.2	27.1	10.8	–
Total	886.5	31.1	15.1	901.5
Rest of world	1,341.0	380.6	199.9	3,061.8

Source: IBRD Mission, *Report on the Economic Aspects of Malaysia* (Kuala Lumpur: Government Printer, 1963), p. 105.

TERMS OF TRADE

The immense influence of changes in the terms of trade on economic welfare needs no reemphasis here.[15] What does need emphasis is that such changes are comparatively more important to economies like Malaysia's with a high GEP/GDP ratio than to those with lower ratios.

The commodity or merchandise terms of trade, or as Taussig calls it, the net barter terms of trade, of West Malaysia for 1955–65, are shown in Figure 8.4, together with the corresponding import and export price indices. Earlier data are not available. The commodity terms of trade show a significant declining trend, an average of 1.37 points per annum. The decline is caused by a fall in the export price index of 1.58 points per annum, slightly offset by a slower decline in the import price index of 0.16 points per annum.

The export price index is the predominant determinant of the commodity terms of trade. The correlation coefficient between the export price index and the terms of trade index must be positive and close to 1. Only in 1962 and 1964 did the commodity terms of trade move in a different direction from the export price index.

The rubber export price index was the main regulator of the export price index, particularly between 1955 and 1961 (see Figure 8.5). Only in the last two years of this period, 1964 and 1965, did the export price index move in a different direction (upward) from the rubber price index (downward). This was because of the spectacular increase in tin prices in these years.

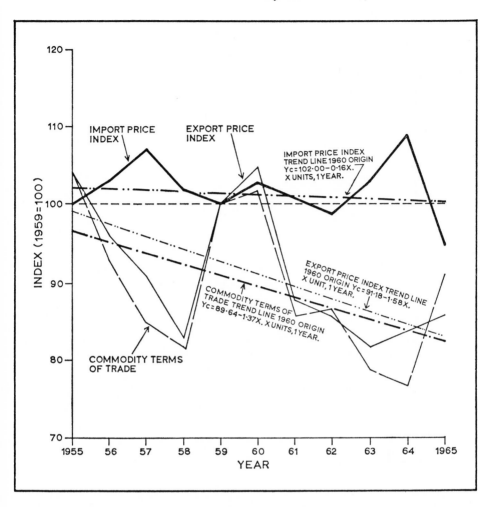

FIGURE 8.4—West Malaysian commodity terms of trade and export and import price indices, 1955–65, with trends

The commodity terms of trade do not show changes in export productivity. No overall export productivity index is available in West Malaysia, but there are data to suggest that export productivity has followed a significantly rising trend. Available statistics on labor and land productivity of the major export industries, including rubber, tin, and palm oil, all show a rising trend, particularly in the all-important rubber sector.[16]

Because an export productivity index would in all probability show a significant upward trend, the trend in the single factoral terms of

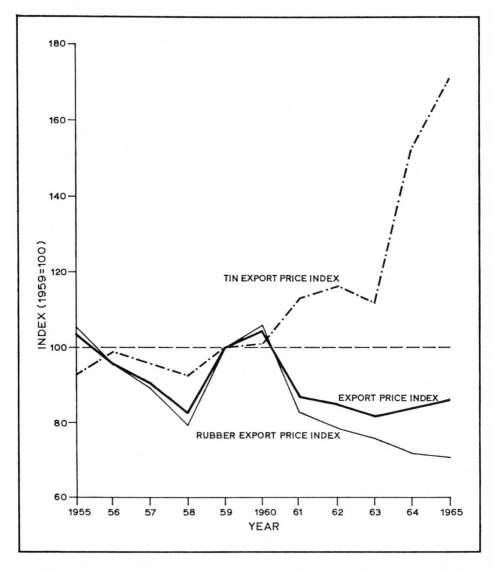

FIGURE 8.5—West Malaysian rubber, tin, and total export price indices, 1955–65

trade probably is in West Malaysia's favor. Therefore West Malaysia is probably better off than shown by the commodity terms of trade.

For the period 1955–65, the export value index shows an average increase of 3.25 points per year, despite a corresponding fall of 1.58 points in the export price index. This seems to be perfectly consistent with our conclusion about a significant rise in the export productivity index. By dividing the export value indices by the corresponding import price indices, we obtain the income terms of trade, or what Imlah calls "export gain from trade." For the period 1955–65 the income terms of trade improved by an average of 3.46 points a year. This is slightly higher than the average export value index trend of 3.25 points per year, because of the slight average yearly decline of 0.16 points in the import price index.

The rising trend in the income terms of trade, and the favorable effects of the rising export productivity index on the single factoral terms of trade, are evidence of our claim that the decline in the commodity terms of trade in West Malaysia is certainly more favorable to economic development and welfare than the figures taken alone would lead us to believe.

Year-to-year statistics on the various terms of trade, import and export prices, and volume indices are given in Table 8.20.

Changes in the gains from trade also operate internally between one industry and another, for instance between rubber and rice; or more broadly between the export sector and the non-export subsistence sector. Just as changes in the internal value of money cause changes in its external value, so do changes in the external terms of trade cause changes in the internal terms of trade both in the income distribution among sectors and in their rates of growth. In West Malaysia, changes in the internal terms of trade are also important because the export and non-export subsistence sectors coincide with the ethnic distribution of the population. The relative incomes of the different states of West Malaysia are also affected because the factor inputs are not distributed equally among the states. The tin industry, for example, is located mainly in Perak and Selangor and to a much lesser extent in Negri Sembilan. All three states are contiguous, and on the central west coast of West Malaysia. The rubber industry, although more widely dispersed, is also mainly on the west coast of West Malaysia.

CONCLUSION

Changes in GDP in West Malaysia were greatly affected by changes in GEP in the 1950's but less so after 1960. Changes in GEP have also had repercussions on import expenditures, the balance of trade, the balance of payments, and government revenue. Changes in GEP have

TABLE 8.20—West Malaysian terms of trade, export and import indices, 1955–65
(1959 = 100)

	Export Indices (1)						
	All exports (i)			Rubber (ii)		Tin (iii)	
Year	Value (a)	Price (b)	Volume (c)	Price (a)	Volume (b)	Price (a)	Volume (b)
1955	96	104	92	106	106	93	86
1956	91	96	95	96	96	99	115
1957	88	91	97	90	90	96	112
1958	76	83	92	80	80	93	87
1959	100	100	100	100	100	100	100
1960	118	105	113	106	103	101	169
1961	106	87	122	83	108	113	170
1962	106	85	125	79	108	116	179
1963	109	82	134	76	115	112	191
1964	112	84	134	72	117	152	159
1965	125	86	146	71	124	170	170

[a] Volume of all imports divided by volume of all exports.
[b] Price of all exports divided by price of all imports.
[c] Value of all exports divided by price of all imports.
Source: See Table 8.1.

been mainly a function of changes in rubber export revenue, itself a function of rubber price changes determined by world supply and world demand conditions.

The commodity terms of trade in West Malaysia are declining, and in all probability will continue to decline in the foreseeable future unless the anticipated declining trend in rubber prices is halted and prices take an upward turn, or cease to fall. Both are unlikely possibilities.

The West Malaysian GEP/GDP ratio has also shown a declining trend and it, too, is likely to continue to decline, with the main growth momentum expected to continue to come from the public sector following the trend set after 1960. The export sector, which played such a strategic role in the economic growth of West Malaysia in the fifties, is likely to continue to be handicapped by the declining commodity terms of trade, although the single factoral terms of trade will probably continue to have some offsetting effects.

The surplus in the balance of trade is also likely to continue to decrease as import expenditures grow faster than the growth in GEP. Again, the terms of trade are likely to have a decisive influence.

TABLE 8.20 (continued)

Import indices (2)					Indices of terms of trade (3)		
All imports (i)			Food (ii)		Cross barter terms of trade	Com- modity terms of trade	Income terms of trade
Value (a)	Price (b)	Volume (c)	Price (a)	Volume (b)	$(2ic/1ic)^a$	$(1ib/2ib)^b$	$(1ia/2ib)^c$
89	100	89	99	94	97	104	96
101	103	98	102	101	103	93	88
104	107	98	108	96	101	85	82
995	102	94	101	102	102	81	75
100	100	100	100	100	100	100	100
124	103	120	101	108	106	102	115
128	101	126	103	107	103	86	105
141	99	143	103	107	114	86	107
145	103	142	106	121	106	80	106
145	109	135	111	123	101	77	103
150	95	156	98	122	108	91	132

How can Malaysia stop her commodity terms of trade from declining? Deterioration in the commodity terms of trade adversely affects the balance of payments and the government budgetary position, thereby necessitating extensive internal and external borrowing, supplemented by the use of accumulated reserves. Furthermore, tax increases are needed for financing public development to maintain the overall growth momentum. The decision of the government to take on greater and greater defense commitments, on top of mounting expenditures for administrative and social services, has certainly made its position much worse. This situation must be considered not only against the background of rising expectations but also against the background of an explosive population growth.

Because of serious competition from synthetic rubber, an international rubber commodity agreement, as in the prewar era, is certainly out of the question. In fact, the effectiveness of such an agreement in raising the export income of that sector is doubtful, although by drastic curtailment of production and exports it might help to slow down the price decline.

Cutting down imports of consumer goods will ease the balance-of-payments situation but without a corresponding increase in the domestic supply of consumer goods the net effect would inevitably be a rise in the cost of living, which has until now remained relatively stable. A serious decline in the internal value of money would probably lead to pressure for higher money wages both in the public and in the private sector, in turn setting off a serious inflationary spiral. Among other results, inflation would weaken the competitive position of the export industries, and in turn worsen the balance-of-payments position. Serious inflationary pressures are also likely to slow down attempts at industrialization of the country.

The answer to the basic structural problem faced by West Malaysia is a successful import-substitution program as well as an increase in the physical productivity of the export industries and the development of new lines of export. The problem has become more acute because of the increasing deterioration in the prices of West Malaysian exports. Even if the industrialization program of West Malaysia is successful, however, it will have at most the effect of decreasing the import of manufactured consumer goods, while capital goods imports will continue to accelerate.

NOTES

1. For instance, read "West Malaysia" for "Malaysia" in the International Monetary Fund, *International Financial Statistics* for recent years, since these statistics do not include "East Malaysia."
2. The major published statistics on the subject of external trade are *Malaysian Quarterly Statistics of External Trade,* States of Malaya, *Annual Statistics of External Trade,* States of Malaya, *Monthly Statistics of External Trade,* and States of Malaya, *Monthly Statistical Bulletin.* Other published statistics are in the Federation of Malaya, *Official Yearbook* (Kuala Lumpur, 1962), Statistical Appendix.
3. GEP refers to gross merchandise exports only. GDP, unless otherwise stated, is expressed in current market prices. The gross national product (GNP) is less than GDP by net factor income paid abroad, which in Malaysia came to about M$185 million in 1964.
4. 1947 and 1948 have been deliberately excluded, primarily because of the distortions caused by the aftereffects of the war.
5. See Lim Chong Yah, *Economic Development of Modern Malaya* (Kuala Lumpur: Oxford University Press, 1967), pp. 267–71.
6. For Malaysia as a whole the cumulative public sector deficit for the five-year period 1961–65 came to approximately M$1,858 million; net domestic borrowing M$1,038 million, net foreign borrowing M$305 mil-

lion, and net use of accumulated assets M$316 million. The balance-of-payments current account shows a surplus of M$424 million in 1960 but a deficit of M$230 million in 1963, and M$122 million in 1964. (See Government of Malaysia, *First Malaysia Plan, 1966–1970* [Kuala Lumpur, 1965], tables 2.8 and 2.9, pp. 32, 33.

7. States of Malaya, *Monthly Statistical Bulletin,* November, 1966, table 2.7, p. 58, "Average Monthly Tin Prices."
8. For Malaysia as a whole although rubber export volume increased at an average yearly rate of 2.3 percent between 1960 and 1965 (1960 used as the base year), rubber export earnings declined from M$2,000.6 million in 1960 to M$1,566.9 million in 1961, M$1,476.9 million in 1962, M$1,475.7 million in 1963, M$1,395.9 million in 1964, and an estimated M$1,454 million in 1965.
9. For background information on the rubber replanting program, see Lim Chong Yah, "The Malayan Rubber Replanting Taxes," *Malayan Economic Review,* October, 1961, pp. 43–52. See also R. H. Mudie, *Report of the Mission of Enquiry into the Rubber Industry of Malaya* (Kuala Lumpur: Government Printer, 1954), 76 pp.
10. See Lim, *Economic Development of Modern Malaya,* pp. 87–92. See also T. R. McHale, "Natural Rubber and Malaysian Economic Development," *Malayan Economic Review,* April, 1965, pp. 16–43.
11. The five-year periods are chosen to coincide with the periods covered by the Five-Year Plans. The first period, 1947–50, of necessity is only four years.
12. *First Malaysia Plan, 1966–70,* p. 46.
13. The crude death rate in West Malaysia declined from 19.4 per thousand of population in 1947 to 12.6 in 1953 and 8.1 in 1964. The infant death rate fell from 93 per thousand live births in 1948 to 87 in 1953 and 48 in 1964. (See States of Malaya, *Monthly Statistical Bulletin,* November, 1966, tables 2.3 and 2.4.)
14. For more information on the subject, see Lim Chong Yah, "The Malaysian-Singapore Currency Split—An Appraisal," in *Ekonomi,* 7 (1966): 5–13.
15. For a comprehensive and informative paper on terms of trade and economic development see Theodore Morgan, "Trends in Terms of Trade, and Their Repercussions on Primary Producers," in *International Trade Theory in a Developing World,* eds. R. H. Harrod and D. Hague (London: Macmillan and Co., 1963), pp. 52–95.
16. See Lim, *Economic Development of Modern Malaya,* p. 68 (tin), p. 123 (rubber), and pp. 135–36 (palm oil).

COMMENT ON CHAPTER 8

I-SHUAN SUN

Exports are more important as a determinant of national income in West Malaysia than in any other country in Southeast Asia. The ratio of gross export proceeds (GEP) to gross domestic product (GDP) is about 40 percent for Malaysia compared with 27 percent for the Philippines, 16 percent for Thailand, and 6 percent for Pakistan. Large fluctuations in this ratio have led to instability in national income in West Malaysia and illustrate how foreign economic forces determine economic welfare in the country.

However, the ratio shows a long-term tendency to decline. In the period from 1947 to 1965, GDP has grown at a compound annual rate of 5.5 percent compared with 4.7 percent for GEP. The reason for the decline apparently is the increasing importance of public-sector investment in West Malaysia, which has been financed by the use of accumulated reserves and external borrowing.

Five major component products account for most of GEP. At one time rubber amounted to 72 percent of total exports, but in recent years the proportion has fallen to 50 percent. Tin exports now account for 25 percent of total exports. Iron ore, palm oil, and timber are relatively less important exports, accounting for 6 percent, 3 percent, and 2 percent of the total, respectively.

The price and quantity behavior of individual exports has been mixed. Rubber prices are definitely falling, although volume has increased greatly. Palm oil prices also show a secular tendency to decline. Increases both in volume and in price have accounted for the increase in tin proceeds. For iron ore and timber, growth has been more in volume than in price.

West Malaysian imports are more diversified and their composition has been changing. Rice imports are declining because of increases in productivity and extension of land under cultivation. Imports of beverages and tobacco, the second largest item in total imports, also shows absolute and relative decline because of import substitution. Chemicals, mainly fertilizers for rice, have registered the fastest rate of increase, and the increase in the imports of capital and consumer goods in recent years has been very striking.

West Malaysia has in the past enjoyed a comfortable surplus in its balance-of-merchandise trade. However, this balance is becoming smaller as the rate of growth of imports continues to exceed the rate of growth of exports. If the surplus continues to decline at the same rate as in the last fifteen years, it will vanish by 1992.

It appears that West Malaysia is coming to the end of one phase of its growth, partly through its own choice and partly because the past pattern cannot continue. Unfortunately, Dr. Lim did not indicate, in view of these problems, what the production and trade policies of West Malaysia should be in the next five or ten years.

Perhaps the experience of Taiwan is suggestive. First, the high commodity and geographical concentration of West Malaysia's exports must certainly intensify the deteriorating terms of trade. A program of diversification may be in order. Second, with its substantial resource base, perhaps West Malaysia could initiate production for exports in rubber products, metal products, soaps, and food products—perhaps even steel production.

CHAPTER 9

PROSPECTS OF INDIA'S TRADE
WITH ECAFE COUNTRIES

D. T. LAKDAWALA AND R. H. PATIL

Inspired by the example of the European Economic Community, many studies have been made of the prospects for regional trade cooperation within the ECAFE region,[1] showing the possible benefits as well as underlining the difficulties. The present study goes one step further, with a detailed examination of the composition and pattern of India's trade with the countries of the ECAFE region and of the scope for its export expansion. The study is in four parts: first, an analysis of the composition and pattern of India's trade; second, the short-term scope for expansion of its export trade; third, policy measures needed to increase trade; and fourth, long-term trade prospects.

COMPOSITION AND PATTERN OF TRADE

The ECAFE region is an important trading partner of India. In the early 1960's, about 21 percent of India's exports went to those countries, and about 17 percent of her imports came from the region (see Table 9.1). The three developed countries of the region—Australia, Japan, and New Zealand—absorbed about 48 percent of India's exports to the region and supplied about 45 percent of the goods that India imported from all ECAFE countries. Japan alone accounted for more than 30 percent of India's total trade with the region.

Afghanistan, Burma, Ceylon, Iran, Malaysia, Pakistan, and Singapore are the other important trading partners. About 44 percent of India's total exports to the region went to these seven countries, with Ceylon absorbing about 11 percent. Approximately 53 percent of

TABLE 9.1—India's trade with other Asian countries
(Average of 1962/63 and 1963/64)

Country	Total exports to country	Total imports from country	Balance of trade	India's exports to country as % of total exports to the region	India's share in country's total imports (%)	Imports from country as % of imports from the region	Imports from country as % of total imports
	(thousand IRs)						
Developed Countries							
Australia	182,019	200,374	− 18,354	12.17	1.61	10.69	1.80
Japan	462,700	626,938	− 164,238	30.94	1.57	33.45	5.65
New Zealand	69,271	15,769	53,502	4.63	1.94	0.84	0.14
Developing Countries							
Afghanistan	68,610	51,197	17,413	4.59	20.24	2.73	0.46
Brunei	2	1	1	negl.	negl.	negl.	negl.
Burma[a]	51,839	88,484	− 36,645	3.47	5.08	4.73	0.80
Cambodia[b]	12,068	5	12,063	0.81	2.42	negl.	negl.
Ceylon	163,106	70,982	92,124	10.91	10.36	3.79	0.64
Hong Kong	44,069	9,231	34,838	2.95	0.72	0.49	0.08
Indonesia	32,295	15,254	17,041	2.16	1.48	0.81	0.14
Iran	54,023	468,922	− 414,899	3.61	2.14	25.02	4.22
Laos[c]	289	negl.	289	0.02	0.22	negl.	negl.
North Borneo	140	10	130	0.01	0.03	negl.	negl.
Pakistan	82,877	130,150	− 47,273	5.54	2.15	6.94	1.17
Philippines	3,613	3,194	419	0.23	0.15	0.17	0.02
Sarawak[d]	233	negl.	233	0.02	0.04	negl.	negl.
Singapore	133,648	67,086	66,562	8.94	2.52	3.58	0.60
South Korea[e]	1,003	1,020	− 17	0.07	0.04	0.05	0.01
South Vietnam	16,355	1,367	14,988	1.09	1.25	0.07	0.01
Taiwan	4,157	1,076	3,081	0.28	0.27	0.06	0.01
Thailand	15,614	8,925	6,689	1.04	0.57	0.48	0.08
West Malaysia	97,428	113,989	− 16,561	6.52	3.36	6.09	1.03
Total	1,495,377	1,873,974	− 378,610	100.00	—	100.00	16.87

negl.: Negligible. [a] Figures in columns 2 and 4 were rounded from 1.7 and 0.7 respectively. [b] The figure in column 3 was rounded from 4.8. [c] The figure in column 3 was rounded from 0.15. [d] The figure in column 3 was rounded from 0.05. [e] The figure in column 8 was rounded from 0.009. Components may not add up to totals because of rounding.

Sources: United Nations, Department of Economic and Social Affairs, *Yearbook of International Trade Statistics* 1963 and 1964 (1965 and 1966); Government of India, Department of Commercial Intelligence and Statistics, *Monthly Statistics of the Foreign Trade of India*, March 1963, Vols. 1, 2, and March 1964, Vols. 1, 2 (Delhi, 1963 and 1964).

total imports from the region came from them, with Iran supplying 25 percent—second only to Japan.

Developed ECAFE Countries

India's exports to and imports from the developed countries of the region for 1962 and 1963 are given in Tables 9.2 and 9.3. More than 71 percent of India's exports to those developed countries were primary products (Standard International Trade Classification [SITC] Sections 0–4). Raw cotton; iron and steel scrap; iron ore and concentrates; and manganese ores were the most important, with iron ore and concentrates accounting for about 40 percent of those commodities.[3] Imports of iron ore and concentrates from India made up only 10 percent of total imports of these products to developed ECAFE countries (mainly Japan), however. Exports of textile fibers (mainly cotton) accounted for 23.2 percent of the exports of primary products and for 16.6 percent of the total exports to the developed ECAFE countries (again primarily Japan). India also exported certain petroleum products, mainly to New Zealand.

Textiles accounted for 86 percent of India's exports of manufactured products (SITC Sections 5–8). Most were destined for Australia and New Zealand. Exports of metals manufactures accounted for about 6 percent of the exports of manufactures to the developed countries.

India's imports from the region's developed countries were mainly manufactures, which made up 76 percent of total imports from them. Thus, India's trade with this group of countries is typical of the trade pattern of a developing country with a developed country. But India's trade structure with Australia and New Zealand, the highest per capita income countries of the region, was contrary to the typical pattern. These two countries supplied almost all of India's imports of primary products from the three developed countries of the region.

Less-Developed ECAFE Countries

Of the less-developed ECAFE countries, the Philippines, Pakistan, and Taiwan have made some progress in industrialization, although heavy industries are not yet important. Hong Kong and Singapore are the two important Asian free ports. Reexports from Hong Kong were estimated at about 20 percent[4] and from Singapore at 75 percent[5] of

TABLE 9.2—Developed ECAFE countries: total imports and imports from India
(Average of 1962 and 1963[a])

SITC code (original)	Total imports (*1*) (thousand IRs)	Imports from India (*2*) (thousand IRs)	*2* as a % of *1*
0 *Food*	4,929,932	88,259	1.79
061 Sugar	941,638	26,729	2.84
07 Coffee, tea, cocoa, spices, and manufactures thereof	637,907	28,292	4.43
081 Feeding stuff for animals (not including unmilled cereals)	221,242	13,436	6.07
1 *Beverages and tobacco*	363,939	3,247	0.89
2 *Crude materials, inedible, except fuels*	13,307,013	378,624	2.84
26 Textile fibers (not manufactured into yarn, thread, or fabrics) and waste	3,926,950	116,881	2.97
27 Crude fertilizers and crude minerals, excluding coal, petroleum, and precious stones	765,233	16,648	2.17
281 Iron ore and concentrates	1,607,889	167,856	10.43
282 Iron and steel scrap	869,184	34,190	3.93
283 Ores of non-ferrous base metals and concentrates	800,659	24,149	3.01
3 *Mineral fuels, lubricants, and related materials*	6,901,611	21,351	0.31
313 Petroleum products	363,217	20,561	5.66
4 *Animal and vegetable oils and fats*	242,943	12,850	5.29
5 *Chemicals*	2,506,903	3,854	0.15
6 *Manufactured goods classified chiefly by material*	5,343,829	192,926	3.61
65 Textile yarn, fabrics, made-up articles, and related products	1,760,678	172,315	9.79
681 Iron and steel	1,068,909	1,598	0.15
69 Manufactures of metals	420,319	11,872	2.82
7 *Machinery and transport equipment*	8,619,711	429	0.01
8 *Miscellaneous manufactured articles*	1,277,564	2,208	0.17
89 Miscellaneous manufactured articles, n.e.s.	598,057	928	0.15
9 *Miscellaneous transactions and commodities, n.e.s.*	192,588	1,563	0.81
Total, all Sections	43,686,033	705,311	—

[a] Because of the nature of the available data, figures in column 3—for SITC Sections and three-digit commodity classifications (original)—are given according to the Indian fiscal year, i.e., April to March. Figures in column 2 are given according to the calendar year, however.
Sources: See Table 9.1.

their total exports. Trade statistics for them therefore have to be carefully interpreted. The other developing ECAFE countries produce mainly primary products. Most produce and export a single commodity as their basic economic activity.

India's exports to these countries were distributed more or less evenly between primary and manufactured products, with primary products accounting for more than 47 percent of the total (see Table 9.4). Food products were about 32 percent of total exports and about 68 percent of primary exports. Exports of fruits and vegetables, sugar, tea, and spices were 12 percent, 18 percent, 15 percent, and 10 percent respectively of the exports of primary products. Indian exports of coal to these countries stood at more than IRs24 million[6] and provided about one-third of their total coal imports. Cotton textiles formed less than two-thirds of Indian textile exports, but they were less than 6 percent of the total imports of cotton textiles of these countries.[7] India's exports of electrical and nonelectrical machinery to these countries were more than IRs12 million, and those of clothing more than IRs11 million.

About 92 percent of India's imports from the developing ECAFE countries were primary commodities (see Table 9.5). Crude petroleum and petroleum products accounted for 50 percent of her total imports from this source. Next in importance were crude materials, with 23 percent. All imported jute came from the developing countries, 66 percent of the rubber, but only 5 percent of the cotton. Seventy-nine percent of India's imported edible oil seeds, oil nuts, and oil kernels came from these countries, 31 percent of its rice imports, and 30 percent of its fruit and nut imports. Lead and tin goods were the other main imports, 63 percent coming from the developing ECAFE region.

Some interesting points emerge from this description. The pattern of trade with the developing ECAFE countries is exports of manufactures and imports of primary products—mainly rice, wheat, petroleum, rubber, vegetable oils, and oil nuts. India's exports of manufactures are predominantly commodities listed in SITC Section 6, particularly textiles. Indian textile exports do not constitute a significant portion of the textile imports of any country in the region, however. New products—including inorganic and organic chemicals, cosmetics, iron and steel products, metal manufactures, machine tools, and electrical machinery—have been appearing noticeably among India's exports. But India still does not compete strongly with the industrially advanced countries of the world in products requiring great skill and highly sophisticated techniques.

TRADE EXPANSION: SHORT-TERM ANALYSIS

Our examination of Indian trade with the ECAFE region gives a perspective from which we can form some idea of the scope for trade

TABLE 9.3—India: total imports and imports from developed ECAFE countries
(Average of 1962 and 1963)

SITC code (original)	Total imports (*I*) (thousand IRs)	Imports from the developed ECAFE countries (*2*) (thousand IRs)	*2* as a % of *I*
0 Food	1,576,670	77,542	4.92
022 Milk and cream: evaporated, condensed, or dried	79,833	8,434	10.36
029 Dairy products, n.e.s.	1,635	735	44.95
041 Wheat and spelt (including meslin), unmilled	973,562	67,722	6.95
045 Cereals, unmilled, other than wheat, rice, barley, and maize	215	215	100.00
1 Beverages and tobacco	2,736	43	1.57
2 Crude materials, inedible, except fuels	1,246,386	112,151	8.99
262 Wool and other animal hair	139,367	91,279	65.49
3 Mineral fuels, lubricants and related materials	962,511	3,266	0.34
4 Animal and vegetable oils and fats	52,490	5,346	10.18
5 Chemicals	944,040	82,719	8.76
511 Inorganic chemicals	148,560	12,306	8.28
512 Organic chemicals	200,423	9,570	4.77
531 Coal-tar dyestuffs and natural indigo	70,899	4,538	6.40
533 Pigments, paints, varnishes, and related materials	13,458	578	4.30
541 Medicinal and pharmaceutical products	87,933	1,194	1.36
561 Fertilizers, manufactured	273,744	46,871	17.12
599 Miscellaneous chemical materials and products	99,866	7,614	7.62
6 Manufactured goods classified chiefly by material	1,970,061	220,798	11.21

(Table continued on following page)

TABLE 9.3 (continued)

SITC code (original)	Total imports (1) (thousand IRs)	Imports from the developed ECAFE countries (2) (thousand IRs)	2 as a % of 1
611 Leather	476	311	65.30
641 Paper and paperboard	123,045	6,115	4.97
681 Iron and steel	881,430	155,797	17.67
685 Lead	30,199	7,403	24.51
686 Zinc	94,379	15,951	16.90
689 Miscellaneous non-ferrous base metals employed in metallurgy	10,823	141,486	13.73
699 Manufactures of metals, n.e.s.	161,594	4,180	2.59
7 Machinery and transport equipment	*3,969,784*	*271,727*	*6.84*
711 Power generating (except electric) machinery	409,434	25,318	6.18
716 Mining, construction, and other industrial machinery	1,676,446	91,728	5.47
721 Electric machinery, apparatus, and appliances	728,175	94,633	12.99
732 Road motor vehicles	27,228	3,553	13.05
8 Miscellaneous manufactured articles	*301,952*	*57,604*	*19.08*
861 Scientific, medical, optical, measuring and controlling instruments and apparatus	78,714	4,227	5.37
891 Musical instruments, phonographs, and phonograph records	1,690	1,358	80.35
892 Printed matter	31,390	2,659	8.47
899 Manufactured articles, n.e.s.	134,251	46,498	34.63
9 Miscellaneous transactions and commodities, n.e.s.	*65,889*	*3,257*	*4.94*
Total, all sections	11,092,519	834,453	—

ᵃ Because of the nature of the available data, figures in column 2—for SITC Sections and three-digit commodity classifications (Original)—are given according to the calendar year, however. Figures in column 3 are given according to the Indian fiscal year, i.e., April to March.

Sources: See Table 9.1.

TABLE 9.4—Developing ECAFE countries: total imports and imports from India
(Average of 1962 and 1963[a])

	SITC code (Original)	Total imports (*1*) (thousand IRs)	Imports from India (*2*) (thousand IRs)	*2* as a % of *1*
0	*Food*	9,190,424	222,477	2.42
03	Fish and fish preparations	286,489	21,192	7.39
05	Fruits and vegetables	614,583	40,597	6.60
06	Sugar and sugar preparations	454,690	58,937	12.96
074	Tea and mate	115,185	50,741	44.05
075	Spices	191,163	32,030	16.75
081	Feeding stuff for animals (not including unmilled cereals)	89,929	4,442	4.93
1	*Beverages and tobacco*	423,251	11,576	2.73
121	Tobacco unmanufactured	112,553	6,058	5.38
122	Tobacco manufactures	161,611	5,518	3.41
2	*Crude materials, inedible, except fuels*	4,290,212	38,797	0.90
263	Cotton	670,082	5,891	0.87
27	Crude fertilizers and crude minerals excluding coal, petroleum and precious stones	85,072	5,029	5.91
292	Crude vegetable materials, inedible, n.e.s.	182,917	12,836	7.01
3	*Mineral fuels, lubricants, and related materials*	2,107,334	43,670	2.07
311	Coal, coke, and briquettes	76,879	24,452	31.80
4	*Animal and vegetable oils and fats*	408,751	12,588	3.08
412	Vegetable oils	76,455	9,469	12.38
5	*Chemicals*	n.a.	17,064	—
541	Medicinal and pharmaceutical products	667,288	6,976	1.04
55	Essential oils and perfume materials, toilet, polishing and cleansing preparations	206,452	2,784	1.35
59	Explosives and miscellaneous chemical materials and products	407,125	2,123	0.52
6	*Manufactured goods classified chiefly by material*	n.a.	276,602	—
629	Rubber manufactured articles, n.e.s.	284,850	5,388	1.89
641	Paper and paperboard	145,262	2,272	1.56
651	Textile yarn and thread	362,916	11,214	3.08
652	Cotton fabrics of standard type (not including narrow and special fabrics)	1,433,254	82,689	5.76
656	Made-up articles wholly or chiefly of textile materials, n.e.s. (other than clothing and footwear)	128,294	42,559	33.17
661	Lime, cement, and fabricated building materials, except glass and clay materials	191,422	4,585	2.39
681	Iron and steel	1,954,530	8,066	0.41

(Table continued on following page)

TABLE 9.4 (continued)

SITC code (Original)	Total imports (1) (thousand IRs)	Imports from India (2) (thousand IRs)	2 as a % of 1
684 Aluminum	72,293	3,466	4.79
69 Manufactures of metals	834,096	10,691	1.28
7 *Machinery and transport equipment*	n.a.	20,699	—
711 Power generating (except electric) machinery	265,568	2,203	0.83
716 Mining, construction, and other industrial machinery	n.a.	8,403	—
721 Electric machinery, apparatus, and appliances	560,781	1,741	0.31
73 Transport equipment	1,878,743	2,628	0.13
8 *Miscellaneous manufactured articles*	1,779,983	35,813	2.01
812 Sanitary, plumbing, heating, and lighting fixtures and fittings	35,165	4,318	12.27
841 Clothing except fur clothing	306,436	11,493	3.75
86 Professional, scientific, and controlling instruments; photographic and optical goods; watches and clocks	329,017	7,090	2.15
89 Miscellaneous manufactured articles, n.e.s.	546,764	11,100	2.03
9 *Miscellaneous transactions and commodities, n.e.s.*	380,251	18,226	4.79
Total, all sections	—	697,512	—

n.a.: Not available for some countries.

ᵃ Because of the nature of the available data, figures in column 3—for SITC Sections and three-digit commodity classifications (Original)—are given according to the Indian fiscal year, i.e., April to March. Figures in column 2 are given according to the calendar year, however.

Sources: See Table 9.1.

expansion during both short and long periods. A short period may be defined as one that allows for relatively small structural shifts in the pattern of production of an economy. Over a short period, the pattern of imports and exports will not change significantly: no new items will be added and no old items will disappear. Because rates of growth of per capita income and technological progress are slow in most of the ECAFE countries, this assumption is likely to be reasonable. Japan is an exception. Japanese demand for the primary products that India produces will increase rapidly.

Imports of consumption goods depend on per capita income, population, the income elasticity of demand for the commodity, the domestic-supply function of the commodity, import-substitution policy, and foreign-exchange availability. The net effect of all these forces is

TABLE 9.5—India: total imports and imports from
developing ECAFE countries
(Average of 1962 and 1963[a])

SITC code (Original)	Total imports (1) (thousand IRs)	Imports from the developing ECAFE countries (2) (thousand IRs)	2 as a % of 1
0 *Food*	1,576,670	170,037	10.78
031 Fish: fresh or simply preserved	58,134	44,712	76.91
042 Rice	208,302	63,469	30.50
051 Fruits and nuts, fresh (not including			
oil nuts)	146,320	32,700	30.46
075 Spices	12,320	3,840	31.16
1 *Beverages and tobacco*	2,736	240	8.78
2 *Crude materials, inedible, except fuels*	1,246,386	230,065	18.45
211 Hides and skins (except fur skins),			
undressed	30,392	18,134	59.66
221 Oil seeds, oil nuts, and oil kernels	94,111	74,113	78.75
231 Crude rubber, including synthetic and			
reclaimed	99,924	66,092	66.14
263 Cotton	529,490	26,720	5.04
264 Jute, including jute cuttings and waste	25,996	25,996	100.00
265 Vegetable fibres, except cotton and jute	12,497	4,667	37.34
292 Crude vegetable materials, inedible, n.e.s.	16,369	5,686	34.73
3 *Mineral fuels, lubricants, and related*			
materials	962,511	478,840	49.74
312 Petroleum, crude and partly refined {			
313 Petroleum products	960,354	478,661	49.84
4 *Animal and vegetable oils and fats*	52,490	32,464	61.84
5 *Chemicals*	944,040	4,828	0.51
541 Medicinal and pharmaceutical products	87,933	1,597	1.81
551 Essential oils, perfume, and flavour			
materials	8,298	2,696	32.48
6 *Manufactured goods classified chiefly by*			
material	1,970,061	58,484	2.97
685 Lead	30,200	12,728	42.14
687 Tin	57,510	42,383	73.69
7 *Machinery and transport equipment*	3,969,784	7,702	0.19
721 Electric machinery, apparatus, and			
appliances	728,175	1,445	0.20
734 Aircraft	120,860	2,000	1.65
735 Ships and boats	27,299	1,908	6.98
8 *Miscellaneous manufactured articles*	301,952	2,706	0.89
9 *Miscellaneous transactions and com-*			
modities, n.e.s.	65,889	7,349	11.15
Total, all sections	11,092,519	992,715	—

[a] Because of the nature of the available data, figures in column 2—for SITC Sections and three-digit commodity classifications (Original)—are given according to the Indian fiscal year, i.e., April to March. Figures in column 3 are given according to the calendar year, however.

Sources: See Table 9.1.

uncertain. Population census studies are available for different countries; we can assume that the present rates of population growth will continue for some time. Family-planning devices will be accepted slowly, and death rates will probably not decline further immediately. The question of income growth poses real difficulties, however. Although information is available in the planning documents of some countries regarding the expected income growth, there are few scientific forecasts.

In any import-projection exercise, certain qualifications must be borne in mind, the first being the definition of a commodity. The available foreign-trade data compel us to take into account only three-digit SITC data, and thus the income-elasticity information pertains to broad commodity groups. When a large number of commodities with different demand and supply conditions are grouped together, one does not know what value to attach to the aggregate demand for the group. We cannot assume that domestic supplies will continue to provide the same proportion of every commodity in the future. Increased import substitution, it is hoped, will mean a slower rate of growth of imports, or, in some cases, it may even result in an absolute decline in the volume of imports. Because of foreign-exchange difficulties, some developing ECAFE countries may attempt to control their imports. In the case of primary raw materials, intermediate goods, and capital goods, there will be the additional complication arising from changes in the production function and perhaps in relative prices.

Even if we were to make an estimate of total import demand for a country, there is the further question of the share supplied by different countries. As P. Lamartine Yates[8] and others have pointed out, this variable is important, but it is difficult to estimate. The import share will depend on the exporting country's capacity to supply a commodity and on relative prices. The necessary information on supply capacity is hard to obtain in economies subject to considerable regulation, where it might be presumed the plans would give sufficient data. Even in India's detailed planning, there is no programming for the creation of exportable surpluses of different commodities.

Foreign-Trade Sector
in Indian Plans

Indian planning has been rather "inward-looking," in the sense that the expansion of various industries has been oriented mainly toward present and future internal demand. The development of a viable export sector on the basis of comparative-cost considerations has not yet been adequately stressed. Until almost the beginning of the Third Five-Year Plan,[9] the planners considered the foreign-trade sector in terms of the import requirements of the Plan, and the gap between import requirements and exports was to be filled by foreign loans and grants. During the Third-Plan period, the importance of the export sector was recognized, but attempts to increase exports mainly took the form of providing subsidies, incentives, and various other concessions. Scant attention was given to creating surpluses for export in addition to providing for a projected expansion in home demand. Sometimes there were statements by the policymakers that export targets would be achieved by depriving the domestic consumers of the normal supply of some commodities. It was not realized that depriving the final consumer is difficult except for a short period, and that starving industrial consumers of their intermediate products is unwise.

Recently, the government and the planning authorities appear to have realized the importance of making the export sector more dynamic. During 1966, the Indian rupee was devalued by up to 36.5 percent, mainly to increase exports. For the first time, the Indian parliament passed a resolution on the question of exports. While stressing export promotion measures, the draft outline of the Fourth Five-Year Plan clearly recognizes the importance of the supply aspects of a plan for expanding exports: "The most important pre-condition for the fulfilment of the export program is the realization of the production targets set for exportable commodities in the agricultural, mineral, and industrial sectors. In the production and investment programs under the Plan, special attention has been paid to this aspect of the problem."[10]

Since the Fourth Five-Year Plan is not yet final, detailed figures on commodities planned for export are not available. The latest estimates of India's global exports in 1970/71 are shown in Table 9.6.

Export Prospects

Given India's supply capacity, the actual possibilities for exporting still depend on prices and exchange rates in many competing countries. Specific elements, such as export subsidies, compulsory exports, and import discrimination, are involved. Therefore, we have made simple estimates showing the extent to which, in our opinion, various

TABLE 9.6—Estimates of India's exports, 1970/71

Commodity	Estimate (Million IRs)
Agriculture and allied crops (including plantation crops)	4,540
Vegetable oils (nonessential)	240
Oil cakes	540
Tobacco unmanufactured	330
Spices	290
Sugar	190
Fruits and vegetables	580
Fish	240
Raw cotton	140
Raw wool	60
Tea	1,640
Coffee	190
Hides and skins (raw)	100
Minerals	1,060
Iron ore	770
Manganese ore	150
Mica	140
Manufactures	5,000
Cotton fabrics	670
Jute goods	2,110
Art silk fabrics	100
Clothings	190
Coir yarn and manufactures	160
Footwear	140
Leather and leather manufactures	380
Engineering goods	480
Handicrafts	320
Iron and steel	200
Chemicals and allied products	190
Cotton waste	60
Other exports	1,640
Total exports	12,240

Source: Government of India, Planning Commission, Perspective Planning Division, *Draft Fourth Plan: Material and Financial Balances, 1964–65, 1970–71 & 1975–76* (New Delhi, 1966), p. 133.

categories of Indian exports to ECAFE countries may increase by 1970/71. The commodities chosen are those that offer scope for expansion (see Tables 9.7 and 9.8). The estimates are based on favorable assumptions with respect to the overall export targets that India has set up.

It is pertinent to ask about the rationale behind the changes pre-

TABLE 9.7—Estimated growth of India's exports to the developing ECAFE countries by 1970/71
(Base: Average of 1962 and 1963ᵃ)

SITC code (Original)	Indian exports in the base period (thousand IRs)	India's share in the market in the base period (%)	Estimated value of exports by 1970/71 (thousand IRs)	Annual compound rate of growth of exports (%)
03 Fish and fish preparations	21,192	7.39	42,384	9.00
05 Fruits and vegetables	40,597	6.60	81,194	9.00
06 Sugar and sugar preparations	58,937	12.96	117,874	9.00
121 Tobacco, unmanufactured	6,058	5.38	12,116	9.00
221 Oil seeds, oil nuts, and oil kernels	458	0.33	6,939	40.50
263 Cotton	5,891	0.87	33,504	24.30
311 Coal, coke, and briquettes	24,452	31.80	48,904	9.00
511 Inorganic chemicals	235	0.32	3,605	40.70
512 Organic chemicals	523	0.38	6,896	38.00
531 Coal tar, dye stuffs, and natural indigo	387	0.62	3,133	29.90
541 Medicinal and pharmaceutical products	6,976	1.04	33,364	21.60
55 Essential oils and perfume materials; toilet, polishing, and cleansing preparations	2,784	1.35	16,704	25.10
621 Materials of rubber	621	11.08	1,232	9.00
629 Rubber manufactured articles, n.e.s.	5,388	1.89	28,485	23.10
641 Paper and paperboard	2,272	1.56	14,526	26.10
642 Articles of paper, etc.	81	0.17	4,684	66.40
65 Textile yarn, fabrics, made-up articles, and related products	271,308	7.36	317,421	2.20
651 Textile yarn and thread	11,214	3.08	45,506	15.00
652 Cotton fabrics of standard type (not including narrow and special fabrics)	82,689	5.76	172,268	9.60
656 Made-up articles wholly or chiefly of textile materials, n.e.s. (other than clothing and footwear)	42,559	33.17	51,317	2.40
661 Lime, cement, and fabricated building materials, except glass and clay materials	4,585	2.39	19,142	19.60
665 Glassware	1,259	4.39	2,867	10.90
681 Iron and steel	8,066	0.41	97,726	36.80
684 Aluminum	3,466	4.79	3,614	0.50
69 Manufactures of metals	10,691	1.28	21,382	9.00

(Table continued on following page)

TABLE 9.7 (continued)

SITC code (Original)	Indian exports in the base period (thousand IRs)	India's share in the market in the base period (%)	Estimated value of exports by 1970/71 (thousand IRs)	Annual compound rate of growth of exports (%)
71 Machinery, non-electric	12,228	0.41	59,550	21.90
711 Power-generating	2,203	0.83	26,557	36.50
714 Office machines	39	0.07	5,294	85.90
72 Electrical machinery, apparatus, and appliances	4,063	0.27	29,745	28.40
812 Sanitary, plumbing, heating, and lighting fixtures and fittings	4,318	12.27	7,033	6.30
841 Clothing except fur clothing	11,493	3.75	30,643	12.20
851 Footwear	762	7.88	1,450	8.30
86 Professional, scientific, and controlling instruments; photographic and optical goods; watches and clocks	7,090	2.15	17,395	10.80
Total	654,885	—	1,364,454	9.60

a Because of the nature of the available data, Indian exports are given for the Indian fiscal year—i.e., April to March—while imports of the developing countries are given for the calendar year.
Sources: See Table 9.1.

dicted by 1970/71. Briefly, the answer is that a study of production statistics reveals that India produces a large number of manufactured, as well as agricultural, commodities. Indeed, India has most of the industries that produce SITC three-digit commodities.[11] India's exports are fairly diversified, including 149 out of the 150 commodities listed by SITC (Original).[12] India's exports in 1962 formed less than 5 percent of its national income,[13] and, except for a few commodities like tea and jute, only a small portion of production is exported. India's ability to export goods of standard quality at competitive prices depends on immediate efforts to supply goods at international prices (through export subsidies if need be) and on possible preferential trading and exchange arrangements.

The import trade of the developing ECAFE countries will increase by 1970/71, and the increase will be exceptionally large for Indian export goods. India now supplies only a modest share of the total imports of these goods into ECAFE countries. Her share can be increased at the expense of developed countries, which can bear their relative decrease.

Among these goods, the potential increase in sales is smallest for commodities in which India's share is already high and scope for further trade expansion is limited by a regional competitor—for example, jute textiles. Although the existing share of coal, 31.8 percent, is quite high, the region is short of coal, which India can supply. For sugar and for fruits and vegetables, a 100 percent increase has been visualized, because the present shares are moderate. For electrical and nonelectrical machinery, the present shares of 0.41 and 0.27 percent are so low that it will not be difficult to raise them greatly. Iron and steel products, and some chemical and pharmaceutical products, have a similar potential. According to our estimates, about 40 percent of the increased exports to the ECAFE region by 1970/71 will be due to the continued rapid growth of iron-ore exports to Japan. Commodities such as motor vehicles are not included in Table 9.7, as India is unlikely to be a large exporter of such goods in the near future.

A potentially important problem is the trade-diverting aspect of India's attempts to increase its trade with the developing ECAFE countries. Increased Indian textile exports to these countries, for example, clash with the interests of Taiwan, Pakistan, and South Korea. Although we do not have conclusive data, two things are noteworthy: a large portion of the textile exports of these countries is directed to the developed countries, and a large portion of the imports of textiles

TABLE 9.8—Estimated growth of India's exports to the developed ECAFE countries by 1970/71
(Base: Average of 1962 and 1963)

Country and SITC code (Original)	Indian exports in the base period (thousand IRs)	India's share in the market in the base period (%)	Estimated value of exports by 1970/71 (thousand IRs)	Annual compound rate of growth of exports (%)
Australia				
03 Fish and fish preparations	1,679.1	2.33	7,202	19.9
074 Tea and mate	21,818.0	16.56	26,354	2.4
121 Tobacco, unmanufactured	0.3	—	5,228	—
65 Textile yarn, fabrics, made-up articles, and related products	122,546.7	10.67	172,216	4.2
681 Iron and steel	137.3	0.05	12,313	75.4
69 Manufactures of metal	90.2	0.03	13,207	86.6
71 Machinery, other than electric } 72 Electrical machinery	155.5	—	25,458	89.1
841 Clothing except fur clothing	16.7	0.05	3,500	95.1
Subtotal	146,443.8	—	265,478	7.7
Japan				
061 Sugar	26,729.7	2.84	235,000	31.2
081 Feeding stuff for animals (not including un-milled cereals)	13,456.6	6.07	22,124	6.4
121 Tobacco, unmanufactured	3,245.1	1.87	9,394	14.2
211 Hides and skins (except fur skins), undressed	698.3	0.24	29,143	59.4
281 Iron ore and concentrates	167,856.6	10.43	875,000	22.9
Subtotal	211,986.3	—	1,170,661	23.8
New Zealand				
05 Fruits and vegetables	791.8	1.04	7,574	32.6
071 Coffee } 074 Tea and mate	2,567.0	4.75	5,398	9.7
652 Cotton fabrics of standard type (not including narrow and special fabrics)	14,652.0	9.99	21,985	5.2
653 Woven textiles, non-cotton	8,760.1	6.31	13,889	5.9
71 Machinery, other than electric	78.8	0.02	9,858	37.1
Subtotal	26,849.7	—	58,704	10.3
Total, developed ECAFE countries	385,279.8	—	1,494,843	18.5

[a] Because of the nature of the available data, Indian exports are given for the Indian fiscal year—i.e., April to March—while imports of the developing countries are given for the calendar year.
Sources: See Table 9.1.

of the developing ECAFE countries (except for jute textiles) origi-
nates from developed countries, including Japan. Therefore, the problems of displacement of other regional textile exporters because of
increased Indian textile exports are not likely to be serious. The rates
of growth projected for these competitive exports are not relatively
very high in any case.[14]

The value of exports to the less-developed countries increases from
about IRs655 million to IRs1,364 million, for the commodities in our
analysis (Table 9.7), or by 9.6 percent a year (compounded). For
the more-developed countries of the region—Japan, Australia, and
New Zealand—separate estimates are made in Table 9.8. Exports of
these commodities to these countries would increase from IRs385
million to an estimated IRs1,495 million, or by 18.5 percent a year
compounded. To the ECAFE region as a whole, exports from India
would rise (assuming the commodities not included above did not
increase at all) from IRs1,495 million in 1962–64 (Table 9.1) to
IRs2,314 million in 1970–71, or by 6.4 percent a year compounded.

For our estimated totals to be achieved, it is, of course, not necessary that exports of each commodity should increase by exactly the
value given in either Table 9.7 or Table 9.8. Some may increase more,
and some less, and lower exports to some countries may be compensated by higher exports to others.

Implications for the
Indian Plans

A trade-expansion policy between India and each of these countries
will have special implications for the successive Indian plans.[15] In
order to increase exports from India, investment resources must be
allocated to create the necessary export surplus. For instance, if Indian exports of iron ore to Japan are to be 25 million metric tons by
1970,[16] a comprehensive plan is required for the development of
mines, of rail lines to transport the ore, of port facilities for bulk
handling, and of berths to accommodate large Japanese ships (carry-
ing 30 to 50 thousand metric tons or more of iron ore). In the case of
textile exports, it will be necessary to modernize the jute and cotton-
textile industries; to import superfine cotton; to produce high-quality
textiles; and also to develop synthetic fabrics, such as terrelyne, that
are increasingly displacing pure cotton fabrics. In some instances, a
number of industries need to be linked. Petrochemicals provide the
famous instance. Efficient production of some chemicals—such as

ammonia, acetic acid, styrene, terrelyne and related products, pigments and paints, and plastic goods—requires the development of a petrochemical industrial complex.

India cannot hope to expand its exports in the ECAFE region without creating opportunities for these countries to export more of their goods to India. A number of ECAFE countries face shortages of foreign exchange, and unless India opens its market to exports from these countries they may not be able or willing to absorb increasing amounts of Indian goods. (Japan is a partial exception.) Care should be taken to avoid needless conflicts with the interests of these countries. One glaring example is the large-scale plans to produce synthetic rubber in India. Since natural rubber remains an effective, and in some uses a superior, substitute for synthetic rubber, rubber-producing countries like Malaysia or Ceylon are bound to resent Indian plans to develop a synthetic-rubber industry.

In short, the plan for the foreign-trade sector has to be closely integrated with the overall development plan of the country; the implications for resource allocation have to be properly worked out; and the interests of other countries have to be duly safeguarded.

TRADE AGREEMENTS AND
ALLIED ARRANGEMENTS

Our estimates require that India increase its exports by about 12.4 percent per annum to the developed ECAFE countries, and by 8.4 percent to the other countries of the region. Between 1960/61 and 1965/66, India's exports increased by about 4 percent per annum to the developed countries of the ECAFE region and by under 2 percent per annum to the rest of the countries of the region. This slow rate of export growth was due, it is true, partly to special circumstances in trade with Pakistan and Indonesia and to the increased competitiveness of Japan. Even so, the much higher estimates we have made for the future will not come by themselves. Achieving higher goals will require persistent, intelligent, and conscious efforts, some of which have already been outlined. Special trade devices are also needed to ensure the removal of obstacles to the growth of exports.

Two major factors limiting export expansion in the region have been exchange controls and great uncertainty about production programs. Many less-developed countries have restricted their nonessential imports by exchange controls. Commodity aid and tied aid from developed countries have reduced their demand for imports further. Partly for these reasons, the relative importance of the intraregional trade of the developing ECAFE countries declined from 24 percent of the import total in 1953/54 to 18 percent in 1961/62.[17]

Trade treaties are a possible way to counteract this trend. The efforts made by India since independence are instructive. The early history of conscious efforts to increase trade with some of the ECAFE countries—such as Ceylon, the then Federation of Malaya, Singapore, New Zealand, and Australia—forms part of the story of the evolution of the sterling area. Historically, the sterling area evolved as a defense against both the interwar Great Depression and the dollar shortage. Along with other sterling countries, India gave preferential tariff and quota treatment to commodities originating in the sterling area, including some of the ECAFE countries. A second favorable factor for trade expansion was the acceptance of sterling for financing trade. During World War II, the great need to conserve dollar exchange acted as a stimulus to intra-sterling-area trade, but enemy occupation of several Asian countries and wartime distortions severely limited this process. In the Indian post-independence period, these preferential trade arrangements withered away substantially for various reasons, among which increasing exchange controls and higher import prices and duties were important. Discriminatory import quotas are no longer used, because of the multilateral convertibility of sterling.

Throughout the 1950's, there was a great spurt in India's trade agreements both with the ECAFE region and with Eastern Europe. In the ECAFE region, India concluded trade agreements with eight countries: Afghanistan, Burma, Ceylon, Indonesia, Iran, Japan, Nepal, and Pakistan. These agreements do not fall into any general pattern as do those with the Eastern European countries. Because of space limitations, we shall mention only a few broad characteristics. For example, the Standstill Agreement of August, 1947, with Pakistan[18] was (as its name implies) not an effort to increase trade, but merely to facilitate continuance of the pre-Partition trade pattern.

The degree of bilateralism differed from one agreement to the next. Bilateralism was quite high in the trade treaties with Pakistan and Burma, in contrast with the treaties concluded with Indonesia and Ceylon. The majority of the trade treaties with Pakistan and Burma until almost the mid-fifties included commitment clauses concerning the quantities of goods to be traded. But a main defect in all of the treaties with Pakistan, Burma, Ceylon, and Indonesia was limited commodity coverage. Sometimes the treaties excluded the most important commodities: the September, 1958, agreement with Ceylon[19] did not include rubber and coconut products, and the agreements with Indonesia did not give sufficient emphasis to exports of her petroleum products. Also, the provisions of the trade treaties were not properly adhered to and so full benefits were not realized. Often, in order to avoid imbalances on their trade account, the countries were unduly cautious in making purchases from each other.

The trade agreements between Iran and India of December, 1954, and May, 1961,[20] were essentially formal declarations of the acceptance by the two countries of the nondiscriminatory principles of the most favored nation arrangements of the General Agreement on Tariffs and Trade (GATT) type. They did not provide either for preferential tariff treatment or for fulfillment of stipulated import and export quotas. These agreements, therefore, may not have done more than smooth the flow of trade between the two countries.

Much the same holds true for India's trade agreements with Japan, Nepal, and Afghanistan. They also were declarations of acceptance of nondiscriminatory principles. For Afghanistan, however, there were two additional features. Payments agreements specified the mode of payment and the maintenance of a balance in the State Bank of India to facilitate trade between the two countries. Facilities were also provided by both countries for transit trade. In the case of Nepal, the main stress was on arrangements for the transit trade passing through Indian territory. An interesting feature of the Japanese arrangement was the sizeable export of iron ores from the State Trading Corporation of India—more recently the Metals and Minerals Trading Corporation of India—to the Japanese steel producers' organizations.

In spite of the agreements, India's trade expansion with these countries has been rather disappointing compared to trade experience with the Eastern European countries. The latter trade has expanded by more than 23 times since 1954/55, increasing from IRs134 million to IRs3,124 million in 1965/66.[21]

A number of factors, apart from the differences in complimentarity of the economies, has been responsible for the unequal performances of bilateral trade agreements with these two groups of countries. In the centrally planned Eastern European economies, trade agreements fitted into national plans. The centrally planned countries were in need of consumer goods, as well as of raw materials, that India could supply. In return, these countries offered credit facilities to India which were helpful in facilitating a large-scale expansion of trade. Arrangements were also made for repaying loans in terms of goods and commodities. Although outside the scope of this paper, political factors may also have been relevant considerations.

Purposeful and determined efforts are necessary in order to increase trade between any two countries. Intricate organizational problems have to be solved to facilitate trade expansion through trade agreements. Credit provisions, willingness of both parties to carry surpluses or deficits, and readiness to exceed the stipulated purchases or sales of certain commodities when unforeseen situations arise are all quite important for successful trade agreements. Experience with the Eastern European countries suggests that state trading agencies facilitate the working of trade agreements. State trading agencies have been created in a number of the ECAFE countries, although the extent of their commodity coverage differs. In some cases, large private organizations have also played a useful role in augmenting trade. The Japanese steel producers' organization is a good example.

The case for systematic and properly planned long-term bilateral trade agreements among the ECAFE countries is quite strong. For instance, India suffers from a shortage of petroleum products, while Indonesia is short of cotton fabrics. Bilateral trade agreements in the past have emphasized trade expansion between the two countries in the goods that are currently being produced. In recent times, a new twist has been given to the concept of bilateral trade. A country needs certain resources to execute economic development plans and to meet increased consumer demand flowing from those plans. The process of planned development can also profitably create surpluses of other goods that can be disposed of through exports. Trade agreements serve the purpose of relieving a country of planned surpluses and of shortages of different goods and commodities. This new trade-agreement concept is receiving increasing attention in the ECAFE region because of special problems arising out of the trade agreements with the centrally planned economies and because of increasing familiarity with the systems of planning and the methods of international trade.

Program of Agreed
Specialization

A second variant of the trade agreement is the "program of agreed specialization" (PAS).[22] The central idea is to avoid concentration on the same development sectors and thereby to avoid some combination of excessive production of certain goods, decline in intraregional trade, and inability to realize the full benefits of economies of scale. It is argued that ECAFE countries would gain more by coordinating their trade and production plans so that countries might specialize in different fields properly fitted into their overall national plans. Comparative cost advantage based on such considerations as natural resources would be taken into account in the choice of sectors. Increased trade among member countries is to be achieved through short-term and long-term trade contracts and agreements.

The case for the PAS is especially strong where free-trade-area or common-market arrangements are unsuitable. There are, in fact, three major obstacles to a common market in the ECAFE region. First, the governments of these countries not only exercise control over the pattern of investment of the private sector but also invest large sums in public-sector undertakings. Second, government interference with the price mechanism through price fixing, resource direction, and distribution controls is considerable. Finally, these countries keep strict control over the foreign-trade sector through import and export quotas, state trading, exchange controls, immigration laws, and restrictions on the movement of short-term and long-term capital.

The PAS is patterned after the Council for Mutual Economic Assistance, which coordinates the trade and development plans of the Eastern European countries. Production, distribution, and foreign trade are centrally controlled in these economies. Trade expansion proceeds on the lines indicated by the PAS. In contrast, none of the ECAFE countries is as centralized. Even Burma's agriculture and her small-scale industrial sector are private, although purchase and export of rice is carried on by state trading agencies. The scope given to the private sector is quite wide in countries like Taiwan, Iran, Malaysia, and the Philippines, despite some government intervention in resource allocation. The mixed economy of India has a well-defined policy specifying the spheres in which the public and the private sectors are to operate. Therefore, the PAS type of arrangement may need some modifications for the ECAFE region, because of the highly divergent roles of governments in the region.

A Suggested Program

What organizational measures will foster closer trade relations between India and other ECAFE countries? The central idea of the PAS scheme cannot be disputed: some amount of coordination in the national development plans of the ECAFE region is essential. The crucial point is the way in which a plan for intraregional trade has to be fitted into the national plans of these countries. We assume that problems of trade expansion among the developing countries will receive special consideration under GATT, and that they will be allowed to depart from the GATT norms so that they can offer preferential treatment to each other's goods. On this assumption, let us indicate briefly the nature of arrangements that would be suitable for augmenting India's trade interdependence with the ECAFE countries.

Bilateral trade agreements will be called for with countries like Burma that have nationalized the foreign-trade sector. The encouragement of industrialization in these countries will be mutually beneficial. India can supply capital goods, and components and parts in exchange for rice initially and for manufactures eventually. The approach must rely on preferential duties with countries like Thailand that encourage private enterprise and have no foreign-exchange problem. Since these countries are less industrialized, India may liberalize imports of manufactured goods from these countries without demanding a *quid pro quo* for Indian manufactured exports, except for complex manufactures. Such arrangements will encourage the export of capital goods and of complex manufactures from India and, at the same time, will provide a wider market for the manufactures of the less-developed countries. Like Thailand, Malaysia enjoys a comfortable foreign-exchange position, but fears a slackening of export growth. She will be on the lookout for trade-expanding arrangements, especially for industrial raw materials.

India's trading position with Japan is quite different, resembling that of the less-industrialized countries with India. Much can be achieved if Japan offers substantial aid to India to develop sectors that will increase India's exports to Japan. Development of iron ore is a good example, for it is in Japan's interest to be assured of a continuous supply of good-quality iron ore for her expanding iron and steel industry.

Indian and Australian industries may be competitors, except in the consumer-durable-goods industry. Preferential duties would help to encourage the growth of complementary industrial sectors in India, Australia, and New Zealand. In 1965, Australia gave unilateral duty concessions on a number of commodities imported from the developing countries. Because Hong Kong and Singapore are free ports, it would be difficult to have special arrangements with them such as preferential duties, trade agreements, or the PAS.

Tariff preferences may not be enough in themselves to ensure the desired expansion of regional trade. Countries that grant preferences will still find it profitable to import from non-ECAFE countries, because of the inferior quality of some regional commodities or higher prices or both. Low quality is bound to prove an insuperable hindrance to trade expansion for some commodities such as medical and pharmaceutical products. But the inferior quality of other types of goods produced in the region may be partly offset by lower prices. These problems do not arise for standard-quality goods, among them a number of Indian manufactures exports. Machine tools and steel pipe produced in India have been well received even in the markets of the developed countries of the West.

Pricing Provisions in
Trade Treaties

The Indian government has attempted to overcome the disadvantages stemming from price differences by providing subsidies and various other concessions to exporters. If bilateral trade agreements are accepted by the ECAFE countries, it would be possible to rationalize the subsidies. Once the obligatory quota limits are fixed by agreement, a general provision stipulating that these goods will be sold at international prices or at some agreed prices may be made. A clause may be introduced in these treaties that will facilitate price changes if international prices fluctuate. Whether these changes should entirely conform to the fluctuations in international prices or be partially adjustable is a decision that may be left to the deliberations of the parties concerned. In the interest of economic stability, however, the prices of the traded goods should not be allowed to fluctuate too widely. Seasonal fluctuations should be smoothed, although secular changes in prices may be fully respected. The latter are particularly important whenever two countries conclude long-term bilateral agreements and integrate their trade plans with their development plans. Even those countries that do not agree to establish state trading agencies to carry on their trade can be brought into this scheme. Whenever a private importer buys a commodity from a member country, the government of that country can arrange to pay the foreign importer the difference between market price and the agreed price.

The advantages of these price arrangements are important. Trade agreements often do not succeed in increasing trade because the trading agencies find it unprofitable to import goods from the trade-agreement partner: prices are too high. Once the agreements include such price arrangements, a great stumbling block to trade expansion will be removed.

Credit Provisions

An international transaction, unless it is of the barter type, requires that the importing country be prepared to pay the exporting country in some acceptable currency or in gold. In bilateral transactions, the currency of one of the partners is accepted by the other, provided that the total value of transactions on both sides balances or that any imbalance is within the limit of the swing credit provided by the partner with the surplus. If the deficit on the balance of trade of a country exceeds the limit provided by the swing credits, the excess may have to be paid in terms of some hard currency, or there may be a provision to carry forward the deficit for adjustment in the next trade-agreement period.

Generally, swing credits are required to facilitate trade between two countries. It is difficult to balance week-to-week or month-to-month trade, because of the variations in delivery periods of different commodities or the skewed pattern of distribution of one partner's exports over certain months. These imbalances of trade account may be small if the state trading agencies operate efficiently in both countries. Even then, if only a small swing credit is available, the country that is afraid to incur a deficit over a given period will always be tempted to reduce its purchases from the other partner, even though it can increase its exports in the long run. A country with limited reserves of hard currency will not risk purchasing beyond the limit of swing credits, for fear of losing hard-currency reserves.

The moral is that India should offer larger swing credits to the developing ECAFE countries and should encourage them to be bold in making larger purchases from India. Fortunately, India also needs a number of commodities that these countries can supply, including tin, rubber, petroleum products, copper, copra, coconut oil, palm oil, rice, and raw jute. There is scope for expanding trade with the ECAFE countries if India takes the initiative in providing credit to buy its goods at international or agreed prices and if India also gives assurance of its desire to purchase increased quantities of the goods which these countries can supply.

As a first step, India can consider supplying adequate swing credits for the purchase of a limited number of commodities like cotton textiles, jute goods, and the newly developing engineering goods. Wherever there is idle capacity in the Indian industries due to lack of demand or wherever there are sectors in which increased supply can be arranged without much expenditure of foreign exchange (for instance, coal), these areas can be brought under this schedule. Second, as part of the long-term objective of increasing exports, India should inform the developing countries that it can also supply, on favorable terms, capital goods required for their development.

The Soviet Union expanded its trade with India through conscious efforts. Similar efforts are necessary if India is to expand its trade with the developing countries.

TRADE EXPANSION: THE LONG RUN

The study of short-term prospects for trade expansion with the ECAFE countries was relatively easy, since the analysis could be based on the existing state of the technological and economic development in the trading countries. A study of the long-term prospects for trade expansion is a difficult task, because structural changes in the patterns of production of the trading countries are likely. These changes will bring corresponding shifts in the composition of imports and exports.

A study of the changes likely in the composition of imports and exports of the ECAFE countries and of consequent effects on India's foreign trade can only be qualitative. It can show only the nature and type of efforts required to exploit opportunities for increased trade with the ECAFE countries. Countries with planned development will proceed, we may assume, along lines that will help them accomplish their objectives. For countries opposed to centralized planning, we have to guess at probable paths of development. The basic assumptions for both types of countries will rely on trends shown by economic history and on some of the highly useful cross-section studies of development patterns.

Developed ECAFE Countries

Our earlier discussion has stressed the importance of iron-ore exports to Japan. While the growth of the Japanese steel industry may not continue at the same rate in the 1970's or 1980's as in the first half of the 1960's, production will increase. In the ECAFE region, the known reserves in Malaysia may become exhausted, but Australia's reserves are known to be quite large (about 6 billion metric tons).[23] Because of her geographical proximity, Australia will be a strong competitor. The advantage of low labor costs may give an edge in competition to Indian mining, however, provided India can be equally efficient in bulk handling, in quick delivery, and in the development of ports capable of taking big ships. India also can hope to enlarge its exports of sugar to Japan, since Japanese consumption is low by the standards of developed Western countries.

Joint Indo-Japanese efforts should be made to develop a two-way trade in manufactures. At present, the Japanese economy is undergoing a rapid structural change. Not only is agricultural labor shifting to industry, but structural changes are taking place in the industrial sector. Rising wages accompanied by growth in the high-productivity sectors such as steel and shipbuilding are creating innumerable difficulties for small-scale, low-productivity industries. Over time, Japanese industries now enjoying a competitive advantage because of relatively lower wages are likely to lose their strong position both in world markets and in their own country. Countries like India, with relatively low labor costs, should exploit the opportunities provided by the import-liberalization policy of Japan. It should be possible to work out a division of labor between India and Japan based on differences in wage costs and resources, as well as in product and process specialization.

Australian and New Zealand industries pay quite high wages to their workers. Their relatively small-scale and labor-intensive industries will increasingly suffer from the major disadvantage of high-wage costs. Even their large-scale industries are said to have some disadvantage. J. B. Condliffe observes that, even if New Zealand and Australia form a common market, their total market would be "too small and too fragmented to offer economies of scale necessary to develop effective industries."[24] Because of many disadvantages, it is maintained by Hunter that "it is unlikely that Australia will ever become a major industrial power."[25] India can reasonably hope to export labor-intensive textiles and similar products, as well as those complex manufactures in which India would gain a competitive advantage because of her huge expanding domestic market. Trade with these countries can also be developed on the basis of exchange of intermediate products.

Developing ECAFE Countries

The developing countries rely mostly on imported capital goods, but the composition of each country's imports differs according to the sectors chosen for development and the type of industries already developed. For example, a more industrialized country like Taiwan is self-sufficient in such intermediate goods as cement, aluminum sheets, soda ash, and caustic soda, whereas other countries import these products. Over the decade 1954–63, total Taiwanese imports increased 70 percent. Imports of capital goods and material required for them increased 112 percent, and consumption-goods imports increased about 5 percent.[26]

In pursuing import substitution, the developing ECAFE countries have been trying to curtail the imports of consumer goods. Consumer-goods imports have not declined in absolute terms, however, for three reasons. First, rising incomes and expanding population have increased total demand. Second, even where it was possible to reduce demand for certain products, other new consumer goods have been imported. Third, food-grain imports have increased because of the slow growth in agricultural output in the face of continual population growth.

Import substitution will give increasing momentum to the production of consumer goods. In relatively less-developed countries, consumers prefer simple consumer goods that can be produced efficiently on a small scale. Such industries are attractive to the entrepreneurs of these countries. Markets for such simple products as textiles are likely to offer less scope for India in the long run. In fact, as their domestic markets expand and as they gain increasing experience and skill, the developing countries may increasingly discourage the import of such goods. The same holds true for products such as cement; tires and tubes; bicycles; paper and paperboard; and simple metal products such as nuts, bolts, and wire. While there is scope for short-term expansion of exports of these products, India's long-term plans should introduce necessary changes so that exportable surpluses of goods meant for these markets can gradually be reduced.

As India becomes more industrialized, and as per capita income increases, industries characterized by significant economies of scale will assume relatively greater importance. Automobiles and petrochemicals are examples. The highly complex techniques and the enormous financial resources required to run these industries efficiently will deter most of the other developing countries from starting them. As an economy develops, the demand for such products increases relatively more rapidly. Most of these products with high growth elasticities of demand are characterized, as Chenery notes, by significant scale economies.[27]

In the long run, it will be profitable for India to concentrate on these industries for export promotion. Because of its huge domestic market, India will be in a position to achieve a high degree of efficiency in these industries. Because these industries are now given high priority, there will be no reluctance to channel adequate resources to them. It has been the experience of many countries that an assured domestic market acts as a springboard for competition in the markets of other countries; it also provides a cushion to absorb the shocks of any fluctuations in export demand. Recent Japanese experience furnishes evidence that successful export industries are those that enjoy rapidly expanding domestic markets.[28] In short, exports of complex manufactures are likely to have better prospects in the markets of less-developed ECAFE countries. Nothing definite may be said at the moment about institutional and other arrangements that may be essential to bring about this trade. Perhaps by then the price mechanism, with a few aids, can be expected to work in the right direction for India.

NOTES

1. Australia and New Zealand have generally not been included in these studies.
2. Government of India, Department of Commercial Intelligence and Statistics, *Monthly Statistics of the Foreign Trade of India, March 1960,* vol. 1, and *Monthly Statistics of the Foreign Trade of India, March 1961,* vol. 2 (New Delhi, 1960 and 1961).
3. Government of India, Department of Commercial Intelligence and Statistics, *Monthly Statistics of the Foreign Trade of India, March 1963,* vols. 1, 2, and *Monthly Statistics of the Foreign Trade of India, March 1964,* vols. 1, 2 (New Delhi, 1963 and 1964).
4. Computed from data in *Yearbook, 1965* of the *Far Eastern Economic Review,* January, 1966, table 4, p. 147.
5. E. L. Wheelwright, *Industrialization in Malaysia* (Melbourne: Melbourne University Press, 1965), p. 89.
6. Throughout this chapter, 4.75 Indian rupees equal one United States

dollar. Even the figures in Table 9.6, though released after devaluation of the Indian currency, should be converted into United States dollars at the same rate.

7. United Nations, *Yearbook of International Trade Statistics, 1963* and *Yearbook of International Trade Statistics, 1964* (1965 and 1966); Government of India, *Monthly Statistics . . . March 1963*, vols. 1, 2, and *Monthly Statistics . . . March 1964*, vols. 1, 2.

8. P. Lamartine Yates, *Forty Years of Foreign Trade* (London: Allen and Unwin, 1959).

9. Government of India, Planning Commission, *Third Five-Year Plan* (New Delhi, 1961). The Third Plan was implemented by the Government of India during the five years from 1961/62 to 1965/66. Total investment in the public and the private sectors was about IRs113,700 million. In comparison with the planned growth rate in national income of 5.5 percent per annum, actual achievement was around 4.4 percent per year during the first four years of the Third Plan.

10. Government of India, Planning Commission, *Fourth Five-Year Plan: A Draft Outline* (New Delhi, 1966), p. 98. The Fourth Five-Year Plan has not so far been implemented. Since the end of the Third Five-Year Plan in 1965/66, annual plans have been framed and implemented. (These annual plan documents have been published by the Government of India, Planning Commission, Delhi.) The present trends of thinking at the official level indicate that the Fourth Five-Year Plan may be implemented from the year 1969/70.

11. India's present classification of industries differs moderately from the one adopted by the SITC, and for comparative purposes a three-digit commodity classification similar to the latter has been adopted in this paper.

12. The majority of countries of the ECAFE region still report in the Standard International Trade Classification, Original (SITCO), but some report in the Standard International Trade Classification, Revised (SITCR). The difference between SITCO and SITCR is mainly in manufacturing categories. Some countries still use the former; most have adopted the latter. India shifted (approximately) to SITCR in 1965. In the SITCO, there are 150 3-digit commodities and in the SITCR, 177. The exports of the following countries reporting in SITCO were recorded in 3-digit commodities as follows: Afghanistan, 10; Brunei, 16; Burma, 20; Ceylon, 16; Indonesia, 23; North Borneo, 23; Sarawak, 11; Thailand, 31. The exports of the countries reporting in the SITCR were recorded in 3-digit commodities as follows: Australia, 45; South Korea, 17; Pakistan, 34; the Philippines, 19; New Zealand, 24; and Japan, 59. Although Cambodia, Iran, and South Vietnam do not report in either SITCO or SITCR, the exports may be classified under the 3-digit SITCO as follows: Cambodia, 10; Iran, 17; and South Vietnam, 15. It should be clear from this that India's exports are more diversified than those of any other ECAFE country. (These counts are based on the information available in United Nations, *International Trade Statistics, 1963* and *International*

Trade Statistics, 1964, and in Government of India, *Monthly Statistics . . . March 1963*, vols. 1, 2, and *Monthly Statistics . . . March 1964*, vols. 1, 2.)

13. Government of India, Central Statistical Organization, *Estimates of National Product, 1960/61 to 1966/67* (New Delhi, 1967), and *Monthly Statistics of Production of Selected Industries in India*, 17, nos. 1–12 (1965); Government of India, Ministry of Food and Agriculture, *Agricultural Situation in India*, 20, nos. 1–12 (New Delhi, 1965/66).

14. The average value of India's cotton textile exports to the ECAFE region for the years 1950/51 and 1951/52 amounted to IRs496 million. By 1965/66, they had declined steeply to IRs155 million—a loss of IRs341 million worth of cotton textiles alone. (Government of India, Department of Commercial Intelligence and Statistics, *Accounts Relating to the Foreign Sea and Air-borne Trade Navigation of India*, March, 1951, and March, 1952, and *Monthly Statistics of the Foreign Trade of India, March 1966*, vols. 1, 2 [New Delhi, 1966].)

15. The international organization measures essential to a policy of trade expansion will be discussed in the next section.

16. The High Authority of the European Coal and Steel Community (ECSC) also predicts that India will be in a position to export 31 million metric tons of iron ore by 1972. In 1965, Japan imported 34 million metric tons of iron ore, and this demand is expected to rise to 57 million metric tons by 1970, an increase of 23 million metric tons (G. E. Pearson, "India Second," *Far Eastern Economic Review,* 51, no. 9 [1966]: 423).

17. ECAFE, "Approaches to Regional Harmonization of National Development Plans in Asia and the Far East," *Economic Bulletin for Asia and the Far East,* 11, no. 3 (1964): table 1, p. 35.

18. Government of India, Ministry of Commerce and Industry (Director, Commercial Publicity), *India's Trade Agreements with Other Countries* (New Delhi, 1949).

19. *Ibid.* (1960).

20. *Ibid.* (1955 and 1962).

21. Sunanda Sen, *India's Bilateral Payments and Trade Agreements* (Calcutta: J. N. Basu and Co., 1965), tables 5.23 and 5.24, pp. 99–100.

22. ECAFE, "Approaches to Regional Harmonization," pp. 33–81. See also D. T. Lakdawala, "Trends in Regional Cooperation in Asia," in *South Asia Pacific Crisis*, ed. Margaret Grant (New York: Dodd, Meade and Co., 1964), pp. 90–100.

23. J. B. Condliffe, *The Development of Australia* (London: Collier-Macmillan, 1964), p. 78. Cf. Leslie Parker, "The Mining Scene," in *The Financial Times* (London), September 3, 1968, p. 17.

24. Condliffe, *Development of Australia*, p. 123.

25. Alex Hunter, "Introduction," in *The Economics of Australian Industry: Studies in Environment and Structure*, ed. Alex Hunter (Melbourne, 1963), quoted in Condliffe, *Development of Australia*, p. 116.

26. ECAFE, *Economic Survey of Asia and the Far East, 1957*, 8, no. 4 (1958): 206, and *Economic Survey of Asia and the Far East, 1965*, 16,

no. 4 (1966): 294. It should be noted that the exchange rate for the 1954 figures was 15.5 Taiwanese dollars to the United States dollar.

27. H. B. Chenery, "Patterns of Industrial Growth," *American Economic Review,* 50, no. 4 (1960): 638.

28. Correspondents of *The Economist, Consider Japan* (London: Gerald Duckworth and Co., 1963), pp. 50–57.

COMMENT ON CHAPTER 9

GERARDO P. SICAT

Although India has been an exporter of manufactured products to the Southeast Asian countries and an importer of raw materials from them, the volume of this trade is rather small. Little or no expansion of exports from India to these countries has occurred in recent years. One wonders whether the optimistic projections of India's trade in Chapter 9 can be realized.

India's development strategy provides one important reason why her export trade has not helped to promote more rapid development. (Exports are only 5 percent of national income according to Professor Lakdawala and Dr. Patil.) India has been implementing an import-substitution policy for development, coupled with many measures that have either discouraged export expansion or given it insignificant attention. The assertion that, as a large country, India may depend on her "large" domestic market for manufactures is belied by the fact that many of India's industries have large excess capacities and inefficient cost positions. Would exposure to world competitive forces through export promotion make at least some of these industries healthier? Moreover, India's low per capita income produces too little demand to support many of the current industries encouraged by contrived import substitution. A large population is not the same as a large domestic market. Perhaps Professor Nurul Islam's discussion of Pakistan's industries describes in some measure the conditions in India's industries as well. However, India does not have an export-bonus scheme, so her industries may be worse off than Pakistan's.

It may still be too early to know the extent to which the devaluation of 1966 will help India's exports and economy, but this is a step in the right direction. Foreign-exchange controls in India may have seriously misallocated India's scarce resources to the wrong kinds of industries.

In Turkey, according to a recent study, foreign-exchange controls have reduced the incentives for exporting in the manufacturing sector because of the profitability of producing for the home market.[1] This same pattern may be valid for many other countries, including India.

India's prospects for trade with other countries in the Southeast Asian region and in the world at large depend more on her internal and external economic policies than on plans for harmonization of national development plans and bilateral arrangements with other countries. Other things elsewhere remaining the same, how can India expand her exports? Professor Lakdawala and Dr. Patil indicate that a reallocation of investment resources within the Indian plan will be necessary in order to develop certain export industries, such as exploiting iron-ore deposits for export. The more fundamental answer lies in shifting to policies that pay greater attention to the allocative power of the price mechanism (e.g., by pricing scarce resources properly) and to appropriate incentives to promote exports.

NOTE

1. Ann O. Krueger, "Costs of Exchange Control: The Turkish Case," *Journal of Political Economy,* 74, no. 5 (1966): 466–80.

COMMENT ON PART III

DOUGLAS S. PAAUW

A general discussant should search for some basis for comparative analysis. This is very difficult in the case of the chapters at hand. In general, they attempt to treat a common set of problems, but the underlying economics of the situations studied are very different. Since this section focuses on export performance, I restrict my comments to this subject, overlooking much in these studies on other subjects—particularly the considerable discussion, in some, of the import side of foreign trade.

The proposition that the economies of the four countries (Hong Kong, the Philippines, Malaysia, and India) are very different requires elaboration. First, the central characteristic under study (export relationships) shows extreme variation among these countries. Malaysia and Hong Kong are two of the world's most export-oriented developing economies, while India is one of the least export-oriented —with the Philippines lying somewhere in between these extremes.

Second, the basic structures of these developing economies vary considerably. To clarify these differences, I employ the taxonomic approach developed by the National Planning Association's research teams in a recent Southeast Asian Research project, in which the Philippines and Malaysia are considered open, dualistic economies with highly significant relationships between their openness and their dualism. These economies are open in the sense of showing high ratios of both exports and imports to total output. In a more fundamental sense, foreign trade plays an important role in the interplay of the dualistic domestic sectors: agriculture and industry. Integration between these domestic sectors depends, to an important extent, upon the performance of the foreign-trade sector.

The open, dualistic economy model appears to be typical of most developing economies. Two economies discussed in this section—Hong Kong and India—do not fit this model, however. At one extreme, Hong Kong represents an economy with a high degree of openness but lacking the typical problem of dualism. Foreign trade is based upon an industrial sector, with its related service activities, but there is no massive agricultural sector with its independent pattern of economic dynamics.

At the other end of the spectrum is India, which exhibits domestic dualism between agriculture and industry to an extreme degree. Domestic dualism is not significantly ameliorated by foreign trade, since the Indian economy shows very low ratios of exports and imports to total output. Hence, we consider the Indian economy to be "closed" or non-trade-oriented.

There is, of course, a fundamental difference between India and the three other countries under consideration. India is a giant with a great variety of natural resources, while the others are comparatively small in size with less variety in resources. India can look forward to a widely diversified pattern of production, with minimum dependence on foreign trade. The others, in varying degrees, will always rely heavily upon trade if their societies are to enjoy a diversified pattern of consumption. This contrast, of course, abstracts from inevitable stresses and strains during the transitional development period when the imported component of development investment is, and will continue to be, high in all these countries, including India.

Such an approach helps us to evaluate the rather striking differences in results reached in the empirical studies under discussion. We can now compare export performance among economies whose economic structures show marked differences, reflected through the role of exports in both the development process and in national development strategies.

In the simplest case—the one-sector model of Hong Kong—the economy's development dynamics are completely tied up with the export sector. Since there is no large agricultural sector on which industry can rely for raw materials, finance, or market outlets, it is essential that the evolving industrial sector maintain and strengthen its external economic relationships. Exports make up a very high share of total output, as we would expect. The export sector has thrived during the postwar period, and exports and domestic industry have become increasingly linked. Between 1946 and 1965, exports grew at an average rate of 14 percent per year. Between 1956 and 1965, a decade of transition from an entrepôt economy, exports have grown at an average rate of something like 10 percent a year. This is a very impressive achievement.

In our frame of reference, this experience stands out as an unusual pattern of export development. Professor Chou describes this achievement as a process of very careful adaptation to specialized markets in developed countries. Special advantages and unique conditions made this success possible: among them were almost unlimited importation of skills; sophisticated entrepreneurship (which evolved for special reasons); and easy access to foreign capital. A significant feature of the Hong Kong one-sector pattern is that the industrial sector itself provides exports that feed industrialization. Industrial exports have earned foreign exchange to finance imported capital goods and raw materials for industrial expansion. The unusual feature of this model is that the industrial sector earns a substantial part of the foreign resources needed to accommodate import substitution and industrial growth. Singapore is another example of this rare phenomenon.

The Philippines and Malaysia[1] combine openness with the problem of dualism. A fundamental difference from the preceding case is the presence of a traditional, backward, relatively stagnant agricultural sector which has been, and continues to be, the dominant source of the economy's relatively high level of export earnings. As we would expect, the export performance of these two countries shows striking differences from that of the unique one-sector economy of Hong Kong. Philippine export performance, according to Dean Castro, has been respectable, showing an average annual growth rate of 5.8 percent for the period 1950 to 1965. The ratio of exports to total output (approximately 20 percent) has been maintained during this period. This is, indeed, a respectable achievement, compared to the export performance of most developing countries.

The Philippine pattern of development has been to maintain and accelerate traditional agricultural exports to feed "import-dependent import substitution" (a term borrowed from Professor Sicat). Little export diversification has occurred, and the Hong Kong phenomenon of ultrasensitivity to new export opportunities has not appeared. Import substitution has not yet had a significant effect on export diversification, since new industries have tended to be competitive with those in scores of other developing countries, especially among the similarly structured economies of the Philippines' ECAFE neighbors.

Nevertheless, the Philippine export sector has been successfully fulfilling its role of feeding industrialization of the import-dependent type. Imports of investment and industrial intermediate goods have increased very rapidly, but the Philippines has not experienced recurrent balance-of-payments crises (as have India and other weak export economies), despite very moderate levels of capital inflow over the past decade. Both exports and imports have grown at a rate close to that for GNP. Professor Castro ascribes the continued buoyancy of traditional exports and of a few new ones to fairly positive export incentives inherent in the whole constellation of postwar external and domestic economic policies.

In the Philippines, the triangular pattern of trade that allows agricultural exports to feed industrialization involves a large part of total output—perhaps as much as 10 percent. This pattern appears to be typical of the early stages of development in the open, dualistic economy. Its success depends on the capability of maintaining a high level of agricultural exports until industrial development can generate adequate thrust of its own. The Philippines seems to be in the middle of this stage during which agricultural exports accommodate import substitution. The studies by Professor Lim and by Mrs. Suparb and Mr. Yune suggest that Malaysia and Thailand are just beginning to enter this stage. Dr. Sun's chapter indicates, however, that Taiwan has almost traversed this stage and is entering a new phase in which industry itself is beginning to provide export earnings to feed its own expansion. Dr. Sun describes a newly evolving pattern of foreign-market-oriented import substitution, leading increasingly towards export diversification.

The Malaysian pattern of development is roughly similar to that of the Philippines, but with somewhat less favorable conditions. As Professor Lim indicates, exports have had much to do with the growth of output during most of the period he reviews. Growth of exports has become increasingly sluggish, however, and domestic expansion programs to take up the slack are beginning to generate balance-of-payments problems. Lim notes a falling trend in the export ratio (although I doubt that this would be reflected in a long-term study going back to the 1920's). He also observes an extreme degree of specialization in a very few primary export products and an unfortunate trend in prices of Malaysia's dominant export, rubber. One conclusion seems stronger for Malaysia than for the Philippines: unless export diversification occurs, Malaysia's open, dualistic pattern of development appears likely to falter. Import-dependent import substitution may very soon produce foreign-exchange bottlenecks similar to those which have plagued development and yielded very low growth rates in many Latin American economies.

India's case takes on considerable significance against this backdrop of radically different economies pursuing development strategies quite alien to India's. I have chosen to view the study by Lakdawala and Patil in the context of India's total export performance, as we have viewed the export performance of the other countries. This requires some reference to data not presented in the paper.

It is well known that India has a very low ratio of exports to total output, perhaps the world's lowest. Lim gives the 1965 ratio of gross export earnings to GDP as .04. Moreover, the low Indian ratio has been falling over the postwar period, as exports have grown more slowly than output. An ECAFE study estimates the postwar growth rate of exports at 2.7 percent per year and employs this figure for long-term projections of the Indian economy.[2] Thus, the target cited by Lakdawala and Patil for the Fourth Plan (1965/66 to 1970/71) of increasing exports to less-developed ECAFE countries by 51 percent (an annual rate of increase of 9.6 percent—see Chapter 9, Table 9.7) would appear to be extremely unrealistic. Lakdawala and Patil obviously have doubts about the feasibility of this target themselves, stressing that the details of the aggregate export target appear not to have been worked out.

In the broader view, India's sluggish export performance reflects the nonexport orientation of a large, diversifying economy. The Indian export sector has not been relied upon significantly to accommodate import substitution and industrialization, thus contrasting with the other three countries discussed. Aggressive import substitution, aimed at a large domestic market, appears to have produced a pattern of growth inconsistent with export expansion. Unlike the other cases under consideration, Indian postwar development has produced enormous balance-of-payments gaps, because the economy has failed to generate foreign exchange to feed industrialization. The Indian strategy has been to fill these gaps by stressing external assistance rather than export promotion. Lakdawala and Patil report, however, that an effort is being made to reverse this situation through export-expansion policies during the Fourth Plan period.

NOTES

1. Thailand and Taiwan, discussed in Part II, also belong in this category of open, dualistic economies.
2. ECAFE, *Review of Long-Term Economic Projections for Selected Countries in the ECAFE Region,* Development Programming Techniques, series no. 5 (1964), pp. 137–39.

IV

Inflation
and Asian Trade

CHAPTER 10

THE IMPACT OF IMPORT AND EXCHANGE CONTROLS AND BILATERAL TRADE AGREEMENTS ON TRADE AND PRODUCTION IN CEYLON

H. N. S. KARUNATILAKE

The impact of exchange and quantitative controls on trade and production in a less-developed economy like Ceylon's is significantly different from the impact of such restrictions on a more advanced country. Both types of countries might introduce trade controls with common objectives in view—e.g., for balance-of-payments reasons—yet the long-term effects may not be the same. A more advanced country might temporarily use restrictive measures to arrest a loss of external assets or to strengthen the exchange rate. In a developing economy, exchange and import controls, initially introduced as temporary measures, may become permanent features; and as long as a very rapid rate of economic development is desired, they may have to remain permanent features of the process of development.

Most developing countries have used tariffs and import and exchange controls to protect domestic markets from foreign goods. New manufacturing industries have been able to establish themselves because of the protection afforded. A general survey of the industrialization of less-developed countries has shown that in the preindustrial stage trade tends to be fully multilateral and there are very few restrictions. As development gathers momentum, there is an increasing tendency to raise tariffs and to introduce import restrictions. As Ceylon's experience will illustrate, most of these restrictions tend to remain in force for a very long time, mainly because in the early phases of industrial growth new industries continue to depend heavily on protection.

THE REGIONAL PATTERN
OF TRADE

Table 10.1 shows the respective shares of Ceylon's import and export trade with the major regional blocs. Although India and Pakistan are shown separately in the table, they are also included in the countries within the sterling area. Ceylon's trade with India and Pakistan has been one-sided. Ceylon does not export very much to either of these two countries, but the volume of imports from each of them, particularly from India, has been considerable.

A significant feature of the changing pattern of trade has been the gradual decline in the proportions of trade between Ceylon and her traditional trading partners of the sterling and dollar areas.

The category that seems to have shown the least variation has been the volume of trade with the OEEC countries, where the decline over the period 1951 to 1965 has been approximately 8 percent.

IMPORT AND EXCHANGE CONTROLS

The legal sanction for import control in Ceylon before 1950 was the Defense (Control of Exports) and Defense (Control of Imports) Regulations of World War II.[1] Thereafter, import controls were functioning under provisions in the Import and Export Control (Continuation) Act No. 27 of 1950. By means of licenses and quotas, the controls limited and prohibited both imports and exports. In addition, conditions were laid down regarding the payment of certain minimum prices by the exporter to the local producer, or by the overseas buyer to the exporter, which had to be duly satisfied before a license to export could be issued.

In September, 1950, the government decided that export and import control should continue, even though the wartime necessities that had brought these regulations into existence were no longer present. One of the primary objectives of the Import and Export Control (Continuation) Act No. 27 of 1950 was the gradual but steady Ceylonization of the import and export trade.[2] The 1950 act was superseded by the Imports and Exports Control Act of September, 1954. The purpose of the latter act was to enforce control over exports and imports, including destinational control and the safe-

TABLE 10.1—Ceylon's trade with selected areas, 1950–65
(Percent)

Area	1950	1951	1952	1953	1954	1955	1956	1957	1958	1959	1960	1961	1962	1963	1964	1965
Sterling area	59.44	63.2	63.6	58.6	60.7	59.7	56.7	59.4	58.2	56.3	56.4	54.5	54.2	51.9	48.1	47.1
Dollar area	17.14	11.5	12.4	7.8	8.7	11.0	9.4	9.2	9.1	12.6	10.3	10.6	9.5	8.9	9.1	8.8
India and Pakistan	10.31	9.9	10.0	8.4	9.0	10.4	9.0	9.0	7.9	8.5	8.8	8.6	8.4	7.6	6.7	4.8
OECD countries	23.41	42.3	41.8	38.0	37.9	38.9	40.6	40.0	43.6	41.4	40.8	38.7	39.0	37.8	35.5	34.1
Bilateral-accounts countries	0.0	0.0	0.0	14.6	12.1	5.9	9.4	0.9	6.1	6.7	7.9	9.3	13.3	14.5	17.1	17.3

Sources: Compiled from the exchange control records (unpublished) of the Central Bank of Ceylon. Figures for the bilateral-accounts countries for the years 1953–56 have been worked out on the basis of data available in the Ceylon customs returns for these years.

guarding of government monopolies of imports and exports; to fix quality standards for export products; to aid the Ceylonization of the export and import trade; and to levy fees for the issue of licenses.

Along with import control, further restrictions were applied on trade and payments through exchange control. The initial exchange control of September, 1939, was partial. It applied only to transactions between Ceylon and the countries outside the sterling area. In June, 1948, exchange control was extended to transactions between Ceylon and countries in the sterling area as well. In 1950 the government department that had previously administered exchange control was absorbed by the Central Bank of Ceylon, which took over the control functions. During the first years after the war and well into the 1950's, regulations were not stringent.[3]

RECENT METHODS OF
IMPORT CONTROL

In 1959 and 1960, the government examined the relative advantages of tariffs and of quantitative methods of import control and decided to regulate imports by monetary methods and by tariffs. (Net balance-of-payments data are given in Table 10.2.) There did not appear to be a compelling need for a comprehensive scheme of import control. To restrict imports, the Central Bank increased the bank rate, in August, 1960, from 2½ percent to 4 percent and raised statutory reserve requirements from 10 percent to 12 percent. Next, in the same month, the government increased customs duties in order to restrict imports. Sharply higher import duties intended both to reduce imports and to augment government revenue were imposed on a variety of imported goods, such as motor vehicles, petroleum, textiles, tobacco, cigarettes, and watches. Higher rates of export duties were imposed on cinnamon, coir fiber, and papain. On the exchange-control side, foreign exchange for foreign travel, study abroad, and capital transfers was restricted.

The effect of these measures was not immediately felt. Monetary methods of import control were introduced at a time when import-control policy was not comprehensive, and they had to be supplemented later by other measures.

The reduction in import volume was not evenly distributed. The fall was most severe in the consumer-goods category, which declined by

TABLE 10.2—Surplus or deficit in Ceylon's balance of payments, net overall position in bilateral accounts, and terms of trade, 1950–65

	1950	1951	1952	1953	1954	1955	1956	1957	1958	1959	1960	1961	1962	1963	1964	1965
Surplus or deficit in the balance of payments (million CeyRs)	137	89	− 446	− 158	306	323	82	− 195	− 153	− 208	− 220	− 94	− 140	− 168	− 160	59
Net overall position of Ceylon's bilateral accounts (million CeyRs)	0.0	0.0	0.0	4.7	9.3	30.9	63.8	90.2	− 14.4	11.7	26.5	− 5.2	12.7	− 34.2	− 51.5	31.1
Terms of trade[a]	114	108	84	86	103	112	104	94	100	102	102	94	98	89	86	88

[a] $\dfrac{\text{Export Price Index}}{\text{Import Price Index}} \times 100.$

Source: Central Bank of Ceylon, *Annual Reports*, 1950–65.

25.2 percent as compared with 1960. Capital-goods imports, on the other hand, fell by 12.8 percent and intermediate goods by 2.5 percent. By the end of 1961 the country reached a point at which, unless either export earnings rose or external liabilities were increased even further, Ceylon would continue to experience severe pressures on her external reserves. Ceylon's external assets at the end of 1961 amounted to CeyRs533 million (CeyRl = 21 United States cents) representing 25.8 percent of the year's import payments inclusive of invisibles—a low amount considering future pressures on imports which would arise out of development needs and the likelihood of further adverse fluctuations in export earnings.

As the program of development gathered momentum (for changes in GNP, see Table 10.3) the need for capital goods and raw materials rose, resulting in further pressure on the balance of payments. In 1961, therefore, the position was that restriction of nonessential imports would have to continue for a long time. Scarcities of various kinds had emerged which, though unintended, hindered economic activity.

There is no doubt that restrictions for balance-of-payments reasons stimulated the establishment of domestic enterprises producing import substitutes. By 1961, the emphasis on import-control policy had shifted from Ceylonization to a more positive object of controlling imports in order to conserve foreign-exchange resources and to stimulate investment.

The external deficit continued to be a serious problem in 1962. In October, it was decided to subject all items, other than five categories of essentials, to individual licensing procedures. The exempted categories were foodstuffs, petroleum, fuel, fertilizers, and drugs.

The cumulative effect of import restrictions and higher duties was pronounced in 1963: prices rose generally and there were severe shortages of some imports. The price rises and shortages were especially harmful because many new industries had just commenced production and had not yet established themselves as going concerns. In the five-year period preceding 1961, the pressure on the domestic price level had eased considerably. There was no substantial restriction on import of goods, and so the impact of the successive budgetary deficits[4] could be siphoned away in the financing of a higher level of imports—at the expense, of course, of the country's external reserves. After 1961, with comprehensive controls on imports, that safety

TABLE 10.3—Ceylon's GNP at factor cost, 1950–65

	1950	1951	1952	1953	1954	1955	1956	1957	1958	1959	1960	1961	1962	1963	1964	1965
GNP at current factor-cost prices, money terms (million CeyRs)	3,524	4,654	4,566	4,560	4,824	5,292	5,152	5,251	5,579	5,854	6,080	6,142	6,418	6,716	7,104	7,388
Percentage change	16.9	32.1	– 1.9	– 0.1	5.8	9.7	– 2.7	1.9	6.2	4.9	3.9	1.0	4.5	4.7	5.8	4.0
GNP at constant (1959) factor-cost prices, real terms (million CeyRs)	4,446	4,704	5,066	4,904	5,002	5,407	5,380	5,418	5,640	5,854	6,066	6,240	6,472	6,599	6,888	7,024
Percentage change	11.4	5.8	7.7	– 3.2	2.0	8.1	– 0.5	0.7	4.1	3.8	3.6	2.9	3.7	2.0	4.4	2.0

Source: Central Bank of Ceylon, *Annual Reports*, 1950–65.

valve was no longer present, and budget deficits had a direct impact on the domestic price level.

By 1964, it was clear that, for Ceylon's economic growth, imports of raw materials and capital goods must increase; any hindrance in obtaining these supplies would jeopardize the country's development.

During 1964 and 1965, there was a positive drive towards import substitution. Industrial raw materials in Ceylon were limited in quantity and types however, and large-scale industrial development could not be sustained without imported raw materials.

Ceylon's foreign-exchange outlays on imported raw materials are inevitably high, and so import substitution in the field of manufactures cannot substantially relieve Ceylon's external-payments problem, but higher domestic production of agricultural commodities such as rice and sugar would immediately result in reduced import charges. These items constitute more than one-third of total imports.

THE EFFECT OF TRADE CONTROLS
ON THE COMPOSITION OF
CEYLON'S IMPORTS

The distribution of imports between consumer goods, intermediate goods, and capital goods in 1950 (as shown in Table 10.4) broadly reflects the pattern of imports that prevailed in the period after the war. In 1950, consumer goods were 59.4 percent of total imports, capital goods were 22.8 percent, and intermediate goods, 17.8 percent. In 1951 and 1952, because of relaxation in import controls, the volume of consumer-goods imports, mainly food, drink, and tobacco, increased slightly. After 1955, the percentage of consumer-goods imports decreased and fluctuated only moderately. The percentage of capital goods imported rose moderately to 1958 and declined thereafter. Attempts were being made, especially during the early years, to increase public-sector investment.

The proportion of capital-goods imports has been subject to marked fluctuations between 1951 and 1965. In 1959 and after, there was a marked fall in the proportion of capital goods, not because of an absolute fall in their volume, but because of an increase in the proportion of consumer goods imported. There have been no deliberate restrictions at any time on the import of capital goods, but other categories of imports have frequently been brought under controls.

TABLE 10.4—Ceylon's imports by major categories, 1950–65
(Percentage of total imports)

Category	1950	1951	1952	1953	1954	1955	1956	1957	1958	1959	1960	1961	1962	1963	1964	1965
Consumer goods	59.4	59.7	60.2	60.8	58.3	54.1	56.0	51.9	55.0	60.0	61.0	57.1	54.6	52.4	63.9	52.8
Food, drink, and tobacco	45.2	44.6	46.4	49.5	47.5	42.8	43.2	40.8	41.6	39.9	38.4	39.5	38.0	42.2	51.0	41.0
Textiles	11.6	11.9	10.5	8.5	8.9	8.9	9.6	8.1	9.3	8.9	10.0	10.1	9.0	5.6	8.4	7.3
Other consumer goods	2.6	3.1	3.3	2.8	1.9	2.4	3.3	3.0	4.0	11.2	12.6	7.5	7.7	4.6	4.6	4.6
Intermediate goods	17.8	17.5	17.0	16.5	17.6	16.4	14.2	19.3	14.1	19.8	20.3	22.5	24.6	25.0	20.1	28.1
Capital goods	22.8	22.8	22.8	22.7	24.1	29.5	29.8	28.8	30.9	19.4	18.1	19.9	20.3	21.7	15.4	17.7

Note: for the years 1959–65 the percentages for consumer, intermediate, and capital goods do not add up to 100 because of a residual figure which accounts for unclassified imports.

Source: Central Bank of Ceylon, *Annual Reports*, 1950–65.

The most consistent upward trend has been in imports of intermediate goods—mainly raw materials for local industries. Raw-material imports (included here) rose sharply after 1960, when import controls were intensified on consumer goods. It was then that a large number of industries in the private sector, requiring such imports, started up production.

TYPES OF BILATERAL
TRADE ARRANGEMENTS

Between 1951 and 1965, Ceylon entered into trade and payments agreements with twenty-four countries. The percentage share of trade with bilateral-accounts countries increased steadily after 1957, and many bilateral trade agreements were concluded between 1958 and 1964. Most agreements with China, the Soviet Union, and the East European countries were strictly bilateral. Agreements concluded with other countries—such as Australia, Austria, and Japan—were far more flexible. (Balance-of-payments data by countries and regions are given in Table 10.5.)

From the payments point of view, trade and payments agreements can be grouped into two categories: comprehensive or fully compensatory arrangements and limited-payments agreements. The distinctive feature of the fully compensatory arrangements is that the trade between the two partners is on the basis of equality and balance. All payments for imports of goods and services are made in Ceylon rupees through clearing accounts maintained at the respective central banks. As long as the agreement is in force, the rupee balances in the central clearing accounts are not convertible into foreign exchange. At the termination of an agreement, the balance may be settled by the movement of goods during a period ranging from six months to one year. If this arrangement fails, the balance is liquidated in some other agreed-on way. The limited-payments agreements are more conventional in character. Only payments for specified exports and imports are made through the rupee accounts. Most of Ceylon's bilateral agreements with the East European countries are of the second type.

Ceylon was not the first country to enter into bilateral trade agreements. For instance, in the postwar period, in order to promote exports, India entered into several bilateral agreements. The object was to supplement dwindling foreign-exchange reserves by finding new markets. Some countries of Southeast Asia were driven to seek

TABLE 10.5—Ceylon's balance of payments: net position, 1950–65
(Million CeyRs)

	1950	1951	1952	1953	1954	1955	1956	1957	1958	1959	1960	1961	1962	1963	1964	1965
Dollar area	297.2	141.7	8.7	88.3	141.7	203.4	181.0	181.9	178.9	192.3	206.1	213.6	199.7	170.0	162.6	151.5
United Kingdom	75.8	62.7	− 81.1	− 38.9	123.5	44.3	− 61.6	− 176.9	− 86.6	− 165.3	− 153.8	− 63.2	− 58.1	39.3	47.4	71.8
India	− 180.6	− 246.5a	− 236.4a	− 226.4a	− 190.6a	− 245.4a	− 211.1a	− 243.9a	− 232.1a	− 239.7	− 242.7a	− 202.0a	− 152.5a	− 161.1a	− 158.3	− 110.1
Other sterling area	− 147.9	− 142.5	− 209.8	− 67.2	158.3	191.8	140.1	83.2	166.4	85.2	60.4	36.4	− 43.1	− 5.3	− 8.6	16.4
Other OECD countries in Europe	51.1	175.8	81.4	11.5	8.5	54.4	− 13.1	− 79.6	− 23.2	− 6.0	− 68.4	− 29.8	− 46.5	− 47.0	− 73.9	− 95.3
Communist China	0.0	0.0	0.0	0.0	0.0	0.0	0.0	0.0	0.0	0.0	0.0	0.0	0.0	0.0	− 27.1	47.5
Soviet area	0.0	0.0	0.0	0.0	0.0	0.0	0.0	0.0	0.0	0.0	0.0	0.0	0.0	0.0	− 41.1	14.0
Other countries	41.2	125.0	32.7	11.2	61.6	69.1	39.8	36.3	− 149.6	− 43.3	− 11.3	− 30.4	− 23.5	− 142.3	− 48.6	− 48.5

a Includes Pakistan.
Source: Central Bank of Ceylon, *Annual Reports*, 1950–65.

markets in nontraditional areas because they found it increasingly difficult to sell products in the usual Western markets. Rubber was a major export of several of these countries, and synthetic rubber presented a severe threat to the natural-rubber industry soon after the Korean War. Since the cost of production of manmade rubber is lower than that of the natural product, the latter could compete only if appreciable cuts were made in selling price. The opening of Eastern markets enabled a few producing countries—first Ceylon and then Indonesia and Malaysia—to offset the impact of synthetic rubber on world prices by selling an increasing proportion of their rubber output to China and the East European countries.

THE TRADE AND PAYMENTS
AGREEMENT WITH CHINA

One of the earliest agreements to ensure a market for natural rubber was the trade agreement of December, 1952, between Ceylon and China.[5] According to this agreement, Ceylon was to supply China with 50,000 metric tons of rubber annually at an average f.o.b. price of CeyRs1.75 per pound.[6] In return, China was to supply 270,000 metric tons of rice per year at £54 per ton for five years. This was essentially a barter arrangement, with settlement of any residual balance in sterling. It operated with two accounts, A and B. Account A was for trade payments only and was to be settled annually primarily in goods. Account B was for the payment of all other transactions, such as freight, insurance, and other invisibles, with the balance at the end of a calendar year to be settled in sterling. This agreement contained several features not commonly found in other bilateral agreements. It mentioned specific quantities of goods to be traded at agreed or predetermined prices. It was valid for five years, whereas most other agreements were valid for only one to two years. Exports and imports were to balance each other very closely.

Under this agreement, the rubber industry of Ceylon was assured of a market for about 50 percent of its total output—or its entire normal output of sheet rubber—at prices appreciably higher than world prices. World-market price was falling, not only because of synthetic rubber, but because the huge stockpiles of rubber built up by the United States and other countries during the Korean War had caused reduced buying and a fall in the price of natural rubber afterwards.

Ceylon, only the fourth-largest rubber producer, had a smaller share of the Western market than her Southeast Asian competitors.

In 1952, China paid a price of 36 Ceylon cents per pound over the Singapore price for rubber, which gave Ceylon CeyRs29 million more in the first year than if it had sold to other buyers. Trade with China continued to expand. The value of rice imports rose from CeyRs28 million in 1953 to CeyRs203 million in 1958. The 132 million pounds of rubber exported to China in 1953 was twice the amount exported in 1952 and was 60.8 percent of total rubber exports, as compared to 31.7 percent in 1952. In 1953, Ceylon earned an estimated CeyRs95 million, or 39.1 percent, more in foreign exchange than it would have received had it sold its rubber to the customary sources at prevailing world prices.[7]

The five-year trade agreement between Ceylon and China expired in December, 1957; a new five-year trade and payments agreement came into force on January 1, 1958.[8] In this agreement Ceylon undertook to export approximately 30,000 metric tons of rubber and other commodities to the value of CeyRs95 million per year, and China undertook to export annually approximately 200,000 metric tons of rice.[9] The prices of commodities to be exported and imported were world-market prices. Provision was also made in the agreement for additional sales or purchases of rice, rubber, and other products to the value of CeyRs70 million. In an economic-aid agreement, which was concluded simultaneously, China agreed to grant Ceylon economic aid in commodities for a period of five years from January, 1958 on, to the value of CeyRs15 million (at world market prices) annually—an offer made in lieu of the premium prices in the first agreement, and partly for the purpose of meeting the cost of Ceylon's subsidies in the rubber-replanting program. China's assistance, whatever its motives, has contributed to the rehabilitation of an industry that was becoming less efficient than that of Ceylon's strongest competitor, Malaysia.

In Ceylon, 35 percent of the rubber is produced by smallholders—those who cultivate less than ten acres. Almost half-a-million people are directly or indirectly dependent on these small holdings. Because the average cost of production of smallholders was about a fifth higher than that of the large producer (the plantation owner), the price fall after the Korean War boom was disastrous to them. One of the factors that drove the government to trade with China was the fear of domestic political instability resulting from a slump in the rubber industry.

Over a twelve-year period, 1953–64, the cumulative favorable balance from the trade with China was CeyRs380 million, the bulk of which was settled by China in sterling, with only a part in goods outside the agreement. In this way, trade with China provided foreign exchange that has been used by Ceylon to make purchases in Western markets.[10]

OTHER BILATERAL TRADE
AGREEMENTS

One of the most important agreements concluded with countries not in the Sino-Soviet bloc was that with Burma. The first trade agreement was signed in September, 1953, and came into effect in January, 1954. In the period 1954–57, Ceylon was expected to purchase 260,000 long tons of rice although commodities to be purchased by Burma from Ceylon were not specified in the agreement. The agreement has been renewed at four-year intervals, with modification of quantities, of commodities involved, and (most frequently) of prices.

This trade agreement does not provide for complete compensation between exports and imports. Ceylon's exports to Burma have been only 10 percent of total imports from that country, and the deficit in balance of trade has had to be settled in sterling or other acceptable currency. The agreement has not substantially affected the normal pattern and direction of Ceylon's trade. Since the end of the war Burma has been one of Ceylon's principal suppliers of rice. The agreement has also enabled Ceylon to find a market in Burma for some of its products such as coconut oil, desiccated coconut, and tea, which Burma had previously imported only in very small quantities.

Another important trade agreement is that with India. For a long time, Ceylon has had a deficit with India, usually between CeyRs300 and CeyRs400 million a year. In 1961, Ceylon entered into trade negotiations with India and signed an agreement in October, 1961. No limits were placed on imports or exports but it was hoped that the volume of imports could be lowered to reasonable proportions and that India could be induced to purchase more Ceylonese products.

The trade agreement in itself has not been successful in achieving this objective. The deficit with India has decreased only moderately. The volume of imports from India has been reduced since 1961 by increased import restrictions and because of increased Ceylonese domestic production, but the volume of exports has not increased much, because of restrictions introduced by India on such Ceylonese products as copra and coconut oil.

The trade agreement of November, 1954, with Egypt is in a slightly different category. In that year, Ceylon had difficulties in selling tea to Egypt—its fourth largest buyer of tea—mainly because Egypt could not pay. To encourage a greater flow of trade between the two nations, a bilateral trade and payments agreement was concluded. Egypt would not purchase Ceylon tea unless Ceylon made a reciprocal arrangement to purchase some of her products. Under the agreement, Ceylon agreed to import rice, cement, potatoes, onions, fertilizers, and cotton goods from Egypt, while exporting tea, coconut, rubber, citronella oil, and spices to Egypt. There was a provision in the agreement for a swing credit of £350,000. Any balance over this limit had to be settled in sterling or in some mutually agreed convertible currency.

The Middle Eastern countries, including Egypt, have been the most important markets for the low-grown varieties of tea. Thirty-five percent of Ceylon's tea output consists of the low-grown varieties, and most of the smallholders and small estates produce these slightly inferior grades of tea. If Ceylon had been shut out from the Egyptian market, a severe crisis would have taken place in the tea industry in Ceylon.

Ceylon is not the only producer of low-grown tea. Cheaper varieties from India and East Africa also enter the Middle Eastern markets, so that Ceylon has to sell its tea under highly competitive conditions. During the ten years preceding 1965 most of the other tea producers have also entered into bilateral arrangements with Egypt, and, as a result, Ceylon could not possibly have pushed sales in the Egyptian market unless there had been a bilateral trade agreement.

PROSPECTS FOR REGIONAL
COOPERATION

During the five years before 1965 Ceylon put an extensive restriction on imports and outward movements of capital. The bulk of the imports that were restricted came from countries of the British Commonwealth and Western Europe and were mostly nonessentials or luxuries. Although it has diminished appreciably since the introduction of restrictions, Ceylon's import trade with the Southeast and East Asian countries has remained important because Ceylon is dependent on those countries for a substantial portion of its essential imports.

Burma and mainland China have continued to remain Ceylon's major suppliers of rice. India has supplied a large variety of subsidiary foodstuffs such as chilies, onions, dried fish, peas, beans, and condiments. Both Japan and India are important sources of supply for a large proportion of the textiles imported by Ceylon.

Since the end of World War II, Japan has become an important source of industrial goods and capital equipment for Ceylon, supplying them on terms that are competitive in price and quality. Since the late fifties, India has also supplied Ceylon with an increasing amount of industrial products, ranging from buses to telephone equipment to textile machinery.

The possibility of Ceylon's participating with advantage in any scheme for economic integration in Southeast Asia, including the creation of a customs union, depends on how much Ceylon will continue to rely on its neighbors for a wide variety of essential products. It is likely that Ceylon will not adequately liberalize its imports of nonessential goods. With the policy of import substitution gathering increasing momentum, it is also likely that Ceylon will produce the bulk of its requirements of cotton and synthetic textiles during the years immediately ahead. The government is also vigorously attempting to cut down on or eliminate imports of rice and other foods such as onions, potatoes, chilies, and cereals. If this policy yields results during the next two years or so, Ceylon will become less dependent on import of foodstuffs and textiles from its neighbors, and the volume of trade between Ceylon and other Southeast Asian countries will decline.

Nevertheless, Ceylon will continue to depend on other countries, for example, India, and (particularly) Japan, for supplies of capital goods and other manufactured equipment that are necessary for its program of industrialization. The demand for capital goods will continue to increase steadily. The overall volume of imports is likely to diminish only a little, with capital goods substituting increasingly for foodstuffs and textiles. Many of Ceylon's neighbors produce the same commodities that Ceylon does. Ceylon has to compete actively with India to sell its tea in foreign markets. Similarly, Malaysia, Indonesia, and Thailand are strong competitors in the rubber market, and the Philippines and Ceylon sell their coconut products competitively.

There is little regional exchange of primary commodities other than foodstuffs, among which rice is outstanding. Though most of the Southeast Asian countries produce rice, inadequate domestic supplies in India, Ceylon, and Malaysia have created a steady regional demand for it. Some industrial raw materials are sold to mainland China and to Japan, and tin and teakwood find a ready market in the region. The volume of trade in such commodities is small, however, compared with that of major products such as tea, rubber, and coconut—each of which is marketed competitively and sold primarily in Western markets.

The creation of a free-trade region presupposes the emergence of two or three strong industrial nations in the region. In return for primary products, such countries would export manufactured and capital goods to their neighbors. If Japan enters such a scheme and decides to purchase its requirements of raw materials for industry mainly from Southeast Asian countries, and if it also becomes a major importer of nonindustrial commodities such as tea and coconut products, then there is no doubt that the volume of trade will increase rapidly and the amount of regional interdependence will grow.

It would appear that the emergence of an effective regional free-trade area would be essentially the by-product of the growth and active participation of industrial nations such as Japan and India. If it is possible also for countries such as Ceylon, Malaysia, and Indonesia to be less dependent on the production of commodities like tea, rubber, and coconut, which are sold competitively—or, alternatively, if it is possible for each of these countries to adopt policies of planned specialization in primary production—then the prospects for the emergence of a free-trade area would be brighter. Such a free-trade area would make countries of this region less vulnerable to fluctuations in commodity prices at the cost, often, of higher production costs and prices.

NOTES

1. The Defense (Control of Imports) and Defense (Control of Exports) Regulations were framed under the Emergency Powers Defense Act of 1939 and were gazetted on October 31, 1939. These regulations created the Department of Import and Export Control. The wartime regulations were framed with a view to (*a*) prohibiting or restricting the importation of nonessential goods, to conserve shipping space for war materials; (*b*) continuing to procure from Empire sources the bulk of goods normally imported from such sources; and (*c*) regulating purchases from non-Em-

pire countries. During the first six months of control licenses were issued fairly freely, and there was little restriction of trade. As the war progressed, import restrictions were tightened, more goods were brought under license, and imports from hard-currency areas were cut down as far as possible. (From Government of Ceylon, *Administrative Report of the Controller of Imports and Exports for 1950* [September, 1951].)

2. At the end of 1950, 1,205 importers had been registered as Ceylonese importers. The table below gives the extent of trade diverted to Ceylon:

Source	Value of trade licensed for Ceylonese (million CeyRs)	Annual value of trade (million CeyRs)
Sterling area and soft-currency regions	40.0	70.0
Japan	67.0	99.0
Switzerland	11.0	19.0
Germany	27.0	56.0

From Government of Ceylon, *Administrative Report . . . 1950.*

3. With the end of hostilities in 1945, import restrictions were relaxed as much as shipping and exchange conditions permitted. Many items were put under open general license, which allowed imports from the sterling area without individual licenses. In 1948, as a result of the Sterling Assets Agreement (published as Government of Ceylon, *Exchange of Letters between the Government of Ceylon and the Government of the United Kingdom, dated April 30, 1948, concerning Ceylon's sterling assets and monetary co-operation between the two Governments*), additional restrictions on imports had to be introduced because Ceylon was committed to contain her balance-of-payments deficit to within £ 3.5 million. In June, 1948, the cabinet therefore decided that, in order to conserve foreign exchange, imports from all sources should be restricted to CeyRs850 million. Dollar expenditure for the same period was restricted to CeyRs100 million. (Government of Ceylon, *Administrative Report . . . 1950*, p. 9.)

The Commonwealth finance ministers agreed that all members of the sterling area should reduce to 75 percent of the 1948 level their dollar expenditure on imports from July, 1949, through June, 1950. In 1948, Ceylon's dollar imports were CeyRs85.37 million; accordingly, expenditure in 1949–50 was restricted to CeyRs4 million. (Computed from published data in the Ceylon customs returns for the relevant years.)

4. Ceylon has had budget deficits since 1955/56. After 1958/59, there was an appreciable increase in these cash deficits. The net cash deficits are as follows:

1955/56	CeyRs1.2 million		1960/61	CeyRs462.5 million	
1956/57	196.4	"	1961/62	456.1	"
1957/58	222.3	"	1962/63	391.7	"
1958/59	413.4	"	1963/64	461.7	"
1959/60	417.5	"	1964/65	442.3	"

(Central Bank of Ceylon, *Annual Report for the year 1965* [Colombo, 1966], table 23.)

5. Government of Ceylon, *Five-Year Trade Agreement relating to Rubber and Rice between the Government of Ceylon and the Central People's Republic of China* (Colombo, 1953).

6. This price was for the first year only. Prices were to be negotiated annually, with the proviso that they would be revised upward if during the course of any year the f.o.b. Singapore price remained above the negotiated price of grades R.S.S. (ribbed smoked sheet) I, II, and III, for a period of one month.

7. The agreed average f.o.b. price for 1953 was CeyRs1.75 per pound, whereas production costs of sheet rubber in Ceylon were then estimated at 88 Ceylon cents. World market price was on the average about CeyRs1.48. In January, 1953, the government introduced a cess of 10 Ceylon cents per pound for the Rubber Stabilization Fund, which was designed to subsidize the domestic industry if world prices were depressed. Rubber sales to China had taken place in 1950–52 even before the agreement was signed. In this period, too, China paid higher prices. (Central Bank of Ceylon, *Annual Report for the year 1952,* pp. 13–14.)

8. See Central Bank of Ceylon, *Annual Report for the year 1958,* p. 20.

9. Of course, not all the rice obtained from China was grown in China. Whenever China found her own supplies inadequate to meet export commitments, she shipped Burmese rice, which was available to her under a bilateral agreement between China and Burma. A considerable part of the rice received from China under the agreement turned out to be of Burmese origin.

10. At the end of 1965 Ceylon had reduced her liabilities with payments-agreement countries by CeyRs68.6 million to CeyRs0.7 million. In addition, Ceylon obtained settlement in 1965 of CeyRs31.7 million in sterling on account of balances in Ceylon's favor in excess of the swing credit in merchandise transactions under payments agreements. In contrast, at the end of 1964 Ceylon had had short-term liabilities amounting to CeyRs69.3 million under payments agreements.

COMMENT ON CHAPTER 10

K. R. CHOU

Mr. Karunatilake works from the premise that, as a developing country moves towards industrialization, exchange and import control tends to become a permanent feature in order to protect new industries. He admits, however, that, at least from the early postwar years up to about 1956, such controls in Ceylon were not primarily for that purpose: Ceylon's controls of imports and foreign exchange during the first postwar decade were mainly for the sake of meeting her obligations as a member of the sterling area. The controls were then rather selective, mainly against imports from the dollar area. After the Korean War boom, Ceylon's direction of trade shifted somewhat, in an effort to preserve some terms-of-trade advantages by agreement on export prices through bilateral trade.

Mr. Karunatilake gives a fairly detailed description of Ceylon's bilateral trade with China. He shows the net gain in the terms of trade, but he does not show how such trade has helped Ceylon's production (either generally or for specific export items) in the long run. Perhaps the higher-than-world-market prices paid by China for rubber had a protective but negative effect, resulting in complacency and in the slowdown of rubber replanting in Ceylon. Bilateral trade agreements with other countries do not appear to have been much more helpful.

In recent years, mainly because of trade deterioration, Ceylon has had serious difficulties in adjusting her import needs to her balance-of-payments position. The difficult years began in 1960 or even as far back as 1956.

A few beneficial aspects of import and exchange control in Ceylon appear to have emerged: increased Ceylonization of trading activities; a slight shift in imports from consumer goods to intermediate goods; and an increased share of industrial production in GNP. I wonder, however, if part of the increase in the GNP share of industrial production might not have been caused by artificially high pricing of industrial products as the control on competitive imports tightened.

The question of how the trade policy and the payments position of Ceylon were tied up with social-welfare programs, and with the socialization of trade and production, does not seem to have been given sufficient attention in this paper, particularly for the decade 1956–65.

CHAPTER 11

DEFICIT FINANCING AND IMPORT
SUBSTITUTION: INDIA, 1951–65

D. V. RAMANA

Less-developed economies are apt to encounter an inflation barrier and a balance-of-payments barrier in the course of planning for economic development, for their investment efforts are not often matched either by domestic savings or by capital imports.[1] The gap between investment and savings—domestic as well as foreign so long as foreign assets or credits last—is filled by deficit financing. The practice of financing a portion of investment by creating a deficit in the budget is justified on two grounds. First, it is argued that the deficit is not inflationary to the extent that it will ensure a fuller use of resources, particularly in the presence of a surplus of agricultural labor, with low or zero productivity, that can be shifted to more productive occupations without appreciably reducing the supply of consumer goods. Second, it is argued that though deficit financing might be inflationary to begin with, nevertheless the inflation is not an unmitigated evil: it is likely to induce a redistribution of income in favor of social groups with a higher propensity to save, thus liquidating itself in course of time through diverting real resources to productive uses. Also the inflation might well improve the efficiency of the price mechanism by making the markets for goods, money, and labor more responsive to the pull of demand.

This paper proposes to demonstrate, with illustration from Indian experience during the period 1951 to 1965, that in practice deficit financing gives rise to a syndrome of undesirable developments: a dislocating rise in prices, a rise in the money rates of interest, an adverse trade balance, and an overvalued exchange rate. The facts show that the strategy of development associated with this particular method of financing, that is, according priority to capital-and-import intensive projects, though it might be a fundamentally sound policy if carried out without deficit financing, only reinforces inflationary pressures if it is preceded or followed by deficit financing. In addition to the restrictive monetary and fiscal measures that are usually taken to cope with the mounting pressures of inflation, administrative attempts are made to control the prices and ration the quantities released for consumption, production, and distribution. Particularly important among these administrative controls is a generalized system of exchange control, which, in the context of a demand-pull inflation, creates the necessary conditions for cost-push inflation. The domestic producers need no longer fear the threat of foreign competition. The productivity of the marginal firm declines but the domestic producers can nonetheless sell their goods for a profit because of the demand-pull rise in prices induced by deficit spending. Import substitutes of indifferent quality are sold in a seller's market.

More often than not, even the production of the import substitutes is threatened, owing to discontinuities in the supply of imported inputs. The supply of import inputs cannot be regular or uniform, for the exports that pay for them do not grow fast enough. On the one hand, a greater emphasis is usually placed on production for domestic consumption than for export. On the other hand, the low quality of domestic production saddles a large burden of export subsidies on the economy thus suggesting a *de facto* exchange rate depreciation.

Inability to export the import substitutes owing to their low quality, plus inelastic foreign demand for the traditional exports of the economy, accounts for the stagnation of export earnings. But demand for imports rises at least proportionately with investment. The mounting trade deficit measures the extent of economic dependence of the country on the rest of the world. Ironically, the very strategy of economic development that is calculated to promote national self-sufficiency may end in making the country more dependent on outside supplies than before.

The purpose of this paper is to furnish data on the chief magnitudes of the Indian economy for 1951–65 and to interpret them in relation to the statements above. The first section describes the changes in income and output during this period. Next, the relationship of money, deficit financing, and the price level is dealt with. The third section outlines a method for measuring the import content of the economy, while the last one contains an account of certain cost-push indicators.

INCOME AND OUTPUT

Data on income, i.e., net domestic product by industrial origin, are available at current and constant prices for four sectors of the Indian economy: (1) agriculture, animal husbandry, forestry, and fishery; (2) mining, manufacturing, and small enterprises; (3) commerce, transport, and communication; and (4) other services (for a discussion of these four sectors, see Appendix B). These data are given for 1951–65 in Tables 11.1 and 11.2, respectively. (On the problem of price deflation, see Appendix A.) Money income rose by approximately 110 percent during the period, real income rose by about 70 percent, and prices rose by about the remaining 24 percent. The sectors of "mining, manufacturing" and of "other services" grew a little faster than the other two sectors; that is, the money incomes of these sectors rose by nearly 140 percent and real incomes by 70 percent and 125 percent respectively. The implication is that the price level of the "mining and manufacturing" sector rose faster than the price level of the "other services" sector. In the "commerce, etc." sector, money and real incomes rose almost by the same margin year after year, and by less than 100 percent during the entire period. The rate of growth of real income of this sector is the lowest, and the rise in its price level also is lowest, a little over 10 percent.

Table 11.3 contains annual data on the output of the four sectors of the Indian economy. The output of a sector is defined as a sum of the "net domestic product by industrial origin" and the material inputs of the sector. The sectoral outputs are projected on the basis of the input-output matrix given in Table 11.4 (see Appendixes A and B). The sectoral outputs are given both in money and real terms. The magnitude of the change between 1951 and 1965 is similar to that of the change in the sectoral incomes (i.e., net domestic products). This is a consequence of the method of projection itself. The same input-output structure was assumed to prevail for the entire period of fifteen years when, as might well be expected, the Indian economy must have undergone appreciable structural changes. At the very modest level of disaggregation used the input coefficients may well remain constant, for plenty of scope is allowed for intrasector commodity substitution due to technical change or relative price movements. The output coefficients are rather likely to remain constant also: these represent the distribution of the output of a sector among

TABLE 11.1—India's net domestic product by industrial origin, current prices, 1950–65
(Billion IRs)

Domestic product	1950/ 51	1951/ 52	1952/ 53	1953/ 54	1954/ 55	1955/ 56	1956/ 57	1957/ 58	1958/ 59	1959/ 60	1960/ 61	1961/ 62	1962/ 63	1963/ 64	1964/ 65
Agriculture, animal husbandry, forestry, and fishery	48.9	49.9	48.1	53.1	43.5	45.3	55.2	52.9	61.9	62.5	68.9	69.6	70.0	81.7	102.7
Mining, manufacturing, and small enterprises	15.3	17.3	17.0	17.7	18.0	18.5	20.0	21.2	21.4	23.2	26.0	28.8	30.8	33.3	36.0
Commerce, transport, and communications[a]	16.9	17.9	17.8	18.0	18.1	18.8	19.6	20.7	21.1	22.3	23.4	24.8	26.5	28.1	29.6
Other services[b]	14.4	15.0	15.4	16.0	16.5	17.3	18.2	19.3	20.4	21.8	23.6	25.5	27.5	29.9	32.9
Net domestic product	95.5	100.1	98.3	104.8	96.1	99.9	113.0	114.1	124.8	129.8	141.9	148.7	154.8	173.0	201.2
Net income from abroad	– 0.5	– 0.1	– 0.3	+ 0.2	– 0.1	+ 0.1	0.0	– 0.1	+ 1.2	+ 0.2	– 0.9	– 0.7	– 0.8	– 1.0	– 1.2
National income	95.0	100.0	98.0	105.0	96.0	100.0	113.0	114.0	126.0	130.0	141.0	148.0	154.0	172.0	200.0

[a] Posts, telegraphs, telephones, railways, organized banking, insurance, other commerce, and transport.
[b] Professional and liberal arts, government services, domestic service, and house property.
Source: Government of India, Central Statistical Organization, *Estimates of National Income*, various issues.

TABLE 11.2—India's net domestic product by industrial origin, constant prices, 1948–49
(Billion IRs)

Domestic product	1950/ 51	1951/ 52	1952/ 53	1953/ 54	1954/ 55	1955/ 56	1956/ 57	1957/ 58	1958/ 59	1959/ 60	1960/ 61	1961/ 62	1962/ 63	1963/ 64	1964/ 65
Agriculture, animal husbandry, forestry, and fishery	43.4	44.4	46.0	49.8	50.3	50.2	52.5	50.1	55.6	55.1	59.0	59.1	57.9	59.7	65.0
Mining, manufacturing, and small enterprises	14.8	15.2	15.8	16.5	17.0	17.6	18.4	18.6	18.8	19.7	21.1	22.1	23.0	24.4	25.5
Commerce, transport, and communications	16.6	17.3	17.9	18.3	19.1	19.7	20.8	21.1	21.9	22.7	24.6	25.4	26.4	27.8	29.7
Other services	13.9	14.3	15.0	15.7	16.4	17.3	18.2	19.2	20.4	21.4	23.1	24.7	26.6	28.7	31.4
Net domestic product	88.7	91.2	94.7	100.3	102.8	104.8	109.9	109.0	116.7	118.9	127.8	131.3	133.9	140.6	151.6

Source: Government of India, Central Statistical Organization, *Estimates of National Income*, various issues.

TABLE 11.3—India's sectoral outputs, 1950–65
(Billion IRs)

Year	Agriculture, animal husbandry, forestry, and fishery		Mining, manufacturing, and small enterprises		Commerce, transport, and communication		Other services		Total output	
	Output, current prices	Output, 1948–49 prices	Output, current prices	Output, 1948–49 prices	Output, current prices	Output, 1948–49 prices	Output, current prices	Output, 1948–49 prices	Current prices	1948–49 prices
1950/51	68.88	61.29	35.16	33.12	21.54	20.91	15.84	15.27	141.43	130.60
1951/52	70.42	62.72	38.20	34.02	22.78	21.73	16.56	15.71	147.96	134.18
1952/53	67.96	64.99	37.38	35.32	22.59	22.50	16.93	16.47	144.86	139.28
1953/54	74.88	70.28	39.55	37.24	23.10	23.18	17.61	17.24	155.14	147.93
1954/55	61.78	71.13	37.68	38.18	22.79	24.10	18.05	17.99	140.30	151.39
1955/56	64.32	70.99	38.92	39.08	23.67	24.79	18.91	18.93	145.82	153.79
1956/57	78.03	74.25	43.42	40.90	25.11	26.14	19.97	19.91	166.52	161.20
1957/58	75.02	71.03	44.66	40.68	26.27	26.39	21.12	20.91	167.09	159.02
1958/59	87.42	78.64	47.20	42.45	27.18	27.56	22.32	22.19	184.12	170.84
1959/60	88.44	78.07	49.96	43.69	28.63	28.47	23.83	23.25	190.86	173.47
1960/61	97.48	83.61	55.40	46.84	30.34	30.80	25.83	25.09	209.04	186.34
1961/62	98.73	83.90	59.53	48.39	32.08	31.77	27.89	26.76	218.23	190.82
1962/63	99.52	82.42	62.61	49.52	34.08	32.89	30.02	28.72	226.24	193.55
1963/64	115.84	85.09	69.05	52.11	36.57	34.61	32.66	30.94	254.12	202.76
1964/65	144.92	92.58	77.99	55.26	39.45	37.04	35.99	33.33	298.34	218.21

Source: Based on the input-output table, 1951–52, prepared by the Indian Statistical Institute, Calcutta, and published in "Inter-Industrial Relations in the Indian Union, 1951–52," *Papers on National Income and Allied Topics* (New York, 1960), 1 : 259–71.

TABLE 11.4—India: transactions matrix on the factor cost basis at current prices, 1951–52
(In crores, or 10 million IRs)

Domestic product	1	2	3	4	Intermediate demand	Final demand	Total demand
1 Agriculture, animal husbandry, forestry, and fishery	1,852.15	933.24	185.60	0.47	2,971.46	4,066.94	7,038.40
2 Mining, manufacturing, and small enterprises	127.27	797.03	155.66	104.02	1,183.99	2,492.15	3,676.14
3 Commerce, transport, and communication	21.50	403.53	108.35	48.22	581.61	2,639.75	3,221.36
4 Other services	53.79	44.29	66.59	13.34	178.01	1,549.07	1,727.08
Total material inputs	2,054.71	2,178.09	516.20	166.05	4,915.07	10,747.91	15,662.98
Net domestic product	4,983.43	1,497.68	2,704.71	1,560.97	—	—	—
Net output	7,038.14	3,675.77	3,220.91	1,727.02	—	—	—

Source: Abridged and modified version of the input-output table, 1951–52, prepared by the Indian Statistical Institute, Calcutta, and published in "Inter-Industrial Relations in the Indian Union, 1951–52," *Papers on National Income and Allied Topics* (New York, 1960), 1:259–71.

all the sectors of the economy including itself. In a traditionalistic and backward economy the pattern of distribution is slow to change; moreover, the high level of aggregation represented by a four sector division of the Indian economy may sufficiently cover many a change in the pattern of distribution of individual goods and services. (On the problem of estimating "value added," see Appendix B.)

MONEY AND PRICES

The data on money supply and prices are given in Table 11.5. There are two sets of data on money supply, M_1 and M_2. M_1 refers to money supply as defined by the Reserve Bank of India, that is, the sum of currency in circulation and adjusted demand deposits. M_2 includes, in addition, the time and savings deposits (suitably adjusted). These

TABLE 11.5—India: money supply and prices, 1950–65

Year	M_1	M_2	WSP	CP	NID	OD
	(billion IRs)		(Base: 1948/49 = 100)			
1950/51	18.01	21.86	109	105	108	107
1951/52	17.13	21.53	108	106	110	110
1952/53	17.09	21.77	107	106	104	104
1953/54	18.32	23.58	102	101	104	105
1954/55	20.47	26.60	101	96	93	93
1955/56	21.79	28.77	99	105	95	95
1956/57	23.06	31.99	107	111	103	103
1957/58	23.77	35.17	112	116	105	105
1958/59	25.46	39.44	118	121	108	108
1959/60	27.11	41.41	120	124	109	110
1960/61	28.40	43.22	125	126	111	112
1961/62	31.14	47.45	125	127	113	114
1962/63	35.41	52.34	128	131	115	116
1963/64	39.06	57.36	135	137	123	125
1964/65	43.00	63.91	153	157	132	137

M_1 = Money supply including demand deposits only.
M_2 = Money supply including demand, time, and savings deposits.
WSP = Wholesale price.
CP = Consumer price.
NID = National income deflator.
OD = Output deflator.
Sources: The Reserve Bank of India, *Report on Currency and Finance*, various years; the input-output table, 1951–52, prepared by the Indian Statistical Institute, Calcutta, and published in "Inter-Industrial Relations in the Indian Union, 1951–52," *Papers on National Income and Allied Topics* (New York, 1960), 1:259–71.

usually go by the name of "near money," since the time and savings deposits can be and are constantly interchanged with demand deposits. Broadening the definition of money supply is also in accordance with the concept of liquidity ratio used by the Radcliffe Committee.

Four sets of data are given on the price index numbers: the wholesale price (WSP), the consumer price (CP), the implicit price of net domestic income (the national income deflator, NID), and the implicit price of output (the output deflator, OD).

The data on the velocity of circulation of money are given in Table 11.6 along with data on the determinants of velocity. Distinction is made among four concepts of velocity (V_1, V_2, V_3, V_4), corresponding to the two concepts of income and output and the two concepts of money supply, M_1 and M_2.

TABLE 11.6—India: velocity and its determinants, 1950–65

Year	V_1	V_2	V_3	V_4	CMR	BR	Y	P^1
1950/51	5.29	4.36	7.83	6.45	2.18	3.28	248	+ 3
1951/52	5.82	4.63	8.64	6.87	2.20	3.69	250	− 1
1952/53	5.75	4.51	8.43	6.66	2.21	3.64	256	− 1
1953/54	5.72	4.44	8.46	6.57	2.45	3.65	266	− 5
1954/55	4.69	3.61	6.84	5.26	2.59	3.72	268	− 1
1955/56	4.58	3.47	6.70	5.07	3.21	3.93	268	− 2
1956/57	4.90	3.54	7.26	5.22	3.71	4.14	276	+ 8
1957/58	4.79	3.24	7.03	4.77	2.96	4.18	267	+ 5
1958/59	4.94	3.19	7.23	4.72	2.74	4.05	280	+ 5
1959/60	4.78	3.13	7.05	4.61	3.67	4.06	279	+ 2
1960/61	4.98	3.27	7.36	4.84	4.35	4.11	293	+ 4
1961/62	4.75	3.12	7.00	4.59	3.69	4.36	294	0
1962/63	4.35	2.94	6.38	4.32	3.77	4.68	294	+ 2
1963/64	4.41	3.00	6.50	4.43	4.00	4.73	300	+ 5
1964/65	4.65	3.19	6.93	4.66	6.28	5.33	301	+ 13

V_1 = Income velocity of circulation of money (including demand deposits only).

V_2 = Income velocity of circulation of money (including both demand and time deposits etc.).

V_3 = Output velocity of circulation of money (including demand deposits only).

V_4 = Output velocity of circulation of money (including both demand and time deposits etc.).

CMR = Call money rate (percent).

BR = Yield on government bonds (percent).

Y = Per capita real income (IRs).

P^1 = Percent change in the wholesale price index.

Sources: International Monetary Fund, *International Financial Statistics*, various years; also, data of Tables 11.1 and 11.5.

The four determinants of income velocity are the call money rate (CMR) (short term), the government bond yield (BR) (long term), the percent change in the wholesale price level (P^1), and the per capita real income (Y). The first three factors represent the opportunity cost of holding money as a substitute for other assets (in so far as the short- and long-term interest rates are concerned) and as a substitute for goods and services (in so far as the percent change in the price level is concerned). Per capita real income (Y) is assumed to be a determinant of velocity because the income elasticity of demand for money, a "superior good," should be more than unity.

The data of Table 11.5 yields the following relationships between money and prices, and money, prices, and income:

Simple Correlation	Partial Correlation	Multiple Correlation
$rM_1.WSP = .93*$	$rM_1WSP.Y = .49**$	$RM_1WSPY = .99***$
$rM_2.WSP = .93*$	$rM_2WSP.Y = .80**$	$RM_2WSPY = .99***$
$rM_1.CP\ \ \ = .95*$	$rM_1CP.Y\ \ \ = .53**$	$RM_1CPY\ \ \ = .99***$
$rM_2.CP\ \ \ = .96*$	$rM_2CP.Y\ \ \ = .78**$	$RM_2CPY\ \ \ = .99***$
$rM_1.NID = .82*$	$rM_1NID.Y = .39**$	$RM_1NIDY = .99***$
$rM_2.NID = .80*$	$rM_2NID.Y = .58**$	$RM_2NIDY = .99***$
$rM_1.OD\ \ = .84*$	$rM_1OD.y' \ \ = .56**$	$RM_1ODy'\ \ = .99***$
$rM_2.OD\ \ = .82*$	$rM_2OD.y' \ \ = .55**$	$RM_2ODy'\ \ = .99***$

    * Significant at the .01 level.
   ** Significant at the .05 level.
 *** Significantly different from zero.
y' = Total output.

The average velocity of circulation of money has exhibited a secular downward tendency. Marginal velocity over time is less than the average velocity.

An estimate of the marginal velocity of circulation of money is given by the estimated regression coefficient, β, below (figures in parentheses are the standard errors of the regression coefficients):

$$Y = \alpha + \beta M_1, \quad \text{and} \quad y = \alpha_1 + \beta_1 M_2$$
$$= 27.8 + 3.79 M_1, \quad \text{and} \quad = 43.1 + 2.24 M_2,$$
$$= \quad (.20) \qquad\qquad\qquad = \quad (.13).$$

The relationship of income and output velocity to its determinants as postulated above is given by:

$$V_1 = a_1 + b_1(CMR) + c_1(BR) + d_1(Y^1) + e_1(P^1),$$
$$= 10.61 + .13(CMR) - .21(BR) - .02(Y^1) - .02(P^1),$$
$$= \quad\quad (.24) \quad\quad (.53) \quad\quad (.13) \quad\quad (.35);$$
$$R_1 = .73 \text{ (significantly different from zero)}.$$

$$V_2 = a_2 + b_2(CMR) + c_2(BR) + d_2(Y^1) + e_2(P^1),$$
$$= 12.76 + .24(CMR) - .05(BR) + .04(Y^1) - .03(P^1),$$
$$= \quad\quad (.23) \quad\quad (.50) \quad\quad (.01) \quad\quad (.03);$$
$$R_2 = .87 \text{ (significantly different from zero)}.$$

$$V_3 = a_3 + b_3(CMR) + c_3(BR) + d_3(Y^1) + e_3(P^1),$$
$$= 16.06 + .24(CMR) - .33(BR) - .03(Y^1) - .02(P^1),$$
$$= \quad\quad (.37) \quad\quad (.83) \quad\quad (.02) \quad\quad (.05);$$
$$R_3 = .72 \text{ (significantly different from zero)}.$$

$$V_4 = a_4 + b_4(CMR) + c_4(BR) + d_4(Y^1) + e_4(P^1),$$
$$= 18.77 + .33(CMR) + .1(BR) - .05(Y^1) - .05(P^1),$$
$$= \quad\quad (.35) \quad\quad (.76) \quad\quad (.02) \quad\quad (.05);$$
$$R_4 = .86 \text{ (significantly different from zero)}.$$

The failure of the postulated determinants to explain the variations in the velocity of circulation of money is due to the fact that the variations themselves are none too pronounced, and there is doubtless strong multicollinearity among the independent variables. Perhaps, in a backward economy like India, the degree of monetization would act as a more substantial determinant, but reliable data on the degree of monetization are hard to come by.

Table 11.7 gives data on the amount of deficit financing, together with data on investment and net capital inflow. It can be seen from the table that, although the foreign capital inflow assumed substantial proportions from 1956 onwards, deficit financing also was resorted to on a large scale. The output of the economy, however, did not increase proportionately; as a matter of fact the marginal capital-output ratio, which was 2.1 in the First Plan period (1951/52–1955/56), rose sharply, to 6.1, during the Second Plan period (1956/57–1960/61). As mentioned earlier, the superimposition of the heavy capital-and-import intensive industry on large-scale deficit financing resulted in an annual increase of the price level of 5 percent during the Second Plan period. The rise in the price level at even a larger rate than 5 percent continued during the Third Plan (1961/62–1965/66) as deficit financing was used without let or hindrance. The magnitude of deficit financing was substantial; it accounted for 80 percent of the increase in money supply, which rose from 18 billion

TABLE 11.7—India: saving, investment, deficit financing, and trade balance, 1950–65
(Billion IRs, current prices unless otherwise stated)

Year	Saving (1)	Net capital inflow (2)	Investment (1 + 2)	Investment at 1948–49 prices	Deficit financing	Cumulated deficit financing	Balance of payments on current account (net)	Cumulated balance of payments on current account (net)
1950/51	5.42	− 0.08	5.34	4.96	negl.	negl.	+ 0.39	+ 0.39
1951/52	5.29	+ 2.24	7.53	6.88	0.02	.02	− 1.63	− 1.24
1952/53	4.08	− 0.17	3.91	3.77	0.45	.47	+ 0.60	− 0.64
1953/54	5.65	− 0.04	5.61	5.38	0.36	.83	+ 0.47	− 0.16
1954/55	7.64	+ 0.47	8.11	8.67	0.93	1.76	+ 0.06	− 0.10
1955/56	9.71	+ 0.63	10.34	10.86	1.57	3.33	+ 0.07	− 0.03
1956/57	10.76	+ 3.78	14.54	14.15	2.53	5.86	− 3.13	− 3.16
1957/58	7.98	+ 4.89	12.87	12.30	4.97	10.83	− 4.31	− 7.48
1958/59	9.31	+ 3.99	13.30	12.30	1.40	12.23	− 3.27	− 10.75
1959/60	11.02	+ 2.58	13.60	12.46	1.12	13.35	− 1.86	− 12.60
1960/61	13.72	+ 4.97	18.69	16.83	− 0.49	12.86	− 3.92	− 16.53
1961/62	13.74	+ 3.81	17.55	15.49	1.84	14.70	− 3.06	− 19.59
1962/63	14.98	+ 4.53	19.51	16.94	1.83	16.53	− 3.46	− 23.05
1963/64	n.a.	n.a.	n.a.	n.a.	2.11	18.64	− 3.35	− 26.40
1964/65	n.a.	n.a.	n.a.	n.a.	1.88	20.52	− 4.37	− 30.77
Total	119.30	31.60	150.90	140.99	—	—	—	—

negl.: Negligible.
n.a.: Not available.
Source: The Reserve Bank of India, *Report on Currency and Finance*, 1965–66.

rupees in 1951 to 43 billion in 1965. In absolute figures the cumulated amount of deficit financing was 20.5 billion, or nearly 15 percent of the total investment made during the period 1951–65. It is also instructive to note that the balance of payments on current account (net) became adverse suddenly in 1956/57 and grew increasingly adverse through 1965, owing mainly to the establishment of import-heavy industries. Though the adverse current account balance of payments was made good completely by the foreign capital inflow, the need for the inflow is a measure of the country's dependence. A current account deficit in the balance of payments implies that the country is dependent on the ability and willingness of the outside world to export to it goods and services on credit!

IMPORT CONTENT OF PRODUCTION

Imports of the Indian economy for 1951–65 are given by sector in Table 11.8. These data are given for only three sectors: "agriculture, etc.," "manufacturing, etc.," and "communications, etc." It is not possible to list from the trade statistics any items that would go in as inputs of the sector, "other services," although some imports indeed would be inputs of this sector. No import-input matrix as such is available. Under the circumstances, the best that can be done in finding out the import content of production is to allocate total imports by commodity to the three sectors, assuming that no part of these imports is used for direct consumption. This assumption is not so implausible as it might seem because in the Indian economy the imports of consumer goods are subject to sharp restrictions, and even the small amount of consumer goods imported is not released for consumption except under compelling circumstances.

Imports as a proportion of net domestic production (net value added) are also given in Table 11.8. In the "agriculture, etc." sector, they form 2 or 3 percent of the net value added (for 10 out of 15 years); in the "manufacturing, etc." sector they form from just under 20 to nearly 30 percent, and in the "communications, etc." sector they form 6 to 15 percent. There is no perceptible trend in the changes of the proportion of imports in the net value added of any of the three sectors.

The import coefficients of output are calculated as the proportion of sector imports to the sector outputs. This is not the same thing as the

TABLE 11.8—India: sectoral import content, 1950–65
(Billion IRs, current prices)

	Agriculture, animal husbandry, forestry, and fishing				Mining, manufacturing, and small enterprises				Commerce, transport, and communication			
Year	Imports	Import coefficient of net domestic product	Import coefficient of output	Cumulated import coefficient of output	Imports	Import coefficient of net domestic product	Import coefficient of output	Cumulated import coefficient of output	Imports	Import coefficient of net domestic product	Import coefficient of output	Cumulated import coefficient of output
1950/51	1.32	.027	.019	.031	3.87	.253	.110	.158	1.32	.078	.061	.075
1951/52	2.56	.051	.036	.056	5.48	.317	.144	.209	1.67	.093	.073	.092
1952/53	1.82	.038	.027	.041	3.48	.204	.093	.139	1.39	.081	.061	.074
1953/54	0.97	.018	.013	.022	3.47	.196	.088	.125	1.23	.069	.053	.064
1954/55	1.07	.025	.017	.029	4.15	.230	.110	.157	1.35	.074	.059	.073
1955/56	0.53	.012	.008	.017	4.31	.233	.111	.174	1.95	.104	.082	.096
1956/57	0.41	.007	.005	.013	5.54	.277	.128	.180	2.54	.129	.101	.116
1957/58	0.94	.018	.013	.024	6.31	.298	.141	.203	3.11	.157	.018	.136
1958/59	1.88	.030	.022	.034	4.22	.197	.089	.136	2.49	.118	.092	.105
1959/60	1.81	.030	.021	.033	5.01	.216	.100	.151	2.79	.125	.103	.117
1960/61	2.14	.031	.022	.035	5.75	.221	.104	.157	3.33	.142	.110	.125
1961/62	1.47	.021	.015	.025	5.76	.200	.097	.146	3.68	.148	.115	.129
1962/63	1.79	.026	.018	.029	5.65	.183	.090	.138	3.87	.146	.114	.128
1963/64	1.63	.023	.014	.024	5.59	.168	.081	.125	4.22	.150	.115	.128
1964/65	2.13	.021	.015	.025	7.23	.201	.093	.139	4.13	.140	.105	.119

Source: Government of India, Central Statistical Organization, *Estimates of National Income*, various issues.

import-input coefficients, for what is imported by a sector is not necessarily used by it in the process of production. Because data on the import-inputs are not available, import coefficients defined as the proportion of sector imports to sector outputs are used as a substitute. The import coefficient of the sector output in "agriculture, etc." shows no perceptible trend of change; in "manufacturing, etc.," it shows a slight downward trend; in the case of the "communications, etc." sector, it shows a rather pronounced upward trend. The cumulated import coefficient of output is calculated according to the procedure outlined in Appendix A. The nature of the change in these coefficients is approximately the same as it is with regard to the direct import coefficients of output.

However, no inferences can be drawn from these coefficients about the rate at which import substitution has been going on. Rather, what can be said is that the structure of imports is probably undergoing a change, as some proportion of the goods hitherto imported is produced and as more goods required for production of import substitutes are imported. These changes in the proportion of domestic production vis-à-vis imports go on continually whether or not a deliberate plan for import substitution is evolved. In the absence of a plan, the import-substitute production takes place in response to relative price changes, and perhaps slowly because of the primitive nature of the market mechanism. If a deliberate plan for producing import substitutes is made in order to accelerate the process, the planner's choice of the commodities to be import-substituted is vastly more important than the mere scale of import substitution. It is the efficiency of import-substitute production that is the relevant consideration; that is, the domestic cost of saving foreign exchange.

INDICATORS OF COST-PUSH

Given the import coefficients of output, it is possible to calculate the addition made to costs, assuming these additions are equal to the average duty imposed on imports of each sector. *Ad valorem* this duty can be calculated, from customs data, as 15 to 20 percent on the imports of the agriculture sector; 40 to 50 percent on the imports of the manufactures sector and 50 to 60 percent on the imports of the communications sector. If we estimate the duty included in the cumulated import coefficients of output, the rise in the cost of production of commodities in general works out to between 10 and 15 percent.

Any cost-push price rises must take place despite extensive under-utilization of industrial capacity due to organizational problems or to the irregular and inadequate supplies of raw materials and semi-finished goods. Details in this regard are given in Table 11.9, according to which only a quarter of industrial productive capacity was fully utilized in the period 1957–64.

TABLE 11.9—India: rate of capacity utilization in selected industries, 1957–64
(Cumulative percentages)

Production as percentage of installed capacity	1957	1958	1959	1960	1961	1962	1963	1964
100 percent or more	20	17	21	25	28	23	27	27
90 percent or more	24	24	28	35	34	33	40	42
80 percent or more	32	35	35	43	49	47	53	57
70 percent or more	49	44	48	53	61	61	63	64
60 percent or more	55	56	61	64	75	76	78	73
50 percent or more	67	72	74	78	82	83	87	88
40 percent or more	78	81	83	87	88	90	91	89
30 percent or more	85	90	91	94	95	95	95	95
20 percent or more	90	95	94	97	97	97	98	97
10 percent or more	95	98	98	98	99	99	99	99
Zero percent or more	100	100	100	100	100	100	100	100

Source: United Nations, "The Financing of Economic Development," *World Economic Survey* (1965), part 1.

Even where productive capacity is fully utilized, the inputs (both domestic and imported) may have been used uneconomically. The inefficient use of resources is indicated by the higher price charged for commodities domestically produced vis-à-vis the import price (without duty) of the same commodities. A few selective details in this respect are taken from a recent report of the Tariff Commissioner and given below for illustrative purposes:

Commodity	*Fair ex-works price as percent of (c.i.f.) import price*
Aluminium ingots	110–120
Piston assembly (Fiat)	120–130
Spinning ring frames	130–140
Acid dyes	140–150
Bicycles	150–200
Ball bearings	Over 200

The technology of production of the commodities mentioned above is simple and has been standardized for a long time, and the production of these commodities has been going on in the country for several years. Still, their ex-works fair price, which is a reasonably good measure of their costs of production, is considerably higher.

It is worthwhile pointing out, in conclusion, that deficit spending and improper choice of commodities for import substitution, along with the deliberate creation of a seller's market through general exchange control, produced both a demand-pull and a cost-push inflation that logically led to the 1965 devaluation of the Indian rupee.

NOTE

1. The views expressed in this chapter are those of the author and not necessarily those of the United Nations.

APPENDIX A

The National Income Deflator and the

Output Deflator

Let

$[Z] =$ a transactions matrix (in terms of value) of the Minkowski-Leontief type

$[\alpha] =$ a matrix of coefficients of quantities of consumption of r for the production of s

$[\beta] =$ the Leontief input-output coefficient matrix (input coefficient matrix)

$[\gamma] =$ a matrix of coefficients of the allocation of r for the production of s (output coefficient matrix)

$[G] =$ a matrix of "value added"

$[\beta^*] =$ a matrix of primary factor cost coefficients per unit of production

$[F] =$ a matrix of accumulated unit primary factor cost coefficients

$[U] =$ a matrix of unit accumulated primary factor costs

$[Y] =$ a matrix of unit primary factor inputs (quantities)

$[\phi] =$ a matrix of accumulated unit primary factor inputs (quantities)

$\mathbf{p} =$ a diagonal price vector

$\mathbf{q} =$ a diagonal quantity vector

$\mathbf{V} =$ a diagonal value vector, i.e. $\mathbf{p}$, $\mathbf{q}$

$d =$ a column vector of final demand (in terms of value)

$\delta =$ a column vector of final demand (in terms of quantities)

$\lambda =$ a vector of unit factor shares

$\mu =$ a vector of unit primary factor requirements

$pf =$ a vector of factor prices

$I =$ a diagonal identity vector

$i, i' =$ an identity column vector and an identity row vector, respectively.

Define

(1) $\qquad [\alpha] = \mathbf{p}^{-1}[Z]\mathbf{q}^{-1}$

(2) $\qquad [\beta] = [Z]\mathbf{V}^{-1}$

(3) $\qquad [\gamma] = \mathbf{V}^{-1}[Z].$

Assuming the relative prices and relative quantities are constant, $[\alpha]$, $[\beta]$, and $[\gamma]$ can be expressed in terms of one another. Thus,

(4) $\qquad [\alpha] = \mathbf{q}[\gamma]\mathbf{q}^{-1}$

(5) $\qquad [\alpha] = \mathbf{p}^{-1}[\beta]\mathbf{p}$

(6) $\qquad [\beta] = \mathbf{p}[\alpha]\mathbf{p}^{-1}$

(7) $\qquad [\beta] = \mathbf{V}[\gamma]\mathbf{V}^{-1}$

(8) $\qquad [\gamma] = \mathbf{q}^{-1}[\alpha]\mathbf{q}$

(9) $\qquad [\gamma] = \mathbf{V}^{-1}[\beta]\mathbf{V}.$

Remark:

$$\text{The inverse matrix of } [I - \alpha] = [I - \alpha]^{-1}$$
$$\text{The inverse matrix of } [I - \beta] = [I - \beta]^{-1}$$
$$\text{The inverse matrix of } [I - \gamma] = [I - \gamma]^{-1}.$$

In equations (4) through (9) the coefficient matrices can be replaced by their corresponding inverse matrices so that the inverse matrices $[I - \alpha]^{-1}$, $[I - \beta]^{-1}$, and $[I - \gamma]^{-1}$ can be obtained in terms of one another by a process of similarity transformation.

At a given set of prices and quantities of output

(10) $\qquad \mathbf{q} = [I - \alpha]^{-1}\delta$

(11) $\qquad \mathbf{V} = [I - \beta]^{-1}d$

(12) $\qquad \mathbf{V} = [G][I - \gamma]^{-1}.$

Remark: The vector $\mathbf{V}$ obtained by (11) and (12) is identical. This follows from the well-known theorem on characteristic polynomials and similarity transformations that the characteristic polynomial, and therefore the characteristic roots, of a matrix are invariant under similarity transformations. Proof

$$\begin{aligned}|\lambda I - \mathbf{V}^{-1}[\beta]\mathbf{V}| &= |\mathbf{V}^{-1}(\lambda I - [\beta])\mathbf{V}| \\ &= |\mathbf{V}^{-1}|\,|\lambda I - [\beta]|\,|\mathbf{V}| \\ &= |\lambda I - [\beta]|.\end{aligned}$$

(13) $\qquad F = [\beta^*][I - \beta]^{-1}.$

Remark: If Z were to be a partitioned matrix,

$$m \begin{bmatrix} X & | & D \\ & n & | & s \\ \hline & G & | & - \\ \end{bmatrix}$$

$$r$$

$$(r = m, \ldots, r)$$
$$(s = 1, \ldots, n)$$
$$\beta^* = Grs\ \mathbf{V}^{-1}.$$

(14) $$[U] = [F]\mathbf{p}$$
(15) $$[\phi] = [Y][I - \alpha]^{-1}$$
(16) $$\lambda = [U] \cdot i$$
(17) $$\mu = [\phi] \cdot i$$
(18) $$\mu^{-1}\lambda = pf.$$

Remark: The sector-wise data on p and pf are not available. Only their index numbers for the economy as a whole—i.e., for all the sectors put together—are used as the national income deflator and the output deflator, respectively.

APPENDIX B

Two Estimates of Value Added

The Central Statistical Organization of the Government of India publishes data on national income periodically (*Estimates of National Income, ENI*). The estimates are based on the "production" method rather than the "expenditure" method. That is to say, national income is estimated by industrial origin. In terms of the national input-output table, the data on national income correspond roughly to the data on "value added," i.e., the total output minus the consumption of materials.

The data on national income by industrial origin are available at both current prices and constant (1948–49) prices. While the data at current prices are given for eighteen sectors, however, the data at constant prices are given for only four sectors. In undertaking any comparative study of the sectoral incomes at both constant and current prices, therefore, only a four-sector classification can be used.

The 1951–52 input-output matrix prepared by the Indian Statistical Institute and published in *Papers on National Income and Allied Topics,* vol. 1 (New York, 1960), 259–71, is rather elaborate compared to the data on national income published by the Government of India. It distinguishes among thirty-six sectors of the economy and seven categories of final demand, including imports. However, this detailed information could not be used for the purpose of this paper. The number of sectors was reduced from thirty-six to four for comparing the data on the "value added" as contained in the ENI. The scheme of aggregation is given in Table 11B.1.

There are two difficulties that relate to the comparability of the data on "value added" in the input-output table and the data on the same given in the ENI. The first difficulty arises in connection with depreciation. The data on "value added" in the input-output table include depreciation, while the data in the ENI exclude depreciation. An estimate of the depreciation allowance of each of the four sectors has been made and sub-

TABLE 11B.1—Scheme of aggregation for the four sectors of the Indian economy

Estimates of National Income (ENI)	Indian Statistical Institute's input-output table
Sector number and name	Sector number and name
1 Agriculture, animal husbandry, forestry, and fishery	1 Agriculture
	2 Plantations
	3 Animal husbandry, fishery, and forestry
2 Mining, manufacturing, and small enterprises	4 Coke and coal
	5 All other mining
	6 Iron and steel
	7 Non-ferrous metals
	8 Engineering
	9 Chemicals
	10 Cement
	11 Other building materials (large-scale)
	12 Food, drink, tobacco, etc. (large-scale)
	13 Cotton textiles (large-scale)
	14 Other textiles
	15 Jute and other fibres
	16 Glass and ceramics (large-scale)
	17 Leather and rubber (large-scale)
	18 Paper, printing, and stationery
	19 Electricity
	20 Metalware and metalworking (small-scale)
	21 Building materials and wood manufacturing (small-scale)
	22 Textile and textile products (small-scale)
	23 Food, drink, tobacco, etc. (small-scale)
	24 Glass and ceramics (small-scale)
	25 Leather and leather products (small-scale)
	26 Other products (small-scale)
	32 Construction
	35 Defense materials (including explosives)
	36 Unclassified (large-scale)
3 Commerce, transport, and communication	27 Railways and communication
	28 Other transport
	29 Trade and distribution
	30 Banks, insurance, and cooperatives
4 Other services	31 Professions, services, etc.
	33 Residential property
	34 Public administration

tracted from the data on the "value added" not only in the first round but also in all the subsequent rounds. This is done in preference to adding depreciation to the data on the "value added" given by the ENI for two reasons. One is that depreciation allowance is a magnitude rather arbitrarily decided on by the industries. Hence, inclusion of depreciation in "value added" introduces an autonomous element and vitiates comparison from one year to another. The other reason for excluding depreciation is simply that it is easier to estimate it for one year than for a string of years. Since the base year for the comparison of the total outputs is 1951–52 and since the data on the "value added" for the other years in the period of comparison are available net of depreciation, it has been decided to eliminate depreciation from the "value added" in the input-output matrix.

The estimate of depreciation is rough and was made mostly on the basis of data from "Estimates of Domestic Fixed Capital Formation for 1948–49 through 1955–56," a table in *Indian Economic Statistics,* part 1 published by the Ministry of Finance, Government of India. The classification of the sectors in "Estimates of Domestic Fixed Capital Formation" and the input-output table is not the same. In the former, a distinction is drawn between private investment and government investment. The private investment has been classified under four heads: (1) construction; (2) agriculture, irrigation, land improvement, and small enterprises; (3) mining and large scale manufacturing enterprises; and (4) transport equipment. Because these four sectors do not correspond to the four sectors in the input-output table, we have made slight adjustments to enforce this correspondence. From sector 2, as defined in "Estimates of Capital Formation" the depreciation allowance of the small enterprises has been separated from the rest on the basis of their relative total outputs as given in the input-output table and that amount has been added to sector 2 in the input-output table defined as mining, manufacturing, and small enterprises. The data on depreciation given under the heading of sector 4, transport equipment, in "Estimates of Capital Formation," have been transferred to sector 3 in the input-output table defined as commerce, transport, and communication.

A lump sum figure was given for the gross and net government investment in "Estimates of Capital Formation." This figure has been broken down by sectors according to the proportions of gross capital formation on government account as available in the input-output table. These are 0.23 percent in "agriculture, etc.," 96.67 percent in "mining, manufacturing, and small enterprises," 3.10 percent in "commerce, transport, and communication," and zero in "other services." The final data on depreciation are given in Table 11B.2.

The second difficulty relating to the comparability of the data arises out of the inclusion of commodity taxes from the second round upwards in

TABLE 11B.2—An estimate of depreciation by sector
(In crores, or ten million IRs)

Sector	On government account	On private account	Total
Agriculture, animal husbandry, forestry, and fishery	0.16	78.07	78.23
Mining, manufacturing, and small enterprises	72.50	222.93	295.43
Commerce, transport, and communication	2.34	74.00	76.34
Other services	n.a.	n.a.	n.a.
Total	75.00	375.00	450.00

n.a.: Not available.

the input-output table and the exclusion of commodity taxes in the data on the "value added" of the ENI. In other words, the inter-industry transactions are given in the input-output table at market prices and the data on the "value added" of the ENI were given at factor costs. (As a result, the total outputs and the interpolated inter-industry transactions would also be at factor costs.) To make the interpolated data comparable to the data in the input-output table, the latter are expressed at factor costs. The first four rows in Table 11B.3 relate to the percentage distribution of the costs of production of each sector. The second three rows relate to the

TABLE 11B.3—The direct and cumulated costs of production
(Percentage of total costs)

Costs of Production	Agriculture, animal husbandry, forestry, and fishery	Mining, manufacturing, and small enterprises	Commerce, transport, and communication	Other services
Direct				
Material inputs	29.56%	52.75%	16.93%	11.10%
Net domestic product at factor costs	68.28	32.45	80.53	88.90
Depreciation	01.07	06.40	02.27	—
Commodity taxes	01.09	08.40	00.27	—
Total	100.00	100.00	100.00	100.00
Cumulated				
Factor costs	96.43	79.66	95.91	98.36
Depreciation	01.74	09.00	03.01	00.76
Commodity taxes	01.83	11.34	01.08	00.88
Total	100.00	100.00	100.00	100.00

data on cumulated factor costs, depreciation, and commodity taxes after the material inputs have been resolved into the primary inputs.

The data for 1951–52 on the "value added" of the ENI and in the input-output table, both brought to a reasonable degree of comparability, are given in Table 11B.4. The discrepancy in the two estimates of the

TABLE 11B.4—Comparison of the estimates of net value added on the basis of input-output and national income, 1951–52
(Billion IRs)

Sector	Input-output, net value added	National income, net value added	Discrepancy (sign neglected)
Agriculture, animal husbandry, forestry, and fishery	49.8	49.9	0.1
Mining, manufacturing, and small enterprises	15.0	17.3	2.3
Commerce, transport, and communication	27.0	17.9	9.1
Other services	15.6	15.0	0.6
Total	107.4	100.1	—

total "value added" is of the order of 7 percent, and in the case of individual sectors, particularly the sector labeled commerce, transport, and communications, it is considerably larger.

Tables 11B.5 and 11B.6 present input and output coefficients for four sectors of the Indian economy for 1951–52, and inverses of the matrices.

TABLE 11B.5—Input and output coefficients, 1951–52

Sector	Matrix of input coefficients based on gross outputs				Matrix of output coefficients			
	1	2	3	4	1	2	3	4
1 Agriculture, animal husbandry, forestry, and fishery	.2631	.2097	.0573	.0003	.2631	.1326	.0264	.0001
2 Mining, manufacturing, and small enterprises	.0219	.2168	.0582	.0744	.0346	.2168	.0423	.0283
3 Commerce, transport, and communications	.0031	.0912	.0336	.0286	.0067	.1253	.0336	.0150
4 Other services	.0075	.0098	.0202	.0077	.0311	.0256	.0386	.0077

TABLE 11B.6—Inverses of matrices, 1951–52

Sector	1	2	3	4
$(I = \beta)$				
1 Agriculture, animal husbandry, forestry, and fishery	1.3691	.3792	.1047	.0319
2 Mining, manufacturing, and small enterprises	.0400	1.2984	.0826	.0997
3 Commerce, transport, and communications	.0085	.1243	1.0436	.0394
4 Other services	.0109	.0182	.0229	1.0098
$(I = \gamma)$				
1 Agriculture, animal husbandry, forestry, and fishery	1.3691	.2397	.0482	.0077
2 Mining, manufacturing, and small enterprises	.0633	1.2984	.0601	.0379
3 Commerce, transport, and communications	.0185	.1708	1.0436	.0206
4 Other services	.0453	.0478	.0438	1.0098

COMMENT ON CHAPTER 11

AMADO A. CASTRO

Dr. Ramana deserves commendation for his neat, thorough, but concise presentation of his argument that deficit financing hurt the Indian balance of payments. In such circumstances I can only ask a few questions by way of clarification.

First, Dr. Ramana studies the relationship of money and prices and shows that there has been a high correlation between the two. I would like to ask whether in making his calculations Dr. Ramana experimented with possible lagged relationships between the different variables, and what the results were, if any.

Second, it is quite definitely shown that deficit financing was a major influence towards bringing about India's balance-of-payments difficulties. However, I wonder whether fortuitous events, such as bad weather leading to crop failures, have been taken into account in the analysis? I understand that in a number of years the food problem was an additional burden on India's resources of foreign exchange and had serious consequences, especially on a marginal basis; that is, it raised the question of whether additional food or machinery and raw materials for industrial production was to be imported.

I also have a minor question concerning the determinants of velocity. Ramana analyzes velocity in terms of four determinants: the call money rate, which is for short-term interest; the government bond yield, which is for long-term interest; the percent change in wholesale price levels; and lastly, per capita real income. I wonder whether I'm being naive in recalling that there may be things which are not susceptible to analysis—such as expectations and other psychological factors. However, this omission is perhaps less important because, as Dr. Ramana points out, the income velocity of money in India does not change much.

Third, I would like to address myself to the larger question which arises in my mind in connection with Dr. Ramana's paper as well as that of Professor Lakdawala. It concerns the long-term economic policy of India in foreign trade. India is one of the countries that have had import controls and exchange controls for a long, long time. In spite of the devaluation of last June, it is one of the decreasing number of countries in this area that still has tight exchange controls. I would look forward to the time when India will dismantle her controls, for I feel that when such a happy event transpires India can progress much more rapidly.

COMMENT ON CHAPTERS 10 AND 11

JOHN H. POWER

Dr. Ramana is both a monetarist and a structuralist, as I think one must be to analyze the inflation problem adequately. Nevertheless I believe that I would put more emphasis on the import-substitution bias and less on deficit financing. Shrinking the deficit would not have contributed to a solution of the basic problem, though it would have reduced the inflationary symptoms. A correct industrialization policy, in contrast, might have rendered the government deficit harmless.

I have in mind a model wherein a policy of encouraging manufacturing for the domestic market behind protection is supposed to force a transfer of saving to industry from the other sectors via higher prices for manufactured goods. If other sectors can protect themselves by raising the money supply for their products, or if they are protected by an inelastic supply (as in agriculture), the attempt to improve the terms of trade for manufacturing may result simply in a struggle for income shares and resulting inflation. And holding back on money creation in such circumstances may only create unemployment.

Bilateral trade agreements are defended by Mr. Karunatilake as providing a market for exports that would have depressed world prices if they had been directed to the free-world market. While I see great advantage for developing countries in increasing trade with Communist countries and others that prefer this kind of trading arrangement, I wonder if there isn't possibly an element of illusion in the rationalization given. If the trading partner buys no more, but simply diverts its demand from the world market to bilateral trade, supply and demand have been withdrawn from the world market in equal amounts and the world price is unaffected. This is perhaps the extreme case, but it serves notice that one cannot expect wholly to avoid a depressing effect on world price by diverting exports to bilateral trade.

CHAPTER 12

INDONESIAN EXPORTS: PERFORMANCE AND PROSPECTS

J. PANGLAYKIM AND KENNETH D. THOMAS

Policies designed to promote economic development came under consideration in Indonesian government circles in the mood of optimism and confidence which affected many levels of society in the months following the abortive coup of September, 1965.[1] In this chapter we assess the contribution that the foreign trade sector can make to any development program in the years to 1970. The general impression is that both the volume and the value of exports have deteriorated rapidly in recent years.[2] A closer examination of the export sector reveals that the situation is more complex than is usually assumed.

We will review the performance of the export sector as a whole from 1950 to 1966 so that the trends can be seen in perspective. We will highlight the contrast between trends in value and volume. Fluctuations in exports, aside from the overall trend, will be related to conditions in the economy as a whole, and to important political events insofar as they have impinged on the country's capacity to export and to reinvest.

Although, as we shall see, the export volume of several commodities was maintained over the final years of this period, this did not encourage an attitude of complacency. If the output of most commodities was to remain at achieved levels or to increase, investment for replacement and expansion was essential. This was especially the case given the trend in commodity prices. Between 1961 and 1965, the fall in the value of Indonesia's exports was due largely to the relatively low world-market prices for rubber. Prices of the other commodities were, in general, more favorable (see Table 12.1) but because rubber accounted for such a large percentage of export value (Table 12.2) the favorable price trends did not offset the depressing effects

TABLE 12.1—Indonesian commodity price indices (United States prices), 1950–65
(1953 = 100)

Year	Coffee	Tea	Copra	Tobacco	Rubber	Tin	Petroleum	Palm oil[a]
1950	87.2	102.8	95.5	94.5	171.4	100.8	94.7	140.3
1951	93.6	98.2	98.3	103.7	252.7	133.6	94.7	205.6
1952	93.3	91.9	71.8	100.6	158.5	126.5	94.7	109.7
1953	100.0	100.0	100.0	100.0	100.0	100.0	100.0	100.0
1954	135.9	146.2	84.1	102.2	97.1	96.7	104.2	108.3
1955	98.5	147.6	75.0	101.6	161.8	96.3	104.2	113.9
1956	100.3	112.6	73.3	105.3	142.3	106.1	104.2	125.0
1957	98.3	125.7	74.3	106.5	129.0	101.3	113.6	125.0
1958	83.6	104.5	93.0	112.2	117.0	99.8	109.4	112.5
1959	63.8	110.5	115.2	117.0	151.0	107.1	107.2	119.4
1960	63.2	114.8	90.9	114.8	159.8	106.4	107.2	112.5
1961	62.2	110.7	74.1	121.3	122.8	118.8	107.2	113.9
1962	58.6	102.2	71.5	122.7	119.1	120.3	112.1	108.3
1963	58.9	104.9	81.0	114.4	109.1	122.6	112.1	113.9
1964	81.8	102.4	85.4	113.0	104.6	165.8	112.1	122.5
1965	77.3	104.3[b]	96.2[c]	117.2	106.6	185.2	112.1[d]	141.3

[a] Import prices of palm oil are c.i.f. European ports in bulk. Price is of Congolese oil until 1963 and Nigerian oil from 1964. The index is spliced at 1964 to account for the change.
[b] Spliced New York price of Ceylon-India tea.
[c] Spliced Manila price of Philippine copra.
[d] Spliced West Texas price.
Sources: *Palm oil:* United Nations, *Monthly Bulletin of Statistics*, various issues; *other commodities:* International Monetary Fund, *International Financial Statistics*, various issues.

of the decline in rubber prices. Assuming that the world market could absorb Indonesia's products, volume had to increase to offset expected price declines (especially for rubber) in the future. The fifties were years of lost opportunity as far as the expansion of productive capacity was concerned. This is attributable for the most part to political instability and the consequent inability of successive governments to act constructively in the economic sphere. For most products, the stage had been reached where, unless a reinvestment program was implemented soon, and if the present trend in world prices continued, export earnings would decline more rapidly than in the past.

General Trends

Eight commodities accounted for 86 percent of Indonesia's exports in 1950, and for 90 percent in 1964 (Table 12.2). Rubber and petroleum clearly dominated the export sector in the early fifties, and in

TABLE 12.2—Indonesian major commodity exports, 1950–64
(Percentage of total exports)

Year	Rubber			Petroleum and petroleum products, gross	Tin ore	Copra	Coffee	Tea	Tobacco	Palm oil	Other	Total
	Estate	Smallholder	Total									
1950	11.9	30.9	42.8	18.4	6.1	7.2	1.9	3.4	5.1	1.2	13.9	100.0
1951	16.7	33.9	50.6	14.3	6.3	10.4	1.7	2.9	1.8	0.9	11.1	100.0
1952	21.5	23.9	45.4	20.5	9.2	5.5	1.9	2.5	2.5	2.9	9.6	100.0
1953	16.5	16.0	32.5	24.3	9.6	6.9	3.7	2.8	3.8	3.4	13.0	100.0
1954	12.1	19.2	31.3	26.2	6.9	5.9	4.5	4.6	4.0	3.1	13.5	100.0
1955	18.2	27.5	45.7	22.8	6.3	3.7	1.7	3.3	3.3	2.5	10.7	100.0
1956	16.7	22.3	39.0	27.6	6.7	4.2	3.3	3.2	3.2	2.9	9.9	100.0
1957	15.3	21.3	36.6	31.7	5.8	4.3	3.1	3.1	3.5	2.7	9.2	100.0
1958	13.8	19.4	33.2	39.9	4.5	2.3	2.3	3.1	3.8	3.0	7.9	100.0
1959	15.4	29.6	45.0	30.7	3.9	3.0	2.0	2.2	2.6	2.1	8.5	100.0
1960	15.9	28.9	44.8	26.3	6.0	3.5	1.6	3.3	4.0	2.4	8.1	100.0
1961	15.5	23.4	38.9	33.1	4.2	4.4	1.8	3.3	3.1	2.7	8.5	100.0
1962	14.9	28.9	43.8	31.7	5.1	2.2	1.8	3.0	2.4	2.6	7.4	100.0
1963	13.5	21.7	35.2	38.6	2.7	1.9	2.9	2.6	2.7	2.8	10.6	100.0
1964	13.6	19.0	32.6	36.9	4.4	3.2	3.7	2.3	3.0	3.7	10.2	100.0

Source: Computed from Table 12.3.

TABLE 12.3—Value of Indonesian exports classified by main commodities, 1950-64
(Million US$)

| Year | Rubber | | | Petroleum and petroleum products | | Tin ore | Copra | Coffee | Tea | Tobacco | Palm oil | Other | Total[b] exports | Total[c] exports |
| | Estate | Smallholder | Total | Gross | Net[a] | | | | | | | | | |
	(1)	(2)	(3)	(4)	(5)	(6)	(7)	(8)	(9)	(10)	(11)	(12)	(13)	(14)
1950	94.9	247.3	342.2	147.5	n.a.	48.7	57.6	14.9	26.9	41.2	9.1	111.3	799.4	—
1951	215.1	438.4	653.5	184.9	n.a.	81.2	133.9	22.3	37.0	23.0	12.2	143.6	1291.6	—
1952	200.6	223.3	423.9	191.3	n.a.	86.1	51.3	18.0	23.5	23.3	26.7	90.2	934.3	—
1953	138.9	133.9	272.8	204.6	n.a.	80.6	57.8	30.9	23.8	31.7	28.6	109.5	840.3	—
1954	104.8	166.4	271.2	227.1	n.a.	59.5	51.4	39.5	39.8	34.6	26.7	116.8	866.6	—
1955	171.9	259.7	431.6	215.8	n.a.	59.5	35.4	16.0	31.2	30.8	24.2	101.0	945.5	—
1956	154.5	206.2	360.7	255.3	n.a.	62.0	39.2	30.0	29.8	29.4	27.1	91.0	924.5	—
1957	145.9	203.6	349.5	302.8	n.a.	55.5	40.5	29.4	29.8	33.6	26.0	88.0	955.1	—
1958	108.8	153.2	262.0	315.2	134.5	35.4	18.3	18.5	24.8	30.2	23.7	62.6	790.7	610.0
1959	143.4	275.9	419.3	285.7	48.0	36.2	27.6	19.0	20.3	24.4	19.2	79.3	931.0	693.3
1960	133.9	243.2	377.1	220.8	70.0	50.6	29.1	13.7	27.7	33.3	20.0	68.5	840.8	690.0
1961	122.4	184.6	307.0	260.9	99.0	33.3	34.7	13.8	25.7	24.6	21.4	66.7	788.1	626.2
1962	101.6	196.9	298.5	215.8	88.0	34.9	14.7	12.5	20.6	16.2	17.9	50.6	681.7	553.9
1963	94.1	150.8	244.9	268.7	n.a.	18.9	13.6	19.9	17.8	18.9	20.0	73.7	696.4	—
1964	98.6	137.2	235.8	267.4	n.a.	31.6	23.5	26.6	17.0	21.8	26.9	73.6	724.2	—

n.a.: Not available.
[a] Net earnings for petroleum have been included, where available, since gross earnings contain an unusually high foreign-exchange component.
[b] Total of columns 3–12, excluding column 5.
[c] Total of columns 3–12, excluding column 4.
Sources: Central Bureau of Statistics, *Statistical Abstract*, 1956; *ibid*, *Warta BPS*, 1, no. 2(1966); Alex Hunter, "The Indonesian Oil Industry," *Australian Economic Papers*, 5, no. 1 (1966): 97.

spite of the government's expressed intention to diversify the economy, these two items continue to provide between 60 and 70 percent of export earnings through 1965.

The total value of exports, averaging $928 million for the period 1950–59, inclusive, declined steadily after 1959. The average for the period 1960–64 inclusive was $746 million, while for 1964 the value was $724 million (see Table 12.3). The reasons for this decline are numerous and will be analyzed commodity by commodity in the next section. In general, the difficulties facing those operating in the export sector in the post-independence period included serious inflation, uncertainty in government policy toward foreign investment, pressures against the Chinese trading community, expulsion of the Dutch and the consequent loss of the Dutch-owned interisland shipping company, internal revolts, and Confrontation with Singapore and Malaysia.[3]

Tables 12.4 to 12.9, which give the main statistics of production and export of the eight commodities discussed below, indicate that for several the performance was better than would have been expected given the political and economic instability of the fifteen years covered. Even in those cases where exports fell, total production of the commodities concerned was less affected than exports, which suggests that growth of home consumption, as well as smuggling, was significant.

Rubber

Indonesian rubber is produced on both estates and peasant smallholdings. The volume of exports from the latter has, since 1936, come to exceed exports from estates by an increasing margin. Because of the lower qualities produced by the smallholders, the difference in the value of output from the two sources has been less significant.

Exports (estimated from production data) of estate rubber declined appreciably after the peak of 304,215 long tons in 1953 (see Table 12.4 and Figure 12.1). This trend was inevitable, at least until the late fifties, because no replanting had been undertaken during the previous decade of war and revolution. Allowing for the fact that the effects of a new planting or replanting program are not felt for seven years, the evidence suggests that little replanting was done, even after independence. Dutch and other foreign interests dominated the estate sector in Indonesia until the end of 1957. The inability of the several governments of this period to provide a favorable climate for foreign

TABLE 12.4—Production of Indonesian and Malayan rubber, 1950–65
(Long tons)

Year	Indonesia		Malaya (Federation of Malaya and Singapore)		Price index, Singapore[a] (1953 = 100)
	Estate	Smallholders	Estate	Smallholders	
1950	175,127	521,345	376,745	317,345	160
1951	222,534	591,872	328,790	276,556	251
1952	294,468	456,026	341,730	242,508	143
1953	304,215	390,335	341,801	232,589	100
1954	283,507	460,861	345,474	241,006	100
1955	262,075	475,013	352,536	286,212	169
1956	261,630	425,037	351,591	274,381	144
1957	253,387	431,128	368,601	268,936	132
1958	239,266	445,932	390,125	272,747	119
1959	220,504	472,983	407,961	289,805	151
1960	212,212	398,240	414,074	294,303	160
1961	219,660	451,739	429,491	307,258	124
1962	205,960	464,849	439,211	312,350	116
1963	205,034	368,063	459,318	329,221	107
1964	219,688	418,765	477,921	347,359	101
1965	220,326[b]	489,034[b]	481,068	379,588	104

Note: For Indonesia, figures for estate production represent reported production; estimates only are available for smallholdings. Total production is taken as being equivalent to total net exports plus an allowance (currently estimated at 23,000 tons per annum) for internal consumption.

[a] Ribbed smoke sheet I.

[b] Exports in metric tons.

Sources: Indonesian Statistical Association in the Philippines, *Journal of Indonesian Statistics*, October, 1966, p. 22; International Rubber Study Group, *Rubber Statistical Bulletin*, 15, no. 1(1960), and 20, no. 11(1966).

investment blocked the implementation of a much-needed replanting program.[4]

The takeover and eventual nationalization of Dutch estates in 1957–58 no doubt had some effect on output during the immediately following years while the inexperienced Indonesian managers were adjusting to their new responsibilities. Proof of this is difficult because Dutch estates accounted for only about 40 percent of the foreign-owned rubber estates and no breakdown of estate production by nationality is available.[5]

Investment policy on the government estates was supervised by a central government authority, and political priorities have apparently prevented an adequate replanting program. Decisions concerning for-eign-exchange allocations for equipment and raw materials for proc-

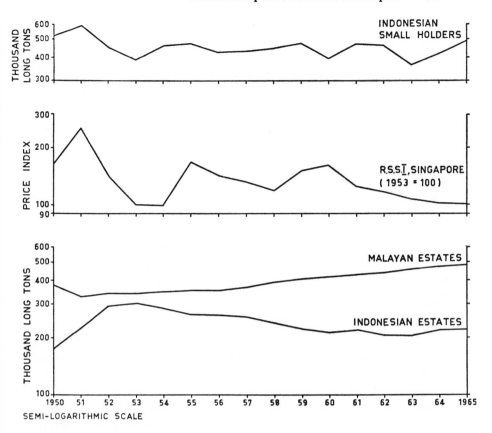

FIGURE 12.1—Exports of Indonesian and Malayan rubber and price index of rubber
(ribbed smoked sheet I, Singapore), 1950–64

essing were outside the responsibility of estate management. An inadequate supply of imported materials has had an unfavorable impact on
estate performance. Foreign-exchange difficulties, moreover, were
only a portion of the problems faced by the estates, because in order
to obtain domestic rupiah finance for replanting, replacement of spare
parts, and other costs, they sold part of their production locally, to
private exporters.[6]

The long-run future of estate rubber depends on large-scale new
planting and replanting with high-yielding rubber. Cutting down old
stands to make way for new rubber usually leads to a fall in output as
the tappable area is reduced. Any delay in implementing a replanting
program is likely to result in a greater decline in total output because

an increasing proportion of the trees left in tap are aging beyond their most productive years.

A new tapping technique, however, has recently become available. It gives highly profitable yields and also prolongs the economic life of the tree. This technique, a system of high- and low-cut tapping, can be used on 1925–30 plantings in good condition, and according to Fleming "There seems good reason to expect *continued high yields* until the trees are between 45–50 years old."[7] Because of the age structure of the trees on Indonesian estates, the importance of this technique and its rapid application cannot be overemphasized.[8]

If this high- and low-cut tapping method or other ways of increasing yield are not adopted on a wide scale, the volume of exports from the estates will continue to decline, since increases in output resulting from past replanting will undoubtedly be offset by the declining productivity of aging trees. Coupled with the expected decrease in volume are forecasts of a steady fall in price. Competition from synthetic rubber (SR) was largely responsible for the fall in the price of natural rubber (NR) between 1956 and 1965. A comparison of the prices for NR in the fifties and sixties reveals a long-run decline and a tendency for price fluctuations to become progressively weaker (see Table 12.1 and Figure 12.1).

Forecasts of the future of NR cannot be considered in isolation from the supply and demand situation for SR. Projections made by the Food and Agricultural Organization (FAO) for 1970 indicate that the overall demand for rubber will increase, with the demand for SR rising at a faster rate than that for NR. The FAO estimates that by 1970 the consumption of all rubber will be between 4.9 and 5.7 million metric tons.[9] Estimates of the increase in world consumption of NR are within a range of 2.3 to 2.9 million metric tons over the period 1962–70, the margin of error being accentuated by uncertainties surrounding the imports of the centrally-planned economies.[10] The prospects for the estate sector in Indonesia make it improbable that the estates will be able to contribute significantly to this increase unless new techniques are adopted quickly.

Future trends for smallholders' rubber are less easy to predict. Exports of smallholders' rubber between 1950 and 1965 (Table 12.4) showed considerable fluctuations from year to year, but no secular trend. Assuming that the figure of 489,000 metric tons for 1965 was too high, and that exports for 1963 and 1964 reflected the influence of Confrontation rather than a decline in capacity, one may take the 1962 figure as a guide. In that year exports of 464,849 metric tons were above the average for the period 1950–62; in fact, they were as high as exports for 1952 and 1954. This suggests that reports in the early fifties to the effect that aging trees would affect exports adversely in the "near future" were based on an incorrect assessment of the potential of the smallholders' rubber industry.[11] The planting of rubber in the shifting cultivation cycle may have been largely responsible for the maintenance of exports at the level of the early fifties (excluding the period of the Korean boom).

A comparison of export earnings from rubber in 1960 and 1962 indicates the magnitude of the problem posed by the price decline in rubber. The volume of exports of rubber between the two years rose from 610,452 to 670,809 long tons, or by 10 percent, reflecting an increase of 14 percent in smallholders' rubber and a decline of 3 percent in estate rubber. But export earnings from rubber fell from $377 million to $299 million or by 21 percent. The increase in the volume of exports from the smallholders' sector was not sufficient to offset the decline in volume of estate exports plus the decline in world prices.

The resilience of the smallholders' sector since 1950 is remarkable when we consider the conditions under which those engaged in producing and marketing the commodity have operated. Inflation has been endemic since independence, and the smallholders have suffered as a consequence. The best indicator of the deterioration of the smallholders' position is the trend in the relative prices of rice and rubber at the village level. Although the rubber/rice price ratio per kilogram on the world market has been consistently in favor of rubber, with a peak of 8.2 : 1, and has not fallen below 4.9 : 1 since 1955,[12] there were occasions in Indonesia when one kilogram of rubber was worth less than one kilogram of rice.[13]

Deterioration of transport facilities also tended to affect adversely the development of the smallholders' rubber sector. There were shortages of spare parts for all types of vehicles, shortages of rolling stock, and an inadequate maintenance of the railway system as a whole.

Our review of the possibilities facing the industry to 1970 underlines the role of the government policy. Assuming that smallholders' capacity is adequate to maintain exports of around 450,000 tons, the main task of the government lies in creating favorable conditions for this level of exports, especially by insuring reasonable relative price ratios for the rubber producer, preventing the disruption of the existing marketing structure, improving communications, and eliminating the numerous unofficial levies on the traders who form the links in the chain to the city.

With the takeover of British and American estates in 1964–65, the government extended its control over the entire estate-rubber industry. The most effective way open to the government to stimulate production in the short run appears to be the widespread adoption of the high- and low-cut tapping system. Simultaneously, the government estates will need to maintain and possibly step up their replanting program in order to insure the long-run earning capacity of the industry. If these two elements are incorporated into some definite plan for the estates there is no reason why output and exports should decline while the newly planted areas are reaching maturity.

Palm Oil, Coffee, Tea, Tobacco, and Copra

These five commodities accounted for between 12 and 22 percent of total exports in the period 1951–64, with 16 percent their share in 1964 (Table 12.2). With the exception of palm oil, these products are produced on both estates and smallholdings. Since independence, the smallholders have improved their position both relatively and absolutely (see Tables 12.5–12.9).

The production of tobacco, coffee, and palm oil fluctuated considerably throughout the period. By 1964, coffee production was much improved compared with the levels reached in the early fifties, but there was a considerable decline in the output of tobacco and a smaller decline in palm oil. Production of copra and tea was much more stable. In both cases output was higher at the end of the period.

Smallholder exports offset the decline in estate exports during the fifties, but since 1960 there has been a tendency for smallholder exports of tea, coffee, and tobacco to stagnate.[14]

PALM OIL. Palm oil is produced only on estates. Production fluctuated considerably during the period under review. There was no secular decline (Table 12.5). Postwar production reached its peak in 1954, but even then it was well below the 1938 level of 226,700 metric tons. The main reason for the decline in production was the failure of the estates to carry out an adequate replanting program.

Exports of palm oil, compared with 1938, declined even more than production. In 1938 exports were 97 percent of production. Between

TABLE 12.5—Estate palm oil, Indonesia: area, production, exports, domestic consumption, and price index, 1938, 1951–65

Year	Area (thousand hectares) Planted	Area Mature	Production (thousand metric tons)	Exports Volume (thousand metric tons)	Volume as % of production	Values (million US $)	Domestic consumption[a] (thousand metric tons)	Price index N.Y. prices 1953 = 100
1938	92.3	74.5	226.7	220.7	97	—	6.0	—
1951	90.2	80.1	121.1	106.2	88	12.2	14.9	205.6
1952	94.0	82.9	146.4	124.8	85	26.7	21.6	109.7
1953	96.4	84.4	160.5	135.8	85	28.6	24.7	100.0
1954	100.2	87.8	168.7	147.2	87	26.7	21.5	108.3
1955	101.4	89.9	165.8	116.3	70	24.2	49.5	113.9
1956	103.0	91.6	164.9	132.9	81	27.1	32.0	125.0
1957	103.0	90.5	160.2	128.9	80	26.0	31.3	125.0
1958	104.5	92.4	147.7	131.3	89	23.7	16.4	112.5
1959	102.9	86.8	137.5	103.0	75	19.2	34.5	119.4
1960	104.3	88.0	141.2	108.5	77	20.0	32.7	112.5
1961	104.9	88.1	145.7	117.6	81	21.4	28.1	113.9
1962	104.7	89.5	141.4	100.4	74	17.9	41.0	108.3
1963	n.a.	n.a.	148.3	109.8	74	20.0	38.5	113.9
1964	n.a.	n.a.	160.6	133.1	83	26.9	27.5	122.5
1965	n.a.	n.a.	n.a.	120.0	—	n.a.	n.a.	141.3

n.a.: Not available.
[a] Production minus exports.
Sources: *Netherlands Indian Report, 1939*, vol. 2; *Statistical Abstracts*, 1938, 1956, *Statistical Pocketbook of Indonesia*, 1957, 1961, 1963, *Monthly Survey*, January and April, 1963, and *Warta BPS*, 1, nos. 1 and 2 (1966) (these four published by the Central Bureau of Statistics); Department of Estates, preliminary figures; United Nations, *Monthly Bulletin of Statistics*, various issues; International Monetary Fund, *International Financial Statistics*, various issues. Value of exports computed from Table 12.3.

1950 and 1964 the domestic market took a much larger share of total output, accentuating the effects of low production on exports.

As with estate rubber, the government now controls the entire palm oil industry. Unless the government undertakes an extensive planting program, the future of the palm oil industry is in jeopardy. Such a program will, in the first instance, reduce current production, particularly if the emphasis is on replanting. Whatever the government does now, a decline in production in the short run seems inevitable, accompanied by a decline also in exports, particularly if domestic consumption is maintained or increased.

COFFEE. Estate production averaged 15,100 metric tons during the fifties (Table 12.6). The maximum of 22,400 metric tons in 1953 was less than half the 1938 output. Prewar production levels could not be regained from the greatly reduced area under production.

By contrast, smallholders increased their output. Much of the increase was, no doubt, due to an extension of the area under cultivation.[15] The data presented in Table 12.6 supports this view, at least until 1961. Local consumption went up, but not so much as to prevent exports from rising.

TEA. Production rose from 68,300 metric tons in 1954 to 83,700 metric tons in 1964. The share of exports declined from 66 to 43 percent (Table 12.7) as home consumption absorbed an increasing proportion. Estate production was fairly steady throughout the period under review, but at a level of about 55 percent of 1938 output. A decline in the area under cultivation was again the main cause. The area of smallholders' tea changed little in the postwar period. Yet under adverse economic and political conditions the smallholders succeeded in maintaining and even improving their overall position.[16]

TOBACCO. Production on estates, which accounted for between 12 and 16 percent of total output, showed no increase over the peak of 10,400 metric tons in 1953 (see Table 12.8). Again, a decline in area largely accounted for the decline in production.[17] Even resort to available techniques for increasing yields per hectare could not have compensated for the reduction in tobacco land. There is no clear-cut evidence to indicate that the expulsion of the Dutch made much difference to the estate output of tobacco. As with rubber, the tobacco estates under government control may have been overcentralized. But on the crucial question of new investment and the expansion of area

TABLE 12.6—Coffee, Indonesia: production, exports, and price index, 1938, 1951–64

Year	Estates Area (thousand hectares) Planted	Estates Area (thousand hectares) Mature	Estates Production (thousand metric tons)	Estates Exports (thousand metric tons)	Smallholders Area (thousand hectares)	Smallholders Production[a] (thousand metric tons)	Smallholders Exports (thousand metric tons)	Total Production (thousand metric tons)	Total Exports (thousand metric tons)	Total Exports as % of production	Value of exports (million US $)	Price index, N.Y. prices (1953 = 100)
1938	103.6	96.1	45.6	28.6	n.a.	61.7	39.8	107.3	68.4	64	—	—
1951	46.9	41.9	12.1	11.3	101.1	39.0	14.0	51.1	25.3	49	22.3	94
1952	48.7	44.0	13.2	5.3	115.3	36.9	13.4	50.1	18.7	47	18.0	93
1953	49.8	44.9	22.4	13.8	119.3	39.6	17.8	62.0	31.6	54	30.9	100
1954	49.5	43.9	14.4	16.7	132.5	43.3	21.1	57.7	37.8	66	39.5	136
1955	48.3	43.0	16.1	9.1	148.6	47.3	14.5	63.4	23.6	37	16.0	99
1956	47.4	41.5	13.0	11.2	163.6	47.0	46.4	60.0	57.6	95	30.0	100
1957	47.1	42.1	15.3	11.8	192.4	60.0	40.4	75.3	52.2	69	29.4	98
1958	47.1	41.7	12.6	5.7	198.9	54.1	23.1	66.7	28.8	43	18.5	84
1959	47.2	42.3	19.0	8.3	208.9	65.3	30.7	84.3	39.0	46	19.0	64
1960	47.1	42.1	18.3	5.6	230.8	77.6	36.6	95.9	42.2	44	13.7	63
1961	46.6	41.3	19.1	7.0	240.2	78.3	60.0	97.4	67.0	69	13.8	62
1962	44.1	39.0	12.3	8.7	n.a.	90.9	49.9	103.2	58.6	57	12.5	59
1963	n.a.	n.a.	18.4	10.4	n.a.	111.5	70.5	129.9	80.9	62	19.9	60
1964	n.a.	n.a.	7.4	15.7	n.a.	90.0	46.6	97.4	62.3	64	26.6	82

n.a.: Not available.

[a] The data refer to robusta coffee only. No information is available for the production of arabica, although exports of this variety were 6,700 metric tons in 1938.

Sources: For smallholders' production in 1938, see C. J. J. van Hall, *Insulinde de Inheemsche Landbouw*, p. 219. For sources of other data, see Table 12.5.

TABLE 12.7—Tea, Indonesia: area, production, exports, and price index, 1938, 1951–64

Year	Estates Area (thousand hectares) Planted	Estates Area (thousand hectares) Mature[a]	Estates Production (thousand metric tons)	Estates Exports (thousand metric tons)	Smallholders Area (thousand hectares)	Smallholders Production (thousand metric tons)	Smallholders Exports (thousand metric tons)	Total Production (thousand metric tons)	Total Exports (thousand metric tons)	Total Exports as % of production	Value of exports (million US $)	Price index, N.Y. prices (1953 = 100)
1938	138.3	137.0	80.5	58.9	66.0	12.2	13.0	92.7	71.9	78	—	—
1951	61.2	68.1	46.5	n.a.	65.0	13.9	n.a.	60.4	45.9	76	37.0	98
1952	78.3	66.9	37.3	n.a.	65.3	38.2	n.a.	75.5	35.8	47	23.5	92
1953	78.3	67.0	37.0	n.a.	64.2	33.1	n.a.	70.1	33.0	47	23.8	100
1954	81.1	67.8	46.9	n.a.	64.4	21.4	n.a.	68.3	45.2	66	39.8	146
1955	80.3	67.7	44.0	n.a.	64.6	21.9	n.a.	65.9	37.7	60	31.2	148
1956	76.9	66.2	42.9	n.a.	59.7	22.0	n.a.	64.9	39.1	60	29.8	113
1957	75.1	65.2	47.6	n.a.	60.1	22.3	n.a.	69.9	40.1	58	29.8	126
1958	74.3	65.9	48.5	n.a.	60.1	23.7	n.a.	72.2	39.0	54	24.8	105
1959	72.9	66.1	44.3	n.a.	62.9	32.1	n.a.	76.4	33.3	44	20.3	111
1960	72.9	66.7	46.1	n.a.	64.3	37.4	n.a.	83.5	39.2	47	27.7	115
1961	72.4	66.2	43.7	n.a.	64.4	37.7	n.a.	81.4	36.2	45	25.7	111
1962	77.8	65.2	47.2	n.a.	n.a.	n.a.	n.a.	n.a.	32.7	n.a.	20.6	102
1963	n.a.	n.a.	38.7	31.6	n.a.	n.a.	n.a.	n.a.	31.6	n.a.	17.8	105
1964	n.a.	n.a.	46.3	36.0	n.a.	n.a.	n.a.	n.a.	36.0	n.a.	17.0	102

n.a.: Not available.
[a] Plucking gardens plus pruned area.
Sources: See Tables 5 and 6.

TABLE 12.8—Tobacco, Indonesia: area, production, exports, and price index, 1938, 1951–64

Year	Estates			Smallholders			Total		Exports as % of production	Value of exports (million US $)	Price index, N.Y. prices (1953 = 100)
	Area (thousand hectares)	Production	Exports	Harvested	Production	Exports	Production	Exports			
		(thousand metric tons)		(thousand metric tons)			(thousand metric tons)				
1938	42.0	40.7	34.7	147.0	66.7	14.5	107.4	49.2	46	—	—
1951	12.3	7.9	n.a.	113.6	47.7	n.a.	55.6	13.3	24	23.0	103
1952	12.3	7.9	n.a.	158.5	64.9	n.a.	72.8	10.3	14	23.3	101
1953	12.6	10.4	n.a.	113.0	46.6	n.a.	57.0	14.8	26	31.7	100
1954	12.1	7.7	n.a.	145.0	60.7	n.a.	66.4	19.8	29	34.6	102
1955	11.4	7.1	n.a.	121.9	43.2	n.a.	50.3	13.2	26	30.8	102
1956	11.5	7.0	n.a.	166.3	53.9	n.a.	60.9	11.8	19	29.4	105
1957	11.1	8.5	n.a.	180.7	68.5	n.a.	77.0	14.7	19	33.6	107
1958	7.6	5.7	n.a.	178.3	61.0	n.a.	66.7	22.1	33	30.2	112
1959	12.4	10.1	n.a.	132.5	49.1	n.a.	59.2	16.0	27	24.4	117
1960	13.1	9.1	n.a.	129.0	49.6	n.a.	58.7	22.8	39	33.3	115
1961	12.5	9.5	n.a.	196.1	75.9	n.a.	85.4	17.5	21	24.6	121
1962	n.a.	n.a.	n.a.	n.a.	n.a.	n.a.	n.a.	n.a.	n.a.	16.2	123
1963	n.a.	n.a.	n.a.	n.a.	n.a.	n.a.	n.a.	n.a.	n.a.	18.9	114
1964	n.a.	n.a.	n.a.	n.a.	n.a.	n.a.	n.a.	n.a.	n.a.	21.8	113

n.a.: Not available.
Sources: See Table 12.5.

under production, the situation after 1957 seems to have been no worse (or better) than before.[18]

COPRA. Estates play an insignificant role in the production of copra. In the postwar period there was no sign of a long-run production trend, either up or down. On the other hand, reported exports fell sharply after 1957, the only exception being in 1961 (see Table

TABLE 12.9—Smallholders' copra, Indonesia: area, production, exports, and price index 1938, 1951–64

Year	Area (thousand hectares)	Production (thousand metric tons)	Exports (thousand metric tons)	Exports as % of production	Value of exports (million US $)	Price index, N.Y. prices, (1953 = 100)
1938	n.a.	523.7	n.a.	n.a.	—	—
1951	1,040.8	722.8	543.9	75	133.9	98
1952	1,237.5	1,119.3	347.5	31	51.3	72
1953	1,284.5	948.1	311.0	33	57.8	100
1954	1,496.1	1,201.8	296.9	25	51.4	84
1955	1,514.2	1,039.1	236.5	24	35.4	75
1956	1,545.1	997.1	266.3	27	39.2	73
1957	1,597.1	1,092.8	312.5	29	40.5	74
1958	1,651.2	1,077.8	127.9	29	18.3	93
1959	1,561.3	1,169.4	133.3	11	27.6	115
1960	1,649.3	1,127.8	169.0	15	29.1	91
1961	1,665.9	1,169.1	251.2	22	34.7	74
1962	n.a.	1,035.1	109.8	11	14.7	72
1963	n.a.	1,050.0	108.5	11	13.6	81
1964	n.a.	1,039.0	175.5	17	23.5	85

n.a.: Not available.
Sources: See Table 12.5.

12.9). Our problem is to explain the decline in exports during a time when production levels have been maintained.

A comparison between the trends in world price and the volume of exports does not help to explain the fall in exports since 1957. Between 1957 and 1959, for example, while the price increased by 55 percent, the value of copra exports fell by 32 percent. Similarly, as prices fell by 36 percent between 1959 and 1961, the value of copra exports increased by 26 percent. Under these circumstances, it is likely that internal factors were more important in determining the level of exports than world prices.

Domestic consumption may well have risen as population increased; unplanned increases in stocks may also have occurred; the withdrawal of the Dutch interisland shipping company (KPM) in 1957 and 1958 undoubtedly resulted in a buildup of copra in the ports—but we cannot be sure how far those problems persisted through the period 1957–65. The intensification of the West Irian campaign may have affected the availability of shipping space between 1961 and 1962.

Singapore was the principal destination for Indonesian copra, taking about half of the copra exported throughout the period 1950–63. Confrontation must have affected exports in the years 1963–65, but the loss of the Singapore market does not seem to have been a decisive factor. Exports in 1964 were higher than they had been in 1960 and 1962 when Singapore was still a major buyer.

Smuggling affords another possible explanation. Obviously there are no data on this. It seems reasonable to assume that smuggling, together with increases in domestic consumption and unplanned stocks, accounted for the decline in reported exports. But we are unable to assess the relative importance of each factor.

To sum up, it is unlikely that exports of palm oil, coffee, tea, tobacco, or copra can be increased substantially in the near future. The gestation period is different for each crop. Coffee and tea require three to four years, tobacco one year, copra takes up to seven or eight years, and palm oil, six years. A tree produces coconuts for about 80 years, coffee should be replanted after 15 to 20 years, tea after 10 to 20 years, and oil palms after 20 years.

The major decisions with respect to estate products for export are within the control of government. The estate sector will remain an important source of foreign exchange only if a vigorous planting program is begun immediately. As for the smallholders, they will continue to produce from existing trees so long as they find it profitable to do so. The available statistics suggest that profits are still to be made from these commodities. Much will depend on the alternatives open to them.

On the demand side, the outlook for these five crops is not encouraging. There is little likelihood that the price of tea on the world market will rise in the near future. Much depends on the demand from the centrally-planned economies, especially China. A like situation exists for coffee. Copra's future is clouded by the increased availability of other oils and fats. The FAO expects total import demand for tobacco to grow at around 3 percent per year as a long-run trend. Export prospects for the developing countries as a whole seem favorable. But if Indonesia and others are to compete with such large exporters as the United States, they must improve the quality of their leaf. Indonesia did succeed in diversifying its tobacco industry to cigarette leaf from cigar leaf, as demand for the latter declined, incidentally dealing a shattering blow to the famous Deli tobacco. The trend in favor of light cigarette leaf is likely to continue, with the European Economic Community a market worth competing for as tariff protection is gradually lowered.

Petroleum and Petroleum Products

As a contributor to Indonesia's foreign-exchange earnings, petroleum was overshadowed in the early decades of this century by the sugar industry. Since independence, oil has in most years taken second place only to rubber, and its contribution has exceeded 25 percent of total exports in most years (see Table 12.2).

All export products contain a foreign-exchange component in their cost structure. This element is proportionately larger for the petroleum industry than for either estate or smallholder agriculture, so the data on gross earnings in Table 12.2 considerably overstate the importance of oil. We have therefore included in Table 12.3 the net earnings from petroleum for the years for which this information is available. These particular figures are derived by deducting all imports required by the industry plus oil company remittances from the gross earnings.[19] It must be noted that the figures now understate the importance of petroleum because the foreign-exchange component of the other products is not taken into account.

Only three major oil companies, Shell, Stanvac, and Caltex, operated in Indonesia up to 1959. Both Shell and Stanvac had explored most of their concession areas before the beginning of the Second World War. Caltex was much better placed because it had only started to exploit its oil discoveries when the Japanese occupied the country.

The production and the exports of crude oil increased considerably between 1950 and 1963 (Table 12.10), while the production of refined products stagnated between 1954 and 1961 and fell by 23 percent from 1961 to 1964. The exports of refined products dropped by almost one-half between 1959 and 1964 (Figure 12.2).

TABLE 12.10—Petroleum, Indonesia: crude production, refinery throughput, exports, and earnings, 1938–40, 1950–64

| Year | Crude petroleum[a] | | Refinery throughput[a] | | | | Total exports[ab] | Gross earnings (million US $) |
	Production	Exports	Domestic feed	Imported feed	Total	Exports		
1938	7,398	52	n.a.	n.a.	7,416	6,015	6,067	n.a.
1939	7,949	90	n.a.	n.a.	8,065	6,335	6,425	120
1940	7,939	299	n.a.	n.a.	7,811	6,049	6,348	n.a.
1950	6,816	8	5,947	1,575	7,522	6,091	6,099	147
1951	8,093	n.a.	7,155	1,495	8,650	6,725	6,725	166
1952	8,523	599	7,480	2,211	9,691	7,284	7,883	181
1953	10,225	2,086	7,937	2,404	10,342	7,689	9,775	207
1954	10,775	2,303	8,408	2,165	10,572	7,618	9,921	227
1955	11,730	3,028	8,420	2,626	11,046	6,515	9,543	216
1956	12,750	4,411	8,108	2,917	11,025	7,814	12,225	255
1957	15,468	6,986	8,047	3,668	11,716	7,328	14,314	303
1958	16,110	7,343	8,328	2,619	10,947	7,446	14,789	315
1959	18,218	4,456	9,852	2,112	11,964	7,969	12,425	231
1960	20,596	7,416	9,794	2,140	11,889	6,514	13,930	221
1961	21,284	9,732	9,461	2,613	12,074	5,759	15,491	261
1962	22,760	12,390	10,124	1,545	11,670	6,549	18,939	216
1963	22,860	12,700	9,484	1,216	10,700	5,770	18,470	269
1964	23,500	15,051	9,588	0	9,588	4,000	19,051	255

n.a.: Not available.
[a] Thousand metric tons.
[b] Equals exports of crude petroleum and exports of refinery throughput.
Source: This table was prepared by Alex Hunter and is reprinted here, with his permission, in essentially its original form, from his article, "The Indonesian Oil Industry," *Australian Economic Papers*, 5, no. 1(1966): table 1, p. 62.

Total exports of petroleum and petroleum products were at their peak at the end of the period because the rise in exports of crude was sufficient to offset the decline in the exports of refined products. The latter was also caused in part by the growing importance of the domestic market which had been encouraged to expand even further than it might have because price control had steadily reduced the real costs of gasoline to domestic consumers.[20] Both Shell and Stanvac were affected by this and their respective contributions to export earnings diminished in consequence.

As a result of the 1963 agreements in Tokyo, Shell, Stanvac, and Caltex began to search for oil in the new areas made available to them. But this phase was short-lived. Confrontation and nationalistic pressures threatened complete expropriation of the "Big Three", although newcomers like Pan American and the Japanese companies were relatively free from the new agitations. The newcomers enjoyed no legal distinction in their situation vis-à-vis the old established

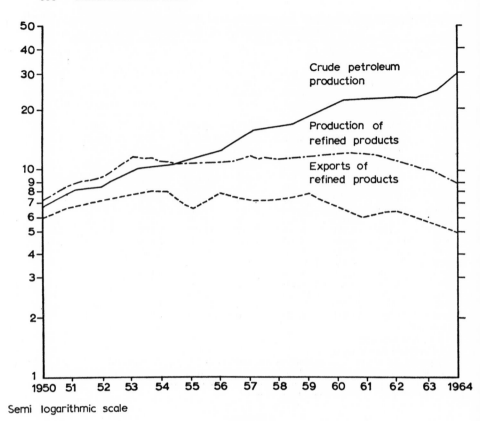

Semi logarithmic scale

FIGURE 12.2—Petroleum: crude production and production/exports of refined products (in million metric tons), 1950–64

companies because contracts on the 1963 model were the same for all. It was simply that the newcomers were not large, had discovered no significant oil fields, and had no conspicuous refining or marketing interests to invite attack.[21]

Shell was bought by the Indonesian government in December, 1965, but because of the recent trend in foreign policy it would be premature to regard this as an irrevocable decision. Rather than speculate on the prospects for the Big Three, we merely emphasize that it is imperative that new wells be found in the near future if petroleum is to continue as an important contributor to Indonesia's foreign exchange.

If the industry does expand further a major change in the composition of marketable products is likely. Political instability in Indonesia, coupled with the ambivalent government policy towards the oil companies in the fifties, induced them to expand their refining capacity elsewhere in Southeast Asia.[22] Greater reliance on crude exports seems inevitable if new wells are brought into production unless the Indonesian government builds its own refineries or encourages others to do so.

A substantial improvement in Indonesian petroleum exports can only occur if (*a*) there is increased exploitation by the three major companies, Pan American, and other "small" foreign companies, or by the state enterprises assisted by foreign contractors, or if (*b*) their exploitation is increased by the state enterprises and their contractors alone. Alternative (*a*) is much more likely to be successful. Alternative (*b*) even if it involved no insurmountable obstacles from the point of view of exploration and production in general, could lead to great difficulties in marketing oil at reasonable prices considering the dominant position of the majors in Southeast Asia and the world in general.

In the short run, Caltex can be expected to increase its production sufficiently to offset further declines in output and exports from Shell and Stanvac, but an overall decline in the output and exports of the industry as a whole will certainly follow within three to five years unless new areas are explored and new wells found.

Tin

Production of tin reached a peak of 53,370 long tons in 1941 in response to war-stimulated demand. Only 1,000 tons were produced in 1945, but recovery after the war was rapid. The producing areas were relatively unaffected by the revolution and an output of 30,600 tons was achieved in 1948. During the last two years of the revolution eight new dredges were installed. By 1948, twenty-six dredges were in operation compared with twenty-eight in 1940. The reinvestment during the period 1945–49, which reflected to some extent the confidence of the Dutch concerning the outcome of the revolution itself, was most fortunate for the industry and for Indonesian export earnings in the following years. After 1949, the foreign tin-mining companies were under constant threat of nationalization and operated in an atmosphere which was hardly conducive to new investment.[23] The Teuku Hassan motion, passed in parliament in 1951, urged the government "to postpone all granting of concession and exploitation permits or extending expired permits, pending the results of the work of the State Commission on Mining Affairs."[24]

It was not until 1960 that a new mining law was passed in parliament. In the meantime no new investment had taken place in the tin-mining industry. In particular, the tin smelters on Bangka were not rehabilitated. During the years 1940–44 an average of 14,513 tons of smelted tin per year had been exported, with a maximum of 21,767 tons in 1940.[25] Throughout the fifties and up to the present, Indonesian exports of tin have been almost exclusively in the form of tin concentrates. The highest output of tin concentrates in the postwar period was 35,861 long tons in 1954 (Table 12.11). This is close to the prewar peak of 37,580 long tons in 1937. After 1954, production declined steadily except for a brief recovery in 1960. This decline occurred on each of the tin-producing islands: Bangka was down by

TABLE 12.11—Indonesia: mine production and prices of tin concentrates, 1950–63

Year	World (long tons)	Indonesia (long tons)	Malaysia (long tons)	£ per long ton[a]	Price index (1920–30 = 100)
1950	162,300	32,102	57,767	744.6	329.4
1951	621,500	30,986	57,396	1,077.3	476.5
1952	165,300	35,003	57,065	964.4	426.6
1953	170,100	33,822	56,404	731.7	323.7
1954	169,000	35,861	60,933	719.4	318.2
Average, 1950–54	165,900	33,555	57,913	—	—
1955	168,000	33,367	61,244	740.1	327.4
1956	166,400	30,055	62,296	787.7	348.4
1957	163,100	27,723	59,293	754.8	333.9
1958	115,800	23,200	38,458	734.7	325.1
1959	119,200	21,613	37,525	785.4	347.4
Average, 1955–59	146,500	27,192	51,763	—	—
1960	136,500	22,596	51,979	796.6	352.4
1961	136,500	18,574	56,028	888.6	393.1
1962	141,600	17,310	58,603	896.5	396.6
1963	141,000	12,947	59,947	909.7	402.4
Average, 1960–63	138,900	17,857	56,639	—	—

[a] London Metal Exchange, cash.

Source: W. Robertson, *Report on the World Tin Position with Projections for 1965 and 1970*, International Tin Council (1965), pp. 58, 65, and 111.

70 percent in 1963 compared with 1953, while in Billiton and Singkep output declined by 55 and 32 percent respectively in the same period.

An important cause of the decline was the lack of maintenance and replacement of equipment. With the expulsion of the Dutch from Indonesia in 1957–58, industrial enterprises which had been equipped with Dutch machinery were cut off from their sources of supply of spare parts. The tin-mining industry was no exception. This situation continued until 1963, when settlement of the West Irian dispute led to more cordial relations between the two countries and the reopening of trading channels.

Tin prices improved considerably following the low level that prevailed in 1957–58. In the latter half of 1957 a world surplus in tin had arisen due to a decline in consumption in the United States and an increase in the amount of tin sold by the Soviet Union on Western European markets.[26] Export controls were introduced by the International Tin Council in December 1957 with Indonesia's quota set at 21 percent.

Export controls ceased to operate after September, 1960, although the council continued to set quotas for its members. In 1962–63, Indonesia's quota was set at 19.73 percent of total exports; by 1966 it was down to 10.79 percent. This decline in Indonesia's share of the total market reflects its inability to maintain the production levels of the late fifties. Indonesia's exports fell from 22,596 long tons in 1960 to 17,310 long tons in 1962 and to 12,947 long tons in 1963. Over the same period, world production increased from 136,500 long tons to 141,000 long tons. Between 1960 and 1963 Indonesian production fell by 9,649 long tons, while Malaya and Thailand increased their output sufficiently to offset this and to contribute a further 4,500 long tons to world tin supply.

Current forecasts of world demand for tin are favorable. Indications in the early sixties were for a demand of about 200,000 tons by 1970. Aluminum presents the greatest threat to the use of tin in the American container market which currently consumes approximately 30 percent of the world tin supply. To some extent, the tin industry has met this competition by the introduction of the double-reduced tinplate process. In other countries the competition from substitutes is less immediate.

Tin cannot regain its old position as an important contributor to Indonesian foreign exchange earnings in the immediate years ahead.

New investment in established mines and the surveying and exploitation of new sources can lead to some improvement in production, but substantial increases will probably emerge only well after 1970.

Other Export Products[27]

In 1938 "other" export commodities accounted for 19.2 percent of total exports. This category comprised some sixty agricultural products including spices, forest products, and such minerals as bauxite, manganese, and nickel. The overall situation remained much the same in the postwar period, but the share of "other" exports fell to between 7.4 and 13.9 percent during the 1950–63 period (see Table 12.2). This occurred despite the relegation of sugar into the "other" category after the war. Hence sugar, once a famous estate product, has faded into insignificance as an export earner. The decline in sugar exports reflected both a decline in total production and a tremendous increase in domestic consumption.[28]

FOREST PRODUCTS. Forest products and several minerals were singled out by the Humphrey team as being potential export earners,[29] subject, however, to extensive surveys that would be needed to provide a realistic picture of the potential of each commodity. These products represented only about 1 percent of the total value of Indonesian exports in 1959 and preceding years.[30] The American team was nonetheless of the opinion that the combined resources of Kalimantan's forests appeared adequate for a large lumber industry, although the forest reserves in both Kalimantan and Sumatra are in heavy jungle areas where it would be costly to separate more-useful from less-useful trees.[31] Aerial surveys were considered advisable and the team recommended American aid for this purpose. Transportation facilities will also have to be provided before large-scale operations are feasible.

Growing Japanese interests in this industry led to a joint exploration venture in East Kalimantan in 1962. The Indonesian government expected that the project would contribute $128 million over an eight-year period to Indonesia's foreign exchange earnings.[32]

MINERALS. Indonesia possesses a wide variety of minerals besides tin. In the interwar period, bauxite, manganese, and nickel were exported. Nickel production became significant again in 1959 when 215 metric tons of nickel content, obtained from some 10,000 tons of crude ore, were produced. Exports rose sharply thereafter to

15,000 metric tons by 1965. The production (and export) of both manganese and bauxite fluctuated considerably in the decade 1952–62, bauxite within a range of 173,000 to 493,000 metric tons of crude ore (dried equivalent), and manganese within a range of 2,600 to 56,000 metric tons (*Mn* content).[33] Production of bauxite expanded steadily but manganese dropped from a peak of 56,600 metric tons in 1956 to 2,600 metric tons in 1962.[34]

The contribution of bauxite, nickel, and manganese to Indonesian foreign-exchange earnings remains very small. The Humphrey team recommended that assistance be given to the Indonesian government to carry out surveys to discover and to prove new bauxite and nickel deposits. But even if extensive reserves are found, it will take several years before exploitation on a significant scale is possible. Transportation facilities would have to be improved before any mines could be operated on a large scale. Under these circumstances, increases in exchange earnings from these minerals cannot change the overall prospects for Indonesia's balance of payments in the near future.

Summary

Export earnings between 1960 and 1962 were sufficient to finance an "austerity" import program of $610 million a year, but not enough foreign exchange was being earned to meet current debt commitments or to finance imports of capital equipment for maintenance, expansion, and development.[35] A development program would require imports well in excess of $610 million.

Foreign-exchange earnings in 1964 were down to $457 million (oil excluded); in 1965 they were lower, $436 million; in 1966 there was recovery to $457 million. The value of total exports fell from $724 million in 1964 to $679 million in 1966. Even if the output of each of the major export products is maintained, a continuation of the current downward trend in the world price of rubber could lead to a further decline in export earnings to a point below that required to finance even a minimum program of imports.

Our survey of the major traditional export commodities gives no ground for optimism for the next few years. For some of them, export volume must be expected to decline, at least in the short run; for others, falling prices are likely to offset increases in volume. Up to 1966, the pattern of Indonesia's exports was for the most part the same as in 1964. Rubber and petroleum exports represented 63 percent of total exports in 1966. The contribution of rubber in 1966 was almost equal to the 1964 level (33 percent), but the contribution of petroleum fell from 37 percent in 1964 to 30 percent in 1966. The share of exports of tin and tea was almost the same in 1966 as in 1964 with 4.5 and 2.5 percent contribution in 1966. Of the remaining four major export commodities, the share of copra fell to 2.22 percent of total exports in 1966, while that of tobacco, coffee, and palm oil rose from 3.0, 3.7, and 3.7 percent, respectively, in 1964, to 3.5, 4.8, and 4.9 percent, respectively, in 1966.[36] Of the minor "other" export commodities only timber appears to have the potential for a significant increase over the next five years. The contribution of other products in this category, especially minerals, can become significant only after 1970.

Even if the prices of some of the major commodities were to rise above the levels currently forecast, the increases would have to be improbably large to offset the depressing effect of the likely decline in the price of natural rubber. Failure to maintain an adequate rate of investment, either for expansion of productive capacity or for maintenance, is the root cause of the inability of both the petroleum industry and the agricultural estates to expand production rapidly in the near future. Exports of smallholder products will continue to stagnate, and may even decline, unless there is a substantial improvement in the conditions under which the smallholders operate.

The conclusion seems inescapable that, even with a comprehensive moratorium on Indonesia's existing debts, much foreign assistance will be required both to finance current exchange requirements and to provide the funds for the country's growth and development for many years to come.

INTRAREGIONAL TRADE

We have referred to the market outlets for export products, especially in Western Europe, the United States, and certain centrally-planned economies. With the emergence of the new order and the gradual elimination of the role of President Sukarno,[37] there was an increasing interest in intraregional trade in the ECAFE area. The ending of Confrontation with Malaysia and Singapore was the most significant political aspect of the new trend, while a significant economic aspect was Indonesia's request to become a member of the Asian Development Bank.[38]

The secretariat of ECAFE has long championed the cause of in-traregional trade. Discussions have focused on trade, both in traditional exports, especially agricultural products, and in new manufactured products. We are mainly concerned with trends in intraregional trade in agricultural products. At this stage of Indonesia's political development we have preferred to forego any attempt to analyze the likely development of manufacturing industry, although it could become important in any future expansion of intraregional trade.

TABLE 12.12—Direction of Indonesia's trade (quarterly averages or quarters), 1958–64
(Value in million US$)

Year	Total trade		Trade with ECAFE countries[a]		Trade with developing ECAFE countries[b]	
	Exports	Imports	Exports	Imports	Exports	Imports
1958	$188.8	$128.3	$100.2 (53%)[c]	$53.8 (42%)	$ 81.4 (43%)	$34.6 (27%)
1959	218.1	114.7	100.0 (46%)	52.2 (45%)	83.8 (38%)	32.9 (29%)
1960	210.0	143.4	101.7 (48%)	71.9 (50%)	85.1 (41%)	46.6 (33%)
1961	195.7	199.0	100.6 (54%)	83.4 (42%)	74.7 (38%)	44.3 (22%)
1962	232.2	185.2	154.4 (66%)	81.4 (44%)	115.7 (50%)	51.1 (28%)
1963	154.1	131.8	63.4 (41%)	43.8 (33%)	36.1 (23%)	29.8 (23%)
1964	167.9	142.4	69.0 (41%)	76.6 (54%)	22.7 (14%)	40.4 (28%)

[a] Of the ECAFE countries, those in the sterling area are Australia, Brunei, Burma, Ceylon, Hong Kong, India, Malaysia, New Zealand, Samoa, and Singapore; those in the non-sterling area are Afghanistan, Cambodia, Indonesia, Iran, Japan, Korea, Laos, Mongolia, Nepal, Philippines, Taiwan, Thailand, and Vietnam.
[b] Includes countries listed above, except for Australia, Japan, and New Zealand.
[c] Figures in parentheses refer to percentages of total Indonesian exports and imports.
Source: ECAFE, *Economic Survey of Asia and the Far East, 1965* (1966), p. 288.

The importance of the ECAFE countries as Indonesia's trading partners is indicated in Table 12.12. Between 1958 and 1964 around 50 percent of Indonesia's foreign trade was with the ECAFE countries. Toward the end of this period there was a tendency for the developed ECAFE regions to increase their shares in both exports and imports. The major commodities in this intraregional trade are rubber, rice, and petroleum. Since most of the exports of crude and refined petroleum go to ECAFE countries, no separate discussion of petroleum is needed here.

Rubber

The main end-users of rubber in Southeast Asia are Japan and mainland China. Singapore had played a significant role as an entrepôt for smallholder rubber until Confrontation and the severance of trade relations in November, 1963.

Between 1950 and 1956, exports to Japan fluctuated within a range of 13,000 to 14,700 long tons. From 1957 to 1963, on the other hand, shipments did not exceed 5,000 long tons per year. In the latter period, Indonesian rubber was replaced by that from Malaya, Thailand, Sarawak-Sabah, and Ceylon. Exports to China were high in 1957–58, and in the 1960's were within a range of 45,000 to 105,000 long tons. Figures in Table 12.13 show the total amount of rubber purchased by both Japan and China in the period 1960–66 and Indonesia's share of the market.

TABLE 12.13—Imports of natural rubber into Mainland China
and Japan, and Indonesia's share of total, 1960–66
(Long tons)

	Mainland China		Japan	
Year	Total	From Indonesia	Total	From Indonesia
1960	119,750	45,375	169,760	3,272
1961	83,250	67,799	182,735	6,624
1962	107,000	55,272	189,935	2,035
1963	107,500	79,206	184,946	5,221
1964	142,000	105,837	211,488	90,473
1965	134,500	89,355	203,993	91,837
1966[a]	(95,500)	(12,312)	(101,304)	(45,879)

[a] Figures are for first half of 1966.
Source: International Rubber Study Group, *Rubber Statistical Bulletin*, various issues.

From Table 12.13 it is clear that Japan reentered the market for Indonesian rubber, especially for smallholders' rubber, in 1964, and continued its purchase in succeeding years. China, on the other hand, began cutting its purchases in 1966, as relations between Indonesia and China became strained.

The most recent development in the rubber trade concerns the possibility of reopening the Singapore market. Up to 1963, Singapore's role in this trade was twofold: (1) a port for transshipment, and (2) a processor of lower grades not saleable on the international market. Most of the ports for smallholder rubber are concentrated in and around Singapore, from Pontianak in West Kalimantan to Labuhanbilik in North Sumatra. These are outports, not located on shipping lanes. As long as rubber could be shipped to Singapore, this was of no consequence. But when trade relations were severed, difficulties arose. For the exporter, turnover was rapid in the trade with Singapore. Rubber exports have continued in the years since Confrontation, but there can be little doubt that transport costs have increased, and, because of a longer turnover period, financing the trade has become more costly.

Remilling factories in Singapore also reprocessed Indonesian blankets and remilled slabs from the Riauw area and elsewhere. Sheet rubber was re-sorted and packed, and the blocked sheets were often mixed with blanket rubber to make smoked sheets. After 1964 no detailed quality breakdown of smallholder exports is available; it is impossible to ascertain what happened to this previously unprocessed rubber. Because Singapore's remilling industry was severely affected, it may be assumed that slab exports were minimal. It is also possible that the quality of sheets was improved.

Rice

Indonesia has become one of the last of the large rice-deficit regions in Southeast Asia. Both India and Pakistan, which were major rice importers before the war, now import only about 800,000 metric tons per year, almost half of which is made available under U.S. Public Law 480. Their imports averaged 2 million metric tons in the years 1934–38, compared with an average of 1 million metric tons for Indonesia between 1960–64. A serious threat to trade with the five major rice producers in the region in particular with Burma and Thailand, is posed by Indonesia's new dwarf-rice expansion effort. Such programs have been a recurring theme in Indonesia's recent economic history, but up to now all have been unsuccessful. The Suharto government has adopted a similar attitude toward the need for increased rice output. The loss of the Indonesian market to ECAFE exporters would be significant should the self-sufficiency program be successful. In 1960–62, rice exports to the developing countries as a whole were 4.2 million metric tons of which approximately 25 percent was imported by Indonesia.

The ECAFE attitude is one of great concern over the possible decline in the intraregional rice trade and the consequences for the producing countries. The secretariat bases its arguments against Indonesia's self-sufficiency drive on the relative inefficiency of Indonesian producers, and their tendency to use land that could be used for export crops.[39] It is true that some sugar land has been turned over to rice, but it has also been argued that Indonesian rice production could be substantially increased in traditional rice-growing areas.[40]

In the short run, the new government will probably encourage the importation of rice. But the long-term objective, already foreshadowed in the *Bimas* project,[41] will be to increase production with new strains, fertilizers, and improved irrigation. Plans are underway to expand Indonesia's fertilizer production, although in the immediate future the stress will be on imports. In the light of such a trend, there seems little likelihood, both for economic and political reasons, of Indonesia's long-run participation in the intraregional rice trade. It is also unlikely that Indonesia's desire to achieve self-sufficiency in rice production will become a matter of negotiation with other ECAFE rice producers. Only if Indonesia is unable to close the gap between domestic consumption and imports, and if the country is unable to increase output and to slow population increase, will the country continue to import large quantities of rice.[42]

NOTES

1. This section of the chapter deals with total Indonesian exports and is a shortened version of J. Panglaykim and Kenneth D. Thomas, *Indonesia's Exports: Performance and Prospects (1950–70)* (Rotterdam: Rotterdam University Press, 1967), adapted by permission of the publisher and the authors. The second section of the chapter deals specifically with Indonesia's intraregional trade.

2. For example, see Alex Hunter, "The Indonesian Oil Industry," *Australian Economic Papers*, 5, no. 1 (1966): 95.

3. For fuller discussions of some of these difficulties, see H. O. Schmitt, "Post-Colonial Politics: A Suggested Interpretation of the Indonesian Experience, 1950–1958," *The Australian Journal of Politics and History*, 9, no. 2 (1963): 196; Bruce Glassburner, "The Attempt to Foster Private Entrepreneurship in Indonesia," *Indian Economic Review*, 6, no. 2 (1962); and Herbert Feith, *The Decline of Constitutional Democracy in Indonesia* (Ithaca, N.Y.: Cornell University Press, 1962), pp. 481–87.

4. No government was able to protect the estates from squatters who took over land for food crops and commercial crops. Several standfast regulations were introduced in the fifties to prevent further encroachments but they were never implemented. For a discussion of the squatter problem, see J. O. Sutter, *Indonesianisasi: Politics in a Changing Economy, 1940–1955* (Ithaca, N.Y.: Cornell University Press, 1959), vol. 3, chap. 18; and

D. Hindley, *The Communist Party of Indonesia, 1951–1963* (Berkeley: University of California Press, 1964), pp. 172 and 243.

5. Overcentralization has presented many problems, among which is the reluctance of some managers to accept the decision-making aspects of their position. For a discussion of this problem and the effects of government bureaucracy on estates in general, see Dahlan Thalib, "The Estate Rubber Industry of East Sumatra," in *Prospects for East Sumatran Plantation Industries: A Symposium*, ed. D. S. Paauw (New Haven: Yale University Press, 1962), pp. 52–53.

6. The rupiah proceeds from exports were not sufficient to finance the day-to-day operations of the estates. Estate managers were often obliged to sell part of their rubber on the local market where they would earn more rupiahs than they could by exporting on their own account.

7. T. Fleming, "Modern Tapping Methods for Mature Rubber" (Paper submitted to the All-Indonesian Planters' Conference—Rubber Seminar, Medan, Sumatra, November 26–29, 1962), pp. 1–3 and 10, our emphasis. Fleming notes that "by skilful use of [the high- and low-cut tapping method], it is possible to carry out large replantings in each of five successive years, and still harvest higher *total* crops for each year, from the decreasing area of old rubber. At the end of five years, when the replantings begin to come into bearing, their production then gives an immediate increase in total crops, and the scale of replanting can be further increased" (p. 13).

8. The *Humphrey Report (Indonesia: Perspective and Proposals for United States Economic Aid* [New Haven: Yale University Press, 1963], p. 199.) gives the following data on the age of rubber trees in the estate sector for 1960: 150,000 hectares 38 years old, 125,000 hectares between 30 and 40 years, and 40,000 hectares between 26 and 30 years.

This means that by 1965, 315,000 hectares were planted with trees over 30 years old, of which 88 percent were over 37 years. In the early fifties, it was customary on estates to consider 35 years as the limit for the productive life of a tree. (*Report of the Mission of Enquiry into the Rubber Industry of Malaya* [Kuala Lumpur: Government Printer, 1954], p. 9, hereafter cited as the *Mudie Report*.) With the new tapping technique, this figure has been drastically revised.

In these terms, Indonesia's replanting problem is considerable. The total area under estate rubber is estimated as 500,000 hectares, of which 48,000 hectares or 10 percent are said to have been replanted up to 1957. Replanting between 1958 and 1960 is given as 33,700 hectares, so that in both periods the rate of the replanting was far below the 3 percent per year recommended by the *Mudie Report* commissioners (*ibid.*, p. 12).

For North Sumatra and Atjeh, the Department of Estates estimated the age structure of trees of 1959 as follows:

more than 35 years	89,000 hectares (33%)
between 25 and 35 years	94,500 hectares (35%)
between 15 and 25 years	54,000 hectares (20%)
under 15 years	32,400 hectares (12%)

From Tan Hong Tong, *Pembinaan Perkembangan di Sumatera Utara/Atjeh,* a pamphlet published jointly by the Agricultural Faculty, University of North Sumatra, and the Sumatra Planters' Organization (Medan, 1965), p. 14.

9. *United Nations, Food and Agricultural Organization, Agricultural Commodities Projections for 1970* (1962), pp. 11–84.

10. Insufficient data are available to forecast demand by the centrally-planned economies, the position of China being the most difficult to assess. Expansion of synthetic-rubber production in the Soviet Union is likely to be considerable, but it is assumed that there will be an absolute increase in the demand for natural rubber. China does not produce synthetic rubber and if the country continues to develop, its role as a consumer of natural rubber may be very important for the producers.

    For rubber, McHale concludes that "present trends suggest that the world's natural rubber market will become increasingly dominated by the Sino-Soviet nations as the traditionally important American, British and Western European buyers absorb less of the world's natural rubber output both relatively and in absolute amounts." (T. R. McHale, "Natural Rubber and Malaysian Economic Development," *Malayan Economic Review,* 9, no. 1 [1965]: 30.)

11. See for example the Bank of Indonesia, *Annual Reports, 1951–52,* p. 165; *1953–54,* p. 108; and *1958–59,* p. 185.

12. This ratio is for ribbed smoked sheet III and Thailand rice. If we substitute Burmese rice, the lowest level reached was 5.7 : 1 in 1963, within a range of 5.7–10.0.

13. It is difficult to draw up a time series to demonstrate this trend in price ratios, but examples are given in K. D. Thomas, "Shifting Cultivation and the Production of Smallholders' Rubber in a South Sumatran Village," *Malayan Economic Review,* April, 1965, pp. 105–6 and 111; and in D. H. Penny, *The Transition from Subsistence to Commercial Family Farming in North Sumatra* (Ph.D. diss., Cornell University, June, 1964), p. 259. Penny notes that in December, 1962, the value of one kilogram of rubber was equivalent to the value of 0.5 kilograms of rice.

14. Since production data for the most recent years may be less reliable than those for the fifties, the recent fall in output may be more apparent than real. In our analysis of smallholder crops we realize that the statistical data are unreliable. To a lesser extent, the same is also true for the estate crops. Indonesian statistics are generally doubtful, but this hardly provides an excuse for permanent agnosticism.

15. It is widely believed that coffee stolen from estates inflates smallholder production, but this is unlikely since estate coffee is grown on Java whereas about 85 percent of smallholders' coffee is produced in the Outer Islands. The same is true for rubber, where estates and smallholders operate contiguously only on the East Coast in North Sumatra.

16. Between 1956 and 1961 output increased by 41 percent, whereas the area under production increased by only 9 percent, indicating a considerable increase in yield per hectare, if the statistics are correct. But, since the

data refer to planted area, bad seasons could account for the low production in the late fifties.

17. Throughout this article no attempt is made to assess trends in quality. Official statistics suggest a decline in the quality of smallholders' rubber, but we have no data for other commodities.

18. A certain percentage of foreign-owned estates were non-Dutch (in the case of estate rubber, around 50 percent). We would require a breakdown of production according to ownership, government or private, to assess the relative performance of the government estates taken over in 1957.

19. The data are from Hunter, "Indonesian Oil Industry," table 6, p. 97. This section rests heavily on that article. We are also grateful to Mr. Hunter for his comments on an earlier draft of this part of our paper.

20. This remains true even though throughout the period many consumers purchased their requirements at prices in excess of the official price. For example, see Hunter, "Indonesian Oil Industry," pp. 93–94.

21. Comments supplied by A. Hunter in private correspondence.

22. This trend was encouraged by a significant technological change that reduced the construction costs of building refineries of 20,000–30,000 barrels per day (Hunter, "Indonesian Oil Industry," pp. 87–88 and pp. 100–2).

23. Sutter, *Indonesianisasi,* pp. 846–50.

24. *Ibid.,* p. 821. This held up investment in the petroleum industry also.

25. W. Robertson, *Report on the World Tin Position with Projections for 1965 and 1970,* International Tin Council (1965), table 2, p. 113. The average for 1960–63 was 1,994 long tons.

26. T. George, "Tin: Is the Price Too High?" *Far Eastern Economic Review,* 53, no. 7 (1966): 321–24.

27. Data in this section are not always comparable with data elsewhere in this paper. We have had to draw on a variety of not necessarily consistent sources.

28. The Bank of Indonesia, *Annual Report, 1956–57,* pointed out that the farmers in some areas in Central Java "do not want to lease their lands (to the sugar mills) but prefer to grow rosella, tobacco or other agricultural products, the reason being that the yields of these crops provide them with a higher income than when leasing their lands" (pp. 154–55).

29. *Humphrey Report,* chaps. 3 and 6.

30. *Ibid.,* p. 64. Table III–3 lists forestry products as logs and sawn woods, firewood, and charcoal. The table on "exports of principal forest products" in the Central Bureau of Statistics, *Statistical Pocketbook of Indonesia, 1963* (Djakarta), p. 94, includes a much wider range of products such as rattan and resins (damar, copal, benzoin, and camphor). The fact that many of the products listed are really groups of products demonstrates clearly that in discussing the future potential of most of the "other exports" it is the individual items in each group which must be analyzed. Rattan contributed Rp136.7 million to exports in 1960, compared with Rp91.3 million for logs and sawn wood and Rp103.5 million for resins. Firewood and charcoal were insignificant in the total.

31. *Humphrey Report,* p. 64.
32. See J. Gibson, "Production Sharing," *Bulletin of Indonesian Economic Studies,* no. 3 (February, 1966), p. 67, for a detailed discussion of Japanese plans.
33. United Nations, *Statistical Yearbook,* various years.
34. United Nations Conference on Trade and Development, *Commodity Survey 1966,* mimeographed (TD/B/C.1/PSC/7/Add.7), May 27, 1966, p. 106. The figure in the original is given as 150,000 metric tons. We have converted this to *Ni* content by assuming a 3 percent conversion factor. For details on the Japanese production-sharing agreements, see Gibson, "Production Sharing," pp. 64–65.
35. In a statement made by General Suharto, Chairman of the Cabinet Presidium, on behalf of the Indonesian Government, to the Multilateral Conference in Tokyo, September 17, 1966, on the question of imports, the general said that "according to our experience an annual import of around $600 million can be considered normal for Indonesia"; see also "Survey of Recent Developments," *Bulletin of Indonesian Economic Studies,* no. 5 (October, 1966), p. 1.
36. Indonesian Statistical Association in the Philippines, *Journal of Indonesian Statistics,* October, 1966, p. 22.
37. President Sukarno transferred all of his authority to General Suharto on February 20, 1967.
38. Indonesia became an official member in November, 1966.
39. ECAFE, "Approaches to Regional Harmonization of National Development Plans in Asia and the Far East," *Economic Bulletin for Asia and the Far East,* 15, no. 3 (1964): p. 80.
40. L. A. Mears, *Rice Marketing in the Republic of Indonesia* (Djakarta: P. T. Pembangunan, 1961), chap. 3.
41. Department of Economic Studies, Research School of Pacific Studies, Australian National University, *Bulletin of Indonesian Economic Studies,* no. 6 (February, 1967), p. 26.
42. We are assuming that there is no switch to other sources of carbohydrates.

COMMENT ON PART IV

D. T. LAKDAWALA

At the outset, I may mention that I see no inevitable connection among bilateralism, planning, and inflation although, I must hasten to add, these are often associated in life. Planning need not necessarily be accompanied by inflation. In fact, in the earlier literature economic development with stability was the ideal. Planning was conceived as a means to achieve this end. If planning is to avoid the consequences that have been ably described by Dr. Ramana in his paper, there should be no resort to undue deficit financing or inflation. If inflation nevertheless occurs, many devices can be used to ward off its effects on external trade. The most convenient devices are import and exchange controls, which act directly on foreign spending. When imports have been rigidly controlled for some time, a stage may come when further restriction only hampers the efficient working of the productive machinery itself, apart from the diminution of consumer welfare. It has been the experience of countries administering exchange control that, as unessential imports become more and more curtailed, the economy tends to become more and more reliant on special types of imports. It is, therefore, necessary under such circumstances to pay greater attention to the promotion of exports. A change in the exchange rate may be thought desirable in such an event, or if more selective commodity discrimination is called for, multiple exchange rates or other export incentives like retention schemes, import entitlements, cash subsidies, or tax reliefs may be relied upon.

If there is inflation in a group of countries, and therefore, balance-of-payments difficulties, bilateralism or limited multilateralism may be the best way out. Such economies have a great propensity to import that which would have to be kept in check as long as they could not earn additional exchange. They will not import more from each other out of fear that the payments would not return to them, directly or indirectly, and might have to be ultimately settled in hard currency. If, however, the exchange earned from additional exports to a country can only be spent in that country, and the country exporting additional goods would like to import more goods from the importing countries, discriminatory devices which would tie purchases to sales could lead to trade expansion. This has been the postwar experience in Europe. When two countries plan to develop rapidly, bilateralism may secure better marginal terms for their exports, and also promote specialization and new lines through assured export markets. A large-scale increase in exports may necessitate changes in the production structure and facilities which could come about easily only if the future is assured.

As the Indian experience shows, bilateralism is not always successful in promoting trade. The bilateral agreements with Eastern Europe have been very successful in expanding India's foreign trade, in obtaining the needed goods for fulfilling its expansion programs, and in enabling it to dispose of its exports on favorable terms. On the other hand, India's experience with limited bilateralism with other countries has been largely unrewarding. The success of the former may partly be ascribed to the complementary economies of the two parties, but there are also more general factors responsible for it. To achieve its dynamic aim, bilateralism must be accompanied by long-term trade agreements, and these in turn depend on the correct forecasting of future commodity surpluses and deficits.

The expansion of exports requires the ability to produce and, more importantly, to export and import according to plan, the setting up of whatever organizations are necessary to implement the plans, the foresight and courage to take the consequence of past errors, and the tolerance not to press too hard on other parties. A number of countries, like Ceylon, Indonesia, Burma, India, and to some extent, Pakistan and Taiwan, could increase their imports profitably if they had an assured export market. Others like Malaysia, Hong Kong, and Thailand find their foreign-exchange situation very easy, but their future may not be as assured as the past. This is obvious from the trade forecast for Malaysia, which expects the same level of exports after five years as now. It will be to Malaysia's advantage to have bilateral long-term trade agreements with countries like India. Thus, if long-term trade agreements and bilateralism are properly exploited without adversely affecting external trade with other countries, they can lead successfully not only to greater trade in the group, but also to the goal of faster economic development.

V

The Possibilities
for Economic Cooperation
in Southeast Asia

CHAPTER 13

VIEWPOINTS FROM THE
BANGKOK CONFERENCE

*Editors' Note: The following eight statements are abridged
and revised versions of the final roundtable discussion at the
Bangkok Conference, during which discussants were asked
to attempt to draw out implications for economic cooperation from the analyses and facts given in the preceding
papers.*

DOUGLAS S. PAAUW

The evidence presented in the conference papers indicates that the
present level of trade among ECAFE countries is very small. In
general, this group of less-developed countries trades mainly with
developed countries rather than with other developing countries. Another general theme of this conference amounts to an indictment of
aggressive import-substitution programs which have been pursued by
many of these countries. The criticism is that import-substitution
programs have tended to freeze foreign trade into patterns that are
both uneconomic and inconsistent with increased regional integration.
Rapid import substitution produces growing import dependence, both
quantitative and qualitative, on more-developed countries. The new
import-replacing industries require intermediate and capital good inputs of relatively sophisticated types, produced predominantly by developed countries.

This pattern is reflected most clearly in the untypical case of Hong
Kong. Her imports have been drawn increasingly from developed
countries to provide intermediate and capital goods for her increasingly sophisticated industry. There is little hope of Hong Kong's
playing a significant role in regional integration so long as her foreign
trade continues to be oriented toward the developed countries.

In the more typical cases of the Philippines and Malaysia we find similar obstacles to regional integration. In pursuing the strategy of feeding import substitution by traditional agricultural exports, neither side of the trade account has shown changes favorable to greater regional trade. Traditional exports have continued to be absorbed by developed countries while they have also provided the bulk of the large increases in imports of intermediate and capital goods for industry. Neither the Philippines nor Malaysia has shown any increase in its trade with developing ECAFE neighbors.

In the open, dualistic economies that have pursued less aggressive import-substitution strategies, however, we find the opposite result. Both Taiwan and Thailand have shown significant gains in trade with their developing neighbors, although they have followed somewhat different varieties of more moderate import-substitution programs. In both cases, industrialization has been tempered by emphasis on agricultural development programs prior to or concomitant with import substitution. In both, substantial achievements have been made in diversifying exports. In the case of Taiwan, export diversification began with the addition of new agricultural exports, with a gradual shift toward the addition of exports with larger components of industrial processing. Dr. Sun describes this experience as a process of combining export-diversification objectives with import-substitution programs. In the case of Thailand, export diversification has been mainly associated with the introduction of new agricultural products. Together with steady increases in rice production this has provided a sound basis for supplying larger volumes of exports to the ECAFE region.

The interesting parallel is that Taiwan and Thailand, which have pursued more moderate import-substitution policies and have open, dualistic economies, have shown the most progress in expanding trade with their developing neighbors. For both countries overall export progress has been outstanding: Taiwan achieved an average export growth rate of about 12 percent annually from 1950 to 1965, Thailand, of 9 percent annually in the same years. Rapidly expanding exports, therefore, would appear to be highly conducive to increasing regional trade.

We also observe the importance of qualitative change. On the latter score, either diversification of agricultural exports (Thailand), or diversification of exports based on increased industrial processing (Taiwan), appears to promote the growth of regional trade.

India's non-export-oriented, dualistic economy is of some interest from the viewpoint of regional integration. India has pursued import-substitution policies that have tended to obstruct the expansion of her trade with developing countries, and India's trade with developing ECAFE countries represents a very small percentage of her total trade. Yet, in India's highly diversified pattern of development there lies real promise of trade expansion with many other developing countries of the ECAFE region.

This is true precisely because the structure of the Indian economy differs radically from that of most of the others in the region. Unlike other less-developed ECAFE countries, India already has a highly diversified pattern of exports—a feature properly given emphasis by Professor Lakdawala. One can envisage a growing volume of trade between India and her developing Asian neighbors, based upon India's capacity to offer a wide variety of Indian products in exchange for the specialized traditional exports of such countries as the Philippines, Malaysia, and Thailand. Progress in this direction will require efficient and high quality production, perhaps even subsidization to meet competition from advanced countries, as well as willingness on India's part to import the predominantly intermediate inputs offered by Asia's other developing countries. It is unlikely that this pattern will emerge, however, until India reaches a stage in which selective export specialization evolves from the many alternatives presented by the domestic diversification emphasis in Indian planning.

JOHN H. POWER

I should like to classify the countries in the region by type of economic policy in regard to industrialization and trade. First we have those which have encouraged industrialization, but not for export—that is, the "inward-looking industrializers." India and the Philippines, would fall in this category, at least before their devaluations. Second are the "outward-looking industrializers," Taiwan and Hong Kong. Third are the "reluctant industrializers," Thailand and Malaysia—though perhaps it is not so much reluctance as a lack of feeling of urgency about industrialization that distinguishes them from the others.

The essence of the argument for regional trade preferences among less-developed countries is to break through what might be called the extended Nurkse dilemma. The simple Nurkse dilemma was based on the difficulties of relying on either traditional exports or new exports to the rich countries as possible engines of growth. The answer, then, was balanced growth for the home market. We are now sufficiently aware of the difficulties of this kind of process within the narrow confines of a national market to appreciate the advantages of import substitution within a larger free market composed of regional or other groupings of poor countries. The result would be new exports for each country representing import substitution for the group.

Clearly, in this kind of arrangement the "inward-looking industrializers" would have to become considerably more outward-looking. What about the "reluctant industrializers"? Wouldn't there be room within a regional grouping for primary-producing countries, just as within a nation there is room for a primary-producing region?

The answer is, I think, no. In a nation the growing surplus labor from a primary-producing region can migrate to industry where employment opportunities grow more rapidly (though this process works far from perfectly even when there are no legal restraints on migration). This is not possible internationally even with favorable international rules.

So all must become more like, say, Taiwan—"outward-looking industrializers." Will this succeed? Can all together do what Taiwan and Hong Kong have done individually? The answer is, I think, yes—especially with a system of intraregional trade preferences. All simultaneously encouraging industrialization and exports is precisely what is needed to meet Nurkse's criterion of balanced growth for the group as a whole.

HIROSHI KITAMURA

The degree of economic interdependence among developing countries in the ECAFE region unmistakably shows a declining trend. This is partly a result of the shortsighted economic policies of the countries concerned, but more important it is also the result of an objective condition: the lack of complementarity in their economic structures. Unless deliberate attempts are made to create new complementary patterns of production and trade, the tendency towards declining mutual interdependence will continue.

The essence of regional cooperation involving adjustments of national economic policies is to attempt deliberately to increase economic interdependence. Why is such a regional approach to the integration problem necessary? Because, as long as economic interdependence is predominantly between the developed and developing countries, the rate of export growth will not be rapid enough to come anywhere near realizing the national aspirations of the developing countries. The experience of the 1950's confirmed that this problem, with which Ragnar Nurkse was so much concerned, is a real one. If it is possible to develop a pattern of economic interdependence among the developing countries in the region—in addition to the already existing interdependence between the developed and developing countries—the developing countries may hope to avoid the pitfalls of agrarian overspecialization and of import substitution in limited national markets. And increased cooperation among countries at similar stages of economic development has been a new and remarkable trend in the world economy since the last World War.

Moves towards integration in a developing region are fraught with greater difficulties than those in a developed region for several reasons. There are the obvious new-born nationalism, and rigidity in economic structure. But difficulties are equally severe for trade liberalization and for adjustment and harmonization of investment and production programs. A scheme of automatic reduction of tariffs and quantitative restrictions is not feasible in the region at the present time. That means that a free-trade-area approach of the West European type is not practicable. Of course, there is scope for approach to "freer" trade through intergovernmental, item-by-item negotiations, but as experience in Latin America has proved, the effectiveness of this approach as a means of integration is narrowly circumscribed.

Thus, regional harmonization of investment and production programs, covering activities in both the public sector and the private sector, remains an important element of integration strategy for the region. It will be less difficult to achieve progress towards economic integration if the approach is flexible; harmonization can first be organized on a subregional scale and can be limited to strategic sectors. A flexible combination of trade liberalization and production adjustments in appropriate doses will be far more effective in increasing the degree of economic interdependence within the group of Asian developing countries than following either approach separately. The two approaches are complementary rather than mutually exclusive.

Progress towards the goal of regional integration will depend on the degree of confidence and trust that can be built up among developing countries in the region through mutual consultation. This is partly a question of new habits of dealing with problems of common interest. An organizational structure providing a framework for mutual consultation may go a long way in implanting habits of mutual consultation in ECAFE countries. And the "confrontation" technique adopted by OEEC and OECD may point to a possible way in which the policy and planning questions of individual countries can be subjected to the joint scrutiny of a group of fellow governments. The Asia in which such mutual consultation has become the rule in conducting intergovernmental business will be a very different world from the present one.

SUPARB YOSSUNDARA

From the foregoing papers and discussions it can be concluded that for the future growth of the developing nations of the ECAFE region some form of integration may be necessary. This may have to start at the production level since liberalization of trade alone, though helpful and basic, may not be adequate for solving the problems now at hand. In the meantime it is also recognized that economic integration on a full scale for the region or subregion is still somewhat remote because of the diversity of economic structure, outlook, and policy that now exists in the region. In this particular instance it would be helpful to try to define an 'ideal' subregion, and what is actually meant by plan harmonization. Should such harmonization apply only to the public sector, or should it also apply to the private sector? In agriculture, especially production and trade in food items, Asian countries seem to have done well on their own, so far, but in industry they may have to seek more cooperation from one another in order to reap the full advantage of economies of scale.

In discussing integration it is difficult to reconcile the principles of efficiency and equity. To succeed, any form of joint (or subregional) investment planning must be based on economic considerations. It is bad enough for one nation to harbor a high cost industry, but for a region to be forced to do so should be deplored. An industry should be located in an area with the highest comparative advantage: this is clearly implied in the concept of specialization.

Within the framework of economic cooperation the domestic policy that a member country pursues is of high relevance. Each country concerned must try to pursue the policies necessary for its own economic growth in such a way that it can think of cooperating with other countries to grow even faster. Attention must always be given to the price-cost structure. As other speakers have already emphasized, if a country does not try, through its own production, trade, and financial policies, to produce high quality articles at competitive costs, its chance for export is very slim.

Economic cooperation should be used as a means of maximizing income—through specialization, making the most economic use of resources, and taking advantage of economies of scale.

The idea of trying to harmonize national development plans down to the last detail of targets and employment of resources may still be unrealistic. However, with a spirit of goodwill and mutual trust countries may very well start by comparing notes on their respective plans, and tell each other in a general way what they are going to do in both the public and private sectors. Plans are eventually published; there is no reason why countries cannot compare notes on them with countries of common interests while the plans are in the process of formulation.

A concrete type of economic cooperation can be joint investment to take advantage of economies of scale. One acceptable form can involve the government's giving its blessing to privately conceived and financed projects. Necessary government policy changes can be made to allow free movement of the capital required to finance the project, to allow free movement also of the finished product, and to achieve compatible taxation of the product. A policy of this type is not too hard to implement with a little goodwill on the part of the people concerned.

EVERETT D. HAWKINS

I should like to suggest that there are two basic types of regional cooperation. One is easier to accomplish, the second is more difficult. On the ground that the first is simpler, I suggest that it deserves greater emphasis now; the second category perhaps will have to wait a while.

In the first category I would put those types of cooperation that do not interfere with a nation's internal sovereignty by requiring common price, monetary, fiscal, or foreign-trade policies, or coordinated international planning. Instead, this type would embrace exchange of persons, training programs—perhaps regional programs for higher education, or such projects as the Asian Highway, the Mekong River project, the Asian Development Bank, and other similar projects. These can be pushed now with real hope that something will be accomplished.

In the second category I would put projects that involve some loss of sovereignty. A free-trade zone, a common market, a currency union, a payments union, or harmonization of planning, all seem at the moment to be very difficult to accomplish in this region.

I make this particular distinction between types of cooperation for two reasons. First, with the exception of Thailand and Hong Kong, all of the countries in this area are newly independent; and all the countries, including Thailand and Hong Kong, have new trade and development plans. As newly independent countries they are trying their wings. Having in many cases just won their independence, they do not wish to give up to other nations the power to determine their trade, their payments, and their planning policies. Second, this conference has demonstrated very clearly the great differences in size, in stage of development, and in economic policy of the countries in the region. For both reasons it will be much more difficult, in the short run, to carry into effect economic cooperation ventures fitting in the second list than those fitting in the first.

In the longer run, the fact that there are differences within the region, may turn out to be, as we like to say in Indonesia, a blessing in disguise. If all of the countries were just alike, the possibilities for trade and cooperation within the region would be considerably less.

I-SHUAN SUN

The classification of types of cooperation offered by Professor Hawkins seems to me very useful. The first type of cooperation mentioned by him is just now being undertaken in the ECAFE region in many areas, such as the newly established Asian Development Bank, the Mekong River project, and the Asian Highway. These easier forms of cooperation are surely the practical way for this region to begin mutual economic cooperation.

Not only is this region composed of many countries with different backgrounds, cultures, and stages of development, but there is also considerable diversity in economic policies—specifically in planning, which is the heart of the proposal for plan harmonization. In the Republic of China, for example, planning is mainly a focus of reference for private and public investment and is not rigidly tied to any fiscal or budgetary policy. With so many types of planning, it will be very hard for the countries of this region to work together on one harmonized plan.

It seems to me that every country should start with a strong domestic policy. In our own experience in Taiwan this has meant that the agricultural base must be built up first and then an industrialization process begun, first with light industry but moving more and more into heavier industries. This is an old and widely discussed strategy; it has proved successful with us. I am not here to preach industrialization, but considering the problems that plague primary-producing countries —falling terms of trade, commodity and geographical concentration —it would benefit this region if each country would start with its own industrialization program.

Industrialization in each country does not necessarily preclude trade cooperation. In the electronics industry, for example, the United States for many years relied heavily on Japan for supplies of electronic equipment. Because of rising wages in Japan, the United States now imports from Hong Kong and Taiwan. This experience indicates that industrialization in one country was followed by a rise in wages which made that country complementary to others instead of competitive. Therefore, it seems to me that, even if all countries industrialize simultaneously, there can still be bilateral and multilateral trade on the basis of free competition, the price mechanism, and comparative cost. The great asset of this region is low cost labor. If we can make effective use of differential labor-costs there should be wide scope for trade within the region and with the industrialized countries.

Given this pattern it might be possible to go one step further and consider each country's production plans in order to avoid excessive regional production of certain standard commodities like textiles, cement, rice, or sugar. This concern is basically secondary to the argument for industrialization accompanied by freer trade.

NURUL ISLAM

The developing countries are beginning to question the high costs of accelerated and indiscriminate import substitution, facilitated by excess demand often created by deficit financing and by restrictive trade practices. At the same time they are finding that a greater reliance on the price mechanism is a desirable tool of planning and policy implementation.

Will a more rational import-substitution policy, coupled with trade practices that pay greater attention to relative costs and prices, widen the scope for economic cooperation and trade in the region? It has been suggested that protection of import-substitution industries should be matched by an equal amount of export subsidies in order that import substitution not unduly restrict trade or hamper the growth of exports. There is a question, though, whether all the developing countries of a region can follow this policy, since the same general groups of industries tend to develop in the early stages of industrialization. But insofar as there are possibilities of complex specialization within the general group of consumer goods industries, the scope for trade expansion remains. There are diversities in resource endowments and differences in factor prices among the countries; wage costs especially vary. These cost variations affect the pattern of specialization in narrow branches of consumer goods industries. Dr. Paauw has advanced a similar thesis: the higher the rate of growth and the higher the degree of diversification of trade, the greater will be the scope for intraregional trade.

The ability to specialize will be enhanced if extremes of discrimination by import duties or export subsidies are avoided among commodities, except where there is a distinct need for differentiation because of differential external economies or differential periods of the "learning process." Moreover, there will be an unavoidable time lag in the establishment of similar industries in various countries, so that in any period a fruitful exchange is possible. Thus, even when simple manufactures are being established in all countries, scope for trade exists, since at any given moment the structure of industries is going to be different. This is the way in which trade has grown historically among the countries that are now more fully developed.

Two special policies may increase intraregional trade: regional payments arrangements and foreign aid. Trade restrictions imposed by the developing countries serve the dual purpose of protecting their domestic industries as well as their balance of payments. Trade liberalization efforts may not be looked upon favorably for fear they might lead to balance-of-payments deficits, with a consequent reintroduction of trade restrictions. Payments arrangements could initially cover a small group of countries, perhaps those that do not have high restrictions on trade and are willing to attempt trade liberalization. Payments arrangements could start with a modest clearing union, so that payments with the partner countries would be settled through book transfers in the accounts of the clearing union, and only net deficit and surpluses settled in foreign exchange. Admittedly, a clearing union alone offers no cushion against the balance-of-payments effects of trade liberalization. On the other hand, it can economize on the use of foreign exchange in the settlement of current transactions.

To be effective, payments arrangements should provide short-term credit facilities which, if necessary, can be limited in various ways. Credit facilities may be linked to the deficits and surpluses arising out of the incremental trade, the increments being measured from a mutually agreed-upon base year. The credit facilities would, therefore, be extended to the deficits and surpluses arising, not from total trade, but from incremental trade among the member countries. The volume of trade taken as the base for estimating increments could be a moving base, increasing by a given percentage each year, irrespective of the trade liberalization measures. The funds for any contemplated payments arrangements have to come from the aid-giving countries, the International Monetary Fund, and the Asian Development Bank, with some participation by the regional member countries.

For developing countries that are heavily dependent on foreign aid from developed countries, there may be some implications of tied aid for intraregional trade. An untying of aid from the developed countries with the provision that such funds can be spent freely only in the developing countries would increase trade among the latter. Such aid funds could be untied either with respect to developing countries within one region, such as Southeast Asia, Latin America, and Africa, or they could be untied globally with the developing countries as a whole. In the immediate future it is unlikely that such untying would greatly divert trade from the aid-giving countries to the developing countries, since the latter are not as yet highly competitive in the field of machinery and intermediate products. But limited untying of aid, coupled with measures for liberalizing trade among developing countries by means of preferential arrangements or regional quotas, would help expand the flow of trade among them. A developing country could repay aid by achieving a surplus with other developing countries rather than by being compelled to expand exports to the aid-giving country.

ROBERT J. LAMPMAN

The ends of economics and politics are generally referred to as improvement of the income level of people and countries, achievement of equality (or a lessening of extreme degrees of inequality), and the increase of liberty or independence or security of people and individual countries. Those ends are at least given broad recognition by all of us, I am sure; but they relate differently to groups *within* countries and to groups *of* countries. One meaning of regionalism is to have concern for the income level of a region rather than of a nation, to have concern for equality among nations, and concern for the liberty of adjoining nations.

The means to these ends could roughly be classified as nationalism, regionalism, and internationalism. The Nurkse discussion of a few years ago was greatly concerned with the distinction between nationalistic economic policy and internationalistic economic policy. Lying somewhere between these two broad means, or patterns, is regionalism.

I am not sure that our discussions have always made a clear distinction among these three patterns. Sometimes the discussions have been about nationalism versus internationalism, or restrictive policies by one country versus the elimination of those restrictive policies. I think it is important to remember that regionalism would aim at a set of regional techniques. Trade liberalization measures would extend only to the members of the region; the measures would actually be trade preferences. There would be harmonization of investment plans only for members of that region. There would be improved factor mobility only vis-à-vis the members of the region.

My comment is aimed at sharpening our definition of regionalism. I am arguing that there is a real difference between regionalism and merely moving away from nationalism, or moderating the extremes of nationalistic economic policies. Regionalism is a third alternative.

Now I would raise the question as to whether this conference has advanced our thinking very much about regions, or about Southeast Asia as a region in particular. My principle criticism would be that I have not heard much about regional goals. I have heard very few people express much concern, for example, about inequalities within the region, or about the independence and security of countries other than their own. If there is real regional thinking it should show itself in concern for the economic performance of neighboring countries and in the realization that inequally of economic performance is a threat to each country's own liberty.

In this conference we have not had a reference to any measure of regional economic performance. Do we know what the regional gross national product is and the rate at which it is growing? Are we concerned about that? Do we know much about regional inequalities?

Are we really concerned with the security and independence of regional members?

Regionalism is not necessarily a natural phenomenon. It usually comes about as a result of some shock from outside, some emergency that brings it into being. It reflects a feeling of mutual need, a recognition that each country's welfare depends upon the welfare of its neighbor. Until that recognition comes, I suppose we cannot really expect regional cooperation.

This brings me to the final note: we should sharpen our thinking on the question as to whether a strategy of regionalism and regional economic cooperation will actually serve the broad economic ends of better living levels, less inequality, and more security and freedom for the members of the region.

CHAPTER 14

SUMMARY AND CONCLUSIONS

Many issues have been raised by or are implicit in the preceding papers and comments.[1] Despite the variety of approaches and emphases in these papers one must be impressed, as Dr. Paauw was, with the dissatisfaction expressed over comprehensive import-substitution policies by a wide spectrum of observers; and also with the substantial uncertainty about the implications of adopting a policy of regional cooperation or integration.

The following comments are arranged around three general topics that are particularly relevant to the theme of national trade and growth experience, and to the possibilities for regional cooperation and integration. First is the nature and accuracy of the data on which analysis must be based and evaluated. Second is the comparative record of past Asian performance in trade and growth, and the role of particular types of commercial policy in accounting for this performance. And third is the policy alternatives relevant to improved economic performance and regional economic cooperation.

ECONOMIC DATA

Almost all of the contributors to this volume have presented data on economic observations in support of their hypotheses and analyses.[2] Anyone who has attempted to study economic development in less-developed countries is well aware of the problem of finding data on relevant economic variables. Most investigators also maintain considerable skepticism toward the data available, particularly those pertaining to levels and rates of growth of income.

However, most economists tend to believe, or at least to hope, that the relatively abundant trade statistics of less-developed countries are among the most important and also the most reliable economic indicators. The goods move under the noses of customs officers and thus can be systematically counted and measured. And because the trade-income ratio in these countries is high and because structures of production and consumption are relatively simple, changes in the levels and composition of foreign trade are used as proxies for other economic variables for which data are either nonexistent or highly suspect. With these not unreasonable assumptions about the nature of the economies in question, economists, with some confidence, make a virtue of necessity in relying heavily on the indications of these trade statistics.

Foreign trade is one of the few economic flows that are regularly counted twice—it is counted once by the exporting country and again by the importing country. Thus a check on accuracy is possible: the statistics recorded by both trading partners can be compared side by side. Conceptually, we should expect that if a given trade flow were identically recorded by each partner, then the ratio of imports to exports should be equal to 1.0 (or slightly more, since imports are usually recorded c.i.f.—cost plus insurance and freight charges—and exports are listed f.o.b.). Deviations of the ratios from 1.0 will indicate the importance of obvious factors such as transportation and other charges, and of uncertain factors such as errors and deliberate falsification.

An empirical test of the consistency and accuracy of Asian trade data for the average of the years 1962 and 1963 reveals that there is wide dispersion and variation in these ratios. Some of the comparative figures are astounding: pairs of recordings of presumably the same trade flow differ by a factor of five or more times! Sometimes the ratio is less than 1.0. In some cases a trade surplus in one recording becomes a trade deficit in other recordings. Note also that these discrepancies are for the *total* trade of a country. Errors in individual commodity flows are bound to be much greater.

Accurate measurement of the direction of trade flows in Southeast Asia is difficult for a number of reasons, such as a large volume of regional entrepôt trade, the statistical treatment of regional commodities that are imported for processing and then reexported, and categories of goods that are treated differently by different countries. A reasonable and fairly undemanding test is simply to compare the average ratio of imports to exports for each Asian country with all of its major trading partners to attempt to determine whether a country's recorded trade statistics accurately represent its total trade. These average ratios for Burma, Ceylon, Indonesia, Malaysia, the Philippines, Singapore, and Thailand, are shown in Table 14.1. A significance test (*t*-test) was made, assuming that a 10 percent discrepancy between imports and exports accurately reflects the effects of known factors such as transportation costs. (The 10 percent margin is used by the International Monetary Fund as an estimate of freight and insurance costs.)

The results show that for four of the seven Southeast Asian countries examined the average ratio of imports with the recorded exports

TABLE 14.1—Comparisons of recorded trade of seven Southeast
Asian countries with trade records of partner countries
(Average of 1962–63)

Country	Number of trading partners compared	Average ratio of country's imports to partner country's exports	Standard deviation	Standard error	Value of "*t*"[a]
Asian imports and partner country exports					
Burma	20	1.43	.71	.16	2.08[b]
Ceylon	21	1.44	1.30	.28	1.21
Indonesia	24	10.47	27.68	5.64	1.70[bc]
Malaysia	27	2.11	2.17	.42	4.31[bc]
Philippines	24	1.34	.61	.13	1.89[b]
Singapore	25	.46	.43	.09	7.53[c]
Thailand	25	1.14	.40	.08	.53
Asian exports and partner country imports[d]					
Burma	23	1.38	1.21	.25	1.08
Ceylon	22	1.30	1.09	.23	.87
Malaysia	28	1.51	.80	.15	2.73[bc]
Philippines	24	.99	.49	.10	− 1.10[c]
Singapore	25	1.49	.52	.10	3.67[bc]
Thailand	26	1.46	.78	.15	2.37[bc]

Note: Ratios involving absolute values less than $20,000 in either exports or imports are excluded.
[a] "*t*" is computed assuming an expected value of 1.10.
[b] Significantly greater than 1.10 (one-tail test).
[c] Significantly different from 1.10 (two-tail test) at the 5 percent level.
[d] Data for Indonesia not available.
Source: Seiji Naya and Theodore Morgan, "The Accuracy of International Trade Data: The Case of Southeast Asian Countries," mimeographed (Madison, 1967), p. 8.

of partner countries' exports is significantly different from 1.10, at the 5 percent level of significance (for a one-tail test; a two-tail test shows that three of the seven differences are significant at the 5 percent level).

Results for the Asian countries' exports in relation to partner countries' recorded imports show that three of the six countries for which data are available are significantly different at the 5 percent level from the expected value of 1.10 (for both the one-tail and the two-tail tests). However, most of those cases that are not significantly different from the expected value are also suspect because the standard errors are high.

These tests of trade data for Southeast Asian countries indicate frequent and large errors. Conclusions are less gloomy if Asian trading partners are divided into two groups—more-developed countries (including Japan) and regional less-developed countries. Variances of

TABLE 14.2—Variability of export and import ratios of seven Southeast Asian countries with regional versus developed country trading partners

Country	Variance of imports and partner's exports			Variance of exports and partner's imports		
	Regional	Developed	F ratio[a]	Regional	Developed	F ratio[a]
Burma	2.80	.30	9.33[b]	.91	.15	6.01[b]
	(11)	(12)		(10)	(10)	
Ceylon	2.58	.33	86.00[b]	.25	2.86	11.44[b]
	(10)	(12)		(9)	(12)	
Indonesia	n.a.	n.a.	–	1,353.01	2.88	469.80[b]
				(13)	(11)	
Malaysia	.93	.27	3.44[c]	7.72	.38	20.32[b]
	(16)	(12)		(15)	(12)	
Philippines	.48	.01	43.00[b]	.28	.48	1.71
	(12)	(12)		(12)	(12)	
Singapore	.42	.08	5.25[b]	.25	.05	5.00[b]
	(14)	(10)		(15)	(10)	
Thailand	1.03	.53	20.60[b]	.15	.16	1.07
	(14)	(12)		(13)	(12)	

n.a.: Not available.

Notes: Ratios involving absolute values less than $20,000 in either exports or imports are excluded. The numbers in parentheses denote the number of trading partners considered.

[a] Each F ratio is computed by placing the larger variance in the numerator.

[b] Significant at the 5 percent level.

[c] Significant at the 1 percent level.

Source: Seiji Naya and Theodore Morgan, "The Accuracy of International Trade Data: The Case of Southeast Asian Countries," mimeographed (Madison, 1967), table 1, p. 11.

import-export ratios for Asian with developed and Asian with other less-developed regional countries are shown in Table 14.2. The ratio of these two variances is the F statistic which indicates whether or not the two variances are significantly different from each other.

For Asian countries' recorded imports compared with partner countries' recorded exports, variances are uniformly higher for trade with regional trading partners than with nonregional partners. All of the F statistics are significant at least at the 5 percent level. Comparing partner countries' imports with Asian countries' exports shows a less uniform pattern, with some regional variances higher than nonregional ones. The F statistic for Thailand and the Philippines is not statistically significant, and the only case (Ceylon) for which the variance with developed countries is greater than that with the region seems to be accounted for by one very extreme value with a European country. The other F ratios show significantly greater variation for regional countries than for nonregional ones.

These tests indicate that data on Southeast Asian countries' intraregional trade suffer much more from discrepancies than data for their trade with developed countries. This additional finding encourages using developed-country trade data to measure Southeast Asia's trade with them.

There are a number of possible reasons for the discrepancies. (1) Transport costs will cause a moderate discrepancy between f.o.b. export and c.i.f. import values. (2) Different definitions are used by different countries in recording trade data. For example, the entrepôt trade of Singapore and other countries of the region is not consistently treated. But the discrepancies are often so large that these innocent explanations plainly fail. (3) There may be a simple error in counting and recording. (4) Countries with considerable tariffs and other trade barriers, and with poorly policed boundaries on land, or extensive shorelines on the ocean, invite smuggling. Smuggling enterprises in the Philippines are said to be notably successful, and Indonesia was, like England, made by heaven for free trade. (5) Customs officers may be encouraged by suitable tokens of friendship to understate quantity and quality of imports, where these are taxed; similarly for exports, where these are taxed. (6) A major channel for illegal transfer of wealth between countries is under-invoicing of exports and over-invoicing of imports, though this will not cause a discrepancy between recorded pairs of data unless different invoice values are recorded in the two countries. The purpose of the capital flight may be to avoid taxation or legal seizure of ill-gotten gains; to avoid the risk of confiscation of property (as of the Chinese in Indonesia in 1959–61 and later); to avoid property destruction from disorder or war; to avoid loss of value of liquid assets through inflation; to transfer funds for the care of relatives abroad, or to meet debts accruing abroad, or to provide for one's retirement abroad—such transfers being illegal under exchange control laws, or difficult, or likely to lead to unpleasant questions about the sources of the funds and whether all taxes had been paid, and to uncomfortable knowledge on the books of the authorities about one's assets.

The basic conclusion from our study is that analysis of the benefits and costs of any integration scheme for the region must rest on the shaky foundation of inaccurate trade totals. We judge, and have confirmed this for one sample country, that errors are greater for sectors and for individual commodities.

Much can be done by energetic customs administration to correct the causes of the discrepancies numbered 2 and 3 above. But 4, 5, and 6 are more resistant: they are likely to be less serious sources of error only as tariffs and other trade restrictions are lowered, and as exchange controls wane; and in fact as economic development in general progresses, and so probity and efficiency improve.

Regional cooperation would bring some improvement in the reliability of statistical measures of the regional economy. For example, the Philippines and Malaysia have discussed a treaty for cooperation in reducing smuggling between their two countries. Although regional cooperation in this form is not dramatic it would provide an essential foundation of basic information for further discussions of regional cooperation, and should in itself lead to better regional understanding.

Another kind of research is very feasible and could accompany efforts to improve standard economic accounts. Micro-studies of resource inputs for producing the same commodity in two or more countries can make a solid contribution towards understanding better the implications of alternative trade and production policies and the possible impact of regional cooperation. Despite an inevitable frequency distribution of cost patterns, and some uncertainties in evaluating differentiated products, variations in costs would often stand out clearly. Numbers could be attached to them, and the change in welfare from freeing trade estimated more concretely. The distribution of welfare gains between two or more countries from dropping trade barriers could also be estimated. Micro-studies of this type have the further advantage of moving us from general matters of policy preference and ideology to emphasis on the concrete and practical.

EXPORT PERFORMANCE AND PROSPECTS

While efforts to improve data and theories continue, plans and decisions must be made using incomplete and imperfect information. Among the main variables or relationships on which to focus for policy guidance are those connected with trade performance and prospects. Trade is essential to understanding national economic growth in Southeast Asia and is the main way in which the benefits of most types of regional cooperation or integration would be achieved.

Southeast Asian Exports to
Developed Countries

The degree of dependence of Asian countries on international trade typically has been and will remain high. Professor Lim's Table 8.2 shows that in many cases the exports of these countries constitute more than 15 percent of their national income. Often 50 percent or more of export earnings are derived from one or two commodities. A large proportion of Southeast Asia's exports has traditionally been and is currently being sold to developed countries, although the importance of this trade varies from country to country. For example, in 1965, according to the International Monetary Fund's *Direction of Trade Annual,* about 95 percent of Philippine exports went to developed countries, 91 percent of Indonesia's, 46 percent of Thailand's, and 31 percent of Burma's.

Recent export performance of the Southeast Asian region as a whole with developed countries has not been good. In a study of eight regional countries for the period from 1956–57 to 1964–65, Seiji Naya found that although Southeast Asian exports to the major developed-country markets increased by about 28 percent, *total* imports by these developed countries increased substantially more, by 76 percent.[3] The difference of 48 percent can be divided into a compositional shift of 32 percent, which indicates the extent to which the changing pattern of the developed-countries' imports moved away from the pattern of the Southeast Asia region's exports, and a residual 16 percent representing a competitive shift, the extent to which the region failed to maintain its share even in individual commodity groups.

The adverse compositional effect reflects a familiar fact: there is high concentration of regional exports in primary products that expand slowly in the world market. The size of the negative competitive effect is unexpected, for it indicates that even when the unfavorable compositional effect is allowed for, the relative position of Asian exports in various commodity groups has declined vis-à-vis third countries.

As Table 14.3 illustrates, there was considerable variation in the performance of individual Southeast Asian countries. The export increases for Taiwan (280.42 percent), Thailand (81.38 percent), and the Philippines (61.57 percent) were outstandingly high compared with that of other countries, some of whose export values fell abso-

TABLE 14.3—Compositional and competitive effects of selected Southeast Asian
countries' exports to developed countries, 1956–57 to 1964–65
(Percent)

| Country | Increase in exports | | Competitive effects $(A - H)$ | Compositional effects $(H - D)^b$ | Difference in growth rates $(A - D)$ |
	Actual (A)	Hypothetical[a] (H)			
Burma	− 1.58%	79.32%	− 80.90%	3.51%	− 77.39%
Ceylon	10.21	26.48	− 16.27	− 49.33	− 65.60
India	16.25	43.62	− 27.37	− 32.19	− 59.56
Indonesia	− .28	38.44	− 38.72	− 37.37	− 76.09
(Malaysia)	(9.19)	(45.80)	(− 36.61)	(− 30.01)	(− 66.62)
Pakistan	− 7.84	31.52	− 39.36	− 44.29	− 83.65
Philippines	61.57	40.78	20.79	− 35.03	− 14.24
Taiwan	280.42	183.54	96.88	107.73	204.61
Thailand	81.38	36.74	44.64	− 39.07	5.57
Total[c]	27.76	43.81	− 16.05	− 32.00	− 48.05

[a] The "hypothetical" figures assume that the listed exporting countries retained the same percentage share of the imports of their trading partners.

[b] Growth rate of developed countries' imports (D) is 75.81 percent.

[c] Malaysia (Malaya-Singapore) figures are not incorporated in the total because of inconsistencies in data and definition. In 1956–57, trade figures for the two countries were combined, but in recent years they generally report separately. Malaysia is defined differently by different partner countries, and often not consistently from year to year. Also, there seem to be serious differences in intra-Malaysian trade, apparently because of the large amount of entrepôt trade.

Source: Seiji Naya, "Export Growth and Commodity Pattern and its Implications for Southeast Asian Economic Cooperation," mimeographed (Madison, 1967), p. 10.

lutely (Indonesia, — 0.28 percent; Burma, — 1.58 percent; Pakistan, — 7.84 percent).

A negative compositional effect is common to all countries except Taiwan (and perhaps Burma), and reflects unfavorable commodity shifts in developed country markets for most Asian countries' goods. But there is a distinct difference in competitive effects: those countries with fast-rising exports (Taiwan, Thailand, and the Philippines) show positive competitive effects; countries with relatively stagnant exports (Burma, Ceylon, Pakistan, Indonesia, Malaysia, and India), negative competitive effects. Furthermore, the relative size of the negative competitive effect is large, in some cases more than or close to one-half the total lag. In contrast, positive competitive effects offset considerably the Philippines' unfavorable compositional change, and offset Thailand's totally. Taiwan's large positive compositional effect was reinforced by a positive, but smaller, competitive shift. This pattern suggests the importance of the competitive effect in influencing the relative export performances, given the unfavorable compositional shift.

Changes in the commodity make-up and export growth of the countries considered are given in Table 14.4 for two broad commodity groups: primary and manufactured products. The rapid increases in primary and total exports of Thailand, the Philippines, and Taiwan stand in clear contrast to stagnation for the other countries. The commonly held view that countries with high concentrations in primary exports perform poorly is not supported here. Thailand and the Philippines have done remarkably well despite a high degree of specialization in primary exports.[4]

Table 14.4 also hints at a possible new feature of the regional economy: the rapid rise of exports of manufactures in all countries except Indonesia and perhaps Ceylon. Exports of some groups of Southeast Asia's manufactured goods have grown at a rate even higher than the relevant import growth of the developed countries, indicating a positive competitive effect. However, the base year values are low, and manufactures were, in 1964–65, still only a small percentage of total exports. Thus, this rapid growth was of course too small to offset the overall deterioration in exports to the developed areas, but it may indicate the beginnings of a significant change in regional trade structure.

Two possible explanations for the overall competitive decline are

TABLE 14.4—Exports of Southeast Asian countries to developed countries by broad commodity group, averages of 1956–57 and 1964–65

Country and commodity group	Value of exports (million US$)		Composition of exports (%)		Percent increase, 1956–57 to 1964–65
	1956–57	1964–65	1956–57	1964–65	
Burma					
Primary	65.9	62.8	97.55	94.33	− 4.83
Manufactures	1.7	3.8	2.45	5.67	127.71
Total	67.6	66.6	100.00	100.00	− 1.58
Ceylon					
Primary	191.6	210.8	98.63	98.49	10.05
Manufactures	2.7	3.2	1.37	1.51	21.36
Total	194.3	214.0	100.00	100.00	10.21
India					
Primary	655.2	641.3	71.62	60.29	− 2.13
Manufactures	259.6	422.3	28.38	39.71	62.64
Total	914.8	1063.6	100.00	100.00	16.25
Pakistan					
Primary	251.5	183.5	94.53	74.83	− 27.05
Manufactures	14.6	61.7	5.46	25.17	324.39
Total	266.1	245.2	100.00	100.00	− 7.84
Indonesia					
Primary	580.6	582.5	97.96	98.55	.32
Manufactures	12.1	8.5	2.04	1.45	− 29.24
Total	592.7	591.0	100.00	100.00	− .28
Philippines					
Primary	437.4	675.2	94.74	90.52	54.36
Manufactures	24.3	70.7	5.26	9.48	191.49
Total	461.7	745.9	100.00	100.00	61.57
Thailand					
Primary	151.2	263.9	99.01	95.24	74.48
Manufactures	1.5	13.2	.99	4.76	769.87
Total	152.7	277.1	100.00	100.00	81.38
Taiwan					
Primary	64.6	209.4	89.65	76.37	224.04
Manufactures	7.5	64.8	10.35	23.63	768.88
Total	72.1	274.2	100.00	100.00	280.42

Note: Primary products consist of Standard International Trade Categories (SITC) 0 through 4—food and live animals, beverages and tobacco, crude materials excluding fuels, mineral fuels, etc., animal and vegetable oils and fats; manufactures consist of SITC 5 through 8—chemicals, basic manufactures, machinery and transport equipment, miscellaneous manufactured goods.

Source: Seiji Naya, "Export Growth and Commodity Pattern and its Implications for Southeast Asian Economic Cooperation," mimeographed (Madison, 1967), p. 13.

high effective rates of tariff protection and overvalued exchange rates.

The concept of effective protection distinguishes between stages of production in assessing the degree of protection granted at each stage. A tariff on a particular commodity not only protects its productive process, but also taxes industries using the commodity as an input. Under the typical policy of import substitution in less-developed countries, the industrial manufacturing sector often enjoys low or zero duties on its inputs and high nominal duties on final output. The resulting rate of effective protection on final goods may be very high.

There are at least two implications of high effective tariff rates. First, to the extent that the final manufactured good is one in which the less-developed country might ordinarily have a comparative advantage and thus be able to export, high effective protection keeps costs and prices high and thus hinders its export. A second implication is that to the extent that the traditional primary export sector must pay high duties on its imported inputs, and costs are forced upward, these products become less competitive in international markets than they otherwise would be. It is conceivable that the pattern of trade of a country could be shifted if, through different rates of effective protection, the traditional export sector had higher costs than the newly established import-substitution sector.

Drs. Islam and Sun, in Chapters 3 and 4 respectively, treat in some measure the question of effective protection. Sun uses conventional techniques in his attempt to estimate effective rates of protection for industry in Taiwan. The heights of some of the rates are impressive, as is the dispersion of rates. Yet Sun finds no correlation between these rates and the growth of output in particular industries.

In some respects this result is not too surprising for, as Dr. Ramana noted in his discussion of Sun's paper, many other factors might also be expected to explain variations in the rates of growth of industrial output.

Aside from the omission of important variables, economists are now beginning to see that the concept of the effective rate of protection is more complicated theoretically and empirically than it first appeared to be. Standard assumptions are that all tariffs are relevant (that tariff protection is not redundant even counting other types of trade control) and that the difference between the domestic and world price is equal to the tariff. As Dr. Sun notes, the first assumption may not be appropriate for Taiwan. There are also several theoretical limitations to this type of analysis: the technique does not allow for substitution among factors of production as the effects of the tariff on relative prices are felt.[5] Nor does the analysis, as usually performed, allow for the fact that many goods are not traded and thus are not subject to the impact of the tariff. Particularly relevant for less-developed countries may be the fact that some traded goods (i.e., imports) are non-competitive—are simply not produced domestically at this stage of development—and therefore the tariff is irrelevant to them as well.

As Dr. Islam notes in Chapter 3, a number of studies have been made of effective rates of protection in Pakistan—most of which have been unavoidably subject to the limitations just mentioned. Islam's own study in this volume is, therefore, all the more welcome, because it attempts to circumvent these theoretical and empirical difficulties with direct evidence on the extent to which tariff protection in Pakistan is associated with higher costs. Although Islam was not able to make close and direct comparisons of his results with those obtained by other researchers, the impression is that the reasons for high costs are to be found in a number of factors other than high rates of effective protection.

Exchange-rate valuation also affects export performance. An exchange rate that overvalues the domestic currency will tax exports and subsidize imports. Therefore, a possible explanation for Southeast Asia's relatively poor export performance is that exchange rates were, on the average, overvalued during the latter part of the 1950's and in the early 1960's. Almost all of the papers touch on the question of the exchange rate. Mrs. Suparb attributes much of the improvement in Thailand's export performance after 1955 to devaluation and to the unification of the exchange rate. Dr. Sun and discussants of his paper emphasize the role that successive devaluations must have played in accounting for Taiwan's consistently good performance in exporting. In contrast, Indonesia, Ceylon, Pakistan, and India have been having balance-of-payments difficulties during much of the postwar period, partly because their exchange rates have been inappropriate for various reasons. India's devaluation in 1966 was intended to ease that country's balance-of-payments problem.

Dean Castro, however, interprets Philippine experience in a slightly different light. He suggests that the Philippine peso was no more than slightly overvalued during most of the period of rapid export growth in the 1950's and early 1960's. Only in the latter part of this period did exchange-rate pressure begin to be felt. For this reason, Philippine exports continued to expand rapidly because the export sector was not being excessively penalized, and indeed, was receiving various other kinds of legal and extra-legal advantages. As Dr. Odawara suggests, there may have been other special features that help explain continued export expansion in the Philippines, including the windfall gain of additional sugar quotas in the United States after 1962, as well as the generalized tariff preference for Philippine goods in the United States market.

Professor Islam's study concludes with an observation that is very relevant for showing some of the complexities in the relationships between various types of commercial policy. An index of the effective rate of protection in the entire economy gives some indication of the extent to which that country's currency may be overvalued. This implicit exchange rate for Pakistan is on the order of PRs8.5 to the United States dollar, compared with the official rate of PRs4.76. Pakistan's system of export bonuses, whereby exporters are allowed to exchange some portion (usually 30 percent) of their foreign-exchange earnings at a higher rate, means that in effect exporters are working with an actual exchange rate of PRs6.19 to 6.91 to the United States dollar. A bonus scheme of this type amounts to a de facto devaluation of the rupee, or correction of the overvalued exchange rate. Thus the level of effective protection as calculated earlier is in fact less onerous than the figures taken by themselves indicate.

The papers in this volume indicate that on the whole our theories for understanding the determinants of export performance plus our attempts at empirical verification and estimates of actual magnitudes need much refinement and improvement. We seem to be able to explain different countries' experiences only with ad hoc reasoning. Until we obtain a sharper understanding of why different countries have performed as they have, it is exceedingly difficult to propose specific alternative policies, including policies for regional cooperation, with any guarantee of being able to predict confidently the results.

Intraregional Trade

The level and composition of intraregional trade is central to any discussion of regional economic interdependence. The two papers in Part I emphasize that Southeast Asian intraregional trade is a relatively small percentage of total Southeast Asian trade and that this percentage has been falling in the postwar period. To Kitamura and

Bhagat this decline reflects a basic lack of regional economic complementarity and offers little prospect that such complementarity will appear as a natural phenomenon. This observation leads them to the case for agreed or planned specialization as the most feasible form of regional cooperation.

As the discussion above suggests, we must interpret these statistics cautiously. Much of the region's entrepôt trade is hard to measure and is not recorded consistently. There are also ambiguities about commodities exported regionally for further processing. Thus, it is difficult to say conclusively that the observed decline of five or so percentage points in the last decade represents a significant feature of regional trade.

Table 14.5 gives some detail on the trade of selected individual countries with the broader ECAFE region.[6] These data and interpretations based on them are of course subject to the limitations described earlier in this chapter.

For individual countries, the apparent share of intra-Asian trade in 1964–65 varies widely, from 79 percent for Laos; 57 percent for

TABLE 14.5—Export growth and shares of intraregional exports, averages of 1956–57 and 1964–65

Country	Total exports (million US$)		Intraregional exports as % of total		Percent increase, 1956–57 to 1964–65	
	1956–57	1964–65	1956–57	1964–65	Total	Intraregional
Burma	239.8	231.5	51.79	50.47	− 3.51	− 5.96
Cambodia	44.5	96.5	35.77	31.55	117.09	91.50
Ceylon	358.7	401.5	5.53	5.82	11.93	17.88
Hong Kong	546.1	1,077.5	50.97	22.01	97.30	− 14.80
India	1,325.2	1,715.5	11.04	9.66	29.45	13.25
Indonesia	925.7	683.0	33.19	10.51	− 26.22	− 76.64
Korea	23.4	147.0	13.67	23.36	528.20	1,073.43
Laos	1.2	1.2	83.33	79.16	.00	− 5.00
Malaysia	726.0	961.0	n.a.	27.00	32.36	n.a.
Pakistan	349.3	510.5	5.15	19.84	41.14	53.83
Philippines	435.5	754.5	2.59	3.67	73.24	145.13
Singapore	1,128.5	943.4	n.a.	57.09	− 16.41	n.a.
Taiwan	133.3	441.5	33.23	28.94	231.20	188.48
Thailand	349.5	610.0	54.17	46.58	74.53	50.06
Vietnam	62.8	42.0	13.37	15.11	− 33.13	− 24.41

n.a.: Not available.

Sources: *Direction of Trade*, 1956 and 1957; *Direction of Trade: A Supplement to International Financial Statistics*, 1964 and 1965. Data for Malaya and Singapore are taken from United Nations, *Yearbook for International Trade Statistics*, 1956 and 1957; and United Nations, *Commodity Trade Statistics*, 1964 and 1965.

Singapore; 50 percent for Burma; to 6 percent for Ceylon and 4 percent for the Philippines. Most countries show an apparent decline in intraregional trade between 1956–57 and 1964–65. The large absolute declines for Hong Kong and Indonesia are particularly noticeable and are in the former case accounted for by the conscious redirection of trade described by Dr. Chou, and in the latter by Confrontation. Pakistan and Korea appear to have enjoyed rapid increases in their intraregional trade shares.

Various papers suggest some of the reasons for the observed decline in intraregional trade and forecast a probable further decline. Chou's figures show an astounding relative decline in Hong Kong's entrepôt trade, and West Malaysia's and other regional countries' efforts to develop their own ports may mean a further decline in entrepôt trade. In the past much regional trade has been in primary commodities, for further processing and then export outside the region. This pattern is changing. Thai and West Malaysian tin has been smelted in Singapore; Indonesian and West Malaysian rubber has undergone processing also in Singapore; East Malaysian and Philippine timber has been processed for lumber and plywood in other countries of the region. The extensive intraregional trade in rice is well known, but has declined both because of declining exportable surpluses from Thailand and Burma (and Vietnam) along with import-substitution programs for this foodgrain in Malaysia, and to some extent in the Philippines.

The significance that should be attached to low regional trade shares can vary. A share may be constant because of low growth rates for total and regional exports, as in the case of Burma. Or a share may fall at the same time that regional trade is rising rapidly, that is, exports to the rest of the world may grow faster than intraregional trade, as in the cases of Taiwan, Cambodia, and Thailand. The latter pattern is more encouraging than the former.

In some ways declining regional trade for the reason above may be less serious and even welcome to the extent that nationalist sentiments can be satisfied, or positive economic gains achieved, at a lower cost than would be involved by some conceivable, alternative policies. Policies to attain near or total self-sufficiency in food production are almost universal among nations. Local processing of raw materials may have important effects on employment and a significant growth impact through the effects of interindustry linkages and labor force training. Declining entrepôt trade in Hong Kong's case indicates a basic, favorable shift in that country's economy.

Thus, a period of declining intraregional trade may, for these rea-

TABLE 14.6—Commodity composition of total and intraregional exports for selected Southeast Asian countries[a], 1962 and 1965[b]

(Percent)

SITC Sections	Total exports		Intraregional exports[c]	
	1962	1965	1962	1965
0–4 Primary products	79.2	75.7	63.4	62.9
0 Food and live animals	26.0	28.1	28.0	27.9
1 Beverages and tobacco	.9	.8	.8	.4
2 Crude materials, excluding fuels	44.9	39.1	23.3	23.5
3 Mineral fuels	5.0	4.6	9.2	9.1
4 Animal and vegetable oils and fats	2.4	3.1	2.1	2.0
5–8 Manufactures	19.6	23.1	34.3	34.9
5 Chemicals	1.5	1.7	3.8	4.6
6 Basic manufactures	13.1	15.9	16.5	16.9
7 Machinery and transport equipment	3.3	3.1	10.2	9.5
8 Miscellaneous manufactured goods	1.7	2.4	3.8	3.9
9 Unclassified goods	1.1	1.1	2.3	2.2
Total	100.0	100.0	100.0	100.0
(in million US$)	(4,011.7)	(4,824.9)	(1,213.1)	(1,400.1

Note: Due to rounding, percentages may not add up to exactly 100.

[a] The Philippines, Singapore, Thailand, Taiwan, Cambodia, Ceylon, Malaya, and Pakistan.

[b] For the Philippines only, 1964 figures are used.

[c] Intraregional trade refers to trade of the eight Southeast Asian countries with all "Other Asia" reported in the *Commodity Trade Statistics*.

Source: United Nations, *Commodity Trade Statistics*, various issues of 1962 and 1965.

sons, open the way economically and politically for other kinds of regional trade. As Professor Islam suggests, nations at slightly different stages of growth or economically similar countries that have emphasized different industries may find large possibilities for increasing trade with each other.

In general, there seems to be a broad correlation between the relative expansion of intraregional exports and exports to the developed countries. Taiwan, Thailand, and the Philippines perform well in export markets of both the developed countries and the region, and consequently in total exports; the reverse is true for Burma, Indonesia, and India. Pakistan provides an exception in which intraregional and

TABLE 14.6 (continued)

Intraregional as % of total exports		Total imports		Intraregional imports[e]		Intraregional as % of total imports	
1962	1965	1962	1965	1962	1965	1962	1965
24.2	24.1	43.0	37.3	79.8	72.7	51.2	37.9
32.6	28.7	16.4	16.5	23.9	28.2	40.3	33.2
27.9	16.6	1.3	1.1	.8	.6	16.0	10.3
15.7	17.5	13.6	9.9	37.4	29.7	75.7	58.2
55.6	56.8	10.3	8.3	16.3	12.0	43.9	28.4
26.2	18.0	1.4	1.5	1.4	2.2	27.6	28.7
52.8	43.8	55.5	60.7	18.4	24.9	9.1	8.0
78.0	78.3	7.8	8.7	2.6	3.1	9.3	7.0
38.1	30.8	20.4	20.9	8.8	13.1	12.0	12.2
92.1	88.7	22.7	26.5	2.4	3.6	2.9	2.7
67.2	48.4	4.6	4.6	4.6	5.1	27.2	21.6
60.6	57.1	1.4	1.8	1.9	2.2	38.8	24.1
30.5	29.2	100.0	100.0	100.0	100.0	27.6	19.5
—	—	(4,739.0)	(5,796.6)	(1,310.6)	(1,120.4)	—	—

total exports have grown rapidly compared to sluggish exports to developed countries, suggesting a directional change towards intraregional trade. Hong Kong's pattern is just the opposite.

The export and import commodity composition and share of intraregional trade for a group of Southeast Asian countries are given, along with the total trade of the region, in Table 14.6 for 1962 and 1965, the earliest and most recent dates for which comparable commodity detail is available. For both exports and imports there is a considerable difference between the composition of total trade and that of intraregional trade. Primary commodities make up the largest share of both intraregional exports and imports: 63 percent and 73 percent respectively in 1965. But relatively small shares of total exports and imports of these primary products go to and come from regional countries (24 percent and 38 percent respectively in 1965). Intraregional exports lean towards manufactured products more than do total exports, and a surprisingly large proportion of total manufactured products, about 50 percent, is exported to other countries of the region. (Of course, the intraregional trade share of manufactured products comprises only a small proportion of the total imports of manufactures.)

REGIONAL COOPERATION AND
SOME ALTERNATIVES

The papers and discussion in this volume illustrate forcefully that not all economists in the region are convinced that regional cooperation is the only solution to regional problems, or necessarily the best. One substantial source of their doubt is uncertainty about the probable effects of various types of trade liberalization or agreed specialization. As we indicated above, much of this uncertainty rests in turn on a lack of reliable information about regional trade and of detailed knowledge about the relation between alternative economic policies and performance.

The preceding sections indicate some of the problems in making detailed or accurate estimates of the probable benefits or costs of various types of regionalism for Southeast Asia at present. In view of the diversity of opinions among Asian economists themselves, it is also clear that substantial further steps toward regional integration will require credible comparisons between regionalism and its alternatives, and among various alternative forms of regionalism. This section summarizes some of the main issues involved in regional cooperation or integration compared with two broad alternatives: a greatly expanded economic aid program for the region; and continued reliance on exports.

Regional Integration

Virtually all contributors to this volume recognize the broad advantages that would result from greater economic specialization and division of labor in the region. Opinions divide sharply, however, on the appropriate institutional framework for achieving these gains, and on the particular implications of various approaches for each country's own economic development.

As Dr. Tang comments in Part I, it is misleading to contrast two idealized cases—regional free trade versus regional planning. These alternatives are not the relevant ones. Few governments anywhere—in economically developed or underdeveloped countries—would be willing (or able, in view of domestic constraints and market imperfections) to implement the free-trade model in its entirety. But it is equally true that few if any governments have the inclination or the ability to engage in the comprehensive national planning that would be required before regional coordination or consolidation of national development plans could be undertaken. The real alternatives lie somewhere in between, and the problem of choice becomes one of finding an economically and politically acceptable "second-best" policy.

For many countries of the region, trade along traditional lines has not been satisfactory for a number of reasons, some within the control of the countries involved, but some clearly not. A number of alternatives to traditional trading relationships have been suggested or tried.

Industrialization through import substitution is one. As the papers in this volume indicate, it has proved less satisfactory than once hoped. If, as Kitamura and Bhagat argue, the failure of import substitution can be traced to national markets too small to allow output to be produced at efficient levels, and also to inadequate national supplies of crucial inputs, regional cooperation to expand both product and factor markets seems very promising. Yet there is a growing body of persuasive evidence, some of which has been presented and discussed above, both from the analysis of unsuccessful case histories and from the example of other Asian countries, that an adequate package of national policies can be devised to promote growth. Certain Asian countries have been able to perform satisfactorily in the wider world market, and are understandably cautious about entering into a regional program that might require significant changes in present policies.

A second concern of proponents of agreed specialization is the nature of appropriate trading relationships. International trade is inherently risky and uncertain. Exporting countries in Southeast Asia must contend with shifting demand schedules from business fluctuations in their major markets, with unforeseen or irregular competition from other countries and from product substitutes, and with possible changes in tariffs or quotas or exchange rates. The consequences of risk and uncertainty are more serious for marginal producers in world markets and for national economies that are highly dependent on trade. Virtually all Asian countries qualify on one or both of these grounds, and their interest in reducing risk and eliminating uncertainty is very understandable.

A third point in the plan harmonization and agreed specialization approach is concern about effects on the structure of production if market forces are allowed more freedom to direct region-wide investment and production decisions. That the market mechanism has led to concentration in production and inequality in income distribution within nations is confirmed by available evidence. The very economies of large-scale production and external economies that are expected as a result of wider markets give rise to the possibility that the gains from integration would not be shared widely. Agreed specialization would provide for a more equitable distribution of new investment: location agreements are thought possible because problems of efficiency are assumed not to be great in large-scale, non-resource-oriented technology. More important in promoting efficient production would be the prospect of assured, stable markets for output, guaranteed by long-term trading contracts.

The case for agreed specialization thus advocates an institutional framework to avoid the equity problems of a free-trade area or customs union.

Contributors have differing views and evidence on the equity argument. As Tang points out, equity has always been a problem during early periods of growth in integrated markets. External and internal economies of large-scale production, by definition, do not spread themselves evenly over a country. Achieving these economies has naturally meant for most countries a period of increasing inequality in the regional and functional distribution of income. In a nation (or in a common market or economic union), factor mobility ordinarily mitigates some of the effects of inequality as factors migrate in response to economic incentives. And problems of deep-seated inequality have usually been attacked at some point in most societies through direct transfers or through a conscious redirection of investment.

Ventures in regional cooperation in other parts of the world have provided for such transfers at the start, usually because the group's low-income countries demand them as a condition for their participation. Further refinements may involve an *ex ante* redistribution of benefits through location of new industry, as in the Central American Common Market. The difference, however, between these proposals and the agreed specialization approach is in the way that location is determined. The Central American "integration industries" are, on the whole, removed from the political arena and depend on market decisions within the institutional constraints. The agreed specialization approach in the form described here seems to have a very strong political bargaining element, and it is difficult to see how efficiency could be ensured for newly established industries.

A second problem related to the rules of equity is the extent to which potential participants would be willing or able to make the required adjustments to agreed specialization. National planning may be structured loosely or tightly, and in either case may be executed efficiently or inefficiently. The diversity in styles of Asian planning mentioned by several authors would seem to be a very great problem indeed.

The kind of proposal for regional cooperation outlined broadly by Kitamura and Bhagat was placed in a particular national context by Lakdawala and Patil. Their account gives some flavor for the kinds of efforts that would be required by the Indian economy to accommodate increased imports from the region and to program more Indian exports to the region. The suggested network of different kinds of trading arrangements needed to accommodate various styles of national economic decision-making seems exceedingly complex and difficult to administer. While India might consider this effort worthwhile, for various reasons, it is not clear that all nations in the region would be prepared to make a corresponding effort.

The Indian case study deals mainly with the short-run adjustments that would be required on the Indian side—i.e., for existing patterns of trade and production. Planning for the introduction of new industries over time in the region is likely to pose different but equally vexing problems. Concern over the outcome of an essentially political bargaining process again becomes important.

Professor Islam's remarks on Rural Cooperation Development planning for agreed specialization reinforce this concern, although the actual experience of this group to date as reported by Kitamura and Bhagat and elsewhere shows that the problems are not insurmountable. But the RCD group may also be favored with a high degree of potential regional complementarity in natural resources and similar-size industrial sectors. In the absence of more detailed studies, the feasibility of agreed specialization in new products in a mainly Southeast Asian subregional group remains uncertain.

External Assistance

The main policy variable that the developed countries control is the rate and condition of transfer of resources—aid. This aid may be in the familiar form of technical or capital assistance, with a choice between grants or loans for the latter. But transfers are also possible through trade preferences to less-developed countries and through support of commodity agreements.

The main question concerning conventional aid is its level: will the future bring higher levels of assistance, or substantially the same levels, or, more likely, lower amounts?

Higher levels of aid would provide considerable additional flexibility and might substantially ease the national costs (or increase the benefits) of regional cooperation. For example, adoption of a regional perspective on aid allocations should allow some economies both in directly productive investment as well as social overhead capital. Proper utilization of this aid might be easier with regional harmonization of national development plans, but such coordination would not be essential. An institutional framework for the region or a part of it could be designed that would give wide scope to market decisions in the location of industry. External assistance could then be used both to support private decisions through investment banking and to compensate slow-growing countries in the region with infrastructure investments through a regional investment fund or development bank.

While the potential flexibility assumed in substantially higher levels of external assistance is great, proposals of this type have two potential and basic difficulties. The first is guaranteeing that the resources required would actually be made available by the developed countries. Recent trends in the levels and conditions of aid mean that this question is an important one. Guaranteeing that the developed countries would supply these resources might well require conditions that some countries would find unacceptable. This leads, of course, directly to the second problem: would a regional group accept aid under those circumstances?

Both of these questions are important and difficult. Speculation on them here seems less useful than considering the alternative of constant or continual declining levels of aid from the high-income countries, and examining the remaining option: continued reliance on export-led growth, perhaps with some alteration of trade and development policies in the regional countries themselves and in their major developed-country markets.

Export Prospects and
Possibilities

The significance of poor Asian export performance discussed previously is sharper when compared with the foreign-exchange needs of countries of the region. Recurrent discussions have emerged from the United Nations and other sources relating to the present and future (prospective) trade gaps of less-developed countries. These discussions run in terms of a growing need for foreign exchange by low-income countries to meet their economic development programs.[7]

There is unanimous agreement about the persistence of deficits; there is disagreement about how large the deficits will turn out to be. According to a study by Bela Balassa, the trade deficit of all less-developed countries combined, under the most likely assumption about income growth in developed countries, will rise from $1.3 billion in 1960 to $4.3 billion in 1970 and to $5.2 billion in 1975.[8] Other estimates indicate an even larger trade deficit: $12 billion for 1970 according to the United Nations Secretariat calculations,[9] and from $8.5 to $12.5 billion in 1975 (excluding the Middle East) according to the estimates by the General Agreement on Trade and Tariffs Secretariat.[10]

Among major regions of the world, the Asian trade deficit is expected to be by far the greatest, rising from $1.5 billion in 1960 to $5.2 billion in 1975, due to the combination of a slow rate of growth of its exports and an increase in the import requirements.

An ECAFE study, assuming a 5 percent growth rate for the region, estimated that by 1980 primary exports will be $12.6 billion, and import requirements $26 billion. The gap is presumably to be met by exports of manufactures, import substitution, or foreign assistance.

The same study estimates that the region's leading exports will obtain the following overall percentage increases between 1960 and 1980 (in constant prices):

Natural rubber	58.5%	Tin metal and	
Petroleum and products	184.0	concentrates	52.0%
Tea	43.6	Wood and lumber	94.6
Vegetable oils	56.0	Cotton fabrics	38.8
Rice	66.5	Jute and jute fabrics	24.0
Sugar	42.6		

The greatest increase is expected for petroleum; then come wood and wood products, rice, natural rubber, tin and tin concentrates; and finally tea, sugar, cotton fabrics, and jute and jute products.[11]

Most of these traditional exports have achieved from 50 percent to more than 100 percent (in current prices) of their projected increases in the four years from 1960 to 1964. There are two important exceptions, however: natural rubber exports from virtually all of the rubber exporting countries have fallen, and exports of tea have stagnated. The following are percentage changes in exports between 1960 and 1964 (in current prices):[12]

Natural rubber	−35.0%	Tin	24.7%
Petroleum and products	17.6	Wood and products	72.5
Tea	1.0	Cotton and fabrics	
Vegetable oils	24.0	and yarn	16.8
Rice	40.6	Jute and products	22.8
Sugar	58.7		

The export gains of several individual countries have been much less satisfactory than these averages, especially for rubber and tea exporters. The overall picture for the region still suggests insufficient rates of export growth. The region's trade deficit was over $3 billion in 1964, double that of 1960. Among individual countries, India had the largest deficit, followed by Pakistan.[13]

Concern over export prospects for primary products encourages investigation of possibilities for exports of manufactures. Although the long-run comparative advantage of less-developed countries for the production of manufactured goods is still inconclusive in detail, there is a strong presumption that it is in the area of modest-skill, labor-intensive products.

An analysis of prospective comparative advantage in manufactured commodities starts with the basic assumption that low-income countries have relatively little accumulated capital. Hence any comparative advantage that they have in manufactures, apart from the resource-oriented ones, must arise from low wage levels. The conclusion then is to specialize in industries with intensive labor requirements and little capital, in the form of either education and training (i.e., human capital), or plant and equipment. Less complex manufacturing groups like textiles and apparel, wood products, leather products, rubber footwear, and other miscellaneous manufactures generally fit this description.[14]

However, the problem is more complex. A clear-cut delineation of certain relatively simple manufacturing groups to the possible exclusion of others (such as metal products; machinery, transport, and other capital goods products; and chemical products) does not seem to be an optimal choice from a long-run developmental point of view. If underdeveloped countries in general and Southeast Asian countries in particular are to avoid an export dead-end road for manufactured goods, long-run projections for the export potential, and of the built-in skill and organization-developing promise of the different manufacturing groups have to be taken into consideration.

The study of future prospects of world trade in manufactures by Maizels projected a declining share of textile and clothing and other miscellaneous manufactures in world trade between 1959 and 1970–75.[15] At the same time, capital goods and chemical products were expected to achieve an increasing share of total trade.

Such forecasts imply a worry: further competition in the production and export of a few manufacturing categories whose future prospects are projected to be dubious may only worsen the situation for those countries.

One criterion for identifying labor-intensive industries, used by Professor Hal Lary of the National Bureau of Economic Research, is the ranking of industries with respect to (1) value added per employee, (2) wages and salaries per employee, and (3) the non-wage value added per employee (the returns to capital and natural resources).[16] Less-developed countries should have a comparative advantage in manufactures that score lower than average on all three criteria. Comparisons of these characteristics of manufacturing groups for a number of countries at various stages of development have shown that textiles and apparel, wood products, furniture, leather, and miscellaneous manufactures consistently satisfied the criteria.

A similar study for six Asian countries (Japan, India, West Malaysia, Pakistan, Indonesia, and the Philippines) indicates that in addition to the above manufactures, metallic products, machinery, and transport equipment also have a lower than average value added, wage and non-wage components per employee.[17] Because there is a large degree of heterogeneity of products included under these industrial classifications, considerable disaggregation will be required to learn which specific commodities hold the most promise.

In addition, one must be sensitive, as Professor Sicat cautions, to the import-dependence of these potential "export-substitutes." Because some manufactured commodities that show low "value added" per employee are undoubtedly "finishing-touches" import substitutes, it does not, of course, follow that these products could become exportable immediately. The capital-labor ratio required at other stages of production will be important, i.e., the total requirements in an interindustry sense.

However, after these qualifications are made, preliminary studies indicate that there still exists a wide range of manufactured goods for which export prospects are good and in which less-developed countries would show a comparative advantage.

Our survey above of the export performance for manufactures for a number of Southeast Asian countries tends to support the abstract argument. Although agricultural products still constitute the highest percentage of total exports, the share of manufactured exports is increasing. For most countries, food manufacture, mainly in the form of simple processing operations, constitutes the largest proportion of total manufactured exports. Textile exports were of no major significance except for Hong Kong and India, followed by Pakistan and Singapore. Metallic products, including machinery and transport equipment, although a small percentage of total exports, have achieved on the whole a higher rate of growth.

One danger for Southeast Asian countries in relying too heavily on exports of labor-intensive manufactures is that the developed countries may raise higher tariffs or establish quotas against these products. In fact, however, there is a strong case for high-income countries to discriminate *for* rather than against manufactured exports of the less-developed countries, by instituting tariff preferences.

Encouragement to regional freer trade measures might take the form of trade preferences extended by the United States and other developed countries on condition of reciprocal lowering of Southeast Asian barriers among themselves. The extension of such preferences by the developed countries, especially the United States, would meet the official and emphatic wish of the low-income countries which is more firmly rooted in fact and analysis than the usual arguments have conveyed.[18]

Trade preferences would provide the large markets required for economies of scale, while avoiding the rigidities implied in programs of agreed specialization and in long-term trading contracts. Because of our limited ability to predict future comparative advantage, much reliance on the price system is necessary. Preferences seem both to meet the economic needs of the less-developed countries and to provide reasonable attention to economic efficiency.

CONCLUSIONS

Unqualified conclusions cannot validly be drawn from facts, analyses, and evaluations with as many aspects of uncertainty as those surveyed above. But, we do need guide lines for policy—guide lines that are neither unduly vague in view of what we know, nor unduly positive in view of what we do not know.

The countries of Southeast Asia have had a diversity of background and experience with economic development. Any meaningful approach must be based on and proceed from such experience in these countries. Among the domestic political aims that have first priority, *national* economic and political integration takes high place. Nationalism is a central fact. Hence, any attempts at regional cooperation must be subordinate to or, if possible, reinforce the major theme of nation building. How can nations and their elites consciously gain as individual units through regional cooperation?

The more formal attempts would compel the countries of Southeast Asia to redefine some of their national goals and to abandon some of their national policies. In the visible future the viability of such attempts is very doubtful.

In contrast, the less formal attempts and partial measures can soften the edge of nationalism. And in time the experience of varied individual forms of cooperation, and, we can hope, the discipline imposed on diverse economic policies by success and failure, can lead to a deepening sense of regional identity and hence willingness to deepen and broaden regional cooperative ventures.

A major commitment to integration in the form of either ECAFE's harmonization proposal or a regional common market, must hold out the promise of great gain for the participants in order to be acceptable; and in fact the gains have been assumed to be substantial. In our view it remains unproved that the economic gains would be large enough, and the political hurdles low enough, to justify integration in either form.

Despite the suggestion that trading contracts specify world prices, the harmonization proposal suffers from not having conspicuously built in the need, which seems to us critical, that a hardheaded test, among other tests, be regularly applied to each industrial project: that of international competitiveness. The common external tariff implied by a customs union is subject to the same criticism to the extent the limitations of national policies are simply transferred to the wider regional context. Price and quality competitiveness need not be achieved immediately: but it should be achievable with a high degree of probability, and within a short period of no more than several years —else the social burden of the project weighs heavily against its acceptance.

A modest attempt at cooperation within the region might be made through analyzing the comparative advantage of the region as a whole along the lines described above, in an effort to discover which products would provide the stimulus to growth through the contributions of current efficiency and of dynamic feedback that traditional exports have failed generally to provide. But even this policy is limited and handicapped by uncertainties of data. Without the correction of existing, sometimes flagrant, errors in regional economic data, and standardization and further refinement, assessment of the consequences of any proposal will be very uncertain. Even with the best data, the practical facts will always turn out to be more subtle than abstract reasoning plus the data can predict.

Finally, diversities, antagonisms, and strong nationalism within the region and the uncertainty of benefits from existing proposals for formal integration all suggest that outside encouragement should be in the main through informal, partial, politically-neutral measures of obvious joint benefit. Outside encouragement of major integration projects should be limited; more emphasis needs to be placed on research and mutual education through discussion of problems and possibilities. Until potential participants in Southeast Asian regionalism see clearly that there is a problem, that the problem can best be met through regional efforts, and that the net benefits to each participant will be significant with incursions on national sovereignty minimal, pressures from outside the region are unlikely to achieve a continuing effect.

There are projects that satisfy these criteria. The Asian Development Bank, many activities of ECAFE, and other ventures in educational cooperation and joint research are examples. Such agencies and projects of regional benefit—ideally with safeguards in planning and execution not unlike those described above—can build up the habits of regional cooperation and expectations of further cooperation and further benefits to come.

NOTES

1. Throughout this chapter we rely on published and unpublished papers by the Wisconsin research staff. The chapter is basically a joint product and incorporates materials supplied by Mrs. Nawal Fag El Nour, J. Clark Leith, Joel McClellan, Seiji Naya, and K. C. Sen.
2. This section draws heavily from Seiji Naya and Theodore Morgan, "The

Accuracy of International Trade Data: The Case of Southeast Asian Countries," mimeographed (Madison, 1967). (Published in *Journal of the American Statistical Association,* Summer, 1969).

3. Seiji Naya, "Export Growth and Commodity Pattern and Its Implications for Southeast Asian Economic Cooperation," mimeographed (Madison, 1967). A preliminary version of this paper was presented to the Southeast Asia Development Advisory Group Seminar on Regional Cooperation (November, 1967, Washington, D.C.), and forms a substantial extension of Naya's "Commodity Pattern and Export Performance of Developing Asian Countries to the Developing Areas," *Economic Development and Cultural Change,* 15 (1967): 420–37.

4. However, both countries have diversified their primary products exports.

5. See J. Clark Leith, "The Specification of Nominal Trade Rates in Effective Protection Estimates," mimeographed (Madison, 1967).

6. The ECAFE region is defined to include Afghanistan, Australia, Brunei, Burma, Cambodia, Ceylon, China (Taiwan), Hong Kong, India, Indonesia, Iran, Japan, the Republic of Korea, Laos, Malaysia, New Zealand, Nepal, Pakistan, the Philippines, Singapore, Thailand, the Republic of Vietnam, and Western Samoa.

7. From Nawal Fag El Nour, "Trade of Less-Developed Countries and Southeast Asian Leading Exports: Prospects and Trends," manuscript, November, 1966.

8. Bela Balassa, *Trade Prospects for Developing Countries* (Homewood, Ill., Richard D. Irwin, 1964), pp. 93–94.

9. United Nations, *World Economic Survey : Part 1, 1962* (1963), p. 6.

10. General Agreement on Tariffs and Trade Secretariat, *International Trade, 1961* (Geneva, 1962), pp. 15–19.

11. ECAFE, *Economic Bulletin for Asia and the Far East,* December, 1963, p. 8.

12. Computed from United Nations, *Yearbook of International Trade Statistics,* various years.

13. Agency for International Development, *Economic Growth Trends for Far East and Near East and South Asia* (Washington: Statistics and Reports Division, 1966), pp. 30–31, 32–33.

14. See Hal B. Lary, *Imports of Labor Intensive Manufactures from Less-Developed Countries* (New York: Columbia University Press, 1968), p. 4.

15. Alfred Maizels, *Industrial Growth and World Trade* (Cambridge: Cambridge University Press, 1963), pp. 402–406.

16. Lary, *Imports of Labor Intensive Manufactures,* pp. 21–22.

17. Nawal Fag El Nour, "Less-Developed Countries' Comparative Advantage in Manufactured Goods," mimeographed, December, 1967.

18. See, for example, Theodore Morgan, "Preferences Revisited," *Malayan Economic Review,* November, 1967, pp. 16–31.

Index

Index